Elections, Parties, and Representation in Post-Communist Europe

Elections, Parties, and Representation in Post-Communist Europe

Frances Millard

Professor in the Department of Government,
University of Essex, UK

First published 2004 by
PALGRAVE MACMILLAN
Houndmills, Basingstoke, Hampshire RG21 6XS and
175 Fifth Avenue, New York, N.Y. 10010
Companies and representatives throughout the world

PALGRAVE MACMILLAN is the global academic imprint of the Palgrave Macmillan division of St. Martin's Press, LLC and of Palgrave Macmillan Ltd. Macmillan® is a registered trademark in the United States, United Kingdom and other countries. Palgrave is a registered trademark in the European Union and other countries.

ISBN 1–4039–0578–9

This book is printed on paper suitable for recycling and made from fully managed and sustained forest sources.

A catalogue record for this book is available from the British Library.

Library of Congress Cataloging-in-Publication Data
Millard, F. (Frances)
    Elections, parties, and representation in post-communist Europe / Frances Millard.
      p. cm.
    Includes bibliographical references and index.
    ISBN 1–4039–0578–9 (cloth : alk. paper)
    1. Representative government and representation—Europe, Eastern. 2. Representative government and representation—Europe, Central. 3. Representative government and representation—Former Soviet republics. 4. Elections—Europe, Eastern. 5. Elections—Europe, Central. 6. Elections—Former Soviet republics. 7. Political parties—Europe, Eastern. 8. Political parties—Europe, Central. 9. Political parties—Former Soviet republics. I. Title.

JF1075.E852M55 2004
324'.0947—dc22   2003064666

10   9   8   7   6   5   4   3   2   1
13   12   11   10   09   08   07   06   05   04

Printed and bound in Great Britain by
Antony Rowe Ltd, Chippenham and Eastbourne

In memory of my father, Ben Millard

Contents

List of Tables

Preface

The study of political change in post-communist countries underwent many changes and shifts of emphasis in the years following the fall of communism. It embraced broad-based international comparative research, regional comparative analysis, and individual country studies. Rich theoretical and philosophical debates assessed the multiple transformations of Central and Eastern Europe from the perspective of institutional design, the role and changing nature of élites, political parties and elections, political economy, civil society, and many other aspects of the wholesale transformation that accompanied the move from the mono-party system and the planned economy. This study contributes to the particular dimension of post-communist representation, as understood through the electoral process. Representation is the fundamental principle of modern liberal democracy.

The book owes its origins to the Project on Political Transformation and the Electoral Process in Post-Communist Europe[1] at the University of Essex. Its focus on representation constituted one element of the Project's study of the nature and evolution of the electoral process and its effects on the broad processes of democratisation. Almost all the quantitative data used here was collected by the Project; it is available at www.essex.ac./elections. That is the work's primary and central source. It is not cited in the text, but it is the source unless otherwise indicated.

I have tried to provide an overview of the complex and diffuse concept of representation and its evolution, seen not merely as a mechanism linking the electorate to a parliamentary representative but as part of a continuing process. Democracy is not just majority rule, but it is a *system of majority rule* and must therefore contain mechanisms within it for its own self-perpetuation. By the same token, a free election does not automatically signal the existence of liberal representative democracy; but successive free elections provide a *system* for the routine reproduction of majority rule coupled with the liberal safeguarding of minority rights.

This notion of process encompasses the determination of the electoral system, the organisation of political parties, the selection of candidates, the appeal of parties to the electorate, the performance of deputies, the interactions of parties, mechanisms of accountability, and the voters' response in successive elections. All these elements affect the ways in which the representative agents of the population are selected and the ways in which they carry out their functions of 'acting on behalf of' the citizenry. This is not a complete view of the process, for a full elaboration would include other factors, particularly in the area of civil liberties. If freedom of expression and the interplay of opposing views are essential to informed electoral choice, then the nature and role of the media is obviously a salient dimension of the electoral process in its widest sense. Such aspects cannot be considered here but will be noted from time to time without systematic evaluation. Unravelling the process is a complex task. In new, dynamic polities all the ingredients are fluid and their interactions may be unpredictable. The point is not merely to identify and examine the various elements of the electoral process and the ways in which they changed and developed, but also to explore how the impact of the separate components and the process of which they are a part affected the quality of representation.

The first part of the book centres on the concept of representation, its historical development, and the ways in which political parties offered distinctive ideological perspectives on its nature and implications. Political parties are seen as the key to representation. The widespread adoption of parliamentarism in the former Soviet bloc gave the Western European experience an immediate relevance, and most post-communist politicians accepted that parties were central to a competitive electoral process. Indeed, identifying mechanisms to foster party development was a major consideration in determining new electoral systems. At the same time new political leaders were also a product of their own societies. In many respects the communist legacy also retained a strong grip on subsequent developments.

So the development of political parties in Western Europe and the pre-democratic context – including the emergence of proto-parties and opposition movements, the crafting of the first democratic electoral systems, the nature of the first free elections, and the broader institutional arrangements – are also important ingredients of this tale. They shaped the political parties, but so did the strategies and actions of the parties themselves. Great emphasis is placed on identifying the kinds of appeals that the parties offered to the electorate, in other words the nature, consequences, and implications of the political menu of choice. The subsequent approach is to provide snapshots of particular aspects relevant to different dimensions of the electoral process. Among others, its aim is to detect the extent to which both parties and voters have adapted their behaviour to the particularities of the electoral process. Then there is a summation of the kinds of party interactions and the structures of competition that have taken shape or – in many cases – remained fluid.

The second part of the book focuses on the representatives themselves – the candidates and the deputies. Candidates in particular are often overlooked, especially for smaller or unsuccessful parties. In post-communist politics, however, the fortunes of parties often changed dramatically. Moreover, candidate data also provide insight into an aspect of political participation without which democracy could not function. The process of representation requires candidates who are prepared to lose elections. Both factors make the changing social composition of the corpus of deputies and candidates of considerable wider interest.

In addition, they cast light on the selection practices of particular types of parties. It seemed plausible to assume that different parties would select different candidates. Generally I tried to identify a scholarly consensus on how individual parties should be classified; but essentially the final judgement was a personal, if reasoned one.

The issue of gender is often neglected in broader studies of democratic development. Data here are more widely available, since the languages of all the countries signify gender and thus make it easy to identify the gender of both deputies and candidates. Again, attention was paid both to overall gender profiles and those of particular types of political party. These data are also used to assess a variety of theoretical findings about women's representation. In general I have mobilised theories and theoretical constructs when they seemed to assist the enquiry, though the tale is essentially an analytical empirical one. The final issue addressed is that of the representation of ethnic minorities and the various strategies they have pursued to gain political representation.

I have used almost exclusively English language sources in the text, but I have tried wherever possible to crosscheck them with primary and original language sources. That has also involved an army of friends and colleagues. I have used the native language acronyms of political parties in order to forestall any problems of party identification, but I have used their English names in the text.

There is a great deal of complex material here. I have maintained a measure of repetition to try to carry the reader with me, but I am conscious that not only may I have failed in that object but also have lost key points in a morass of detail. The examples used are drawn from a wide range of countries, but not all are treated with equal depth and not all countries are examined in each section. I have tried to indicate where illustrations appear 'typical' and where diversity of experience is the norm. Falling between stools is a common hazard for academics, but perching on one stool also has its own pitfalls.

I owe a great deal to my colleagues on the project, Kieran Williams, Sarah Birch, Marina Popescu, and Robertas Pogorelis, all of whom contributed unstintingly to its success. I would like to follow the usual custom and practice and thank all those others who assisted me, but the list would be overwhelming. Those who are omitted have had my personal thanks, and my immeasurable domestic debts will also be acknowledged privately. But I would like to express my gratitude to Gábor Tóka, Sándor Gallai, Wojciech Czaplicki, Henryk Bielski, Zdenka Mansfeldová, Petr Kopecký, Adam Fagan, Vladimír Krivý, Tim Haughton, and most of all to Marina Popescu. The weaknesses, as well as the eccentricities, are all mine.

Frances Millard
University of Essex

Note

1. Grateful acknowledgement is made to the ESRC's 'One Europe or Several?' Programme and its Director Helen Wallace. The project was funded by grant L213252021.

List of Party Acronyms

Bulgaria

BBB	Bulgarian Business Bloc (*Bulgarski Biznes Blok*)
BCP	Bulgarian Communist Party (*Bulgarska Komunisticheska Partiya*)
BSP	Bulgarian Socialist Party (*Bulgarska Socialisticheska Partiya*)
BZNS	Bulgarian Agrarian National Union (*Bulgarski Zemedelski Naroden Sajuz*)
DL	Democratic Left (*Demokratichna Levitsa*)
DPS	Movement for Rights and Freedom (*Dvijenie za Prava i Svobodi*)
EL	Euro-Left Coalition (*Koalitsija Evrolevitsa*)
NDSII	National Movement Simeon II (*Natsionalno Dvijenie Simeon Vtori*)
SDS	Union of Democratic Forces (*Suyuz na Demokratichniti Sili*)

Czechoslovakia

HSD–SMS	Movement for Self-Governing Democracy–Society for Moravia and Silesia (*Hnutí za samosprávnou demokracii–Spolecnost pro Moravu a Slezsko*)
KDU–ČSL	Czechoslovak People's Party (*Křest'anská a demokratická unie-Československá strana lidová*)
KDH	Christian-Democratic Movement (*Krest'ansko–demokratické hnutie*)
KSČS	Communist Party of Czechoslovakia (*Komunistická strana Československa*)
KSS	Communist Party of Slovakia (*Komunistická strana Slovenska*)
OF	Civic Forum (*Občanské fórum*)
SNS	Slovak National Party (*Slovenská národná strana*)
VPN	Public against Violence (*Verejnost' proti násiliu*)

Czech Republic

ČSSD	Czech Social Democratic Party (*Česká strana sociálně demokracie*)
DEU	Democratic Union (*Demokratická unie*)
KDU–ČSL	Christian Democratic Union–Czechoslovak People's Party (*Křest'anská a demokratická unie-Československá strana lidová*)
KSČM	Communist Party of the Czech Republic (the Czech Lands and Moravia) – (*Komunistická strana Čech a Moravy*)
LB	Left Bloc (*Levý blok*)

ODA	Civic Democratic Alliance (*Občanská demokratická aliance*)
ODS	Civic Democratic Party–Christian Democratic Party (*Obcanská demokratická strana*)
SPR-RSČ	Rally for the Republic–Republican Party of Czechoslovakia (*Sdružení pro republiku – Republikánská strana Československa*)
US	Freedom Union (*Unie svobody*)

Estonia

EK	Estonian Citizen (*Eesti Kodanik*)
ER	Estonian Reform Party (*Eesti Reformierakond*)
ERSP	Estonian National Independence Party (*Eesti Rahvusliku Sõltumatuse Partei*)
I	Homeland (*Isamaa–Pro Patria*)
KK	Secure Home (*Kindel Kodu*)
KMÜ	Coalition Party and Rural Union (*Koonderakond ja Maarahva Ühendus*)
M	The Moderates (*Valimisliit 'Môôdukad'*)
MKE	Our Home is Estonia (*Meie Kodu on Eestimaa*)
P	Right-Wingers (*Parempoolsed*)
PE&EK	Better Estonia & Estonian Citizens (*Parem Eesti ja Eesti Kodanik*)
TEE	Future's Estonia Party (*Tuleviku Eesti Erakond*)

Hungary

FIDESZ	Federation of Young Democrats (*Fiatal Demokraták Szövetsége*)
Fidesz–MPP [ex-FIDESZ]	Fidesz–Hungarian Civic Party (*Fidesz–Magyar Polgári Párt*)
FKGP	Independent Smallholders Party (*Független Kisgazda-, Földmunkás-és Polgári Párt*)
KDNP	Christian Democratic Party (*Kereszténydemokrata Néppárt*)
MDF	Hungarian Democratic Forum (*Magyar Demokrata Fórum*)
MIÉP	Hungarian Justice and Life Party (*Magyar Igazság és Élet Pártja*)
MSzMP	Hungarian Socialist Workers' Party (*Mágyar Szocialista Munkáspárt*)
MSzP	Hungarian Socialist Party (*Magyar Szocialista Párt*)
SzDSz	Alliance of Free Democrats (*Szabad Demokraták Szövetsége*)

Latvia

JL	New Era (*Jaunias Laiks*)
JP	New Party (*Jaunā Partija*)
LC	Latvia's Way (*Savienîba 'Latvijas Celð'*)
LNNK	Latvian National Independence Movement (*Latvijas Nacionalas Neatkarîbas Kustîba*)
LPP	Latvia's First Party (*Latvijas Pirmâ Partija*)
LSDP	Latvian Social Democratic Party
LSDSP	Latvian Social Democratic Workers' Party (*Latvijas Sociâldemokrâtiskâ Strâdnieku Partija*)
LVP	Latvian Unity Party (*Latvijas Vienîbas Partija*)
LZS	Latvian Farmers' Union (*Latvijas Zemnieku Savienîba*)
PCTVL	Alliance for Human Rights in a United Latvia (*Apvienîba 'Par cilvçka tiesîbâm vienotâ Latvijâ'*)
TB	For Fatherland and Freedom (*Tevzemei un Brîvîbai*)
TB/LNNK	LNNK Fatherland and Freedom Alliance (*Apvienîba "Tçvzemei un Brîvîbai"*)
TKL	People's Movement for Latvia (Siegerist Party) [*Tautas kustība Latvijai (Zīgerista Partija)*]
TP	People's Party (*Tautas Partija*)
ZZS	Green and Farmers Union (*Zaïo un Zemnieku Savienîba*)

Lithuania

LCS	Lithuanian Centre Union (*Lietuvos centro sajunga*)
LDDP	Lithuanian Democratic Labour Party (*Lietuvos demokratinė partija*)
LKDP	Lithuanian Christian Democratic Party (*Lietuvos krikśćionių demokratų partija*)
LKDS	Lithuanian Christian Democratic Union (*Lietuvos krikśćionių demokratų sajunga*)
LLS	Lithuanian Liberty Union (*Lietuvos laisvės sajunga*)
LLS	Lithuanian Liberal Union (*Lietuvos liberalų sajunga*)
LMP/NDP	Lithuanian Women's Party/New Democracy Party (*Lietuvos moterų partija/Naujosios demokratijos partija*)
LVP	Lithuanian Peasant Party (*Lietuvos valstiečių partija*)
MKDS	Union of Modern Christian Democrats (*Moderniujų krikščionių demokratų sajunga*)
NKS	Union of Moderate Conservatives (*Nuosaikiujų konservatorių sajunga*)
NS(SL)	New Union/Social Liberals [*Naujoji sajunga (Social-liberalai)*]
TS(LK)	Homeland Union (Lithuanian Conservatives) [*Tėvynės sajunga (Lietuvos konservatoriai)*]

Poland

AWS	Solidarity Election Action (*Akcja Wyborcza Solidarność*)
AWS–RS	Solidarity Election Action–Social Movement (*Akcja Wyborcza Solidarność–Ruch Społeczny*)
AWSP	Solidarity Election Action of the Right (*Akcja Wyborcza Solidarność Prawicy*)
BBWR	Non-Party Reform Bloc (*Bezpartyjny Blok Wspierania Reform*)
CD	Christian Democracy (*Chrześcijańska Demokracja*)
KLD	Liberal Democratic Congress (*Kongres Liberalno-Demokratyczny*)
KP	Polish Convention (*Konwencja Polska*)
KPN	Confederation for Independent Poland (*Konfederacja Polski Niepodległej*)
LPR	League of Polish Families (*Liga Rodzin Polskich*)
MN	German Minority (*Mniejszość Niemiecka*)
OKP	Citizens' Parliamentary Club (*Obywatelski Klub Parlamentarny*)
PC	Centre Alliance (*Porozumienie Centrum*)
PChD	Christian Democracy (*Partia Chrześcijańskiej Demokracji*)
PiS	Law and Justice (*Prawo i Sprawiedliwość*)
PL	Peasant Alliance (*Porozumienie Ludowe*)
PO	Civic Platform (*Platforma Obywatelska*)
PSL	Polish Peasant Party (*Polskie Stronnictwo Ludowe*)
PZPR	Polish United Workers' Party (the Communist Party) (*Polska Zjednoczona Partia Robotnicza*)
ROP	Movement for the Rebuilding of Poland (*Ruch Odbudowy Polski*)
SdRP	Social Democracy of the Polish Republic (*Socjalno-demokracja Rzeczypospolitej Polskiej*)
SKL	Conservative-People's Party (*Stronnictwo Konserwatywno-Ludowe*)
SKL (AWS)	Conservative-People's Party–Solidarity Election Action (*Stronnictwo Konserwatywno-Ludowe–Akcja Wyborcza Solidarność*)
SLD	Alliance of the Democratic Left (*Sojusz Lewicy Demokratycznej*)
SO	Self-Defence (*Samo-Obrona*)
SP	Labour Solidarity (*Solidarność Pracy*)
UD	Democratic Union (*Unia Demokratyczna*)
UW	Freedom Union (*Unia Wolności*)
ZChN	Christian National Union (*Zjednoczenie Chrześcijańsko-Narodowe*)

Romania

CDR	Romanian Democratic Convention (*Convenţia Democrată Română*)
FDSN	Democratic Front of National Salvation (*Frontul Democrat al Salvării Naţionale*), renamed PDSR in July 1993.
FSN	National Salvation Front (*Frontul Salvării Naţionale*)

PD   Democratic Party (formerly FSN, FSN-Roman) (*Partidul Democrat*)
PDAR   Democratic Agrarian Party of Romania (*Partidul Democrat Agrar din Romania*).
PDSR   Party of Social Democracy of Romania (*Partidul Democratiei Sociale din Romania*), formerly FDSN, since 2001 PSD.
PNL   National Liberal Party (*Partidul Naţional Liberal*)
PNŢCD   National Peasant Party–Christian Democrat (*Partidul Naţional Ţărănesc–Creştin Democrat*)
PSD   Social Democratic Party (*Partidul Social Democrat*), formerly PDSR.
PUNR   Party of Romanian National Unity (*Partidul Unităţii Naţionale Române*)
PSM   Socialist Party of Labour (*Partidul Socialist al Muncii*)
UDMR   Democratic Union of Hungarians in Romania (*Uniunea Democrata Maghiară din Romania*)

Russia

DVR   Russia's Democratic Choice (*Demokraticheskii vybor Rosii*)
KPRF   Communist Party of the Russian Federation (*Kommunisticheskaya partiya Rossiiskoi Federatsii*)
KRO   Congress of Russian Communities (*Kongres Russkikh Obshchin*)
LDPR   Liberal Democratic Party of Russia (*Liberal'no – demokraticheskaya partiya Rossii*)
–   Inter-Regional Movement Unity (Medved) [*Mezhregional'noe dvizhenie 'Edinstvo' 'Medved'*]
NDR   Our Home is Russia (*Nash dom-Rossiya*)
OVR   Fatherland-All Russia (*Otechestvo-vsya Rossiya*)
PRES   Party of Russian Unity and Concord (*Partiya Rossiskovo Edinstva i Soglasiya*)
SPS   Union of Right Forces (*Soyuz Pravykh Sil*)
        Strong State (*Derzhava*)
VR   Russia's Choice (*Vybor Rossii*)
ZhR   Women of Russia (*Zhenshchiny Rossii*)

Slovakia

ANO   Alliance of New Citizens (*Aliancia nového obcana*)
ESWS   Co-existence (*Együttélés-Spolužitie-Wspólnota-Souižití*)
HZD   Movement for Democracy (*Hnutie za demokraciu*)
HZDS   Movement for Democratic Slovakia (*Hnutie za demokratické Slovensko*)
KDH   Christian Democratic Movement (*Krestanskodemokratické hnutie*)
KSS   Communist Party of Slovakia (*Komunistická strana Slovenska*)
MOS   Hungarian Civic Party (*Mad'arská Občanska strana*)
PSNS   The Real Slovak National Party (*Pravá Slovenská národná strana*)

SDA	Social Democratic Alternative (*Sociálnodemokratická alternatíva*)
SDK	Slovak Democratic Coalition (*Slovenská demokratická koalícia*)
SDKÚ	Slovak Democratic and Christian Union (*Slovenská demokratická a krestanská únia*)
SDL'	Party of the Democratic Left (*Strana demokratickej l'avice*)
SMK	Party of the Hungarian Coalition (*Strana Mad'arskej koalície – Magyar Koalíció Pártja*)
SNS	the Slovak National Party (*Slovenská národná strana*)
SOP	Party of Civic Understanding (*Strana obcianskeho porozumenia*)
ZRS	Association of Slovak Workers (*Združenie robotníkov Slovenska*)

Slovenia

DEMOS	Democratic Opposition of Slovenia (*Demokratična Opozicija Slovenije*)
DeSUS	Democratic Pensioners' Party of Slovenia (*Demokratična Stranka Upokojencev Slovenije*)
DS	Democratic Party (*Demokratska Stranka*)
LDS	Liberal Democracy of Slovenia (*Liberalna Demokracija Slovenije*)
NSi	New Slovenia–Christian People's Party (*Nova Slovenija – Krščanska ljudska stranka*)
SDS	Social Democratic Party (*Socialdemokratska stranka Slovenije*)
SKD	Slovenian Christian Democrats (*Slovenski Křčcanski Demokrati*)
SLS + SKD	Slovene People's Party (*Slovenska ljudska stranka*)
SMS	Slovene Youth Party (*Stranka mladih Slovenije*)
SNS	Slovenian National Party (*Slovenska nacionalna stranka*)
ZLSD	United List of Social Democrats (*Združene liste socialnih demokratov*)
ZS	The Greens of Slovenia (*Zeleni Slovenije*)

The Ukraine

KUN	Congress of Ukrainian Nationalists (*Konhres Ukrains'kykh Natsionalistiv*)
NDP	Popular Democratic Party of the Ukraine (*Narodno-Demokratychna Partiya Ukraïny*)
PDVU	Party of Democratic Rebirth of Ukraine (*Partiya Demokratychnoho Vidrodzhennya Ukraïny*)
PSPU	Progressive Socialist Party of the Ukraine (*Prohresyvna Sotsialistychna Partiya Ukraïny*)
Rukh	Popular Movement of the Ukraine (*Narodnyi Rukh Ukraïny*)
SDPU (o)	Social Democratic Party of the Ukraine–United (*Sotsial - Demokratychna Partiya Ukraïny–ob''yednana*)

SPU	Socialist Party of the Ukraine (*Socialistychna Partyia Ukraïny*)
For Our Ukraine	(*Za Nashe Ukraïne*)
ZYU	For a United Ukraine (*Za Yedinu Ukraïne*)
UNA	Ukrainian National Assembly (*Ukrains'ka natsionalna asambleya*)

1
Introduction: Representation, Political Parties, and the Quality of Democracy

Representation, secured through routine, regular competitive elections, lies at the heart of parliamentary democracy, the main institutional framework of European political systems. Elections provide the mechanism for selecting those who will act *on behalf* of their electorates. One 'free election' is predicated upon the notion of a subsequent free election, ensuring that power continues to reside with the people, providing them with both a means for judging the quality and responsiveness of their representation and a method of orderly succession in government. It is this assumption of continuation that builds representation and accountability into the liberal democratic system: the electoral mechanism becomes a continual process for ensuring that representatives act for those whom they were elected to serve and are accountable to them (with accountability tested at the next election). Elections 'implant uncertainty in the minds of representatives'.[1] Thus the routinisation of the electoral process is a condition of modern democracy.

The role of elections

The role of elections in new or aspiring post-communist democracies differed however from that of an established democracy. The first reason for this is that the conditions of democratic elections needed to be established simultaneously and in parallel with their implementation. With the gradual democratisation of Western Europe, by the time the concept of 'free, democratic elections' gained currency, a whole series of these prior conditions was already in place for their realisation, if only imperfectly. 'Free, democratic elections' do not occur in a vacuum. An ideal-typical free election is a microcosm of democratic process and practice, both confirming and sustaining 'democracy'.

A free election requires a capacity for public administrative efficiency and integrity to establish a register of eligible voters, to demarcate constituency boundaries, to confirm candidacies, to set up polling stations, to print ballots,

1

to count votes, and apply electoral formulae. It requires the capacity for free expression and public debate to ensure that the electoral mechanism embodies competition, that is, that issues have been aired and choices are meaningful. It requires freedom of association and assembly to develop some set of organisational linkages with society in order that candidates may be trawled/extracted and offered as 'representative'. Historically political parties provided such linkages and evolved and developed with major extensions of the franchise.[2]

A free election requires sufficient sense of political community and consensus to ensure acquiescence in, if not positive acceptance of the results. The rule of law must be embedded to ensure that rules are upheld impartially, that disputes are resolved non-violently, and that the winners take their seats. If elections are free and democratic, then governments generated by the electoral process constitute the effective decision-makers for society. Authoritative control of a territory, the rule of law, and the enjoyment of civil liberties are all fundamental features of the democratic state.

Historically in Western Europe the gradual constitutional embodiment of liberalism – with its emphasis on the rule of law, limited government, and individual rights – provided these prior conditions. Gradually the ensuing challenge of democracy – with its stress on popular sovereignty – to liberalism – emphasising the autonomy of the individual citizen and the need for limited government – created representative liberal democracy, replete with both philosophical and practical tensions.

Although the growth of 'democracy' was closely associated with the extension of the franchise, in states where liberalism was weak the 'democratic institutional context' making representation 'fair' and 'meaningful' was not necessarily in place: there were many 'electoral non-transitions'. The franchise was quite wide for the Russian Duma in 1906, but the Duma had virtually no power. Prussia had universal adult male suffrage from 1867, but again, parliament had little authority. Neither could be regarded as a democracy. The prerequisites were not in place and élites were not committed to democratic processes. This is also why contemporary concepts such as 'electoral democracy', 'delegative democracy' or 'illiberal democracy' are not very useful. Such polities are not democracies, though they share some features with democratic polities. Rather they are what used to be called 'quasi-democracies' or 'facade democracies'. Elections are a necessary but insufficient condition of representative democracy, which must be liberal *in order to be* representative.

In some respects, this basic condition of routine competitive elections was indeed rapidly met in all the countries of the former Soviet 'bloc' and in a number of European Soviet successor states. Over the first post-communist decade, elections generally improved in regard to the efficiency of their administration and in providing the necessary conditions for genuine electoral choice. Electors also demonstrated their ultimate sanction by frequently failing to re-elect the parties of incumbent governments. However, the fact of routine competitive elections does not ensure the quality of democratic representation. Elections only ensure that identifiable persons are elected to parliament to serve as the people's representatives, legitimised by the very fact of the competitive electoral process. But that process has remained badly flawed in certain countries and it has presented continuing problems for many.

Democracy and democratisation

In examining the electoral process and its implications for the quality of democracy, we deliberately eschew much discussion of democratic 'consolidation'. In a broad sense the concept may be useful to suggest a process of the institutionalisation and routinisation of democratic rules and practices. But the distinction often made between transition and consolidation appears to have become hopelessly confused. The widely quoted study by Juan Linz and Alfred Stepan, for example, sees 'tasks of consolidation' as including the development of the autonomy of civil and political society, constitutionalism and the rule of law[3] when surely these are tasks of democracy-building itself. Nor is there agreement on how consolidation should be measured or assessed.[4] Clearly there is no single indicator of consolidation. It is an aggregate concept that involves judging when a variety of institutions and attitudes at various levels are both 'democratic' and 'stable' (yet not static).[5] Yet serious disagreements remain about just what institutions and just whose attitudes are crucial.

The role of political parties provides an example: stable parties are not part of Linz and Stefan's widely cited consolidation menu, but they are often attributed a key role in consolidated democracy.[6] The underlying premise of this book is that the nature of the parties and the party system is absolutely fundamental to modern democracy. Parties are the agents of democratic representation, and we agree with Gábor Tóka that 'the influence of parties and party systems on the quality of democracy can hardly be overstated'.[7] Despite assertions of party decline in Western democracies[8] and parties' often ineffective performance of their functions, no institution challenges their centrality to the democratic process. In the circumstances of post-communism, where alternative mechanisms of representation such as pressure groups remained undeveloped or ill-linked to national decision-making processes, parties were virtually the sole agents of representation.

Political developments in post-communist Europe

Although our focus is on representation, the argument that parties are central to democratisation means that we need some attention to the factors that explain the development of political parties. Traditionally three types of explanation have predominated, none of which are mutually exclusive and all of which are relevant in the post-communist context. Historical factors are vital for explaining the socio-economic and political circumstances in which parties develop. No one studying Central and Eastern Europe can remain in any doubt that 'history matters', though 'what history' and how it matters remain hotly disputed. A second type of explanation stresses the significance of institutional factors. The overall structures of the political system itself and the type of electoral system establish rules of behaviour and provide incentive structures within which political actors operate. Thirdly, the nature of the actors themselves have been given primacy, especially where socio-economic structures are breaking down and institutions are in flux. This stress on élites characterised wider studies of democratisation, as well as studies of party development. Rational choice approaches also focus on élite interests, often with little attention to how they themselves have been shaped. We will make use of all three, while also assuming the importance of their interaction and no uniform direction of causality. It is worth a brief detour to suggest at the outset the significance of institutional factors. The significance of history and legacy for institutional development and political behaviour and the role played by élites will recur throughout this book.

The dominant form of political system adopted in Central and Eastern Europe was the parliamentary system. Inter-war experiences of democracy, however short-lived, had been based on parliamentarism; and in a formal sense the communists also maintained the supremacy of parliament. In most states constitutional amendments had already taken place when the first free elections were held; and subsequent institution-building occurred in parallel with the development of political parties. While many presidents were directly elected (Poland, Lithuania, Romania, Bulgaria, Slovenia, and Slovakia after 1999), and some had considerable powers of legislative initiation and veto (the first three are often regarded rather misleadingly as semi-presidential or premier-presidential[9]), the basic parliamentary principle of government accountability to parliament remained intact. Russia and the Ukraine constituted exceptions to this, with far stronger presidencies and concomitantly weaker parliaments than those elsewhere.

Parliamentary systems are party-friendly because parties structure both parliament itself and the government. Where government is accountable to parliament and (at least in part) drawn from it, parties have proved the only effective organisational mechanism for constructing the necessary support, whether to generate and sustain a government or to criticise and evaluate it. Parliaments provide powerful office-seeking incentives for political parties. In the post-communist parliamentary systems many constitutions such as the Czech and Lithuanian explicitly noted the importance of parties and provided their legal legitimacy. In the Czech Republic the political system is 'based on the free and voluntary establishment of democratic political parties and their right to compete freely' (Article 5).

The position was rather different where strong presidencies emerged, and presidentialism proved less conducive to party development in both Russia and the Ukraine. Indeed, Steven Fish has been the most vigorous advocate of the view that that these states should be viewed as 'super-presidential': A large executive apparatus overshadowed other state agencies and also parliament in its size and resources. The president enjoyed powers to legislate by decree and controlled most levers of public expenditure, as well as exercising considerable influence over the judiciary; impeachment rules made removal difficult, if not impossible.[10]

Part of the explanation of post-Soviet presidentialism lies in the absence of a clear break with the previous regime, making for institutional continuity but also providing a context of ambiguous relations between president and parliament. Mikhail Gorbachev had introduced the Soviet presidency in 1990 as part of his efforts to shift the locus of power from the Communist Party to the state, and many constituent republics of the USSR followed suit. In Russia, Boris Yeltsin won the first direct presidential election in June 1991 and by December had spurred the final break up of the Soviet Union. Conflicts between president and parliament developed throughout the following spring, with mounting political crisis culminating in the bombardment of parliament. These events enabled Yeltsin to effectively impose a highly president-centred constitution, confirmed in a referendum held simultaneously with the parliamentary elections in December 1993. The Duma retained little role in determining either the prime minister[11] or the composition of government. Indeed, President Yeltsin changed prime ministers frequently and with alacrity. Even the Duma's legislative function was weakened because all laws also needed the support of the Federation Council (initially an appointed body), while the president had extensive decree powers. The effect of elections was limited, argued Vladimir Gelman, and they provided 'no more than a façade for the real process of decision-making'.[12] This was not an isolated view: others too saw elections as 'largely worthless, in so far as their results determine neither the composition of the country's government, nor the internal and external policies that it carries out. The absence of real plenary powers makes deputies more radical and irresponsible'.[13] Although there were some signs that the Duma expanded its prerogatives,[14] it is more difficult to sustain the view that Russian legislators and parties could check or tame executive power.

In the Ukraine the 1996 Constitution also established a more clearly presidential system, which President Kuchma sought to shift still further in favour of the presidency. As in Russia, the Supreme Council (*Verkhovna Rada*) did not play a genuine role in appointing the government but was merely required to confirm the president's nomination for prime minister and the government's annual programme. In both cases presidential vetoes also undermined the strength of parliament. The broad institutional framework affected both the type of parties that emerged and their evolution. Political parties remained weak, and in both countries strong presidents attempted to hinder their development and to maintain their own local patronage networks. Parties could not ensure channels of access to decision-makers; indeed those seeking influence had other means, both direct and indirect, of gaining access to power.

In neither Russia nor the Ukraine, however, should strong presidencies be associated with strong states. In the Ukraine in particular what remained of the state under Communism were elements that as a constituent Soviet Republic had never functioned autonomously or with full responsibility. Yet in both cases the rapid decline of state capacity was one of the startling features of post-communist development.[15]

So parliamentarism is party-strengthening, although a parliamentary system does not guarantee strong parties. Of course, even a weak parliament such as the Duma or the Rada may have some party-fostering impact because of the advantages and privileges associated with parties, especially larger parties. Positions such as those of speaker or chairs and membership of parliamentary committees are usually determined on the basis of party, and so too are some patronage opportunities and resources such as offices, equipment, and funds. Committees of parliamentary party leaders may determine the parliamentary agenda. Independents may sit in parliament, but they lack both benefits and influence; in consequence they may also form parliamentary groups (caucuses, clubs, or factions). In Russia parliamentary factions' organisational resources were crucially important to their members' electoral interests; thus factional status was a resource for both ideologically motivated and office-seeking parliamentary factions.[16] Yet in Russia and the Ukraine, party or faction membership did not give automatic access to the patronage resources enjoyed by parties on whose support the governments in parliamentary systems depended. Such patronage was dispersed by the president and his chosen associates.

The type of electoral system[17] also affected party development, though its independent effect is hard to determine when other factors are working in a similar direction[18] (we shall explore this further in later chapters). In parliamentary systems based on proportional representation (PR) parties became the central vehicles of representation and recruitment and, where permitted to stand, the number of Independents fell with successive elections. Governments were formed largely from among the governing parties' own deputies. Independents played no political role in the Czech Republic, Slovakia, Latvia, Estonia, Poland, Romania, Bulgaria, or Slovenia.

In Russia and the Ukraine the combination of presidentialism and the new mixed-parallel electoral systems proved detrimental to political parties. The mixed electoral system encouraged both independent candidates and locally popular parties to stand in the single-member districts. Different parties often stood in the PR and single-district elements, leading to an overall increase in the numbers of parties represented in parliament.[19] At the same time Independents retained a presence in the single-member element. In Russia in 1999, half (51.3 per cent) the candidates in the single-member districts were Independents, and they won 105 of the 225 seats (46.7 per cent). Regional élites in Russia had little incentive to engage in party-building, since they could secure access to power by mobilising their resources for the single-member constituencies, through their own personal connections, as well as through lobbies and other channels.[20]

Party development in the Ukraine was affected by similar factors. But whereas Russia had a mixed system from 1993, the Ukraine used a wholly majoritarian system for the 1994 election, and in addition made it extremely difficult for parties to nominate their candidates.[21] Half the deputies elected to the Ukrainian parliament in 1994 had no party affiliation. The use of a mixed system in 1998 and 2002 meant that half the deputies now automatically owed their election to a party label, but the single-member element still provided scope for large numbers of Independents. In 1998 Independent deputies still won more than half the single-member seats, and in 2002 they won 41 per cent.

Similar mixed-system effects were also seen in parliamentary Lithuania, but they were rather more muted. The small size of the country may also have been a factor hindering the development of local fiefdoms; though parties' support varied widely from region to region, Independents found little purchase. However, the availability of single-member districts for small parties with popular leaders did contribute to party fragmentation. Small parties tried to remain in contention since winning even a few seats could be important in coalition formation.

The existence of separate direct presidential elections in Russia, the Ukraine, and Lithuania (and also in Poland, Slovakia, Slovenia, and Bulgaria) may also be relevant here. When presidential elections are not held simultaneously with parliamentary elections, parties must reorient themselves to a different type of competition. In Russia and the Ukraine strong presidentialism, separate presidential elections, and the mixed-parallel electoral system all worked together to promote personalism and hinder institutionalisation,[22] with serious implications for the development of political parties.

Representation and the electoral process

Most studies treat representation primarily as a *relationship* between the representative and his or her constituents. Mostly the relationship has been conceived as that between an individual voter and his/her member of parliament or between the voter and a political party. The focus is on parliament itself and what representatives actually do during their time there. This is certainly appropriate for the study of mature, stable democracies. Here, however, we take a far broader approach. We aim to demonstrate that for post-communist countries the whole of the electoral process bears on both the development of political parties and the quality of representative democracy.

Of course, parties are not simply vehicles of political representation. Clearly the recruitment of candidates by political parties is a crucial party activity; candidates provide the pool from which representatives are chosen. However, other roles identified by (idealised) functional approaches to parties are also closely related to the process of 'acting on behalf' of those they represent. Parties set the political agenda through their aggregation of interests, their priorities, and their policies. They actively seek to structure public choice. Parties are also mechanisms of integration, bringing people into the political process by providing channels of communication between society and political leaders. They may also articulate certain moral or social values or a concept of the wider community. When their role is effective, the legitimacy of the political system is enhanced and the likelihood of violent social conflict is reduced.

In well-established parliamentary democracies, political parties are fundamental as mechanisms for structuring the institutions of parliament and government. The 'party in public office' constitutes the decision-makers of executive and legislature in parliamentary systems. Governing parties govern and opposition parties offer a critique of their performance. The mettle of party accountability is tested in the electoral cauldron.

Although we do not equate democracy with periodic free elections, we do argue that each stage of the electoral process is relevant to the quality of representative government. The nature of electoral competitors determines the choices available to voters. Representation is affected by electoral strategies of contenders and by their number and type. Voters need to distinguish them and to know what they stand for. In addition, numbers are important. Large numbers of individual politicians and large numbers of parties mean more participants in the legislative bargaining process, 'making it harder to initiate and sustain collective action in pursuit of public goods'.[23]

Nomination regulations and candidate selection procedures determine the pool of potential representatives; but these are also affected by the readiness of individuals to offer themselves as candidates. In circumstances of constant upheaval and dislocation certain types of people may be more prepared than others to seek political office. This is often deemed a particular problem for women's political participation (see Chapter 8). The nature of the choice offered on the ballot is part of this sequence, as are factors such as turnout, electoral volatility, and voters' learning about the effects of the electoral system. How elected deputies act in parliament is another dimension. Where parties are weak focuses of loyalty, important collective goods may be undersupplied or not supplied at all.

Finally, there is the question of how voters can call their elected representatives to account. Accountability is not automatically ensured at the time of each successive election. Voters may be constrained in their choices, particularly when parties disappear or reconfigure themselves. Voters may misunderstand the workings of the electoral system in particular or the political system in general. Radosław Markowski has argued that civic education and socialization are crucial dimensions of developing citizens' capacity to make use of elections as mechanisms of accountability;[24] but few governments carried out such programmes. Nor should one assume that accountability mechanisms apply only to incumbents, judged by the voters with a broad retrospective evaluation. Of course, if the government loses an election, then something clearly has gone wrong. Indeed, voters in post-communist states have not hesitated to 'throw the rascals out'. But accountability may be undermined or obviated by other institutional arrangements. As Przeworski and Cheibub put it, 'Rulers are accountable if the probability that they survive in office is sensitive to government performance; otherwise they are not accountable.'[25] However, electors are not simply evaluating governments or governing parties but also the effectiveness and competence of the opposition. Indeed, poorly functioning governments may win simply because the opposition looks weak or incompetent; and doubtless there are also examples where reasonable governments are displaced by more convincing opposition forces.

In sum, we are concerned first with what is offered to the electorate. Parties and candidates not only reflect but also themselves structure public opinion; their nature affects the range of different choices from which the voter must select. Secondly, we are interested in who is offered to the electorate. The nature of the candidates determines the social composition of parliament, as well as its views. Thirdly, we examine the electorate's response to these offerings. Then we look at the behaviour of deputies themselves, particularly in regard to faction formation and party discipline. Finally, we look at how voters have called their representatives to account at successive elections. Representation is affected by the process through which it takes place and is renewed.

Elections, parties, and representation

The task, then, is fundamentally analytical and empirical: identifying the ways in which relevant aspects of parliamentary elections are pertinent and exploring how they have operated in the first decade since the fall of communism in Europe. It is theoretically grounded, but it is not a work of theory-building. Indeed, for all its centrality to the concept of liberal democracy, political science has little theory of representation. There are diverse *concepts* of representation, based on more or less explicit normative principles; but there is no theory explaining its genesis or evolution or establishing the conditions of its effectiveness. This book contains a great deal of thick description.

This should not be taken to imply that we have no points of departure. This is an area of rich philosophical debate and numerous explanatory insights about the effects of certain historical conditions and institutional developments. Traditionally, much of this debate centred on questions about the appropriate basis of representation, what type of persons would best represent their electorates, and how those elected should behave once in parliament. In the following chapter we first examine the development of the idea and practice of representation from the point of view of the Western European historical experience and explore some implications of the way parties developed. We also explore the rather different concept of representation used by the communist regimes. This provides some reference points and conceptual markers.

Chapter 2 also reviews the ways in which the post-communist departure point differed in significant respects from earlier European experiences of democratization. All these countries began with some fundamental similarities arising from their shared communist experience. However, there were also profound regional and country-specific differences. The initial conditions arising from the 'revolutions' of 1989–90 on the one hand and the disintegration of the USSR on the other gave rise to very different circumstances of democracy-building. This also affected how representation was viewed in the initial debates on electoral systems and the particular systems devised for the first fully free, competitive parliamentary elections.

The first free elections were seminal occurrences in all countries, but not all countries had 'regime-choice' elections. Both the timing of these elections and the wider institutional context also varied substantially, as well as the electoral mechanism itself. The contenders in this proto-democratic phase also determined the early shape of political parties in the subsequent period. Most, but not all, emanated from within parliaments following the semi-competitive elections of the dying days of the *ancien régime* or the first fully competitive elections that marked a break with communist mono-partism. In Central Europe the key factor in the first stage of party development was the nature of anti-communist opposition movements and the manner in which they later split. All these movements gave rise to some enduring political parties.

This was not the case in Russia or the Ukraine, where the first elections were delayed for several years and opposition movements had already crumbled. In Russia, Yeltsin's dissolution of parliament eliminated many advantages to incumbent deputies, including media access. Parliament was not the central site of initial party formation, but neither were there conditions for a 'bottom-up' process of party formation. The residual organisation of the Communist party provided a partial exception. While the Ukraine escaped the trauma of violent intra-élite confrontation, there too parliament was an unpropitious arena from which to launch new political parties. The communists were again in the best position to mobilise the electorate, and fragments of the opposition movement also survived. We have already alluded to the weakness of parliament and the importance of the majoritarian electoral system in strengthening the role of powerful individual candidates with entrenched bases of local support. These differences provide us with some intra-regional comparative benchmarks.

Chapter 3 investigates the kinds of parties that emerged in the first post-communist decade or so. It does so on the basis of their 'electoral' appeal and the array of choices offered to the voters. Maurice Duverger observed that in 'countries new to democracy', parties were normally generated from within parliament, and thus maintained the greater role of the parliamentary party.[26] This was certainly true of post-communist politics. Parties remained essentially top-down creations, though they essayed different strategies for wooing voters. Many parties fit neatly into the ideological 'party families' characteristic of Western Europe's development. However, divisions and mergers shaped the configuration of parties, and so too did the challenge of outsiders. By no means all parties assumed (some) ideological or philosophical underpinnings.

In some cases the pattern of electoral competition influenced the reconstitution of broad disparate *electoral parties* that mimicked earlier opposition umbrella formations. New and old élites in Russia and the Ukraine mobilised their manifold resources in nefarious ways, but the electoral party was also the favoured format of those in power: their 'parties of power' appealed on the basis of patronage relations and broad promises of security and continuity. In most countries communist successor parties also played a significant role, but they too adapted to new circumstances in different ways. Ideological parties vied with electoral parties and various types of populist parties, with a broad anti-establishment appeal. What becomes clear from this evaluation is just how unsettled the political landscape remained in many countries even after three, four, or even five elections. The menu of choice was often confusing and it frequently changed from one election to another, muddying not only electoral choice but electoral accountability.

Chapter 4 explores the ways in which voters responded to the novel experience of electoral competition. It is not concerned with voting behaviour in relation to support for particular parties but rather with the mechanics of the electoral process. The major indicators used here are turnout, the casting of valid ballots, the level of vote 'wastage' in party-list voting, and the use voters made of preference voting in open or semi-closed list systems of proportional representation. Voting is the fundamental act of political participation for many voters, but voters also need to know how to use their vote and to assess the implications of their choice.

Turnout fell in Central and Eastern Europe over the first decade or so, but the decline was neither steady nor uniform. The most persuasive explanations focus on contextual factors rather than institutional ones to explain changes in turnout. When voters did go to the polls they generally cast valid votes from the outset, but this was not always the case. This raised the question of the role of institutions such as the Permanent Electoral Commission but also had implications for civic education in several countries.

Electoral volatility presents particular problems of analysis. Rational-choice views of voters' behaviour are limited in their usefulness because they often depend on some basic assumptions of environmental stability: they assume that voters have a sense of what follows from their actions. In the post-communist context voters often found it very difficult to judge outcomes, and few countries offered them a stable framework for their choices. Electoral systems and political parties changed. Voter learning was harder in a dynamic context and the pattern of wasted votes was difficult to interpret.

Finally, Chapter 4 explains and examines the various complex mechanisms of preference voting available to voters. Choice may have given voters an increased sense of efficacy, but optional preference voting made little difference to electoral outcomes, except in Latvia, where voters' choices did determine the winners from each party. Slovenia, Poland, and Estonia made candidate-choice compulsory, but often with unexpected and unintended outcomes.

Chapter 5 analyses the act of voting from this perspective of outcomes. With the partial exception of certain communist-successor parties, voters failed to develop affective attachments to political parties. In Western Europe, where many parties had arisen to serve and represent certain sections of the community, much of the electorate retained a sense of party ownership, with loyalty transmitted from generation to generation through family and party socialisation processes. In Central and Eastern Europe the top-down creation of political parties created a situation more like a market stall where voters could choose from diverse offerings. Voters neither liked nor trusted their political parties much, and electoral volatility remained high through-out the region. Incumbency did not prove an advantage in circumstances of profound transformation. Time and again voters punished governing parties by removing them from office and even from parliament.

Yet some parties were markedly more successful than others, both in their electoral results and in their participation in government. Successor parties were notable in this respect, especially in Poland, Hungary, Slovenia, and Lithuania. But not all countries had a clearly defined successor to the ruling communist party and some communist parties sought to retain a 'communist identity', stressing their links with the communist past more emphatically than their adaptation to new political and economic circumstances. The electoral success of the communist parties of Russia and the Ukraine was not rewarded by government positions or decision-making influence.

At the same time anxieties that (other?) anti-system parties would gain credibility, while not unfounded, did not have the consequences that many had feared. Support for such parties was considerable, but their sheer numbers invited a dispersal of their support and it was often fragmented. With a few notable exceptions they too proved unable to retain enduring support.

Chapter 6 examines the interaction of political parties. The concept of the 'party system' is central to this discussion, but it is not one that can be applied to all countries. Many factors combined to lead to an absence of systematic party interaction. These included changing numbers of parliamentary parties, rapid alteration of their relative strengths, the introduction of new, often ill-defined actors, the lack of party cohesion, and the concomitant phenomenon of 'party tourism'. Many party configurations lacked coherent patterns of interaction, and all were dynamic. Hungary, the Czech Republic, and Slovenia appeared to have moved in the direction of greater stability and a degree of predictable interaction, that is, to have party systems. Elsewhere, as in Poland, Estonia, and Romania, there was also a measure of continuity-within-change and a measure of partial predictability. Other countries had more fluid party configurations, more uncertainty, and little sign of 'systemness' in party interactions.

The final chapters of this study shift our attention to the character of individual candidates and deputies. The emphasis here is on social representation, and they address three rather different dimensions of generating representation through the electoral process. Chapter 7 focuses on the nature of those standing for office. Although studies often centre on the social composition of parliaments, we analyse the occupations not just of deputies but the wider candidate pool for a number of post-communist countries. If democracy is to work, individuals must contest elections, though most will fail. Although the deputies' occupational profile was by no means uniform, it showed a very rapid shift away from the diverse composition of communist parliaments. The candidate pool was far more socially diverse. Political parties fielded candidates with rather different occupational profiles.

Chapter 8 is also concerned with 'who' represents the electorate. It focuses explicitly on the issue of women's political representation, the reasons for its rapid decline, and the changes that occurred over successive elections. In the absence of strong women's movements, gender too was addressed from the top down by some responsive party élites. Increasing numbers of prominent women politicians provided evidence of women's competence in many Central European parties. More often the issue was not addressed, with traditional male power centres in the economy and in the state administration echoed also in the political arena. Social democratic parties proved particularly receptive to quota arrangements for strengthening women's presence. The 'parties of power' remained overwhelmingly male.

The issue of minority representation is the last to be considered. The first section discusses the issues raised for democracy by minority rights and the evolution of international provisions. It then examines the constitutional frameworks in Central and Eastern Europe, focusing on citizenship issues. There were two basic strategies for ethnic minorities, either forming an ethnic party or seeking accommodation with others capable of serving as a vehicle for minority interests. Ethnicity formed the basis of significant political parties in Bulgaria, Romania, and Slovakia. Yet these should not be regarded as societies divided along ethnic lines. All three ethnic parties found common ground with other parties not only on minority issues (urged by international bodies including the crucial European Union) but on wider issues of democratic development and the economy. In all cases they participated in government – in 2002, two of them, in Bulgaria and Slovakia, were full coalition partners, while the Democratic Alliance of Hungarians in Romania supported the minority social democratic government. The Roma, by contrast, remained an excluded minority. Though placed firmly on the political agenda by the European Union, this had little initial impact on their political representation.

In the Baltic states, with thorny and difficult issues of nation-building in an uncertain international environment, Latvia and Estonia followed an exclusionist path, limiting the citizenship of their large Russian minority (and other small ones). Nationalist fears dominated the early period of restored independence, and minorities remained largely excluded from national political representation. Yet as virulent nationalism waned there were some signs of accommodation and integrative processes, to ease naturalisation and to bring (citizen) Russians into existing political parties.

The concluding chapter focuses on some of the broader themes discussed earlier. The first section reviews the electoral process and the extent to which one can identify general characteristics. This is important because the format of the individual chapters does not match the sequence of questions posed earlier – What and who are offered to the electorate? How did the electorate respond? How did deputies behave once elected? and how did voters call their representatives to account?

It places greatest emphasis on the overall institutional structures of governance, especially the differences between the parliamentary and presidential systems. It reaffirms the view of those who have stressed the workings of presidentialism as an impediment to democratic development, including the development of political parties. Parliamentary government requires the winning of elections as the key to political power. It mitigates, though it does not remove, the persistent elements of patronage and clientelism. It strengthens, though it does not ensure, the functioning of elections as crucial mechanisms of accountability.

The combination of presidentialism and the mixed-parallel electoral system proved mutually reinforcing in hindering the development of political parties and maintaining patronage politics. Indeed, electoral systems were of major significance in shaping the contours of representation. They did not act as a uniform causal mechanism, but they provided an array of differing incentives in parliamentary systems too. Similarly, the communist legacy and the dislocations of transition also remain powerful explanatory factors in both presidential and parliamentary systems. Popular disillusion with democratic institutions, if not with democracy itself, helped create a cycle of electoral and party volatility.

The data

Finally, we need a comment on our case-selection procedures and on the data used in this study. Those countries with some claim to democratic elections have been included, but not those where war or violent upheaval occurred (as in the Caucasus and most of former Yugoslavia) or where the boundaries of state territory remained contested (as in Moldova). Albania's upheaval was of a rather different order than that elsewhere. Its first elections were seen as reasonably fair, but by the mid-1990s the position deteriorated. Not only was the 1996 election blatantly fraudulent, but the collapse of an infamous pyramid scheme led the country into several months of virtual anarchy.[27]

These exclusions leave a rather lopsided selection. It includes all countries of the former 'Soviet bloc': Poland, Hungary, the Czech Republic, Slovakia, Romania, and Bulgaria. It includes only one country of the former Yugoslavia, namely Slovenia, and only five from the former Soviet Union, Latvia, Lithuania, Estonia, the Ukraine, and Russia. Eight of these countries were well-nigh universally regarded as democratic by the end of the twentieth century: Poland, Hungary, the Czech Republic, Slovakia, Slovenia, Latvia, Lithuania, and Estonia. These eight were confirmed in December 2002 as meeting the requirements for membership of the European Union, including stable democratic institutions and safeguards for human rights.

Romania and Bulgaria attracted more mixed assessments, while Russia and the Ukraine were even more problematic. Steven Fish regarded Romania as democratising in 2000, with Bulgaria, Russia and the Ukraine viewed as 'backsliders'.[28] But Zoltan Barany called Bulgaria 'a robust democracy' by the standards of the region, with élites genuinely committed to the constitution and a 'record of democratization...far superior to that of Bucharest'.[29] Certainly both Romania and Bulgaria enjoyed unquestionably free elections. The institutional mechanisms of the separation of powers functioned, not only in the capacity of the opposition to oppose the government, but also in respect of judgements of the Constitutional Court. As of late 2002 both governments appeared to be seeking to implement genuine anti-corruption strategies. Romanian dissatisfaction with the functioning of its institutions led to serious constitutional debate (not always well informed).

There was rather more consensus regarding Russia and the Ukraine. Presidential candidate and leader of the Yabloko party Grigory Yavlinski effectively concurred with Fish that 'political time in Russia is flowing backward...(by 2001 Russia) had become an artificial, formal, sham democracy'.[30] Indeed, Russia was widely viewed as mired in some protracted and uneven process of transformation, witnessing a 'transition from Communism but not yet a transition to *democracy*'[31] – a 'state of uncertainty',[32] 'an unstable electoral democracy',[33] not electoral democracy but 'electoral clanism',[34] or 'bureaucratic quasi-authoritarianism'.[35] Judgements about the Ukraine were not dissimilar. For example, it was seen as a variant of 'semi-authoritarianism' coexisting with 'vibrant elements of a nascent civil society'.[36] Russia and the Ukraine were both dominated by personalistic government, with elements of the Soviet bureaucracy, though disintegrated into various clans, still holding sway.[37] Much of our discussion also provides support for such judgements.

It must be stressed, however, that coverage of these countries remains rather uneven, in part depending on the accessibility of data. Most data utilised here are electoral data (see http:\\www.essex.ac.uk\elections) but they are often patchy, with gaps for certain countries for certain elections or in certain respects. Sometimes these lacunae appear unavoidable. The University of Essex datasets gathered national election results for all elections, but constituency results and candidate data varied widely in their availability. It also proved impossible to gain full election results for the first competitive elections in Bulgaria (1990) and Russia (1993), where these were never published and do not (apparently) exist in any archive collections. The complete results for Czechoslovak elections also appear to be officially 'missing'. All national-level election results are available for Romania, but not all constituency data, nor all candidate data. Restrictions of time and resources also played a role. Generally if I have data, I have tried to include them, even where they are not always strictly comparable. Candidate data are available for all elections only for Poland, Lithuania, Estonia, and independent Slovakia. Countries varied widely in the information collected from candidates and its availability.

The picture that emerges is one of many flaws in the quality of democratic representation. In the context of multiple transformation political leaders faced enormous challenges, but transformation also provided exceptional opportunities for political entrepreneurs. Political parties were shaped not by their societies but by élites, who were repeatedly weighed in the balance and found wanting. Parties split and re-formed, and new parties appeared overnight in a way that would not have been possible without modern media communications. Party-strengthening incentives operated, but they were not sufficient to produce stable party systems across the region. Social insecurity did not manifest itself in a backlash against democracy, but party membership and sustained party support remained low, and turnout declined. Voters continued to search for politicians and parties of integrity and efficacy.

At the same time the gap between the two giants of the former USSR and the rest widened. On virtually every dimension Russia and the Ukraine were different from the others.[38] The issue there was not one of the quality of democracy but of fundamental obstacles to democratic practice. Both countries had competitive elections, but their élites did not ensure their democratic functions. Elsewhere the new democracies had the basic institutional framework of democratic governance in place and operating according to the rules. The main difficulties lay in developing a quality of democratic representation and diffuse political support to ensure the legitimacy and further deepening of the democratic process.

2
Representation and Elections

The concept of representation has remained central to democracy but it is neither easy nor uncontested. Historically several different notions of representation have coexisted in different political systems. For two centuries debates have continued in Western Europe over what is being represented, who should be doing the representing, and how they should do it. Much of Eastern Europe joined these debates in the inter-war years; after 1989 it joined them once again. The Soviet concept of representation, transmitted to Eastern Europe after the Second World War, was less heterogeneous but not without its own contradictions. It remained a minor but persistent influence.

Representation in Western European democracies

The historical context

By the end of the fourteenth century, representative institutions were part of the machinery of government in some dozen European states.[1] Aristocrats, bishops, and burghers met as 'communes' or 'estates' to advise the monarch, providing embryonic forms of political representation, albeit for the few. This was also the origin of the notion of the representative as an agent of a particular community. As far afield as the Dutch United Provinces and Poland, the States General and the *Sejm* were meeting places for mandated delegates, bound by instructions.[2]

Gradually revolutionary demands for representation of wider (property-owning) strata took root in Europe. The first radical extension of the suffrage came with the ratification of the 1789 Constitution in the United States, where more than half the adult male white population was enfranchised. By the end of the Civil War the United States could claim to be a full (masculine, white) democracy. In France the Revolution introduced a complex system of indirect elections (until 1817)[3] and strict property qualifications. Full male suffrage came with the renewed turmoil of 1848.

The idea that members of the legislative assembly were agents of their estates or communities largely expired with the abolition of the Estates-General in France and the replacement of boroughs and shires as the basis of representation in England; but it did not disappear altogether. Moreover, the traditional estates system persisted in Sweden until 1866, and in the Austrian element of the dual Habsburg Monarchy the estates (*curiae*) remained until 1907. In France after 1789 and Britain after 1832 the most widely accepted view was that parliamentarians were elected representatives of 'the nation'. Indeed, new French constitutional provisions prohibited mandates and instructions. According to the 1791 Constitution, the National Assembly embodied the will of the nation, while deputies elected in the departments 'will not be representatives of a particular department but of the whole nation'. The election process itself legitimised the role of representatives as 'collective trustees of national sovereignty'.[4] This fictional principle remained enshrined throughout continental Europe, and it reappeared in Central Europe after 1989.

Arguments about the nature of representation were central to conflicts over extending the franchise. Edmund Burke conceived the national interest as the sum of the objective economic interests represented in the localities, with the summing achieved through processes of parliamentary deliberation.[5] Burke saw parliament as 'a *deliberative* assembly of one nation, with one interest, that of the whole nation' which should be guided by 'the general good, resulting from the general reason of the whole'.[6] All citizens were 'virtually' represented because their interests were assured, 'though the trustees are not actually chosen by them'.[7]

Jeremy Bentham saw Burke's justification of the narrow franchise as a cover for the 'sinister interest' of the propertied minority. For Bentham the national ('universal') interest could only be ensured by adult (manhood) suffrage representing all interests. The *individual* was the unit to be represented, and parliament should mirror the myriad interests and opinions of individuals.[8]

Other key issues of emerging liberal democracy were also articulated as debate intensified in the nineteenth century. For John Stuart Mill representative democracy was not merely the embodiment of the majority will. A permanent majority could ride roughshod over dissenters, who would thus remain unrepresented. Mill, approving Thomas Hare's work on formulae to ensure proportional representation, saw the 'first principle of democracy (as) representation in proportion to numbers. It is an essential part of democracy that minorities should be represented.'[9]

By the middle of the nineteenth century, then, concepts of representing economic (constituency) interests, individuals, society, and the nation vied with one another. At the same time, incipient political parties were developing, albeit at variable rates. Distinct Catholic and Liberal parties appeared in Belgium in the 1830s, but national parties in France remained inchoate until the end of the nineteenth century and generally undisciplined right up to the Fifth

Republic. In Switzerland as in France it was long customary to speak of *tendances* rather than parties. In Britain the 1867 Reform Act provided a huge fillip to party development, notable not least for Conservative efforts to woo the new working-class voters.[10] In Sweden the first election contested by nationally organised parties took place in 1887.

The rise of political parties

As political parties developed in Western Europe as the major institutions of electoral competition, *de facto* ideas of representation by parties took root, although there was never a single theory of party representation. Nor should this be surprising. Parties themselves held different views of representation, and their complex historical adaptation and mutation often resulted in contradictory strands of thought even within a single party. Parties differed on whom they sought to represent and on how the function of representation should be carried out. Yet their developing role caused a shift, as the concept of representation by a political party joined the notion of representation by a particular individual.

Conservative parties proved pragmatic in their adaptation to the competition they faced from the inclusion of new voters. But their underlying belief in a natural social hierarchy remained intact, along with the idea that their deputies would embody the 'national interest'. Conservative parties denied the salience of class and presented themselves as best equipped to serve the public good through strong leadership, offering the maintenance of order, stability, and tradition, with a dose of paternalism thrown in. As one observer wrote of British Conservatism, 'its very genius affirms on the one hand the Solidarity of the nation and the unity of all classes...(and) on the other hand the propriety of leaving predominant political control in the possession of those who are...best fitted to exercise it.'[11]

Liberal parties developed in the nineteenth century as radical groupings of the new middle classes, seeking representation to secure their interests against the aristocratic landowning class that still controlled the state. They aimed to remove state restrictions on the production and trading of goods, and to secure secular constitutionalism with guarantees of individual rights, notably the protection of property, as well as recognition of legal equality and freedom of association. Liberals gained from the initial extensions of the franchise, but the mass franchise created serious difficulties: some declined rapidly, as in Belgium and Italy, or they 'carved out a place for themselves with a sure, if restricted, clientele'.[12]

Emerging socialist parties stressed the significance of class in contrast to liberal individualism. Marx of course saw class conflict as the salient feature of society. He viewed political parties as vehicles of class interests and, with many other socialist thinkers, strived for increased working-class organisation in both trades unions and parties. Socialist parties were needed to represent the working class, as liberal parties represented the bourgeoisie, agrarian parties the peasantry, and conservative parties the landed aristocracy. Workers' struggles also provided arenas in which the oppressed classes could acquire revolutionary awareness.[13] Of course 'working-class interests' had a material dimension involving wages, working conditions, organisational rights, and the like; but there were strong underpinning values in the commitment to equality and liberation from exploitation. The 1918 split between socialist or social democratic parties and communist parties was initially, at least primarily, a division over means rather than ends. Communists supported the revolutionary strategy of the Communist International and the violent defeat of the bourgeoisie, and social democrats the use of electoral and parliamentary means to promote workers' representation within the existing political framework.

Christian parties had a great deal in common with conservative parties, including a hostility to permissive social values and an emphasis on social order. Historically they emerged as a general response to liberal anti-clericalism, to defend Catholics or the Church itself, and to counter growing support for socialist parties. They were ostensibly representatives of 'values' rather than class interests, though their defence of the Catholic Church could also link them strongly to landed interests. These parties in turn generated reactive parties, as with the mobilisation of Dutch Protestants against the Catholic Conservatives. The modern equivalent – the Christian Democratic parties that emerged after 1945 – retained many characteristics of the early religious parties; but their social welfare orientation was especially pronounced.

Political parties, then, appealed to the electorate on the basis of interests, values, and trust in their leadership. As electoral competition increased, parties began to develop programmes and policies. Of course issues were not absent before this – not least the issue of the suffrage itself. Nor were the new programmes necessarily specific. The first programme of the German Catholic *Zentrum* in 1870 'was a deliberately vague document, and, perhaps for this reason, it remained a successful basis for the party's political activities for several decades'.[14] This vagueness also characterised many other parties, and programmes of party principle tended to be enduring.[15]

Leaflets, election addresses, and campaign slogans conveyed a broad message and general image of the party. After 1867 British Conservatives established an extra-parliamentary organisation to mobilise support from the new electorate; in six years it distributed some 800,000 pamphlets and circulars.[16] Many other right-wing parties, with strong local bases and a prior presence in parliament, remained loose associations of local notables, with little attention to issues of organisation or membership: these were Duverger's 'cadre parties'.[17] Their emphasis was on the quality of members, whose resources – prestige, money, connections, expertise – could be mobilised for electoral success. Mass suffrage initially led to some greater opening up of such parties, but they needed voters rather than members; they tended to remain decentralised and loosely knit. Throughout the Fourth Republic, French 'political feudal chiefs' continued to appeal on the basis of the local influence of individual *notables* in areas where the leadership of the old ruling class remained a political asset.[18]

Other parties operated within a distinct milieu, such as that provided by the labour movement for socialists and the churches for Christian parties. A burgeoning number of associations, pressure groups, and civic organisations were often linked to parties. The religious and social democratic 'social-moral milieux' in particular developed close relationships with these associations and fostered a broad socialisation process with their own trade unions, adult education structures, newspapers, and the like.[19] Many parties, most notably socialist parties, developed as membership parties (Duverger's 'mass parties'[20]) seeking the widest possible recruitment to finance elections and educate their members politically. They developed complex institutional structures to relate the parliamentary party, its members, its bureaucratic structures, and its affiliated organisations. The problems of German liberalism prior to the First World War have been attributed in part to its lack of a clear-cut milieu.[21] Similarly in Britain 'the Liberal Party's success before the war was possible because the new class politics had not yet fully taken hold'.[22]

Institutional change also assisted the development of political parties as the central vehicles of representation in Western Europe. Chief among these was a shift from majoritarian electoral systems to proportional representation, often with closed party lists. Many countries had used two-ballot systems, a legacy of the practices of the Catholic Church. Britain was rare in retaining a form of majoritarianism and France also mostly maintained double-ballot systems. But proportional systems came rapidly to predominate, and they firmly shifted the basis of representation from individual to party. They both reflected and assisted the 'segmented division' of the electorate. They also encouraged the strengthening of party structure and internal discipline.[23] The notion of accountability was now, implicitly at least, a collective one: accountability of political parties to their electorates.

Following the First World War the countries of newly independent Eastern Europe built on their (often very limited) experience of party development under imperial rule. Proportional representation was also the norm in these new but short-lived democracies. Parties developed rapidly, resembling the 'party families' of Western Europe, including Christian democratic parties, liberal and conservative parties, and social democratic and communist parties. Peasant parties reflected tensions with the dominant conservative landowners, notably over land reform. Ethnic minority parties pressed for the protection of their own cultural and linguistic communities, while nationalists opposed them. For both nationalist and ethnic parties the 'interests' to be represented were not simply material interests, but also spiritual and cultural values associated with the community itself. In the defeated states – including Germany/Prussia, and also Austria, Hungary, and Italy – irredentist nationalism contributed to the success of fascist movements in the 1930s.

Fascism, which also developed strong domestic permutations in Spain, Romania, and the Croatian territories of Yugoslavia, was anti-democratic and anti-parliamentarian, as well as nominally anti-capitalist. Fascist parties nonetheless competed in elections on the basis of a varied ideological admixture of anti-democratic nationalism, imperialism, anti-Semitism, and anti-socialism. But effectively the fascist idea of representation was based on the leadership principle, with the leader serving as the 'brain' for society as a whole.

Despite the brevity of the democratic interlude in Central and Eastern Europe everywhere save Czechoslovakia, some authoritarian regimes permitted a limited role for political parties and continued to hold flawed or rigged elections throughout the inter-war period. Czechoslovakia and Hungary also held free elections in the interval between the end of the Second World War and the communist assumption of power. However, the lands incorporated into the USSR in the 1920s had no practical experience of democracy: Soviet concepts of representation remained their basic point of reference.

Contemporary party representation

Numerous post-war developments generated varied scholarly approaches and emphases relevant to our concern with representation. The first stressed the stability of historic cleavages, the institutionalisation and continuity of political parties (the 'freezing hypothesis'[24]). Strong party identification linked segments of the electorate to their parties. Parties were bearers of ideology, offering the voters programmes consonant with their broad philosophies on a clear Left–Right continuum.[25] Voters chose on the basis of packages of policies presented by parties, and their representatives obliged themselves to pursue those policies. It followed that members of parliament should support their party's policies by voting in parliament as a disciplined bloc. In Britain this was increasingly formalised from 1945 onwards as the 'doctrine of the mandate'. By voting for a party, the electorate collectively endorsed the policies laid out in the party's manifesto and thus provided a mandate for the governing party. Since the largest party (almost always) formed the government, the lines of accountability were clearly identified and the party could be called to account at the next election.

Where political parties were involved in coalition governments, responsibility for government action remained less clear-cut. However, mandate theories of sorts also made their appearance, also known as the 'responsible party' model of representation.[26] The importance of party programmes and election manifestos generally grew in tandem with the growth of government, while election programmes also became increasingly specific in content.[27]

By the late 1960s, however, scholars were detecting a shift in the nature of West European parties and their electoral strategies. Otto Kirchheimer identified a new breed of 'catch-all "people's party"', emerging as a response to softening class divisions and less salient religious conflicts. The mass parties were 'abandoning attempts at the intellectual and moral *encadrement* of the masses (and) turning more fully to the electoral scene, trying to exchange effectiveness in depth for a wider audience and more immediate electoral success'.[28] Kirchheimer stressed the 'drastic reduction of the party's ideological baggage', a further strengthening of the top party leadership, the reduced role of individual members, a broadening of the party's clientele, and increased links with a variety of interest groups.[29] He feared that the evolution of catch-all parties would erode the representative role of parties, making them '...something too blunt to serve as a link with the functional power-holders of society'.[30]

This analysis struck a strong chord. Some parties were already highly successful in their appeals to a wider society. The British Conservative Party attracted high levels of working-class support, and the post-war German Christian Democrats included both Catholics and Protestants in their electoral constituency. Puhle identified two main trends associated with the development of catch-all parties: Programmes and milieux became less important as societal links weakened, and the representation of particular interests diminished. Campaigns became more professional as parties adopted marketing strategies to maximise votes. In consequence parties became 'more centrist, more moderate, and more similar to one another...'.[31] Yet although the catch-all party was often added to the growing repertoire of party types, its implications for parties as vehicles of representation lay unexplored.

Clearly not all parties could be described in this way, and not all countries witnessed this type of party evolution.[32] Many cadre-like or elitist parties remained; others developed their organisational structures, yet could not be described as member-oriented 'mass parties'. Communist parties adapted but remained distinctively ideological (most transformed themselves into social democrats following the fall of European communism). Many social democratic parties in particular faced the dilemma of how far they could move to the centre without alienating their traditional supporters. Even catch-all parties needed some means of differentiating themselves from their competitors. Ideology and policies did not disappear, and they had always been supplemented with appeals to professional competence and the quality of leaders.

Yet the development of new strategies seeking to build more heterogeneous coalitions implied an erosion of the view of representation that emphasised the diverse values and interests of particular elements of society. Moreover, from the 1980s the catch-all party was seen as further evolving, with less organisation, increased fragmentation, and a further decline in the anchoring of parties in social cleavages. Panebianco identified the increasing professionalisation of party élites in the 'electoral-professional party', with the use of modern media channels to appeal to less-segmented electorates.[33] Richard Katz and Peter Mair identified the presence of 'cartel parties',[34] emerging as a result of the capacity of parties to manipulate the state in their own interests [*sic*]. Cartel parties did not represent elements of the electorate, nor even act as brokers between state and society. As parties in power they colonised the state and allocated themselves large subsidies, obviating the need for individual members or wealthy donors to finance them. Notably in Austria, Italy, and Germany, through collusion and power-sharing of privilege and patronage, political parties became part of the 'party-state'. These parties no longer represented society's interests, making it 'necessary for societal interests to be represented by different groups and organisations, which, in turn, approach the parties in their function as *representatives of the state*'.[35]

At the same time new parties challenged the old bases of representation, as well as the catch-all strategists and the cartel parties. Between 1980 and 1984 Green parties emerged in twelve countries of Western Europe.[36] They brought a new emphasis on the representation of ('post-materialist') values, including the representation of future generations. One strand of greenery introduced a new style of left-wing politics and links with representatives of social movements, such as feminists and gay rights' activists. Greens entered national parliaments in Belgium in 1981 and in Germany, Switzerland, and Finland in 1983, after which they became familiar features of the parliamentary scene and governing partners in several countries.

A wave of rising parties of the extreme right also provided new reference points both for parties and voters. These new parties were widely held to be 'anti-system parties', an element shared with their neo-fascist counterparts.[37] Like the fascists and neo-fascists these were often leader-parties offering the promise of national salvation with 'a messianic, crusading recipe of national redress and redemption . . .'.[38]

Extreme-right parties (ERPs) were certainly anti-establishment parties whose values conflicted at various points with those of liberal democracy. There was widespread recognition of ERP hostility to the functioning of socio-political institutions, including the bureaucracy, but also to other political parties, which were condemned as self-serving and corrupt.[39] They were nationalist, often racist, with an obsessive xenophobia and a central stress on anti-immigrant policies. Strong populist elements also surfaced in ERP claims to speak for 'the people', many of whom had been 'deceived by the mass media and political leaders to a point where they are incapable of expressing their real interests'.[40] In part, at least, the dramatic (if temporary) success of Haider's Freedom Party (FPÖ) in Austria in 2000 stemmed from a reaction to the cosy, entrenched position of the two major parties.[41]

We see, then, that political parties are not uniform vehicles of political representation, and that some scholars see the parties' crucial representation function as having been eroded or even abandoned to other organisations. Wolinetz has suggested three types of political party as a heuristic device for comparative analysis.[42] Policy-seeking parties include parties with well-defined programmes and/or well-articulated ideologies, single-issue parties, and protest parties. Policies are their priority, and they generally give greatest weight to the articulation or defence of their policies. Vote-seeking parties want above all to win elections, and they regularly manipulate their policies to maximise electoral support. Office-seeking parties are satisficers rather than maximisers, preferring low-risk strategies to maintain their attractiveness as coalition partners, and more concerned with reaping the benefits of office than with any policy agenda. Although there are undoubtedly grave difficulties with the application of these overlapping and hardly mutually exclusive categories, this conceptualisation reinforces the view that some parties take representation of interests and values very seriously. Others, more concerned with organisational or personal self-aggrandisement, stand in violation of the very principles of representative democracy they profess.

The nature of the representative

As parties first developed, offering programmes based on the values and interests they sought to serve, so too they offered a view of the nature of the representatives themselves. Socialist parties in particular stressed that *workers* should represent the interests of working people, just as bourgeois represented bourgeois. This view was later echoed by feminist thinkers (see below) who argued that democracy was undermined by the small numbers of women in parliaments. National minorities, whether cultural or linguistic, also tended to doubt whether non-members could effectively represent their interests (see Chapter 9).

These ideas dovetailed with the view expressed earlier that parliaments in general should be reflective of social diversity, although the two strands are not essentially interwoven. Hare and d'Hondt, the main architects of proportional representation, were the effective progenitors of descriptive[43] (or characteristic[44] or microcosmic[45]) representation. But they did not advocate it. Both liberals and conservatives agreed with Mill's anxieties about the behaviour of the masses and the potential 'tyranny of the majority'. The notion that parliament should have a majority of working-class deputies was anathema to him. He argued that the representatives should be 'more highly instructed' and 'wiser' than their electors, bringing voters the benefits of their 'superior intellects'.[46] Liberals emphasised the importance of diversity, but they did not seek diversity of characteristics from their candidates. Conservative parties maintained the view that politics should remain an élite affair, with the natural hierarchy of society reflected in the dominance of the superior stratum of society. These elements would be the agents of society, acting on its behalf and in its best interests. Parties thus held differing views on the quality of the individuals serving as political representatives: they ranged from the view that interests of social groups are best expressed by representatives drawn from their particular milieu to the view that 'superior' individuals could best translate the interests they sought to represent.

The representation of women

Ideas regarding social representation faded rapidly with the professionalisation of parties, but they gained new impetus with the emergence of feminist scholars of representation. First, there were issues of democratic justice or 'symbolic equity'.[47] In the words of Anne Phillips, 'Any system of representation which consistently excludes the voices of women is not just unfair; it does not begin to count as representation.'[48] Symbolically it clearly makes a difference if women are visible in politics, especially given the 'traditional' view that politics is a man's game. In a broad egalitarian sense it also matters if women are deprived of opportunities in certain spheres of life. A country cannot lay claim to genuine democracy if there are identifiable categories effectively excluded from the political process.[49]

Secondly, broad arguments centred on society's effective utilisation of the resources possessed by women. Effectively, valuable human resources are wasted if society fails to tap the talents of half its population. Women bring a more compassionate and more collaborative style to politics.[50] Moreover, women are more public-spirited and less prone to corruption.[51]

Finally, there is the issue of the representation of 'women's interests'. This area aroused wide debate, and there is no consensus about how far women *qua* women have common 'interests'. However there is a measure of agreement among feminist writers that women must have the capacity to construct their own interests. They must be politically visible as women, and empowered to act as women because they may have needs and attitudes on vital issues which differ from those of men.[52] Phillips argued that if women are not represented (by women), then 'their needs might then be defined from above and not even explored by women themselves'. Moreover, women share at least one interest: 'They need improved access to every sphere.'[53]

Some findings indicated that women do make a difference to the outcomes of parliamentary deliberations, that is, increased representation of women could affect the political agenda and policy outcomes.[54] Norris and Lovenduski used the notion of a 'critical mass', such that 'things happen' after the 'mass' has been reached.[55] However, there is some difference as to how massive the mass must be. In this respect, however, the argument clearly shifted over the years from symbolic to substantive equity, though the symbolic dimension cannot be ignored.

The role of the representative

Debate about the nature and character of representatives still left open the question of how those individuals would act 'on behalf of' the electorate. Mill had no doubt that his wiser representatives should be free to exercise their own discretion.[56] In this respect he echoed Burke, who also stressed that conscience and judgement would determine his vote, not the dictates of constituents. In France 'rampant individualism' long undermined the parties' capacity for effective parliamentary organisation.[57] In general the tradition of the independence of deputies proved enduring there, with the exception of the Communist Party, even as party discipline increased in the 1960s.[58]

In contrast, some 'mandate theories' viewed representatives as agents, but of their parties rather than of their constituents. In some socialist parties this approach became entangled with the view that deputies' loyalty was owed via the party to that segment of the electorate which had elected them. At the same time parties and deputies also portrayed their pro-grammes as best designed to serve the 'national interest'.

Individual deputies were not robots, and party sanctions could never make discipline absolute. Members of parliament faced multiple and sometimes conflicting demands: as individuals, as party members, from those who elected them, from all their constituents. In Britain the problem was partly resolved by stressing two separate roles. First, as party members MPs would support their party's programme in parliament. Second, they would serve their individual constituents by providing them with assistance for their difficulties, giving advice, intervening with national or local government departments: this social care function became a significant part of the British MP's role. In post-war West Germany, with its mixed-member electoral system, those deputies elected in single-member constituencies were also expected to work to maintain strong personal links with the voters. In France deputies maintained and made much of their local linkages, often seeking multiple offices at local and national level. Political leaders often served as mayors of major cities. In PR systems the idea of territorial/consti-tuency representation was further weakened, and less emphasis was placed on the individual deputy.

Representation and its export

We have identified significant philosophical differences in approaches to how individuals and parties should seek to act 'on behalf of' or represent others. Moreover, we identified enormous tensions in the exercise of repre-sentation by collective bodies, that is political parties. Parties are not unitary actors, and they have their own institutional interests and concerns with self-preservation and self-aggrandisement. There is no 'model' of representation that can easily be adopted and transferred from one political context to another.

For the independent states of Central and Eastern Europe historical, cultural, and institutional reference points included the observed West European experience, which had influenced their own inter-war institutional develop-ment. Many of them also had more contact with Western post-war Europe, and in the 1990s they rapidly established links with both individual parties and European-level bodies such as the Socialist International. Their own experience of communism was far from irrelevant, however. The basic conceptual and institutional framework laid down by the Soviet Union was adapted to varying degrees by individual countries, and elements of the underlying 'theory' of representation persisted in a number of countries. Soviet successor states outside the Baltic region lacked any prior experience of democratic practices and had little knowledge of the workings of democratic states. It is therefore not surprising that following the disintegration of the USSR, debates over the nature of parliament and the electoral process drew heavily on their own experience of 'socialist democracy'.

Communist approaches to representation

When the Bolsheviks came to power in 1917, their ideas of representation were often ill-formed, utopian, and ad hoc. They drew on concepts developed by Marx; the practices of the emerging European socialist parties; the views of Plekhanov (the 'first Russian Marxist'); Lenin's own battles with the 'revisionism' of German Social Democrats and with his domestic left-wing opponents; and the experiences of the 1905 Revolution. Lenin was also a masterly tactician, and he readily abandoned ideas developed in earlier periods in the light of current circumstances.[59] However, Stalin adapted a number of key Leninist precepts to Soviet practice. We can summarise the core ideas without too much oversimplification.

First, the working class was the central historical actor of the capitalist period and class struggle was the motor of history. The revolutionary task was its emancipation through the dictatorship of the proletariat, with the Party as the organisational vehicle of the most enlightened section of the working class. Second, parliamentary democracy had many strengths, but at base it remained a cloak for masking the interests of the (bourgeois) ruling class, so the separation of powers was a sham. As socialist democracy developed, individual freedoms would become genuine with economic and social emancipation from capitalist exploitation through workers' control of production. In the meantime, the success of the revolution was the highest law, and particular democratic principles might need to be sacrificed.[60] Third, the key political institutions would be the soviets (councils) representing workers and peasants and combining executive and legislative functions on the lines of the Paris Commune.[61] The links of soviet deputies with their electors would be sustained because deputies would still keep their jobs while serving and by the mechanism of recalling them for unsatisfactory performance.

As the Soviet Communist Party tightened its grip as the single party of power under Stalin, the electoral mechanism operated in the context of the 'leading and guiding role of the Communist Party'. Both Lenin and Stalin accepted the principle that parties served as the representatives of class interests. Lenin used this as a justification for the banning of parties serving the 'enemies of the working class' and indeed by 1921 a ban on all other political parties. Class enemies were seen as a real and present danger in circumstances of foreign intervention and civil war. From 1922 to 1936 Soviet elections were indirect and conducted on the basis of a weighted franchise that favoured urban workers and excluded those deemed to have been tainted by association with the old regime. This disenfranchisement of 'class enemies' subsequently reappeared in the immediate post-war elections of independent Eastern Europe, when 'fascists' or collaborators were excluded.

Stalin declared the achievement of socialism in 1936, when the class enemies were deemed to have been defeated. Direct elections and universal suffrage were restored. Stalin actually prepared for genuinely competitive elections, but he reversed his position after receiving local reports of potential centres of opposition.[62] The formal justification for single candidates was a clear exercise in sophistry: Since parties represented classes, and class harmony was the prevailing order in the new socialist phase, only one party was necessary to electoral politics. In this context there was no need for competing candidates.

This view meshed well with the concept of the Party's 'leading role'. Thus from 1936 to 1989 Soviet national elections were held in single-member districts, with a single candidate standing in each. The voter's task was to endorse (or delete) the candidate, whose democratic legitimacy was confirmed by the absolute-majority requirement for election. The deputy's accountability was then ensured through his/her 'mandate', specifying the issues and tasks to be undertaken for voters, and the electors' formal right of recall. A turnout requirement of at least 50 per cent of the electorate constituted an additional 'guarantee' that deputies would represent a majority of their constituents.

The communist assumption of power in Eastern Europe after 1945 entailed the adoption of the 'superior' Soviet political system, including its electoral practices. Other political parties were often permitted,[63] but they remained subordinate to the Communist Party in 'popular front' formations. Majoritarian electoral systems based on single-member districts were introduced in all but Poland and the GDR, which had multi-member districts for much of the post-war period.[64]

Alongside the representation of individuals in territorial constituencies, the USSR gave formal recognition to ethnicity in elections to the Soviet second chamber, the Soviet of Nationalities. Not all nationalities were represented. Nor did nationality deputies necessarily belong to the nationality they 'represented': a Russian could represent Kazakhs as well as Russians. But a complex system of federal and sub-federal units did give opportunities for representation of the larger Soviet minority groups. There also remained some element of functional representation in the role played by social organisations and the workplace in the nominating and recall procedures. This took on a specific form in 1989, when one-third of the seats in the USSR's new Congress of People's Deputies was reserved for social organisations, including the Communist Party.

The basic precept underlying the socialist concept of representation remained, however, the cross section or mirror image. As far as possible representatives should be 'like' their voters in terms of occupation, age, and gender and should maintain strong local ties. To achieve this 'reflection' the Party issued guidelines regarding composition to 'assist' nominating committees. Assemblies in communist states had large numbers of (formally) working-class deputies and a broader occupational profile than that in Western European parliaments, as well as more women.

Thus there was a particular emphasis on the representative function of elections, accompanied by perennial concerns with improving the quality of 'socialist democracy'. Under Nikita Khrushchev (1957–64) there was greater emphasis on deputies' mandates and on the right of recall.[65] It was also under Khrushchev that discussions again took place regarding the possibility of multi-candidate elections.[66]

Such developments had already taken place in Poland. One response to political upheaval in 1956 was the practice of having more candidates than seats, as well as the inclusion of independent lay Catholics (Tadeusz Mazowiecki, the future Solidarity prime minister in 1989, gained parliamentary experience as a Catholic deputy). Electoral reform also constituted a persistent theme in Hungary from the mid-1960s.

The Hungarian regime first retained proportional representation, though this was irrelevant from 1949 with a single 'government list' and no opposition candidates. In 1966 Hungary adopted the Soviet-type majoritarian system as a means to 'strengthen links between deputies and their constituents'. Its provision for multiple candidacies was little utilised, and in 1970 the Party called for more competition to generate an 'improvement in the electoral mechanism'.[67] In 1971 only 49 of 352 districts saw contested elections; but the provision was not entirely irrelevant.[68]

When concerns about political participation and the strengthening of 'socialist pluralism' placed electoral reform on the agenda in the early 1980s to 'enhance the political maturation and voluntary participation of the citizenry',[69] increased electoral choice was the centrepiece of the new proposals. Choice would enliven elections, provide better quality representation, and rejuvenate parliament. At the same time, the revised Hungarian electoral law of 1983 included mechanisms to ensure continuing Party control. Alongside new provisions for mandatory multiple candidacies in each constituency sat a new, uncontested national list to ensure the election of selected luminaries. Party control of nominating procedures also remained considerable[70] and proved sufficient to ensure the defeat of prominent dissidents. Local party committees often persuaded incumbents not to stand as part of the proposed 'renewal', but they had difficulty in finding 'matching pairs' of competing candidates to generate the desired social composition of the new Hungarian parliament.

Multiple candidacies improved the quality of political debate, and local issues emerged as central to the campaign.[71] In 1985, 35 genuine Independents won seats along with the new breed of party members. Parliament became increasingly active, both in the work of its committee system and in its public profile.[72] The concept of constituency service developed; it became an important reason for the subsequent emphasis on single-member districts in the 1989 electoral law. The need for a close connection with the electorate and concern with local matters was 'deeply rooted in the Hungarian public mind'.[73]

Yugoslavia departed considerably from the Soviet model, with a distinctive emphasis on functional representation. The idea of a 'democracy of soviets' was a manifestation of their specific 'self-managing' socialism superior to both Soviet and bourgeois practices.[74] Electoral laws changed frequently, but voters were essentially regarded as citizens granted political representation, while workers enjoyed economic representation and members of a nation had representation for their republics. The system was a complex combination of direct and indirect elections. Throughout the 1960s the League of Yugoslav Communists wrestled with the tension between party control and increased voters' participation and choice. Some 'undesirable' candidates got through in multi-candidate elections, especially in 1967, while the party's ability to ensure broad social representation was also undermined. The 1974 Constitution reverted to indirect elections in a complex 'delegation system' that ultimately failed,[75] and by 1988 elements of direct election were again planned for 1990.

Western observers largely dismissed 'socialist' elections up to the late 1980s. There was little, if any, genuine competition;[76] elections served socialisation, recruitment, mobilisation, and legitimation functions[77] that benefited the Party rather than the electorate. Elections could not alter the composition of government. Increasingly many ruling parties themselves came to realise the inadequacies of the system. The stress on deputy service, the notion that different milieux had different needs, and provisions for recall were democratic elements that had lost their democratic force with the dominance and control of the ruling party.

Reforms aimed at improving deputy–constituency links by providing elements of competition and choice had some impact in Poland, Hungary, and Yugoslavia and a profound impact on the USSR, where the 1989 elections marked the first stage of the disintegration of the communist system. In the post-communist period advocacy of single-member districts to improve the quality of representation persisted in continuing debates on electoral legislation. It was one reason for the prevalence of mixed electoral systems in the post-communist period. In 2002 discussions favouring a shift from proportional to mixed or majoritarian systems were still salient in Poland, Romania, Slovakia, and Lithuania.

The post-communist context and the founding elections

The context of democratisation in communist Europe was very different from the evolutionary circumstances of democratisation in Western Europe.

It was not the gradual extension of the franchise but the mobilisation against communism that provided the opportunity for free, competitive elections and the process of democracy-building. For individual countries much depended on the timing of elections, the institutional framework, and the outcome of the first elections; but there were also significant common features.

The suddenness and near simultaneity of change in Central and Eastern Europe thus provided the first major contrast with Western Europe. Two other contrasts pertained throughout the region and persisted as a legacy of the old system. First, the rule of law and constitutional norms had not governed communist regimes. Theirs was a culture of arbitrary power. It could be very efficient, as in the highly developed administrative arrangements for conducting elections. Yet law was not a supreme principle but an instrument of politics. Secondly, the communist systems were highly centralised. There was no tradition of strong local government to provide a mechanism for popular, 'bottom-up' political input. Local government was the prisoner of the centre, incapable of providing local forums of representation or of providing a school for new political parties.

The third arena of difference, that of civil society, was one of considerable variation within the region. One feature of communist regimes was the contrast between their emphasis on mobilising the population while simultaneously prohibiting its autonomous social and political action. There was an official 'ethos of participation'. People were urged to participate in political manifestations; to serve as local government volunteers; to join trades unions and ancillary organisations; and of course to provide the highest possible turnout for elections. On the other hand, the Communist Party prohibited spontaneous voluntary groups and controlled existing organisations by licensing and monitoring them, appointing their leaders and setting their tasks through the *nomenklatura*, and censoring their public pronouncements. Society was made up of controlled subjects rather than active citizens.

The particular nature of each regime and the pattern of social mobilisation had a profound effect on the ways in which communism was challenged in 1989–92 and the ways in which political parties developed. At the same time the long-term suppression of social activism provided a fundamental contrast with the West European experience. There were few distinct 'milieux' or embedded social institutions to provide a basis for political parties.

The fall of communism and the mode of exit

The 'revolutions' in Central and Eastern Europe in 1989–90 and the collapse of the Soviet Union at the end of 1991 inaugurated the multifaceted transformation of communist political and economic systems and international relations, with profound consequences for social and cultural developments. Not all the revolutions embodied democratic aspirations, but outside Central Asia élites articulated a commitment to liberal democracy, at least in rhetoric. Their break with communism came, however, in rather different ways.

After Mikhail Gorbachev became leader of the USSR in 1985, his reform programmes released Soviet society from vigorous censorship and existing constraints on voluntary social organisation. Strikes and demonstrations became commonplace occurrences as the Soviet Union began to unravel. Gorbachev urged reform on his East European colleagues, though not all reacted positively. In Poland and Hungary, Gorbachev legitimised and further stimulated the greater tolerance of dissent that had emerged earlier; both these countries had already developed as variants of soft authoritarianism. In Bulgaria and Czechoslovakia the regimes responded hesitantly with small measures of relaxation. In Romania the regime remained extremely repressive, and did not respond at all; the space between the public and private spheres remained empty.

In the Soviet Union the ferment caused by the rapid release of earlier restrictions gained organisational focus in the periphery. Increasing economic chaos provoked responses at the level of the federal and sub-federal units; republics and regions began to assert claims to control their own resources. In 1988 the Communist Party resolved to redesign Soviet federalism, with more rights given to the republics and a clearer division of powers. But Gorbachev was rapidly left behind as republics began to declare their own 'sovereignty' and assert the superiority of republican over all-union law (the 'war of laws'). In the Baltic republics in particular the original Popular Fronts for the support of *perestroika* rapidly became movements for political independence. Key elements of their communist parties allied themselves with national aspirations.

At the same time the 1980s marked the start of ferment in Yugoslavia. The highly decentralised model of federalism had lost its key integrative force with the death of Tito. Slovenia in particular saw the rapid emergence of an active, diverse civil society with a 'self-management consciousness' and strong reform communism under Milan Kučan, with the two elements increasingly allied against centralising tendencies emanating from Serbia.[78] As with the Balts, national and democratic aspirations intermingled and reinforced one another. But in Slovenia decisions about multi-partism could be taken at the republic-level. Proto-parties emerged from the growing *de facto* pluralism. The League of Slovene Communists published its Renewal Programme in March 1989, confirming the abandonment of one-party rule. By December the Slovene Assembly had adopted new laws on political association. Free elections were scheduled for April 1990.

Poland was an exceptional case, not least because it was the first to change its political regime. In this regard it was also the exemplar for its neighbours, showing that genuine change was possible. Poland had had a national opposition movement, the Solidarity trade union, for almost a decade. Prohibited under martial law after December 1981 and weakened by its underground existence, Solidarity never the less provided an alternative focus of loyalty for much of the population. After successive failed efforts at both repression and reform, the ruling party adopted a strategy of coopting Solidarity into the political process.[79] When the regime negotiated measures of institutional change with Solidarity in spring 1989, among them were semi-competitive elections designed to ensure that the communists and their satellite parties retained a parliamentary majority. The arrangements backfired during the election of June 1989, when communist miscalculations and powerful popular support for Solidarity led to the defection of the satellites and the construction of a Grand Coalition under Solidarity leader Tadeusz Mazowiecki. In the newly elected parliament communist deputies participated in a reform consensus supporting radical measures to speed both democratisation and the move to a market economy. It was this 'contract parliament' that generated the system used for the first free parliamentary elections in 1991.

In Hungary the Communist Party, as in Slovenia, endorsed the concept of genuine multi-party pluralism. Although lacking Slovenia's wider social activism, Hungarian proto-parties had emerged from 1988, along with the strengthening of reformist elements within the Communist Party. The regime negotiated systemic change with key elements of the opposition at the Round Table in summer 1989, including new institutional arrangements and a new electoral system.[80] In both these socio-economically advanced and relatively liberal communist regimes the incumbents faced a relatively strong pro-democratic opposition that was ideologically differentiated while retaining a capacity for concerted action.

In Czechoslovakia and Romania reform communists played a negligible role, nor was their contribution much greater in Bulgaria. In Czechoslovakia the communists fell in late 1989 through escalating public demonstrations to which they proved incapable of responding. Small erstwhile dissident groups provided leadership and rudimentary organisation for Civic Forum (the Czech wing) and Public against Violence (in Slovakia). The communists' effective abdication permitted the election by parliament of dissident playwright Václáv Havel as president in December. The composition of governing institutions changed with the cooptation into parliament and government of Civic Forum and Public against Violence. By early 1990 about half the deputies were newly incorporated oppositionists,[81] positioning their combined forces for free elections in June.

The Romanian 'revolution' differed not only in its violence and bloodshed, but also in the key role played by the military, elements of which refused to defend the repressive regime in the face of spontaneous popular mobilisation.[82] The military formally transferred its allegiance to the newly created National Salvation Front (*Frontul Salvării Naţionale* – FSN). The summary execution of the Ceauşescus on Christmas Day 1989 brought an end to violence, but the role played by former communists in creating the

Front led many to question the authenticity of its democratic aspirations. The Front took the lead in a new, more broadly based council to determine the shape of the electoral system, along with other constitutional issues. The long period of repression had prevented the emergence of a potential counter-élite and the FSN reaped the electoral benefits of incumbency.

In Bulgaria, the Communist Party's ditching of its leaders has been likened to a 'palace coup', followed by a rapid rechristening as the Bulgarian Socialist Party. The Bulgarian Union of Democratic Forces (SDS) brought together some ten disparate dissident groups shortly after the removal of communist leader Todor Zhivkov and rapidly demonstrated their ability to mobilise the (urban) population in mass demonstrations. The opposition movement was new, weak, and inexperienced but nonetheless able, with the threat of strikes and mass protest, to position itself as interlocutor in round-table talks on political reform in winter–spring 1990.[83]

We see, then, that Hungary provided an example of change through what has become known as 'pacting', with agreement negotiated successfully between reform elements of the communist party and the opposition. Poland also had elements of a 'pacted transition', but the participants did not address systemic transformation; moreover, given the centrality of electoral mobilisation to regime-change, this cannot be categorised simply as 'revolution from above'; Solidarity's support meant that it could act as the agent of dis-affected society. Elsewhere, spontaneous popular mobilisation was central to the defeat of communism and pacts were absent or of secondary importance.

The new electoral laws: representation and other matters

Naturally, states needed new electoral laws for their first competitive elections. This applied to Hungary, Czechoslovakia, Slovenia, Romania, and Bulgaria, as well as to Poland in 1991. The Soviet republican elections of 1990 were effectively competitive in Latvia, Estonia, and Lithuania; but only Estonia altered its electoral law significantly, unusually moving to the single trans-ferable vote.[84] Electoral reform did not feature either in Russia or the Ukraine, where elections were semi-competitive (see below).

The conditions, the timing, and the forums of decision-making varied with particular circumstances. The balance of power between 'reformers' and 'conservatives' in ruling communist parties also varied considerably, and the outcomes were not always what rational choice or strategic bargaining models would suggest.[85] Four countries moved directly from their variants of 'socialist majoritarianism' to a list system of PR: Czechoslovakia, Romania, Poland (1991), and Slovenia for the key Socio-Political Chamber of its still tricameral system. Both the Czech Republic and Slovakia maintained PR after independence. Latvia also introduced list PR for its first post-independence election, as did Estonia, but (as we shall see in due course) with some highly distinctive 'bits and pieces with little rhyme or reason'.[86]

Hungary adopted a mixed system of enormous complexity. It introduced the German format of single-member and proportional elements, though with no mechanism for establishing overall proportionality. It provided two votes, but it had three elements of seat allocation from 176 two-round single-member districts, 20 regional list constituencies with a maximum of 152 seats, and from national party lists. All these elements were linked both by nomination requirements and seat allocation procedures.[87]

Bulgaria also adopted a mixed system in 1990, with equal numbers of seats elected in single-member districts and by list PR. Here the two elements operated in parallel, with no formal linkages between them. The Polish parliament also preferred a mixed system for its first fully competitive election, but its conflicts with President Wałęsa over electoral reform led to the adoption of PR as an acceptable fallback position. Bulgaria moved to PR in 1991, while Russia and Lithuania adopted mixed parallel systems after independence.

Several prominent themes emerged in early debates on free elections. First, there was a professed desire to open up the political process as widely as possible to maximise the representation of diverse views and interests. The first new laws on political parties were highly permissive. Many new electoral laws also retained the right of 'social organisations' to present candidates. In Poland the emphasis on the historic contribution of the Solidarity trade union was a significant factor in maintaining this provision until 2001.

The basic architecture of the electoral system proved highly contentious everywhere. There was no question of simple mimicry of Western Europe's dominant form of PR. The legacy of the communist period proved strong, both from self-interest (from those with strong organisation, local connections, and prominent personalities) and also from a normative perspective. Many saw single-member districts as providing the best form of representation by giving voters a personal choice of deputy, and deputies a direct interest in nurturing their constituencies. It was widely accepted that in circumstances where new political parties were often inchoate and largely unknown, and where the idea of 'party' evoked the old practices of mono-partism, a direct shift from representation-by-individuals to representation-by-parties would be difficult. In Lithuania the opposition movement Sajūdis took an 'anti-party', 'pro-personality' position and favoured the retention of majoritarianism in 1992.[88] Within Civic Forum in the Czech Lands prominent voices also advocated single-member districts to provide greater opportunities for independents so as to 'improve the quality of representation'. At the same time the decision-makers also recognised that the essence of modern representative democracy lay in the existence of competing political parties. The question was not whether parties should be fostered, but how and when. In Czechoslovakia many saw PR as second best in terms of its representative qualities, but sought in the (provisional) electoral law to stimulate party development before reverting to a majoritarian system. In the Ukraine the left and the moveable 'swamp' of non-aligned deputies elected in the USSR in 1990 agreed that PR was desirable, but only later, when parties were more developed.

Perhaps it is not surprising, then, that the mixed system attracted such favour. Not only could it offer a compromise satisfying opposing views, but it seemed to provide personal representation while fostering party development. New liberal parties in Poland and Hungary, the Democratic Union and the Alliance of Free Democrats, also endorsed the mixed system as the 'best of both worlds'. Yet it would be inaccurate to say that participants in these debates understood the potential dynamics of the mixed system for party development. After all, Germany stood as a lone exemplar, and its actual mechanisms were rarely understood or appreciated. The complex three-tiered Hungarian variant emerged from a tortuous process of ad hoc compromises at the Round Table. The mixed-parallel system, with no formal linkages between the single-member and PR elements, was essentially new, first adopted in Bulgaria.[89] No one was quite sure how either would work.

Only in Poland's 'contract Sejm' did majoritarianism fail to find strong defenders. The successor social democrats strongly favoured PR, stressing its superior representative qualities, while most Solidarity deputies supported a mixed system. The PR system finally adopted retained the element of personal choice by the mechanism of the open list. President Wałęsa bitterly opposed this, arguing that closed lists would strengthen the weak parties. The biggest shift came in Romania, where the dominant National Salvation Front wished to retain the majoritarian system. It agreed to PR, favoured by the revived but weak historic parties, to ensure its own legitimacy and that of the forthcoming election. With majoritarianism, the obvious strength of the Front raised the spectre of a parliament with a tiny, impotent opposition. This consideration also became the determining factor in Bulgaria, where the Bulgarian Socialist Party (BSP) initially favoured a dominant single-member element but then agreed a fifty-fifty split. As in Romania, the BSP shifted to ensure parliamentary representation for the opposition so as to confirm Bulgaria's new democratic credentials.

Thirdly, the decision-makers acknowledged the need to promote effective government. Openness of competition was a virtue, but too much openness risked fragmentation and potential problems of government formation. The main mechanism used to prevent excessive fragmentation was the threshold (in all save Romania) for the list or list element: 4 per cent in Hungary, Bulgaria, Lithuania, and Latvia; 5 per cent in Czechoslovakia and later for Russia (1993), as well as for Poland's (1991) and Estonia's (1992) national-list tier. Thresholds would not only eliminate parties with little support, but they were seen as encouraging party mergers and alliances.

We can see that although representation remained a key focus, the architects of these new institutions embraced a variety of concerns, including systemic considerations such as legitimacy. Some countries sought to enhance the legitimacy of their elections by retaining turnout requirements characteristic of the Soviet system. Hungary, Lithuania, Russia, and the Ukraine maintained this practice. In Lithuania it was Sajūdis deputies who opposed a proposed reduction of the minimum turnout requirement on the grounds that the elected deputies 'might not be representative'. In Romania, Bulgaria, and the Ukraine debates were also sensitive to the perceptions of the international community. These three countries, along with Russia, were most explicitly concerned with systemic legitimacy, including issues of corruption and electoral administration.

The first free elections

The challengers

The 1990 elections were distinctive, with large umbrella formations uniting opposition forces in surrogate parties. In these regime-choice or founding elections the communist–anti-communist political fault line was based on clashes of values rather than on the conflicts of interests characteristic of West European evolution. Civic Forum/Public against Violence in Czechoslovakia, the Union of Democratic Forces in Bulgaria, Sajūdis in Lithuania, the Popular Fronts of Latvia and Estonia, and Democratic Opposition of Slovenia (DEMOS) represented the forces of change (in Poland, Solidarity had played this role in the semi-competitive election of 1989 and was already the linchpin of government). In Hungary opposition proto-parties stood separately, while Romania lacked a unified opposition movement. The adversaries of these movements were the communist parties, already transformed in some measure in Slovenia, the Baltic republics, and Hungary. Despite this general polarisation, however, the openness of competition left room for numerous other contenders. Many proved ephemeral, others were to maintain a presence for longer or shorter periods, while some became enduring political parties.

These new movements and nascent parties were profoundly resource-poor. They had neither money nor infrastructure. Their organisation was ad hoc and election-oriented. With few exceptions their leaders were largely unknown. They had nothing to offer their supporters in the way of material incentives or rewards. They had ill-developed programmes, promising only the prospect of change and some opaque model of democracy and the market.

However, their electoral preparedness also depended partly on how and when they emerged, itself a function of the state–society relations of late communism. We have stressed Poland's long history of political dissent. The Balts and Slovenes had seen the awakening of civil society in the 1980s, along with the emergence of reform-communists sensitive to the atmosphere of national threat as relations with Moscow and Belgrade deteriorated. In Latvia, Lithuania, and Estonia popular fronts were the main vehicle of political mobilisation, while in Slovenia six proto-parties united for the elections. In Czechoslovakia and Bulgaria opposition movements had existed for barely a few months before the electoral contest, but in Czechoslovakia they had already assumed a role in government.

The incumbents

The communist parties that contested the free elections of 1990 (or in Poland the semi-competitive regime-change election of 1989) had varied in their responses to Gorbachev's reform initiatives. They differed in their historical legitimacy and their degree of unity, particularly in the role played by reformist elements within their ranks. They varied in their penetration of society and in their willingness to use repressive measures. They 'ranged from the ossified ideologues of the stagnating Czech party to the pragmatic technocratic experts of its relatively liberal Hungarian counterpart'.[90] All were indubitably political parties, highly structured, reaching deep into society with mass (if eroding) memberships, and controlling immense resources. All accepted, however reluctantly, the principles of free elections and multi-partism; sharing power was better than losing it altogether. They thus subjected themselves to the novel experience of competition.

The Hungarian party was indeed the most liberal; it also made the greatest changes by the time of the election. In February 1989 it abandoned its leading role, in May it virtually abolished the *nomenklatura*, from June it negotiated with the opposition at the Round Table. The culmination of the growing influence of reform circles within the party was the final congress of the Hungarian Socialist Workers' Party (MSzMP) and the birth of its successor, the Hungarian Socialist Party (MSzP) on 8 October.[91]

Unlike the Hungarian party, the Polish communists never succeeded in achieving anything more than fleeting periods of legitimacy.[92] Despite their power and privilege, they lacked authority. They also lacked cohesion. Intensely divided throughout their history, they oscillated between repression and reform in the 1980s; neither could resolve acute economic and social crisis or soften popular alienation. The party's reformers did not dominate but remained rather isolated until the leadership itself embraced a new strategy of coopting Solidarity into the political process. Above all, party leaders appeared to overestimate the credit they would gain for partially competitive elections. They expected to win in 1989 (after all, the election was rigged), and they did not expect Solidarity to monopolise the opposition role.

We have already signalled the more nationally oriented approach of the Baltic and Slovene communists. The Baltic parties, however, saw acute divisions between hardliners and reformers, often on ethnic lines. (In Latvia Russians comprised some two-thirds of party members.[93]) In Estonia one group of reform communists were closely associated with the Popular Front, while another stood as the Free Estonia coalition in 1990. The conservative wings in both Estonia and Latvia formed pro-Soviet Interfronts to counter the radicalisation of the popular fronts and their growing demands for independence.

The Bulgarian Communist Party (BCP) was the most deeply entrenched of all; indeed, Bulgaria experienced few manifestations of discontent before 1988. But Zhivkov's removal, along with the departure of others of the older generation, 'set off a wholesale critique...primarily focusing on extensive nepotism and corruption'. The new leaders promised respect for the rule of law, a reversal of policies directed against the Turkish minority (see Chapter 9), and the transformation of the party.[94] Unlike the position elsewhere, opposition newness and weakness enabled the BCP to retain control of the early processes of change. Its change of name to the Bulgarian Socialist party (BSP) did not, at the start, signal much departure from old habits and practices.

In contrast, in Czechoslovakia the communists had withdrawn in the face of mass mobilisation. They were discredited but unrepentant. The founding congress of the Communist Party of Bohemia–Moravia (March 1990) saw continuing domination of anti-reform regional leaders and apparatchiki.[95] In Slovakia, where hitherto unknown intellectual reformers assumed a key position in the Communist Party of Slovakia in January 1990, this made no difference to electoral performance (see Table 2.2).

The Romanian regime under Nicolae Ceauşescu was the most distinctive, with its combination of repression and grotesque personality cult. The Communist party served largely as an appendage to its dynastic 'socialism in one family'.[96] Yet in the winter of 1989–90 the party effectively vanished without trace. The leaders of the hastily constituted FSN were mostly dissident communists who rapidly assumed control as a self-styled caretaker government, initially promising not to contest the forthcoming free elections. New parties and returning émigrés with links to historic parties tried to mobilise anti-communist sentiment against the FSN, but they made little headway in forming a nascent counter-élite. The government took rapid measures to alleviate the hardships of the population, while asserting its democratic credentials and its commitment to some vague form of socialism without Ceauşescu.

The results

Where the dividing line between communism and anti-communism was clear, it created a measure of unity that undercut other potential social divisions and resulted in large victories for the forces of change (see Table 2.1). In Poland, Solidarity had won all the freely contested seats in the semi-competitive elections of June 1989, leaving the communists unable to form a government once their erstwhile satellites had defected. The Baltic popular fronts took control in their respective republics of the USSR in *de facto* competitive elections. Although they suffered persistent Soviet pressure up until the abortive *coup* of August 1991 (formal international recognition came only with the *coup*), the 1990 elections constituted a radical break. By independence the three republics had already effectively dismantled Soviet

Table 2.1 Results for opposition movements in founding parliamentary elections, 1989–90

Country/Republic	Election	Main opposition contender	% Share of PR vote	% Share of seats	Outcome
Poland	June 1989	Solidarity	n/a	35.0[1]	Grand Coalition under Solidarity
Latvia[2]	March–April 1990	Popular Front[3]	n/a	67.0	Majority PF government
Lithuania[2]	February–March 1990	Sajūdis[3]	n/a	68.5	Majority Sajūdis government
Estonia[2]	March 1990	Popular Front	n/a	40.6–44.6[4]	PF government with effective majority[5]
Slovenia[2]	April 1990	DEMOS	54.5	52.5	Majority coalition of 6 DEMOS components
Hungary	March–April 1990	Hungarian Democratic Forum, MDF[6]	24.7	42.5	Majority coalition, Forum + Christian Democrats + Smallholders
Romania	May 1990	Democratic Alliance of Hungarians[7]	7.2	7.3	National Salvation Front majority government
Czechoslovakia[8] Czech Lands	June 1990	Civic Forum, OF	53.2	67.3	CF/VPN majority coalition with Christian Democrats
Slovakia		Public against Violence (VPN)	32.6	38.8	
Bulgaria	June 1990	Union of Democratic Forces, SDS	36.2	36.0	Socialist majority government
Bulgaria	October 1991	Union of Democratic Forces	34.4	45.8	UDF coalition with Party of Rights and Freedoms

[1] Maximum possible seats under Round Table Agreement. [2] To republican parliaments. [3] Sajūdis and the Popular Front did not stand in their own right but 'supported' candidates. [4] From Bernard Grofman, Evald, Mikkel, and Rein Taagepera, 'Electoral System Changes in Estonia, 1989–1993', *Journal of Baltic Studies*, vol. 30, no. 3, 1999, p. 230. The system was STV but without candidates' affiliations, which were not always clear. [5] See n. 4; but many reform communists of the Free Estonia Coalition largely supported the Front. [6] The Forum had the strongest first-round result. [7] The strongest single opposition force. [8] To Czech and Slovak sections of the Chamber of the People.

restrictions on political and economic organisation and declared their commitment to democratic capitalism.[97]

The Slovene election within Yugoslavia was a *de jure* competitive election,
won by the six-party coalition DEMOS (from *Demokratična Opozicija Slovenije*).
The presidential victory of the former communist leader (now the Party of
Democratic Renewal) Milan Kučan showed that the electorate valued his
role in the unravelling Yugoslav Federation and also encouraged his cooperation with DEMOS. Slovenia declared its independence in June 1991, when
the Yugoslav army launched a brief abortive attempt to reassert control. The
psychological impact of the 'ten-day war' was profound, but its brevity meant
that the new parliament could embark on system transformation in a context of *de facto* independence and a measure of national consensus.

Hungary and Czechoslovakia saw the most radical ruptures with the old
regime. In April the Hungarian Democratic Forum emerged as the strongest
of the fragmented opposition contenders. It placed a relatively narrow first
in the list vote (24.7 per cent to the Free Democrats' 21.4 per cent), but in
the second round of the single-member element voters moved to it in large
numbers.[98] In June in the Czech Lands, Civic Forum gained a majority, and
though in Slovakia Public against Violence also won most votes, Slovakia
saw rather more fragmentation.

In Romania the FSN won easily and formed its own super-majority government. The renamed BSP also capitalised on its strengths, running a more
professional campaign for responsible, conservative, and painless change
than the disjointed, poorly organised, inexperienced Democratic Forces,
whose support for a radical break was concentrated in urban areas.[99] Both
the Romanian and Bulgarian elections attracted allegations of impropriety
(in neither were complete election results published), but there was no
suggestion that the opposition could have won.[100]

Yet as the Bulgarian economy deteriorated, public unrest increased. The
government survived only until November, when it was replaced by a caretaker
administration. By the October 1991 elections[101] the largest ('Movement')
element of the Union of Democratic Forces won 34.4 per cent of the vote to
the socialists' 33 per cent. Bulgaria thus had two 'founding elections', still
based on polarization over overriding issues of system-change.

In the broadest sense all these election results were 'representative': there
is no doubt that the results mirrored the aspirations of the majority. In the
short term, only in the Baltic republics did reform-communists gain credit
for promoting change – in this case supporting the interests of their republic
against the centre (see Table 2.2). The Hungarian Socialists did worst of all,
having seen their support ebb steadily from the summer of 1989.

Semi-competitive elections in Russia and the Ukraine

The republican parliaments elected in March 1990 also came to constitute
the first parliaments of independent Russia and the Ukraine, but here

Table 2.2   Results for communist and successor parties in founding elections

Country/Republic	Contender	% Share of PR vote	% Seats
Poland	Polish United Workers' Party, PZPR	n/a	38.0[1]
Latvia[2]	Communist Party of Latvia	n/a	
Lithuania[2]	Communist Party of Lithuania[3]	n/a	32.6
Estonia[2]	Communist Party of Estonia	n/a	25.7[4]
Slovenia[2]	Party of Democratic Renewal	17.3	16.7
Hungary	Hungarian Socialist Party, MSzP	10.9	8.6
Romania	National Salvation Front, FSN[5]	66.3	66.4
Czechoslovakia[6]	Communist Party of		
Czech Lands	Czechoslovakia	13.5	14.9
Slovakia		13.8	16.3
Bulgaria 1990	Bulgarian Socialist Party, BSP	47.2	52.8
Bulgaria 1991	Bulgarian Socialist Party	33.1	44.2

[1] Seats allocated to PZPR under Round Table Agreement. [2] To republican parliaments. [3] No longer part of the federated Communist Party of the Soviet Union. [4] Pro-Soviet deputies; from Riina Kionka, 'Elections to the Estonian Supreme Soviet', *Report on the USSR*, no. 14, 1990. The use of STV permitted candidates to stand as individuals and their affiliations were not always clear. However, many reform communists of the Free Estonia Coalition largely supported the Front. [5] The Front was not legally a successor party. [6] To Czech and Slovak sections of the Chamber of the People.

communist deputies continued to dominate. Russia lacked the popular front of other republics, and its opposition groups were fragmented, weakly organised and ill-prepared; reformers won about one-third of seats in the Russian Congress of People's Deputies. Following the abortive Soviet *coup*, Russian President Yeltsin served as the architect of the Soviet Union's formal dissolution in December 1991. The first post-independence election came two years later (see Chapter 3).

In the Ukraine the popular front Rukh was established late and with greater influence in the west of the republic. The democratic opposition won about one-quarter of the seats in the Supreme Soviet in 1990, leaving most other deputies, as in Russia, to become part of a 'moveable swamp'. The declaration of independence in August 1991 resembled desertion of a sinking ship rather than genuine national aspirations, though part of the élite clothed itself rapidly in national garb. Confirmation of independence in the December referendum thus left power in the hands of the old élites, adapting themselves to greater or lesser degrees to the circumstances of Soviet dissolution. The first free election came only in 1994, and it was neither a founding nor a regime-choice election, effectively confirming the continuing entrenchment of parts of the old *nomenklatura*.

Conclusion

Representation never lost its basic meaning of 'acting on behalf of', but it developed a myriad of ideological underpinnings and practical overlays in the course of its long historical evolution. As the political community expanded to include society at large, both the concept itself and the forms of its embodiment in the political process also evolved. Representation became a key legitimating concept for modern democratic polities, with elections providing the fundamental mechanism of civic participation. New ideas of liberty and equality challenged its basic precepts, and both old élites and the new social strata demanding incorporation developed fresh ideas about whom and what was being represented and how the process should best take place. As political parties emerged in Western Europe, from élites reaching out for the support of the newly enfranchised or from social groups demanding representation, they offered distinctive arguments. Conservatives stressed the people's delegation of decision-making to the wise and the experienced, to provide stability and order and secure the 'national interest'. Socialists wanted their working-class representatives to further workers' interests. Christians defended the institutional interests of the church and its values. Party colonisation of distinct segments of the population was made easier by systems of proportional representation, but generally parties became closely associated with the representation of diverse interests in diverse societies.

Institutionalised political parties in Western Europe both reflected and shaped political attitudes and their inter-party competition drew them closer together in developing programmes and platforms for public choice. Parties became virtually the sole actors in electoral competition, and the new inter-war democracies followed the same path of party organisation into distinct socio-ideological families with (philosophically) often-incompatible principles of representation. The concept was in a muddle, but it did not matter much. Large sections of the population developed affective attachments to their political parties. Normative philosophers did not develop a theory of representation that took parties into account.

The Soviet Union used the concept of class representation as the basis for single-candidate competition in its system where classes coexisted in official harmony. Workplace, ethnic, and territorially based representatives would promote the needs of their electors within a framework of class cooperation and Party leadership. The Party stressed the social care function of deputies, much as did British parties in their single-member districts. This was the approach exported to Eastern Europe, where it became part of the received wisdom and where some serious attempts were made to go beyond its earlier formalism.

As Western European parties developed, political science caught up by introducing some rather unsatisfactory models of 'responsible party government' or 'rational voters', both predicated on the notion that voters chose parties on the basis of their programmatic offerings. Kirchheimer used implicit vote-seeking arguments when he observed that party differences were waning as many larger parties reached out beyond their traditional constituencies. He called into question the representative capacities of parties in this context, but this was essentially still the 'interest-based' view of representation.

In Central and Eastern Europe the immediate post-communist environment was more conducive to value-based divisions, and the first elections in 1990 reflected the divide between supporters and opponents of the old regime. Despite some more enduring popular mobilisation in Poland, Slovenia, and in the Baltic republics and some spontaneous activism elsewhere in 1990, civil society was embryonic and incapable of serving as the basis for interest articulation, especially given the sudden and compressed nature of developments. In the short term the spokespersons of wider mass movements expressed the widespread dissatisfaction of the population and gained control of freely elected parliaments.

Where there were no forces capable of articulating opposition sentiments, as in Romania, disaffected elements of the old élite took on that role and appropriated much of the power base of the former regime. In Bulgaria the socialists won the first election, but lost the second after failing to survive a full term. In Russia and the Ukraine old and new élites dismantled the state from above, but they did not hold immediate elections for their newly independent states. Republican parliaments, still dominated by those elected in 1990, now assumed the role of national parliaments.

Despite these variations, the legacy of mono-partism proved enduring. Parties formed, not gradually as vehicles of social groups, but from within 'accidental' new parliamentary élites offering 'accidental' representation. It is to the nature of these new parties that we now turn.

3
Political Parties and their Evolution

The previous regime cast a long shadow on the development of competitive party politics after the fall of communism. 'Party' evoked all the negative connotations of communist control and manipulation, especially in Central Europe. Politics was seldom equated with the art of compromise and negotiation. Yet the new institution-builders recognised the ubiquity of political parties in modern democracies and what is more, the absence of any obvious alternative. When elections became the key to political power, groups of aspiring politicians set out to mobilise the population. In the absence of a developed space between the public and private spheres, these groups bridged the gap. Politics was of necessity élite-driven. The élites both reflected and shaped the political opportunity structure. They structured the choices available to voters. This chapter analyses the types of parties that emerged in post-communist states. It examines the bases on which aspiring élites sought electoral support. It centres on the post-communist menu of choice and its evolution. It demonstrates the diversity of ways in which parties adapted to the demands of political competition.

Two criteria were traditionally adopted to generate typologies of European political parties: organisation and ideology were seen as the key to differentiating parties, understanding their internal dynamics, and explaining their change and adaptation. We referred to several of these approaches in Chapter 2. In Duverger's argument the two dimensions of ideology and organisation were interlinked.[1] Panebianco focused on the ways in which formative organisational development affected the process of party institutionalisation.[2] Lipset and Rokkan were more concerned with how ideology matched the cleavage structures in society, itself shaped by critical pre-democratic conflicts.[3] Recognisable 'party families' became a widespread basis for categorising political parties.[4] Yet neither approach can offer a single criterion for identifying the range of post-communist parties. Many parties were hard to differentiate by organisational type, though in their initial stages they often resembled Duverger's parties of notables – a sort of *faute de mieux* cadre party. New parties' organisational capacity remained weak and their structural penetration limited. They found it difficult to attract and retain members, and they lacked the resources to develop as 'electoral-professionals'. Nor were all parties 'ideological'.

The typology presented here is based on a central criterion, the nature of a party's electoral appeal. However, four caveats are in order. First is the problem of extracting the *core appeal* from what were commonly multi-pronged strategies to reach the electorate. Secondly, there are instances where categories overlap. Thirdly, party history is an implicit dimension of this typology. Parties emerged and developed in particular contexts and those that survived carried their history with them. The nature of political institutions, parties' resources, and the character of their competitors affected the framing of their electoral appeal. None of these will be explored systematically, although they will be frequently noted in the course of our discussion. Fourthly, not all these types were present everywhere, nor were they necessarily linked to particular stages of the democratisation process.

Party types in Central and Eastern Europe

Many parties came to resemble their Western European counterparts, adopting the common philosophical underpinnings identified in Chapter 2, even though their ideological bases rarely 'fit' existing social or economic cleavages in these rapidly changing societies. Ideological hybrids were also common.[5] The first category therefore is that of the *ideological party*. Within this category we find parties whose programmes were linked to their broad values and aspirations. We also find a distinctive group of less prevalent milieux-parties that sought to appeal to the values and interests of a specific segment of the population. Both may also be regarded as weak variants of policy-seeking parties (see Chapter 2).

But not all electoral contenders could be described as 'parties', and not all parties sought to base their electoral appeal on ideology. Thus we cannot use a simple dichotomy of 'ideological' and 'non-ideological parties'. The 'non-party non-ideological contenders' were new types of umbrella formations whose electoral appeal was closely linked to their organisational format. They established vote-seeking *electoral parties* or *blocs*, promising to deliver on valence issues of broad general concern, though without clear programme specifications. This is the second broad category in our typology. One manifestation of this type of formation was the distinctive 'party of power' that emerged in post-Soviet Russia and the Ukraine from within the institutions of the state. Another was the 'new umbrella' formation that brought existing parties together to defeat a common enemy; they were heterogeneous and unstable (see below).

Thirdly, the political scene was littered with a variety of *populist parties*. Indeed, one feature of the changing political scene was the frequency with which new parties emerged. In its contemporary variant, populism had no intellectual or historical base. Its central feature was a strong anti-establishment, 'pro-people' outlook. Traditionally populism in Central and Eastern Europe was associated with agrarian parties, based on the mystique of peasant virtue and offering a 'Third Way' superior to liberalism and Marxism.[6] Historically the peasants *were* the people in Eastern Europe; but modern-day populists had no historical linkage to these movements and indeed no historical baggage. Although the 'people' remained central, the people could be viewed as coterminous with the nation, as in right-wing variants of populism, or with the 'common man' in more egalitarian left-wing variants.[7] In addition, there was a distinctive type of 'liberal populism', summed up as 'better, deeper, quicker economic reform'. Populists focused on notions of injustice, and redress of grievances allegedly caused by (say) politicians, bureaucrats, or minorities. But one should not assume philosophical underpinnings, or ideological or programmatic coherence.[8] These parties were pragmatic opportunists in a context where parties lacked social roots, where politicians were mistrusted and often untrustworthy, and where voters were available.

Many such parties were effectively the creature of a particular leader. This was 'trust me' politics writ large, though the basis of such appeals was none the less quite varied: from 'trust me, I am competent and honest'; 'trust me, I will deal with the Jews, Hungarians, IMF, communists, foreign capitalists...'; 'trust me, I will raise pensions and wages and reduce unemployment and inflation'; 'trust me, I am not like the others' to the admittedly unique case of 'trust me, I am the former tsar of Bulgaria'.

Most political parties fit quite easily into these three broad categories and their subsets. The ways in which they emerged also saw significant similarities, although we shall explore the configurations of parties that characterised individual countries further in Chapter 6. Initially much depended on the 'mode of exit' from communism, for in most cases the first new parties came primarily from the opposition forces of the late 1980s. Despite the broad polarisation of the first 'regime-choice' elections, the openness of competition left room for numerous other contenders, with some parties seeking a niche electorate as well as frivolous miscellaneous 'parties', often alongside pressure groups and regional organisations. Many proved ephemeral, others were to maintain a presence for longer or shorter periods, while some became enduring political parties. But it was the subsequent disintegration of the mass opposition movements and the adaptive capacity of the successor parties that constituted the major factors in party development and provided the new axes of competition in most of Central and Eastern Europe.

The first stages of party development

Elections provided the main spur to party development, with major changes occurring within the large anti-communist umbrella formations. In Central

Europe the great value battles were resolved by a new élite consensus on democracy and the market, coupled with and reinforced by an emerging pro-European Union orientation. This was also true of Slovenia and the Baltic states (we shall discuss the exceptional 'ethno-democratic' elements of the Estonian and Latvian regimes in Chapter 9). This consensus was strongest among the countries marked by the clearest break with communism: Poland, the Czech Republic, Hungary, Slovenia, and the Balts. Slovakia was distinctive in this regard (see below). Yet élite consensus was not matched in society, where high popular expectations gave way to gloom and disappointment.

Industrial recession struck hard everywhere without exception, and massive disruption of trade resulted from the break-up of the USSR. Though the pace of economic change varied, all post-communist states had to find new ways to manage state-owned economies without the mechanisms of state planning and price setting. Price liberalisation led to high inflation, and unemployment accompanied economic restructuring. Widespread economic hardship, the erosion of state welfare, and rising levels of crime generated issues to which politicians responded. The rate of economic change, the nature of privatisation, and the extent of state welfare provision emerged as 'issues of transition' around which the new parties structured their agendas. By the second free elections the anti-communist opposition movements had split, and many parties were already aligned on recognisable ideological lines.

The emergence of ideological parties

Aside from the communist parties themselves, nascent ideological parties were present in many of the first free elections in 1990. Their presence was most marked in Hungary. Proto-parties emerged early from strands of the intellectual opposition, and historic parties such as the Smallholders had also begun their 'rebirth' by 1988. Seven 'parties' formed the 'Opposition Round Table' to coordinate negotiations with the regime, though intending to campaign separately in the forthcoming elections. Only the Hungarian Democratic Forum (MDF) established a 'truly national movement',[9] though it lacked a formal programme. In the course of the negotiations the Forum won substantial by-election victories with united opposition candidates. The Young Democrats (Fidesz) and the Alliance of Free Democrats (SzDSz) also gained recognition, enhanced later in the autumn in a successful referendum campaign on presidential elections.[10] Thus several viable competitors had emerged before the election.

All major contenders had relatively clear ideological profiles,[11] even where programmatic clarity was absent. The Free Democrats (SzDSz) and Fidesz, seeking the youth vote in particular, were both liberal parties, committed to the rapid development of capitalism and the securing of individual rights. The (successor) Socialist Party (MSzP) began to associate itself with European models of social democracy. The Forum was diverse, but it was essentially conservative-nationalist in cast. Smallholders and Christian Democrats sought to revive a segmented 'milieu-base' for their parties: The Smallholders stressed land rights and defence of the traditional family to woo their rural constituency. The Christian Democrats aimed both to re-create and represent a Christian subculture.[12]

Christian Democrats in Czechoslovakia also found an identifiable niche in 1990 with their stress on religious freedoms, the reassertion of religious values, and the restitution of church property. In the Czech Lands the successor Czechoslovak People's Party (KDU–ČSL) and the Christian Democratic Party stood together (and later merged), winning 8.7 per cent of the vote in the Czech section. Christian Democrats were even stronger in Slovakia, with historical traditions of clericalism and where the Church had provided a focus of opposition in the 1980s. Already in December 1989 the Christian Democratic Movement had detached itself from Public against Violence; in June it gained about one-fifth of the vote.

Class appeals remained rather rare, though the Hungarian Smallholders, the (successor) Polish Peasant Party (PSL), and the Latvian Farmers' Union (LZS) were more explicit class parties from the outset, with programmes clearly tailored to their rural constituencies.

Ethnic and nationalist parties also made an early appearance. In Romania and Slovakia large Hungarian minorities supported their own political parties. In Romania the nationalists of the Party of Romanian National Unity (PUNR) initially made little impression, standing in the Romanian Unity Alliance. In Slovakia, however, minority mobilisation was fostered by the (re)emergence of the Slovak National Party (SNS), which was pro-independence and anti-Hungarian. The Bulgarian Turks' Movement for Rights and Freedoms (DPS) arose from a series of mass protests in 1989, aiming at the redress of anti-Turkish communist policies; but no strong nationalist party emerged in Bulgaria (see Chapter 9). Most of these parties survived, and we will return to them in various contexts. But we turn now to the stimulus to party development created by divisions within the anti-communist movements, the surrogate parties of the founding elections.

The disintegration of the umbrellas

The mass anti-communist formations split in different ways in the new parliamentary democracies. The first to split was Solidarity, the earliest 'governing umbrella'. Solidarity divided over the competing presidential candidacies of Solidarity leader Lech Wałęsa and Prime Minister Tadeusz Mazowiecki in late 1990, then again in preparations for the first fully free election in October 1991. Solidarity crumbled into many small ideological 'parties' competing for the same political space. Most dissociated themselves from the radical liberal policies of the interim Solidarity governments of 1989–91. They included several Christian democratic and Christian nationalist groupings, several peasant parties, and some social democratic or socialist parties (and two liberal parties).[13] Other groups formed outside parliament. The Polish Sejm elected in 1991 was intensely fragmented, with deputies chosen under 29 different labels. Often referred to as parties, even a lax definition could count only some sixteen as 'parties', along with trades unions and local and regional groupings. Mazowiecki's Democratic Union became the largest party (13.5 per cent of seats), but it could not muster a coalition.

In Lithuania attempts to transform Sajūdis into a party also failed. Early divisions accelerated from late 1990 and by mid-1992 Sajūdis' increasing fragmentation[14] meant intense factional division and the loss of its parliamentary majority. With parliamentary decision-making effectively paralysed, early elections were scheduled for October. This decision fostered a new wave of proto-parties based on existing parliamentary factions: the Lithuanian Centre Union (LCS), the Moderates' Movement, the National Progress Movement, as well as the first ethnic party, the Union of Lithuanian Poles. The Sajūdis that stood on its governing record in 1992 was effectively its mainstream right-wing (the 'Homeland Union [Lithuanian Conservatives]' TS[LK] after May 1993).

As with Sajūdis the splits in Civic Forum, Public against Violence, and the Union of Democratic Forces also gave rise to one large party. The Czech Civic Democratic Party (ODS) under the Federation's finance minister Václav Klaus swiftly became the dominant party of the right in Czech politics, with a clear profile of radical economic liberalism.[15] In 1992, indeed, 77 per cent of ODS supporters placed their party 'somewhat' or 'clearly' on the right.[16] Klaus retained strong support in 1992 in the Czech Lands. Six months later he took control of the new independent Czech government, along with another small 'civic' offshoot, the Civic Democratic Alliance (ODA), and the Christian Democrats.

One large party also emerged in Slovakia from the disintegration of Public against Violence. Under the popular Vladimír Mečiar the profile of the Movement for Democratic Slovakia (HZDS) was far from clear, but it rapidly became the largest Slovak party. In 1992 it campaigned on a dual platform of more cautious economic reform, including slower privatisation and a more decentralised form of (con)federalism. The irreconcilable differences between the two victors, ODS and HZDS, sealed the fate of the Czechoslovak federation.[17]

In Bulgaria too the Union of Democratic Forces (Movement) retained the dominant position in (the second founding election of) 1991, when its smaller offshoots failed to enter parliament. However, this remained a coalition of smaller parties, of which the Democratic Party was the largest and best organised,[18] with some acute divisions, including over the restoration of the monarchy.

Democratic Opposition of Slovenia (DEMOS) fell apart in December 1991, largely on policy issues: it was divided over the pace of privatisation and along secular-religious lines. Critics accused Prime Minister Lojze Peterle, a Christian Democrat, of 'spending too much time reopening churches and not enough mending the economy'.[19] Slovenia differed from other countries, however. First, DEMOS had been constructed of identifiable proto-parties and collapsed into its constituent elements, Christian Democrats, the People's Party, the Democratic Union, the Social Democratic Party (SDS), Greens, and Liberals. Secondly, the Christian Democrats remained in government, with two successor parties joining a coalition crossing the communist–anti-communist divide. One of these, the centre-left Liberal Democratic Party of the new Prime Minister Janez Drnovšek, emerged as the largest party in the 1992 elections.

In Estonia the Popular Front stood again in the first post-independence election, gaining 12.3 per cent of the vote in 1992. Various groupings had emerged within the Front, the most important of which was the Centre Party (*Keskerakond*) of former Prime Minister Edgar Savisaar. Disillusion with the Popular Front (it had been replaced by a non-partisan government in January 1992) paved the way for 'nationalist opposition parties to capitalize on this discontent by promising to "clean house" through market reforms and Western integration'.[20] The Centre Party stood in its own right in 1995. In Latvia, however, the Popular Front came to an end with a whimper. In 1993 it failed to enter parliament with 2.6 per cent of the vote. Former Prime Minister Godmanis later returned to parliament for Latvia's Way.

In four cases, then, popular movements gave rise to a single large party of the right. Economic liberals dominated the Civic Democrats in the Czech Lands. The HZDS was more economically interventionist and more nationalist. The Lithuanian Homeland Union was a self-styled conservative party. The Union of Democratic Forces (Movement wing) combined radical anti-communism with a broad pro-reform stance on the economy.

The Centre Party emerged later in Estonia and did not assume the same dominant position. Slovenia had six parties. Poland had (roughly) eight from Solidarity, with the intellectual ex-dissidents of the Democratic Union closely associated with economic liberalism. Latvia had none. Along with the new Hungarian parties, these parties had recognisable, if still indistinct, ideological profiles in the second free elections in 1991 (Bulgaria and Poland's first) and 1992 (Czechoslovakia, Lithuania, Estonia, Slovenia, and also Romania). Latvia had its second (first post-independence) election in 1993. Neither Russia nor the Ukraine had had a free, competitive election by this time.

The reshaping and development of the successor parties

The communists did not stand idle in the face of these political perturbations, and their successors remained significant actors everywhere save Latvia and Estonia. Despite falling membership and shrinking resources, they worked to rebuild their grass-roots support. They retained major assets, including finance, organisational skills, a political base, and networks of informal relations. Although all remained relatively well-defined ideological/ programmatic parties, they responded to the challenge of democratic competition in various ways.

In Lithuania (1992), Poland (1993), and Hungary (1994) the former communists returned immediately to power after convincingly refashioning themselves as the effective counterparts of West European social democracy.[21] Already dominated by reformist elements in 1989, they rapidly committed themselves to democratic multi-partism, pro-'European' orientations, economic reform, and strong welfare policies – in short, to capitalism with a human face in the context of severe economic hardships and anxiety, with their own strong claim to 'professionalism' and expertise.[22] Early electoral success restored their legitimacy and henceforth they dominated the centre-left, taking part in successive alternation in government.

The successors benefited from their opposition role. The first new governing élites, drawn from Sajūdis, Solidarity, and the Forum, had failed to fulfil the high popular expectations associated with rapturous farewells to the old regime. The latter campaigned largely on patriotic anti-communism, no longer the prime concern of the population. In addition, these three successor parties carried their remaining members with them, as well as keeping links with ancillary organisations. In Poland the social democrats brought the 'old' trade union into a broad electoral Alliance of the Democratic Left (SLD). The Hungarian socialists (MSzP) and Lithuanian Democratic Labour Party (LDDP) also retained close links with the largest ('old') trade unions.[23] Thirdly, they projected an image of competence and experience. On this basis they were able to win support from the working class, the former *apparat*, traditional left-wing supporters, the so-called 'losers' of transition, but also its winners, including the new red capitalists benefiting from insider *nomenklatura* links. This was not the class appeal of the 'old' European social democrats; but the egalitarian ethos, concern with trades unions and the plight of public sector workers, and penchant for state regulation placed these parties clearly on the left.

Credible leaders were also a factor. LDDP leader Brazauskas regained much credit for Lithuania's variant of 'velvet transition'. In February 1993, victory in the presidential elections confirmed his popularity, a feat emulated by Poland's Aleksander Kwaśniewski in December 1995 and again in 2000.

The parties also adapted their organisations to new conditions. In 1999 the Polish SLD reconstituted its broad alliance format as a unified political party and – allied with the small Labour Union (UP) – won some 40 per cent of the vote in 2001. In 2000 the Lithuanian party (LDDP) strengthened its credentials as a programmatic left-wing party by merging with the small (historic) Social Democratic Party,[24] which had stood under Sajūdis' banner in 1990, but separately gained seats in 1992 and 1996. After winning in 2000 the LDDP was excluded for a time by a united alliance against it, but it returned to power when that unity dissolved. In 2002 the Hungarian MSzP also celebrated its second election victory.

The position in Slovenia was rather different, since the Party of Democratic Renewal, although embracing a social democratic strategy, did not establish a rapid monopoly of left political space. The Liberal Democratic Party emerged from the Federation of Socialist Youth to woo the emerging business class and become Slovenia's enduring governing party with a successful gradualist economic strategy. Except for the first government and with a brief hiatus in 2000,[25] the Liberal Democrat leader, pragmatic economist Janez Drnovšek, served as prime minister until his election to the presidency in 2002.

Drnovšek presided, often uneasily, over some unusual coalitions of left and right parties. After DEMOS broke up, his new government included both anti-communist Christian Democrats and former communists. His own party merged in mid-1994 with three smaller centre-left groups as Liberal Democracy of Slovenia (LDS). But space also remained for the former communists. In mid-1992 the Party of Democratic Renewal concluded an electoral alliance with some smaller left-wing groupings; in May 1993 they established the United List of Social Democrats as a unified party. The United List remained a junior coalition partner, and it left the government in January 1996, complaining of lack of influence; but from November 2000 it was again a member of the governing coalition.

Both the Bulgarian Socialist Party (BSP) and the quasi-successor Romanian Social Democrats (PDSR, originally the National Salvation Front) also proved highly successful. Without the initial spur of defeat, their ideological and structural adaptation proved slow. They retained the loyalty of considerable swathes of voters, especially in rural areas. Bulgarian political culture in particular had never shared the anti-Soviet cast of the Central Europeans. For Romanians life had improved in the aftermath of the 1989 upheavals. The FSN-Social Democrats remained in government (1990–6), utilising to the full the advantages of office and the patronage opportunities of a state-owned economy. But the Bulgarian socialists also returned early to power after victory in 1990 and defeat in 1991, with the Union of Democratic Forces (SDS) failing to provide an effective reform agenda. In both cases economic reform was slow, partial, and far from transparent. The lack of legal regulation and the entrenchment of the old *nomenklatura* in the economies gave rise to 'red millionaires' arising from the asset-stripping and insider deals of 'hidden privatization'.

Both parties weathered splits and defections. The BSP's internal divisions were acute, though it largely contained its factional struggles. Despite shifting to a new younger leadership, the BSP chose the slow road to change, only rejecting the class struggle and 'reviewing its past' in autumn 1994. It benefited greatly from the mistakes of its opponents. The priorities of the Union of Democratic Forces (SDS) in government, including radical decommunisation, property restitution, and a reluctance to deal with the grievances of the Party of Rights and Freedoms (DPS, see Chapter 9), left the SDS isolated and unpopular.[26] After two caretaker governments the BSP returned easily to power in December 1994, when it (again) promptly led the country into its deepest economic crisis.

Internal party conflicts intensified over Bulgaria's relations with the International Monetary Fund and the inefficiency of Videnov's government.[27] Mass demonstrations engulfed the streets. The BSP split, losing a section of its reform wing. It gained 23 per cent of the vote in 1997 (the new Euro-Left gained 5.5 per cent). The BSP's decline continued with the ex-tsar's appearance on the political scene, and in 2001 its vote fell to 17.2 per cent. Yet three months later its new, young, reform-minded leader, Georgii Parvanov, won the presidential election. The BSP Congress in December appeared at last to marginalise the conservative elements and to confirm the party's social democratic direction.

In Romania the National Salvation Front (FSN) did not claim to be the heir of the Communist Party, but its composition and ideology made it at least a distinctive successor-variant. It remained the largest single party at four successive elections (but not the governing party during 1996–2000). The FSN maintained its strength in successive mutations as the Democratic National Salvation Front (FDSN), the Party of Social Democracy of Romania (PDSR), and the Social Democratic Pole (PSD). How far the party made a 'genuine' conversion to social democracy remained contentious, though a more explicit 'pro-European' orientation gradually came to dominate. Certainly observers at the outset stressed the party's propensity to mobilise fears of rapid reform with national-populist rhetoric.

Gallagher saw it as a 'nationalist party run by ex-communist apparatchiks who emphasise nativist themes and criticise the wholesale adoption of western economic and political models'.[28] Its 1992 split saw the departure of former Prime Minister Petre Roman to a new centre-left creation which did well in 1996 (13 per cent). Roman's alienation left the PDSR's nationalist wing in a stronger position, and President Iliescu sought the support of nationalist parties for the now-minority government. The 1996 election programme was more notably pro-reform but continued to stress 'national-patriotic' themes.[29] After losing the election the party split again in 1997, with the departure of yet another reform element. However, the now Social Democrats found a ready strategy in a sustained, disciplined attack on the weaknesses of the government. They survived their first electoral defeat and learnt to be an effective opposition. Their potential social democratic opponents in Roman's Democratic Party lost through their participation in the unpopular government of 1996–2000. By 2000 the Social Democrats were firmly on the 'European track'[30] and once again ensconced in government and the presidency.

The Slovak Party of the Democratic Left (SDL') was the only successor party to serve in government yet not to survive in parliament. Initially it appeared to have several advantages. With a less anti-socialist political culture in Slovakia its historical legacy was less onerous than the repressive nature of the Czechoslovak communist regime might suggest; and it too had joined the forces of social democracy, albeit somewhat hesitantly. Hoping to gain respectability amongst sections of the electorate,[31] the SDL' participated in the broad-based coalition that governed briefly after Mečiar's fall in March 1994. Yet its role in a largely centre-right government promulgating austerity measures provoked a split but failed to broaden its electoral appeal.[32] It stood in 1994 as Common Choice, muddying its identity further.[33] The SDL' continually found it difficult to carve out a space from or define its relation to Mečiar and the Movement for Democratic Slovakia (HZDS)'s own brand of caring reform.[34] In 1994 as a member of an unpopular government it faced competition from HZDS as well as from its own hard-line offshoot, L'upták's anti-capitalist and anti-NATO Association of Slovak Workers (ZRS). Common Choice gained 10.4 per cent of the vote, ZRS 7.4 per cent, and SDL' rejected Mečiar's political advances.

In 1998 the SDL' recovered somewhat (14.7 per cent), but its popularity ebbed again. Again a minor governing coalition partner, it took the poisoned chalice of the finance ministry and remained uncomfortably allied with liberal reform and Christian elements. In November 2001 the party elected Pavol Konkoš of the 'conservative' faction, determined to 'table a socialist alternative for Slovakia'.[35] But members of the reform wing left early in 2002 to form the Social Democratic Alternative (SDA). In the autumn election neither the SDL' nor the SDA crossed the parliamentary threshold.

The Czech Communist Party (KSČM) did not play a governing role. It remained largely unashamed of the repressive character of the regime it had led, and it sought to retain the core of its communist principles while embracing democracy and adapting to new circumstances.[36] The party provided a rare example of an institutionalised mass party with a core electorate,[37] albeit losing its former trade union link. The new leaders developed a reasonably coherent neo-communist ideology. But its history and anti-capitalist radicalism kept it unattractive even for a population moving to the left.[38] The tiny Social Democrats (ČSSD) rose rapidly to overtake it as the major Czech party of the left. Though seeking recognition as a 'normal political party', in parliament the KSČM remained largely isolated. However, in 2002, the communists' role as the 'party of protest' gained them some 18 per cent of the vote.

Only in Estonia and Latvia was a clear, immediate social democratic 'successor' indistinguishable. In Estonia a small Russian-speaking rump remained after the defection of pro-independence reformers, who contested the 1990 elections as 'Free Estonia'. Subsequently leading figures from the communist period found a home in the Coalition Party, making 'an apparently effortless transition' to the (social) market economy.[39] Similarly in Latvia one prominent group of former reform-communists joined returning émigrés, 'career seekers', and Popular Front members in the influential liberal party Latvia's Way.[40] Another remained with the Nationalist Latvian Communist Party, later the Latvian Democratic Workers Party. It took a more reformist direction after 1995 as the Latvian Social Democratic Party (LSDP) and established good relations – and in 1999 merged – with the 'historic' Latvian Social Democratic Workers' Party (LSDSP).

The Russian and Ukrainian communists also offered exemplars of the ideological category. Their position and the context in which they developed was substantially different from their East European counterparts, however. The communists did not contest the first elections as incumbents, though most incumbents were former communists. The incumbents sought to utilise their advantage, and the communists and other incipient parties faced a new type of party, the party of power. We shall return to the communists and other new parties after a diversion to this distinctive type of electoral party.

Electoral parties: the parties of power

In Russia and the Ukraine existing élites were able to defuse or neutralise weak opposition forces, and they wielded power for longer, delaying the first democratic elections. In these pre-democratic systems, delayed elections in Russia (1993) and the Ukraine (1994) meant fraying or already defunct mass movements and weak, uneven party development. Relations between parliament and President Yeltsin deteriorated rapidly, culminating in September 1993 in a presidential *coup* against the legislature and a profound political crisis. No consensus characterised Russia or the Ukraine, where stark divisions on issues of capitalism-building and state formation remained salient. The continuing presence of strong regional bosses and central coteries gathered around key central institutions fostered clientelism and political rent-seeking.[41] Élite continuities meant continuing opportunities for party-voter 'linkage by reward'.[42]

New parties were weakly prepared for the first free elections. With no election immediately following independence they had had no effective basis for mobilising the population and few resources with which to do so. In Russia most proto-parties that had proliferated from 1989 onwards had disappeared or taken refuge in wider blocs. The anti-communist mass movement Democratic Russia had orchestrated Boris Yeltsin's campaign in the first direct presidential election in June 1991, gaining a membership of hundreds of thousands.[43] Yet with its objective achieved, and with no rewards and no influence ensuing, Democratic Russia withered. By January 1992, with the inauguration of the independent Russian Federation, 'parties' constituted weak, shifting factions within parliament and patchy groupings of activists in the regions. The December 1993 elections rapidly followed Yeltsin's assault on parliament, providing a mobilising incentive but little time to respond. Only thirteen 'parties' mustered the support needed to register a list;

eight won seats in the list element of the mixed system (the single-member battles were more fragmented).[44]

In the Ukraine *apparatchik* Leonid Kravchuk won the presidency in December 1991, when a referendum also confirmed Ukrainian independence. The opposition Rukh (Movement) had already fragmented; outside Kiev it was virtually non-existent in vast swathes of southern and eastern Ukraine. Power remained centred in that part of the old *nomenklatura* élite which had chosen the nationalist route and still controlled central and local government, the media, and the large state enterprises and collective farms. Rukh supported Kravchuk in his nationally oriented policies against the still pro-Soviet communist establishment. But part of the price it paid was only limited economic reform; privatisation 'remained confined to the realm of rhetoric'.[45] Heavy subsidies for loss-making enterprises and collective farms continued to give regional bosses and enterprise directors a stake in continuity rather than change. The entrenchment of local élites also created vested interests in maintaining an electoral system based on single-member constituencies, where they could use their local dominance to good effect. In both countries a new phenomenon emerged, that of the electoral 'party of power'.

Parties of power were formed from within the polity, whether from the central administration or from regional bosses. They varied in their composition and relative cohesion. Few had features of ideological parties; most displayed little sign of programmatic or ideological content. They appealed to the authority of incumbency and to the benefits they could provide. 'Imagine', wrote Duverger, '....if no one creates or develops active committees capable of securing the confidence of the new electors, these will inevitably tend to vote for the only candidates of whom they have any knowledge, namely the traditional social élites'.[46] With weak civil societies and little political mobilisation Russian and Ukrainian elections offered continuing opportunities for clientelist strategies based on long-standing social networks; Sarah Birch described this as *nomenklatura democratization*.[47]

The 1993 victor (with most seats but only 15.5 per cent of list votes) Russia's Choice was the first to be labelled a 'party of power'. It was an electoral bloc extending its own state and economic networks to those of smaller 'parties'. Formed from within governing circles under Yegor Gaidar, architect of Russia's variant of 'shock therapy', Russia's Choice could also be placed in ideological terms. It seemed to promise the development of a coherent liberal 'party of notables' based on Gaidar's laisser-faire market orientation with a stress on civil rights, associated with Sergei Kovalev. There was also Sergei Shakrai's Party of Russian Unity and Concord (PRES), 'the party of the regions', formed from a network of state officials, with the support of associated interest groups such as the Union of Small Cities. As Minister of Nationalities, Shakrai gained advantages from his capacity to distribute subsidies among the Russian republics.[48]

In the Ukraine the powerful worked through the constituencies of the still majoritarian electoral system: the 'party of power' was essentially fictitious, a virtual 'non-party' party of power whose candidates stood mainly as Independents. It none the less controlled many constituencies locked-in by patronage and clientelism, though it was divided along both regional and bureaucratic lines.[49] Indeed, even with all other political forces ranged against it, the 'party of power' won an estimated 77 seats, enough to 'leave the legislature malleable'.[50] The Ukraine lacked an identifiable party of power until 2002. After 1998, parliament lacked a clear division between government and opposition, with 'ephemeral interest groups, all of which support(ed) the president and compete(d) for presidential favor...'.[51]

Ideological parties in Russia and the Ukraine

The main opposition to the parties of power came from the communist parties. In both Russia and the Ukraine they re-emerged after periods of illegality and managed to reconstruct their resource base with some success. In 1993 the ban on the Russian Communist Party (KPRF) was lifted only shortly before the election. Its rural wing had formed the Agrarian Party to avoid the ban and also won seats. The development of the KPRF was fraught with ideological and strategic contradictions as it struggled to adapt to new political circumstances. It was an anti-system party opposed to capitalism and democracy, with anti-system competitors from other communist-successors and the 'national-patriotic camp' reducing its capacity for ideological flexibility.[52] In the Ukraine the communists were anti-market but also anti-state, supporting a (new type of) union with Russia. The (non-successor) Socialist Party of the Ukraine stressed the need for gradual market reform with the transformation of ownership to workers. But aside from these parties and Rukh, oriented above all to preserving Ukrainian statehood, parties were of little import in the first Ukrainian elections.

Personal politics was notable, and parties in Russia too were closely identified with their leaders. Yabloko (Apple) was a compilation of its leaders Yavlinski, Boldyrev, and Lukin. But more than most, Yabloko had organisational resources[53] (from the remnants of the broad democratic movement) and an economic reform strategy. The Liberal-Democratic Party, the vehicle of the charismatic Vladimir Zhirinovskii, could be regarded as a leader-party. But Zhirinovskii was indubitably part of the nationalist camp, with a particular brand of fiery imperialism. Zhirinovskii also provided a rare example of a Russian politician making a sustained attempt to recruit members and develop his party's structures.[54] To the shock of the reform movement his party came first in the list element in 1993, though its unknown candidates performed badly in single-member districts.

The Communist Party of the Russian Federation (KPRF) remained the largest political party (possibly the only 'political party') in Russia, rapidly rebuilding its network of primary party organisations and (re)attracting over half a million members. It remained statist and patriotic, with its 1995 programme an 'intellectually incoherent synthesis of Marxism and the national idea', and its leader Zyuganov's own thinking 'a heady mix of statism, *Slavophilism* and populism'.[55] Despite the presence of strong communist (pro-Soviet) sentiments among a considerable proportion of the population, the KPRF did not rely solely on nostalgia; but it had difficulty generating a set of coherent alternative policies.[56] Electoral participation brought it within the ambit of democratic practice, and it 'began to adapt to the conventions of parliamentary politics'.[57] At the same time its pragmatic stance within the Duma gave it a degree of access to informal clientelist processes, at least when its support was advantageous to government.[58]

The Communist Party of the Ukraine (KPU) was the strongest party in the Rada in 1994 and again in 1998 (with 24.7 per cent of the list vote). Unlike the KPRF it did not seek the 'patriotic' vote. It was 'unreformed' not only in its strong opposition to capitalism but also in its anti-state, pro-Soviet (Russian) orientation. In 2002 its popularity fell to 20 per cent, second place in the list element; but it remained the largest single party.

The further shaping of the centre-right

We noted above that save for Russia, the Ukraine and Romania the break-up of opposition umbrella formations led to several large parties with relatively clear ideological orientations similar to Western European 'party families'. The successor parties mostly dominated the centre-left or the left; and their successes were also a product of the failure of their competitors. This was also the case in Russia and the Ukraine; but the non-communist opposition parties faced different challenges and again warrant separate discussion. In this section we examine the development of the parties of the centre-right and the right elsewhere. Then we will explore a second, later variant of the electoral party and the emergence of new populist parties.

Liberal and conservative parties

The evolution of parties of the right was in some measure a function of how closely they were linked to the incumbents after the first free election. Economic misery caused a reaction against governments everywhere save in the Czech Lands, where economic crisis was delayed. Only Václav Klaus and the Czech Civic Democratic Party succeeded from a position of incumbency in mobilising voters in favour of a clear platform of radical economic liberalism.

In Estonia and Latvia, where new parties distinguished themselves from the Popular Fronts, the liberals of Homeland (*Isamaa – Pro Patria*) and Latvia's Way also did well, emerging as the largest groupings in the first post-independence elections. Latvia's Way even survived blame for a major banking collapse in 1995. Although in 1998 the new People's Party

(*Tautas Partija*) won the Latvian election (21.3 per cent) as the party of dynamic capitalism,[59] Latvia's Way remained strong (18.2 per cent). But in 2002 although the People's Party remained credible with 16.6 per cent of the vote, Latvia's Way fell below the threshold.

In Estonia the Coalition Party was closely associated with the interests of the Soviet-era industrial élite. Its leaders Jaak Taam and Tiit Vähi had been members of the Popular Front government. The party was primarily concerned with issues of privatisation and land reform. In 1992 it contested the election as an element of Secure Home, securing a respectable 13.6 per cent of the vote, rising to 32 per cent in a new broad electoral alliance in 1995. It faced a challenge from 1994 from the new liberal Reform Party, a product of the new young business élite, and by 2002 the Coalition Party had effectively disappeared.

In Bulgaria the Union of Democratic Forces (SDS) failed to make economic reform its governing priority after 1991 and lost to the Socialists in 1994. By 1997, when the Socialists' ineptitude effectively ceded the election, the Union's strident anti-communism had given way to something more positive. It began to resemble a unified political party with a coherent economic reform strategy, an anti-corruption programme, and an unambiguous pro-European Union foreign policy orientation.[60]

Several erstwhile market-liberal parties shifted their emphasis over the course of the first decade, particularly where – within a broad pro-reform consensus – transition-shock appeared to make the population less receptive to radical capitalism. Some parties adopted a more obvious conservative line, stressing the importance of traditional values and also taking on a nationalist hue. Thus, while retaining its commitment to a laisser-faire economy, Klaus's occasional nationalist outbursts and lack of enthusiasm for 'civil society' gave the Czech Civic Democratic Party (ODS) an increasingly conservative tinge. The ODS remained the largest right-wing party, adding a more nationalist, Euro-ambivalent message to its 2002 election campaign (its vote edged down from 27.7 to 24.7 per cent).

Klaus's leadership style and the party-finance scandals of 1997 had seen an earlier split, with the new Freedom Union (US) often seen as 'the ODS minus Klaus'. The US also maintained its pro-capitalist stance, but its 1998 campaign for a less confrontational style of politics, greater decentralisation, and more sensitive minority policies distinguished it from its parent[61] (it gained 8.6 per cent of the vote). Klaus's continuing rightward shift made the US's liberalism more distinctive, but the Freedom Union did not stand alone in 2002 (see below).

In Estonia Pro Patria (Isamaa), which had spearheaded the first wave of radical economic reform, lost votes in 1995 and shifted its emphasis to 'family, cultural and national values'.[62] But this tendency to blend conservatism and economic liberalism was not repeated in Hungary. The Free Democrats (SzDSz) remained secular and pro-market; they chose the centre-left option, joining a governing coalition with the Hungarian Socialists in 1994 and again in 2002. Fidesz, however, abandoned its original liberalism, moving steadily to appropriate the Hungarian centre-right space. Both its market rhetoric and its civil libertarian orientation weakened. Its 1998 election campaign combined a stress on national and religious values with promises to lower taxes and restore many universal welfare benefits, along with law and order promises and support for Hungarian minorities abroad. By 2002 it had sharpened its nationalist rhetoric still further.[63]

In Poland two liberal parties emanated from Solidarity. Of these, the Liberal Democrats (KLD) failed to enter parliament in 1993. They merged with former Prime Minister Mazowiecki's Democratic Union (UD), which had lost votes but maintained a parliamentary presence. Increasingly their new Freedom Union (UW) appeared an enduring, stable party with a core electorate drawn from the urban intelligentsia. The Liberals and the Democratic Union were in government in 1991 and 1992–3, and in 1997 the Freedom Union returned to government with Solidarity Electoral Action (see below). But with its controversial leader Balcerowicz again at the Finance Ministry, the UW was increasingly associated with stringent fiscal policies. This rendered its alliance of market liberals with old Solidarity-dissident human rights' liberals increasingly fragile; and the UW split in 2001. Several months later it failed to cross the electoral threshold.

Despite its position as the largest parliamentary party after 1993, Russia's Choice, the liberal 'party of power' lost presidential support, its governing role, and the accompanying resources. Gaidar began to build a 'proper' political party, Russia's Democratic Choice; but in the process he alienated 'those democratic celebrities and state officials who did not want to subject themselves to any party discipline'.[64] A mushrooming of new 'democratic' parties followed, and Russia's Democratic Choice failed to cross the threshold in 1995. In 1999 it was part of the Union of Right Forces.

Nationalist parties

New nationalist parties emerged for the second elections, notably in Romania. Both the Party of Romanian National Unity (PUNR, now under its own name) and the new Greater Romania Party (PRM) offered communist-era nostalgia and a counter to the 'Hungarian threat' in 1992. PUNR had its origins in Transylvania, with a large Hungarian population and considerable ethnic tensions (see Chapter 9). It did well enough (7.7 per cent) to encourage aspirations to become a national party.[65] The PRM was cut from much the same cloth. Led by former communist 'intellectuals' (Corneliu Vadim Tudor was Ceauşescu's 'court poet'[66]) and retired army and former Securitate officers, the PRM was still more extreme. It had many characteristics of a far right party, including overt anti-democratism, xenophobia, the glorification of strong leaders (including Ceauşescu and wartime dictator Antonescu); it viewed the inter-war fascist Iron Guard positively and stressed a litany of dangers to the Romanian nation from Hungarians, Jews, the IMF, and the West.[67]

Both nationalist parties supported the 1992–6 minority (Democratic National Salvation Front) government first informally, then in coalition; but within six months of the next election both had been removed as Iliescu sought to distance himself from their radical rhetoric. In 1996 each gained just over 4 per cent of the vote, but their subsequent fortunes were rather different. PUNR failed in its bid to become a centrist party with a more moderate national stance and rapidly disintegrated. The PRM stormed into second place in 2000, with 19.5 per cent of the vote, and Tudor contested the presidential run-off against Iliescu.

Elsewhere far-right parties waxed and waned. Few gained enduring success. The Republicans entered the Federal Assembly from the Czech Lands in 1992. They were xenophobic and 'vitriolically and wholeheartedly anti-communist',[68] but being pro-Czechoslovakia, they were more statist than nationalist. For a time their attacks on democracy and their predilection for violent confrontation made them distinctive among parliamentary parties in Central Europe. But they did not cross the electoral threshold in 1998. The party went bankrupt, and two new 'republican' formations contested the 2002 elections; together they received just over 1 per cent of the vote. In Hungary István Csurka's radical nationalist Hungarian Justice and Life Party (MIÉP) gained representation in the 1998–2002 parliament with 5.4 per cent of the list vote. Though its vote held, the higher turnout meant that MIÉP failed to cross the threshold in 2002.

Milieu parties

Parties seeking the support of particular segments of the electorate tended to fare badly in the 1990s. No new milieu parties emerged. The Polish Peasant Party (PSL) provided a rare example of a successful class party.[69] As a successor party it retained a large membership, considerable property, and organisational penetration of the countryside. At first it mobilised its class electorate quite effectively. In 1989 it enjoyed reserved seats, but in the 1991 free elections the PSL attracted 8.7 per cent of the vote (several small Solidarity peasant parties gained 5.5 per cent). In 1993 after nearly doubling its vote (15 per cent) it entered government with the social democrats (SLD). Yet the PSL earned little credit in government, with its greedy exploitation of patronage and its disloyalty to its coalition partner. Nor did it nurture its members in the manner of a mass party. It lost half its vote again in 1997 and did little better in 2001, when Self-Defence mounted a successful challenge in rural areas (see below). It returned to government with the SLD until its exclusion from the coalition after voting with the opposition in March 2003.

In Hungary Fidesz's successful sweep to the right incorporated elements of the Forum, Christian Democrats, and Smallholders along the way. The

Christian democratic parliamentary party dissolved in July 1997. Despite successive splits and an increasing extreme-rightist cast under József Torgyán after 1991, the Independent Smallholders saw off three other small-holder-competitors in 1994. In 1998 they still attracted 13 per cent of the list vote and became Fidesz's junior coalition partners. But Torgyán's leadership remained divisive and they finally imploded in a cloud of corruption scandals. Three smallholders' parties contested the 2002 election; none entered parliament.

Christian Democrats in the Czech Republic, Slovakia, and Slovenia did maintain their electoral niche and all played a governing role. The Czech Christian Democrats (KDU–ČSL) stressed the 'social market', expressing a desire to emulate the German Christian Democrats, and maintained an unambiguously pro-European Union stance. Its leader Josef Lux positioned the party firmly in the centre as a possible coalition partner and hence counterweight to either the left (i.e. the Social Democrats) or the right (the Civic Democrats). The Christian Democrats enjoyed a relatively large membership and attracted a loyal electorate in the first four elections.[70] In Poland the clearest Christian identity was that of the Christian National Union (ZChN), although they never stood under their own name in national elections. The ZChN disintegrated in the early months of 2001, ceding the traditional religious-clerical vote to the new League of Polish Families (LPR).

The development of electoral parties

The evolution of the parties of power

Unlike Russia's Choice with its clear reform messages, subsequent parties of power were notably lacking in the clarity of their electoral appeal. They made general appeals to security, continuity, and order. After Russia's Choice 'Our Home is Russia' emerged as a new party of power from under the wing of Prime Minister Viktor Chernomyrdin, with precisely this statist technocratic message of order and stability. But for the 1995 election numerous other challengers had also appeared, and Independents continued to dominate the single-member districts. This was a 'crowded market with "low product differentiation"'.[71] 'Parties' made little attempt to develop organisational structures, and those like Gaidar and Zhirinovskii who tried, largely failed. In 1995 only Zhirinovskii's party (187) and the Communist Party (129) proved able to nominate candidates in more than half the single-member districts. Only four electoral blocs managed to cross the list threshold. The Communists 'won'. Our Home is Russia, gaining 45 list seats (10.1 per cent of the vote) but none in single-member districts, performed worse than had Russia's Choice in 1993.

If after two attempts in Russia the incumbency appeal of the party-of-power appeared rather unsuccessful, in 1999 it yielded very different results. Unity (the Inter-regional Movement of Unity or 'Bear') emerged in September. Too late to register officially for the election, Unity drew in seven associations that had already registered. It held a founding congress ten weeks before the election, but it remained to all intents and purposes a virtual party. Michael McFaul described its programme as 'mysterious'.[72] But in Vladimir Putin, Unity gained the endorsement of a massively popular politician; and its leader Sergey Shoygu also leapt high in public esteem.[73] Unity came from nowhere to take 23 per cent of the list vote (just behind the KPRF's 24 per cent). Like Russia's Choice and Our Home is Russia, Unity possessed copious financial resources from government and business, and privileged access to the mass media. Unlike its predecessors, it had a clear campaign strategy designed to maximise these advantages. It was '...a campaign first, and an electoral bloc and political-party-in-the-making second'.[74] It conveyed a fresh professional image designed (successfully) to target new and unattached voters, and it played effectively on President Putin's own themes of pride, patriotism, and territorial integrity. Myagkov and Ordeshook noted the 'influence of regional governors and their abilities to direct the votes of their electorates in a nearly wholesale fashion' – 'almost as if those political bosses themselves filled out the ballot forms'.[75]

The Ukrainian situation was complicated by the development of regional 'parties of power', as regional élites sought access to parliament (to supplement avenues to ministries and the presidential administration), and national élites sought regional fiefdoms. The Russian term 'oligarch parties' gained currency in the Ukraine. Kimitaka Matsuzato identified the resources used by wealthy entrepreneur Viktor Medvedchuk of the Social Democratic Party (United) [SDPU (o)] to establish that party's (temporary) dominance in Zakarpattya. His large personal wealth permitted him to pour funds into the region; vote-buying; the possession of his own mass media; connections with 'law enforcement' that enabled him 'to jail, or at least blackmail...his political antagonists'; up-to-date election technology; charitable work; administrative pressure; and an 'almost coercive enrolment' of party members.[76] SDPU (o) adopted left-wing rhetoric, but it was widely regarded as part of the amorphous centre in the 1998–2002 Rada, taking a pragmatic and pro-presidential stance.[77]

In 2002 the main party of power, 'For a United Ukraine', was also a disparate pro-presidential creation, initially of five 'parties' with an array of regional and institutional support and obvious presidential backing. These were often little more than the vehicles of regional bosses. For a United Ukraine used a typical incumbency electoral appeal to the need to preserve 'civic stability and social unity, stable national currency and economic growth...'[78]; but it had great difficulty in building a coherent image. While local machines were crucial to the single-member vote, 'their presence made it harder to reinvent the bloc for the list vote'.[79]

Electoral parties: the new umbrellas

While incumbent groupings used appeals to stability and order, a second type of electoral party had emerged earlier in Central Europe. For these 'parties' too structure was a key dimension, as they also brought together disparate entities; but their central election promises were largely negative. Essentially their appeal was based on a plea for unity against an incumbent foe. The 2002 Ukrainian elections provided several examples of this use of the umbrella formation by those palpably too weak to achieve much on their own. These 'electoral parties' lacked coherence, and so too did most of their constituent elements. We will discuss the Central European variant below (see below), but the Ukraine in 2002 also provided some interesting exemplars. Even the best known of the twelve electoral blocs that contested the election (alongside numerous 'political parties') were themselves composed of varied parties, proto-parties, coteries, and cliques. The major battle was that between former Prime Minister Yushchenko's 'Our Ukraine' bloc – reuniting the two main wings of Rukh, along with liberal, patriotic, and Christian democratic groupings, as well as the trade union federation – and 'For a United Ukraine', the 'party of power'. 'Our Ukraine' had a programme of radical economic and political reforms, including Ukraine's integration into European and trans-Atlantic structures to complete the 'revolution' begun in 1989–91. But the key issue was still the guarantee of Ukrainian democracy, Yushchenko argued.[80] Though he did not attack the president directly, the implicit premise was the need to counter Kravchuk's control of parliament. Indeed, the multifarious composition of the two leading blocs pushed specific policies into the background. Yushchenko's track record as a previous reforming prime minister and his personal credibility were more important.

Yulia Tymoshenko's bloc by contrast fought an openly anti-presidential election with a group of national-democratic and nationalist parties.[81] Yushchenko's former deputy energy minister, Tymoshenko was a vigorous opponent of Ukrainian 'anti-democratic super-presidentialism'. Despite her personal popularity[82] she failed to draw other anti-presidential parties, notably the Socialist Party, into a wider bloc.

The elections were marked by violence, including the murder of two candidates, intimidation, media bias, accusations of US and Russian plots, corruption charges against party leaders and the president, prolonged allegations of scandal surrounding presidential complicity over the murder of a prominent journalist, and disqualification of candidates and parties. Still the pro-democratic parties recorded their greatest success to date. Yushchenko's bloc came first (the Communist Party was second). Yet as we shall see in Chapter 6, there were elements of a pyrrhic victory here. 'For a United Ukraine' mustered only 12 per cent of the list vote, but presidential resources proved a strong pull once deputies took their seats.

In Central Europe the strategy of creating a new umbrella formation to unite against a powerful incumbent was also evident in Romania, Slovakia, and Poland. In Romania the anti-social-democrat alliance also sought new impetus to 'reform'.[83] Their initial success showed that voters could still mobilise against a perceived foe, but in Romania and Poland this mobilisation proved only temporary. The Romanian Democratic Convention (CDR, 1996) and Solidarity Election Action (AWS, 1997) displaced social democrats, and in Slovakia the Democratic Coalition (1998) removed Mečiar's Movement for Democratic Slovakia (HZDS). Neither the remains of the Convention nor the AWS rump entered parliament in 2000 and 2001. Neither managed to transform heterogeneous electoral parties into enduring party formations, and their governments paid a high price for factional infighting, lack of coherence, and manifest personal ambition. AWS shattered, with many seeking refuge in successful new parties, especially the Civic Platform (PO), Law and Justice (PiS), and the League of Polish Families (LPR).

The Democratic Convention (CDR) was an uneasy shifting alliance of up to six 'parties' and a dozen or so other groupings with the National Peasant Party–Christian Democrat as its fulcrum.[84] It positioned itself as the main opposition force, stressing the need for urgent economic reform; but its programme was vague in other areas. It gained 20 per cent of the vote in 1992 before winning both parliamentary and presidential (with Constantinescu) elections in 1996. Its government was a 'coalition of coalitions', with the Hungarian Democratic Union and the Social Democratic Union, the latter also an alliance of the Democratic Party (formerly Petre Roman's National Salvation Front) with the small Social Democratic Party.

Coalition politics proved volatile as the constituent elements bickered over the allocation of posts and failed to generate coherent policies. Following the Social Democratic Party's success in 2000 and the CDR's exclusion from parliament, the core of the Convention, the Christian Democratic-Peasant Party (PNȚCD) split, with former leaders spearheading a new Popular Christian Party (PPC). The Romanian Liberals (PNL) had already defected, remaining in parliament after 2000. In January 2002 the PNL merged with the extra-parliamentary Alliance for Romania (a social democratic reformist splinter) but then promptly resumed their factional infighting.

The Slovak Democratic Coalition (SDK) was nominally a 'party', forced to register as such by prohibitive new coalition thresholds set by Mečiar's then government; but it never functioned as a single entity.[85] Although the SDK performed respectably in 1998, Mečiar's HZDS remained the largest party. As in Romania this forced a government 'coalition of coalitions': the five-party Democratic Coalition with Social Democrats (SDL'), the Hungarians (SMK), and the new Party of Civic Understanding (SOP). Tensions within the government were a constant feature of Slovak political life from 1998 to 2002.[86] The SDK disintegrated; and new parties proliferated, both from splits within the coalition and outside it. But unlike Poland and Romania, one such offshoot proved successful.

Prime Minister Dzurinda inaugurated the Democratic and Christian Union (SDKÚ) soon after coming to power, adding to Slovakia's list of right-wing parties. He threw his own government into disarray, taking leading figures from other parties, including the liberal Democratic Union, whose origins lay in early departures from Mečiar's HZDS. But Dzurinda's gamble paid off. The clear division of the parties on distinctive pro- and anti-Mečiar lines gradually became more blurred. By the 2002 election the new SDKÚ had begun to develop a more positive vision.[87] Although it came second to the HZDS, it formed the basis of a smaller, less diverse governing coalition.

In the Czech Republic efforts to create a broad electoral party were short-lived; the 'enemy' was not uniformly defined. The Christian Democrats (KDU–ČSL) and Freedom Union constituted the core of the 'Quad-coalition' (4K), formed with two small parties for the 1998 Senate elections. 4K became 3K when the Freedom Union merged with the extra-parliamentary Democratic Union in December 2001. But it became 2K with the withdrawal of the Civic Democratic Alliance (ODA, an original Civic Forum offshoot) over a crisis over the party's debts and a record of dubious sponsorship. The KDU–ČSL and the US–DEU stood as 'the Coalition' in 2002, but proved reluctant to submerge their distinct identities, and differences rapidly emerged in the course of negotiations with the victorious Social Democrats, to whom the Christian Democrats were more favourable.

This example shows how 'new umbrella' electoral parties may be difficult to distinguish from other forms of electoral alliance. Many smaller parties sought strategic electoral alliances, and some major parties sought to increase their votes by adding other parties to their coat-tails (see Chapter 6). For example, we saw that the Polish Social Democrats concluded a formal alliance with the Labour Union in 2001. In these cases, however, the identity of the core party remained intact and constituted the main basis of the alliance's electoral appeal. This distinguished them from electoral parties, which tried to present a new identity separate from that of their constituent elements, while retaining any voters loyal to their constituent members.

The emergence of populist parties

We encapsulated the electoral appeal of populist parties as based on broad notions of serving the 'people' and healing their ills. Such parties began to emerge as part of the 'reactive politics' of disillusion, hardship, and insecurity. In most such parties leaders appeared from within the new élites. Many failed or proved ephemeral, as aspiring leaders overestimated their magnetism. In Latvia, Joachim Siegerist typified right-wing populism. Expelled from Fatherland and Freedom (LNNK) for extremism, his new People's Movement for Latvia (Siegerist Party, TKL) gained 15 per cent of the vote in 1995 with vehement nationalist rhetoric (Ironically Siegerist was a German, ejected from parliament for inadequate knowledge of Latvian). TKL went from success as the second-largest party in 1995 to ejection from parliament with a vote share of 1.7 per cent in 1998.

In Slovakia Rudolf Schuster's Party of Civic Understanding (SOP, 1998) and Róbert Fico's Smer (Direction, 1999) illustrate the leftist variety of populism. SOP was a one-parliament wonder founded just before the election. Based on its leader's undoubted popularity, SOP won 8 per cent of the vote. Although it gained Schuster enough visibility to win the presidency in 1999 and SOP remained a junior coalition partner, its efforts to define a clearer profile[88] bore no fruit; it did not contest the 2002 election.

Unlike Schuster, Fico was a parliamentary deputy, elected from the SDL'. Smer promised 'order, justice and stability' along with 'new faces' for the voters.[89] The charismatic Fico and Mečiar were the country's most popular politicians before the 2002 elections. Smer with a vague farrago of authoritarian, anti-corruption, anti-establishment, and anti-minority rhetoric was second to HZDS in opinion polls. It performed less well than expected, however, gaining 13.5 per cent of the vote.

The most striking case of liberal populism was provided by Bulgaria in 2001. Ex-tsar Simeon Saxecobburgotski had demonstrated no obvious political ambitions until his return in April, but he proved a capable strategist for his Simeon II National Movement. Refused registration for his party, Simeon formed a formal coalition with two innocuous small parties, the Party of Bulgarian Women and the Movement for National Revival (*Oborishte*). Simeon's moral appeal was central, but his entourage of young, Western-trained technocrats also helped bolster his economic credibility.[90] While stressing historical ideals, moral values, and the need to abandon political partisanship, Simeon maintained a neutral image, attacking neither of his major opponents. His extraordinary success (42.7 per cent of the vote) would plausibly have been higher but for the presence of the Simeon II Coalition (3.4 per cent) and the National Union for Tsar Simeon II (1.7 per cent).

In few instances did genuine outsiders succeed even temporarily; but such breakthroughs did occur. In Estonia, US army veteran Jüri Toomepuu took the country by storm in 1992 with his 'anti-party'[91] Estonian Citizens' group (*Eesti Kodanik*), founded a month before the elections; in 1995 its alliance with Better Estonia failed to win seats.

Self-Defence (SO) in Poland provides a case of a left-populist leader-party where the persistence of a long-standing outsider finally paid off. Andrzej Lepper's party was notorious for its style of confrontational direct action and radical rhetoric in defence of the 'poor and the disadvantaged'. SO had a demonstrable anti-establishment record, targeting the 'losers' of transition with an ambiguous 'programme' offering simple solutions to complex problems. After a derisory performance in all previous elections (0.8 per cent in 1997), in 2001 SO achieved what the Peasant Party had failed to do, namely to attract voters from urban areas as well as the beleaguered countryside. SO came third (10.2 per cent).

Some parties remained very difficult to categorise. The most notable example was the Movement for Democratic Slovakia (HZDS), led by Vladimir Mečiar, central to Slovak politics from 1991 to 1998. It was deemed a 'non-standard party'[92] but also 'populist'.[93] Tim Haughton placed it on the centre-right, 'with a touch of populism thrown in...'.[94] But its concern for the losers gave the party's appeal an egalitarian cast, though references to 'enemies of the nation' did not. However, Mečiar's tenure in government also gave HZDS some features of a 'party of power'. It exhibited a disdain for liberal constitutionalism and offered a central economic policy role and opportunities for insider privatisation to key industrialists.[95]

Conclusion: the menu of electoral choice

We have identified a wide variety of political parties in this survey. Parties appealed to voters on the basis of ideology and programme. Some ideological parties sought to represent distinctive milieux, others to gain a wide electoral appeal. Electoral parties in Russia and the Ukraine were parties of power, using their vast administrative and patronage resources for conservative appeals. In Central Europe electoral parties formed new umbrellas with a negative appeal against a perceived political enemy. Populist parties evoked ordinary folk and their sufferings or asked for trust in their particular abilities or orientation.

Many parties therefore did not offer a set of highly specific programmatic choices. Indeed, Abby Innes argued that in Central Europe too successful parties were 'instant catch-all parties', whose lack of mass membership and developed ideology distinguished them from the Western European variant. This catch-all nature resulted from constraints arising from the failure of communist economic reform (necessitating capitalist development) and the imperatives of European Union membership (adherence to EU policy requirements and minimising redistributive issues).[96] This meant that parties endorsed the same aims, engendering competitive style without competitive substance. In consequence, parties failed to offer programmes but defined their policies after the election, leaving party competition at an 'extremely high level of political abstraction' and undermining a 'sense of personal political agency'.[97] Jiri Pehe argued similarly that the 2002 Czech election campaigns were 'devoid of any real issues...', with politicians effectively telling voters, 'You cast your vote in our favor [*sic*], we will do with it what we want.'[98]

This is a useful perspective, not least in drawing attention to the importance of the shared, overarching aims of many political parties in Central Europe. Accepting the entire EU *acquis* removed many issues from politics, though not all would have reached the political agenda. Issues like intellectual copyright are hardly the stuff of politics. It is also true that left-wing parties did not manage to offer a strategy for building capitalism without supporting capitalists nor a coherent egalitarian vision of the future while encouraging entrepreneurial initiative. Opposition parties also found it hard to develop specific policies because of their lack of resources, political inexperience, and inadequate information. Much competition centred on general issues of how far and how fast to proceed with the agenda of change, how best to provide a measure of protection for vulnerable social groups, as well as with issues of the quality of democracy, including leadership competence and integrity.

Yet conflicts of values remained salient, and electors had ample opportunity to choose between egalitarianism and paternalism, cosmopolitanism and nationalism, individualism and collectivism, or to support explicitly anti-capitalist and anti-EU parties. Restoration of national pride may be as important to voters as proposals to reform the education system. Nor were specific policy commitments absent. Preoccupation with valence issues can hardly be regarded as a criticism: Means may be as important as ends in offering solutions to unemployment, inflation, or crime. Parties offered their manifestos with greater or lesser degrees of clarity, and incumbent parties had a record the voters could judge (see Chapter 5). Indeed, sectional (milieu) parties did not normally have more specific programmatic commitments than the larger ones.

A clear division emerged between Russia and the Ukraine, and those elsewhere. In the still semi-democratic context of these two countries major issues of structural change remained central, but parties could not assume any ability to carry through their programmes. Delayed elections delayed party development, which remained weak, and the role of 'parties of power' retarded rather than promoting it. Economic and political power remained closely linked, and ad hoc blocs formed electoral parties defending or challenging institutional vested interests, including those of the presidency and regional barons. The old communist parties remained strong, but not sufficiently strong to determine the direction of policy in the 'super-presidential systems'.

We have done no more than allude to explanations for party development, nor have we examined the mix of parties in individual countries. In some cases the number of electoral contenders fell, and rising thresholds also had an effect on the numbers of parliamentary 'parties'. However, new – mainly populist – parties and shifting alliances meant a broad fluidity in the menu of choice. In Chapters 4 and 5 we shall assess features of the voters' reaction to the menus described here. We shall examine particular country configurations and their evolution in Chapter 6.

4
Voters and the Electoral Mechanism

The willingness of the electorate to take part in the electoral process and voters' ability to cast their votes effectively constitutes an important dimension of representation. We reviewed the variety of political parties and their offers to the electorate in Chapter 3. Now we turn first to issues of citizens' participation and then to the nature of voters' choices in terms of their relationship to the electoral process. Participation is gauged by levels of electoral turnout and the proportion of invalid votes. Wasted votes and the use made of preference voting give some indication of voters' strategic response. None of these indicators may be regarded as decisive, but they provide an overview of key elements of the process of representation.

Turnout

It is self-evident that in liberal democracies the political process is quintessentially participative. Without participation, democracy cannot exist, though 'how much' participation is desirable remains a subject of debate. The view that apathy could be functional or that a sudden influx of voters could be highly destabilising was current for a time.[1] But more recently, emphasis on the quality of democracy again stressed its importance and the dangers of low levels of participation for system legitimacy and the perpetuation of civic values.

The most important basic indicator of participation is turnout at elections, reflecting the voters' decision to go to the polls and cast a ballot. Yet declining turnout appeared to be a feature of many liberal democracies,[2] creating anxieties about popular alienation from politics. In the new democracies, turnout also became a cause of concern, both for politicians fearing a loss of legitimacy and for scholars who stressed an engaged population and democratic political culture as necessary features of democratic development.

Regime-choice elections
We would expect the initial regime-choice elections to constitute the highpoint of turnout, with the prospect of change and the novelty of competition. Such

elections were full of drama and symbolic import. Some drop in turnout was to be expected following a period of high expectations. But not all elections were classic regime-choice elections, and the regime-choice element was not always obvious. Earlier we viewed regime-choice elections as including both those semi-competitive elections that led to the Communist Party's removal from power (Poland in 1989 and the Soviet Baltic Republics in 1990) and the first *fully* competitive elections (Czechoslovakia, Hungary, Bulgaria, Romania, and Slovenia in 1990). In Russia in 1993 and the Ukraine in 1994 the choice between the 'old' regime and a 'new' one was less clear cut, as profound changes had already taken place by the time of the first fully competitive elections. But there were still contenders promising to halt or even reverse change, however improbable their goals. In the Ukraine key issues of state-building and the constitutional order remained unresolved.

This use of two criteria (outcome and process) for a regime-choice election means that we cannot assume identical content for these elections. In particular, where semi-competitive elections resulted in the accession of an élite committed to regime-change, it was not clear how far voters realised the profundity of the electoral stakes. In retrospect we know that Poland and the three Baltic republics had their founding elections as a chorus of the swansong of the old regime, but this was not apparent at the time. In Poland the 'rigged' nature of the 1989 election and the supposedly pre-determined outcome neither presumed nor even intimated a serious opportunity to remove the communists from power. The Balts had seen a partial dress rehearsal for competitive elections in 1989; but independence was not a foregone conclusion in the republican elections of 1990.[3]

Turnout[4] was indeed high in the first *fully* competitive elections (see Table 4.1), with the Czech Lands, Slovakia, Bulgaria, Romania, and Slovenia recording levels above 85 per cent and the Czechs highest of all at almost 97 per cent. But Hungary's turnout was far lower at 65 per cent. The four semi-competitive regime-change elections saw lower turnout than the competitive elections, but the Balts still recorded higher turnout than that in Hungary. Ukrainian turnout for its highly ambiguous 1994 election was low considering the great divides in Ukrainian politics, but it was higher than that in Hungary, Lithuania, Poland, or Russia.

Low turnout in Hungary and Poland may be partly explained by the negotiated element of the 'mode of exit' from communism. In neither country was there mass popular mobilisation in 1989, and the new institutional arrangements were created by a small group of regime and opposition élites largely insulated from public scrutiny. In Poland the electoral outcome appeared assured in advance. In Hungary the public had remained largely passive in the face of change, and the new electoral system was particularly complex.

In Russia circumstances were highly specific. The 1993 election followed an intense political crisis, it aroused little interest, and it was a rather miserable affair. Indeed, a special commission set up to investigate electoral fraud

Table 4.1 Turnout in the first competitive or regime-choice elections (%)

Country	Turnout
Czech Lands 1990[1]	96.8
Slovakia 1990[1]	95.4
Bulgaria 1990	90.8
Romania 1990	86.2
Slovenia 1990	85.7
Latvia 1990[2]	81.2
Estonia 1990[2]	78.2
Ukraine 1994	75.8
Lithuania 1990[2]	71.7
Hungary 1990[3]	65.1
Poland 1989[4]	62.1
Russia 1993	54.3

[1] To the Federal Chamber of the People, Czechoslovakia.
[2] To the Supreme Soviet of the Republic. [3] First-round list element. [4] semi-competitive for the Sejm according to the Round Table Agreement.

suggested that the turnout figure had been falsely inflated by the authorities because of the higher minimum turnout requirement for the simultaneous constitutional referendum.[5]

The dynamics of turnout

In subsequent elections the dynamics of participation also varied (see Table 4.2). In the Czech Republic, Romania, Slovenia, and the Ukraine turnout declined at successive elections; but elsewhere there were reversals or sudden upsurge: in 1994 and 2002 in Hungary, in 1993 in Poland, in 1995 in Estonia, in 1998 in Slovakia, in 2000 in Lithuania, and in 2001 in Bulgaria. However, the general trend was clearly downwards, sometimes dramatically so, as in the third (the second post-independence) elections in Latvia and Lithuania. Although turnout rose in Latvia's first fully competitive elections, it fell in Lithuania and Estonia, pushing them into the low-turnout bracket. Poland – with a history of societal mobilisation and political activism under the communists – sank into a pattern of non-voting that placed it in the democratic outlier category along with Switzerland and the United States.

A variety of factors are often adduced to explain changing turnout at elections. The most relevant for our purposes are those that focus on institutions and contextual factors. Some have offered individual-level explanations. In stable democracies there is some indication that those who routinely do not vote are less educated and less interested in politics than their voting

Table 4.2 Changing turnout for elections to lower chamber, 1989–2002 (%)

Country	Election 1	Election 2		Election 3		Election 4		Election 5	
	Turnout	Turnout	Change	Turnout	Change	Turnout	Change	Turnout	Change
Czech Republic	96.79[1]	85.08[1]	-11.7	76.29	-8.8	73.86	-2.4	57.95	-15.9
Bulgaria	90.78	83.87	-6.9	75.23	-8.6	58.87	-16.4	66.77	+7.9
Slovakia	95.41[1]	84.21[1]	-11.2	75.65	-8.6	84.15	+8.5	69.99	-14.16
Latvia	81.2	91.18	+10.0	72.65	-18.5	71.00	-1.65	72.5	+1.5
Poland	62.1	43.2	-18.9	52.08	+8.9	47.93	-4.2	46.18	-1.75
Romania	86.19	76.92	-9.3	76.01	-0.9	65.31	-10.7		
Lithuania	71.72	75.29	+3.6	52.92	-22.4	58.63	+5.7		
Estonia	78.20	67.84	-10.4	68.91	+1.1	57.43	-11.5		
Slovenia	82.80	85.67	+2.87	73.7	-12.0	70.36	-3.34		
Hungary									
1st round	65.09	68.92	+3.8	56.26	-12.7	50.5	-5.76		
2nd round	45.51	55.12	+9.61	57.01	+1.89	70.53	+13.5		
Ukraine	75.81[2]	70.78	-5.0	69.26[3]	-1.5				
Russia	54.32	64.37	+10.0	61.68	-2.7				

[1] To the Chamber of the People. [2] 1st round. [3] List 69.27%, smd 69.24%.

Legend

Bulgaria: 1 = 1990; 2 = 1991; 3 = 1994; 4 = 1997; 5 = 2001
Czech Republic: 1 = 1990; 2 = 1992; 3 = 1996; 4 = 1998; 5 = 2002
Estonia: 1 = 1990; 2 = 1992; 3 = 1995; 4 = 1999
Hungary: 1 = 1990; 2 = 1994; 3 = 1998; 4 = 2002
Latvia: 1 = 1990; 2 = 1993; 3 = 1995; 4 = 1998; 5 = 2002
Lithuania: 1 = 1990; 2 = 1992; 3 = 1996; 4 = 2000
Poland: 1 = 1989; 2 = 1991; 3 = 1993; 4 = 1997; 5 = 2001
Romania: 1 = 1990; 2 = 1992; 3 = 1996; 4 = 2000
Russia: 1 = 1993; 2 = 1995; 3 = 1999
Slovakia: 1 = 1990; 2 = 1992; 3 = 1994; 4 = 1998; 5 = 2002
Ukraine: 1 = 1994; 2 = 1998; 3 = 2002
Slovenia: 1 = 1990; 2 = 1992; 3 = 1996; 4 = 2000

co-citizens. There is some evidence that this applied to Poland, Hungary, Lithuania, and Russia,[6] and it could well have been the case elsewhere. However, factors such as education, wealth, or occupational profile cannot explain changes within or between countries. Clearly country profiles do not change within three or four years, and 'high-turnout countries do not have richer or better educated people than low-turnout countries'.[7]

Franklin and his colleagues identified three aspects of the institutional dimension. First was that of 'salience', reflecting the importance of outcome: their studies confirmed that elections that 'do not decide the disposition of executive power' were likely to be viewed by the electorate as less important, while a close election determining the composition of the executive would see higher turnout.[8] Second was the nature of the electoral system: if a high proportion of votes were wasted, then motivation to vote would be reduced. Therefore PR should be more conducive to higher turnout, since single-member plurality systems have high 'wastage', particularly with large numbers of candidates. The third factor was the cost of voting: the difficulty of the registration process and the act of voting itself. [9]

These explanations can be only partly applied to post-communist elections. The cost of voting remained low in post-communist Europe. Indeed, registration, access to polling stations, and other dimensions of the mechanics of voting showed only minor variations across the region, and in many cases (such as voting on board ships or in hospitals) provisions remained more or less intact from the communist period. No country introduced compulsory voting – in this case a reaction against previous communist practices of intensive voter mobilisation, if not formal compulsion.

Some differences remained, of course. Russia and the Ukraine provided an 'against all' negative voting option intended to foster turnout.[10] We cannot say whether turnout would have been still lower without it; but clearly it did not function to raise turnout in comparison with systems lacking such provision. Two-day voting persisted in the Czech Republic and Slovakia and for a time in Latvia, but this did not prevent a major drop in the fifth Czech and Slovak elections, making it difficult to see a consistent discernible impact.

Countries using PR did not show higher turnout rates than those with a mixed element. Nor can we attribute causal effects to changes in electoral systems, whether large- or small-scale change. Only the Ukraine retained a fully majoritarian system for its first fully competitive election, and the notion of safe seats remained dubious for most single-member seats in countries with mixed systems. In the event, we found no significant relationship between turnout and type of electoral system or proportionality, whether taking all elections into account or including only 'non-founding' elections.

The most important variable identified by Franklin was electoral salience, with a 'salient election' affecting the disposition of executive power. Since all parliamentary systems enjoyed this salience, other measures were used to assess salience by the degree of competition. But Kieran Williams, using Pérez-Liñán's measure of competitiveness, found no relationship between party competition and turnout.[11] The closeness of election result, as measured by the difference in vote share of the top two parties, proved similarly unilluminating (see Table 4.3).

Using a wider data set than ours, Marina Popescu's analysis[12] endorsed the finding that elections that matter show higher turnout. She found that legislative responsibility was the only institutional variable to prove significant in post-communist elections; but her conclusions were very tentative, especially given the small number of cases. Nor did Popescu's more broadly conceived 'experience of elections' model, based on Franklin's later stress on competitiveness as the key to the salience of an election,[13] yield significant results, though the novelty of elections (years since the first free elections), majority status,[14] disproportionality, and legislative responsiveness had a moderate impact in the expected direction.

If institutional factors seemed to play little role, there did appear to be some major contextual factors at work. Many observers noted a strong antipathy to political parties as a key legacy of the communist system.[15] Mobilisation activities by political parties proved a significant dimension of turnout in the new democracies of Latin America, where both the state and political parties were seen to have a key role as agents of mobilisation.[16] Gray and Caul linked the decline in turnout in older democracies to demobilisation, including declining trade union membership, weakening party ties, and the proportion of (less active) younger voters.[17] Siaroff and Merer also stressed the link between party and trade union membership and higher turnout.[18] Yet these activities were largely lacking in Central and Eastern Europe. Parties' lack of resources, their weak links with society, and their poor reputations did not facilitate a mobilising role.[19] The continuing weakness of civil society provided little scope for other intermediary bodies to fill the gap, though some have stressed the importance of trade union links for the electoral success of the Alliance of the Democratic Left in Poland or the Hungarian Socialists (see Chapter 3).[20] The Confederation of Independent Poland (KPN) and the more successful Movement for Democratic Slovakia (HZDS) also established party-linked trade unions. Yet the initial decline in turnout following most first free or regime-choice elections may certainly be broadly linked to the weaknesses of parties in their incipient stages of development.[21]

Moreover, processes of social withdrawal and increasing apathy set in as the process of transformation generated severe economic hardship, widening inequalities, and social insecurity.[22] The newness of the new political parties, their inexperienced leaders, the focus on personalities, seemingly endless corruption scandals, and the atmosphere of dislocation and hardship all contributed to a region-wide lack of trust in politicians, political parties, and

Table 4.3 Turnout and electoral competition in parliamentary systems, 1990–2002

Country	Turnout (%)	Competition index[a]	Competition index[b]
Bulgaria			
1990	90.79	52.16	10.94
1991	83.87	92.95	1.22
1994	75.23	30.75	19.27
1997	58.87	17.87	30.23
2001	67.03	17.01	24.56
Czech Republic			
1990[1]	96.79	6.79	39.67
1992[1]	85.08	21.76	14.78
1996	76.29	80.0	3.18
1998	73.86	73.0	4.57
2002	58.0	67.13	5.73
Estonia			
1992	67.84	36.24	8.4
1995	68.91	23.28	16.04
1999	57.43	44.18	7.32
Hungary			
1990[2]	65.09	48.98	3.34
1994[2]	68.92	19.75	13.25
1998[2]	56.26	75.49	3.44
2002[2]	70.53	90.90	0.98
Latvia			
1993	91.18	17.16	19.06
1995	72.65	87.43	0.25
1998	71.00	74.56	3.15
2002	72.50	76.56	4.86
Lithuania			
1992[1]	75.29	22.73	22.81
1996[1]	52.92	11.09	20.91
2000[1]	58.63	40.61	11.44
Poland			
1991	43.20	94.2	0.33
1993	52.08	58.24	5.01
1997	47.93	67.27	6.70
2001	46.29	9.94	28.36
Romania			
1990	86.19	1.2	59.08
1992	76.29	48.67	7.69
1996	76.01	53.2	8.55
2000	65.31	28.83	17.13
Slovakia			
1990	95.39	42.27	13.56[1]
1992	84.20	15.44	19.09[1]

Table 4.3 (Continued)

Country	Turnout (%)	Competition index[a]	Competition index[b]
1994	75.65	8.83	21.08
1998	84.15	95.23	0.67
2002	70.06	60.13	4.41
Slovenia			
1990	82.8	71.84	39.0
1992	85.60	42.13	8.95
1996	73.70	60.27	7.63
2000	69.90	17.89	20.2
Average	71.37	46.44	13.59
Average 1990–6	76.08	41.89	15.32
Average 1997–2002	64.23	53.54	10.86

Source: [a] Kieran Williams, 'PR's First Decade in Eastern Europe', *Representation* (forthcoming, 2004), [b] Author's calculation (vote share of largest party – vote share of second largest party).
[1] Chamber of the People, Czech/Slovak section. [2] List vote.

parliament itself.[23] The Czech Republic remained an exception until 1997, when party corruption and economic downturn struck it too.

Party identification remained low, reducing the impetus to turn out to support a strongly preferred option. Voters in the former Soviet Union were less likely to identify a party 'that represents my interests and views' than those in East Central Europe. In the Ukraine where parties were least developed (see Chapter 3) voters were less committed to particular parties than in any other country.[24] Yet the problem was a wider one, with few voters expressing attachment to or confidence or trust in political parties.[25] Rose found 61 per cent of respondents in EU candidate countries very or fairly dissatisfied with the way their 'democracy was working'.[26]

Continuing party splits and the emergence of new parties often increased the number of choices available to voters (we will discuss this further in Chapter 6). But they did not increase the clarity of choice; the constant movement in many countries was extremely confusing. Yet there were no significant statistical relationships between turnout and support for particular parties, the number of electoral contenders, or the number of new parties.

It is easier to provide plausible ad hoc explanations for sudden rises in turnout, therefore, than it is to explain the reasons for decline or the differences between countries. Obviously the nature and circumstances of each election itself does constitute an important factor. In Poland, the 1991 election witnessed a record number of 111 contenders at national and constituency level. Most voters knew only a few of them and their disorientation was often profound.[27] The 1993 election offered rather clearer choices and more salient political parties and turnout rose. But 1997 was also an 'important' election, reflected in the polarisation of left (SLD) and right (AWS), yet turnout fell. In Slovakia the high turnout in 1998 was seen as part of an intensive politicisation of society into pro- and anti-Mečiar camps, with extensive activity by non-governmental organisations to mobilise the population.[28] In Bulgaria in 2001 turnout rose despite a subdued campaign because the sudden entry onto the political scene of ex-tsar Simeon II offered a qualitatively new and unexpected dimension to political life. In Hungary the 2002 campaign was both closely fought and very bitter, with a clear divide between two camps offering different versions of 'identity politics';[29] the uncertain outcome brought more voters into the second round. These particularistic explanations are both relevant and important additions to general regional factors. However, they do not take us much further in trying to understand the general decline in voter participation in the new democracies – or why (say) Poles were reluctant to vote despite their tradition of political activism.

Declining turnout across the region constituted a clear trend; but it cannot be regarded as definitive or necessarily stable. If disillusion was a factor, it is not necessarily permanent. If party identification were to increase and parties devoted greater efforts to mobilisation, and if genuine party–civil society linkages developed, this could make a difference in the longer term. Yet in the meantime such signs of political disengagement must be regarded as inimical to the development of strongly democratic political culture.

Next we turn to the capacity of voters. Once a voter has decided to go to the polls, he/she must be able to cast his/her vote in accordance with the electoral rules. He/she need not understand them but needs to comply with them. One clear measure of this type of civic capacity is the share of invalid votes cast.

Invalid votes

Invalid votes are simply votes cast on valid ballot papers but not in the correct manner: the voter puts the mark in the wrong place or votes for two parties or several candidates or punches or stamps the voting card inadequately. The most prominent instance of this problem will undoubtedly long remain the infamous Florida chads of the US presidential election of 2000.

Although ease of understanding is often cited as a positive attribute of electoral systems, the variety of electoral mechanisms did not affect voters in Central and Eastern Europe. Judging by the total of invalid votes cast, most voters had no difficulty in correctly marking their ballots, even with Estonia's major shift from Soviet majoritarianism to STV in 1990.[30] Of course voters may cast invalid votes for reasons other than ignorance or error. They may deliberately decide to spoil their voting slip as an act of protest,

Table 4.4   Against all (%)

Election	Against all, single-member districts	Against all, list element
Russia 1993	15.39	4.22
Russia 1995	9.85	2.77
Russia 1999	11.76	3.32
Ukraine 1998	7.46	5.26
Ukraine 2002	7.43	2.55

including writing slogans or comments on their ballot paper. We cannot judge how far the capacity to cast a valid vote 'against all' reduced this sort of voting; but it was widely used in the two countries where it applied, especially in single-member districts (see Table 4.4). Indeed in Russia in 1999 'against all' received the most votes in eight constituencies and those elections were rerun.

If a low proportion of invalid votes constitutes a rough indicator of familiarity with the voting system and inclusiveness in the process of seeking representation, then we may be partially reassured. Most countries had few spoiled ballots. Table 4.5 shows those elections where invalid votes constituted more than 3 per cent of the total. These are high figures by

Table 4.5   Invalid votes above 3 per cent in parliamentary elections

Election	Invalid votes (%)
Romania 1992	12.93
Slovenia 1992	7.98
Romania 1990	7.54
Slovenia 1990	7.40
Russia 1993	6.81
Romania 1996	6.49
Ukraine 1994 (1st round)	6.29
Romania 2000	6.23
Slovenia 1996	5.89
Poland 1991	5.63
Lithuania 1996 (list)	4.93
Lithuania 2000 (list)	4.44
Poland 1993	4.23
Poland 2001	3.99
Poland 1997	3.88
Bulgaria 1990 (smd – 1st round)	3.86
Ukraine 2002 (list)	3.72
Hungary 1990 (list)	3.55
Slovenia 2000	3.31
Lithuania 1992 (smd – 1st round)	3.10
Ukraine 1998 (list)	3.09

West European standards;[31] but in Bulgaria and Hungary only the first free elections saw relatively numerous spoiled ballots. Voters there adapted very quickly. Only in Romania were there substantial numbers of invalid votes cast, especially in 1992. Still, all Romanian elections appear in this list, as do all Polish, Lithuanian, Slovene, and Ukrainian elections.

No obvious factor links these four countries. Romania, Poland, and Slovenia used list PR (though Poland used open lists, in Slovenia voters chose a single candidate from a ballot resembling that used in single-member districts). The Ukraine had a double-ballot majoritarian system in 1994 but a mixed-parallel system thereafter. The issue remained most serious in Romania, where the exceptionally high figure for 1992 was deemed by some to be an expression of electoral irregularities[32] and was noted with concern by the Organisation for Security and Co-operation in Europe (OSCE). Romania had complex ballots, not least because of the minority contenders (see Chapter 7); but most of the problem in 1992 was attributed to double-stamping of ballots, whether by voters confused by similar logos or illegally by 'ruling party agents', as Carey suggests. The counting of votes was better monitored in 1996, and there was no serious suggestion of fraud,[33] though the share of invalid votes remained rather high. The OSCE repeated its call for a Permanent Election Commission and for simplifying the format of the ballot paper.[34] This would have helped ensure greater national conformity in judging ballot validity; but no action followed.

In the Ukraine in 1994, the mechanics of voting in the majoritarian system were very cumbersome. The voter had to strike through all the names of unwanted candidates, leaving just one (or none). Poles had an exceptionally thick ballot-booklet in 1991 because of the large number of contenders. Anecdotal reports also suggested that some voters failed to understand why they had two votes for the Senate (a plurality system with two votes for two-seat districts) but only one for the Sejm. Yet the ballot grew gradually shorter, and one would have expected voter learning over successive elections. Coupled with its notoriously low turnout, Polish figures reduced effective political participation even further.

In the Ukraine the 'against all' figures after 1998 also increased the share of voters not contributing positively to determine their representatives. Since both 'against all' and invalid votes were included in the total from which parties' list proportions were officially calculated, this did make a difference to the outcome.[35] By contrast Czech voters cast few spoiled ballots: by the elections of 1998 and 2002 invalid votes were less than half of 1 per cent.

Wasted votes

If most voters had few problems with the process of voting itself, how rapidly did they learn about the implications of the electoral process? One common indicator of voters' learning is change in the proportion of wasted votes – votes not used to elect any candidate – at successive elections. This is easiest to see with PR systems, and it is generally calculated as the sum of votes cast for parties failing to win parliamentary seats. Of course technically more votes than these are 'wasted' because of unallocated remainder votes for successful parties. But in theory voters should 'learn' not to vote for parties that are unlikely to win seats. If their party is tiny or sinking in the opinion polls, voters should shift their votes to a second-best party where votes will make a difference. In this view the proportion of wasted votes should decline over time, as voters become familiar with the vagaries of the electoral system and the likely fortunes of political parties.

In plurality or mixed systems one can also calculate single-member district 'wastage' as the proportion of votes cast for those who did not win. However, with elections more personalised, with high numbers of new contenders at each election, and with the option to vote also for a party in mixed systems, this does not appear a useful indicator of voters' adaptation to electoral rules (though we shall see that it affected party strategies). Moreover in Hungary's complex mixed-linked system (more party oriented and with greater continuity of parties) losing-votes for parties in both single-member and list elements are transferred for national list allocation; so votes for candidates standing for small parties below the threshold are 'wasted', while others are not. Effectively then, it is practical to assess wasted votes only for parties failing to cross the threshold in the list element.

At the same time we should note the factors working to maintain rather high levels of wastage. Uncertainty remained a general feature of most post-communist elections. Voters who learned that the smallest parties do not win seats also discovered that expectations about who would win and lose often proved unfounded. Voters moved in considerable numbers, not least because electoral contenders often changed radically from one election to the next. The electoral parties in particular created problems. Thus high levels of both electoral and party volatility also obstructed voters' capacity to behave 'rationally'.

Moreover, information about the parties' standing was often limited by prohibition of the publication of opinion polls. These rules changed considerably as election laws were modified, and they differed from country to country. In Lithuania in 1992 such a ban (later rescinded) lasted throughout the campaign, while in Latvia, which effectively reinstated its inter-war electoral law, there was no mention of opinion polls and little on campaign regulation. The Czech Republic maintained its seven-day ban after independence. Slovakia also reduced its ban from 23 days as a constituent republic of Czechoslovakia to 14 days in 1994 and to 7 in 1998. Poland began with 7 days, moved to 12, then settled in 2001 for 24 hours. In Bulgaria the initial prohibition was 8 days prior to polling day, then 14 days from 1991 to 1997, and then one day in 2001. Russia introduced a ban of 3 days in 1999.

Most of these bans were long enough to hinder voters from assessing the effects of campaigning on electoral preferences, but clearly the tendency was for the length of this information blockade to be shortened. The Internet also made late polls available in some cases to voters with computer access.

In addition, it was unlikely that voters could consistently assess the impact of changes in the electoral system. Where there were 'big' changes, as with Bulgaria's shift from a mixed system to PR in 1991 or the Ukraine's move from a majoritarian to a mixed system in 1998, a 'learning lag' could be expected. Only Russia and Hungary retained their initial competitive systems virtually intact. Others saw changes in district magnitude, the level of thresholds, and the formula for translating votes into seats (though not in the size of the assembly). We ignore the issue of formulae here as too technical to affect voters' choice. Thresholds appear most important in this regard.

The impact of rising thresholds was easier than their first introduction for voters to assess *if* we assume reasonably reliable information. Voters did not respond effectively to Poland's jump from no constituency threshold in 1991 to 5 per cent in 1993. Generally thresholds did tend to increase, often ostensibly as a measure to reduce the number of parties in parliament. At the same time increased thresholds offered protection for the larger parties, both from small parties and from the challenge of outsiders – though effects could be unpredictable.

Thresholds changed not only for individual parties but also for parties standing together in electoral alliances (see Table 4.6). The Czech Republic Slovakia, Poland, Romania, and Lithuania all introduced differential thresholds that made voters' calculations more complex. With other changes, including changes in district magnitude, it was harder still for voters to calculate the cumulative impact on election results. In Hungary the complexity of the electoral system made it extraordinarily difficult to predict electoral outcomes. Voters probably did not understand the complex allocation of wasted votes for the national tier allocation or the transfer of unfilled list seats to the national level. We shall also examine some idiosyncratic features of the 'Byzantine'[36] Estonian electoral law. These complexities complicated but did not necessarily rule out attempts to maximise the utility of the vote as in more orthodox electoral systems.

Of course as with spoiled ballots, voters could well 'waste' their votes for reasons other than ignorance.[37] Even with sound expectations about party performance, voting for a failing party need not be a sign of irrational behaviour but rather the result of strong ideological or personal reasons. Voters have different aims. Some party-oriented voters may seek to maximise the national vote of their party, however small. In many cases the threshold for state funding of parties provided an incentive, since it was less than the threshold for entering parliament. Other voters may vote to gain a preferred

Table 4.6 Changing list thresholds in fully competitive elections, 1990–2002

Country	Election 1	Election 2	Election 3	Election 4	Election 5
Bulgaria	4%	no change	no change	no change	no change
Czech Republic	5%[1]	5% (one party), 7% (2-party alliance), 9% (alliance of 3), 11% (alliance of 4+)	no change	no change	5% (one party), 10% (2-party alliance), 15% (3-party alliance), 20% (alliance of 4+)
Estonia[2]	5% for national list	no change	5% for national list; electoral coalitions prohibited		
Hungary	4%	5%	5% (each party, allied or not)	no change	
Latvia[2]	4%	5%	no change		
Lithuania[2]	4%	5% (party), 7% (alliance)	no change		
Poland	5% (national list)	5% (party), 8% (alliance), 7% (national list)	no change	5% (party), 8% (alliance)	
Romania	none	3%	no change	5% + 3% for the 2nd party in alliance and +1% for each additional party, to a maximum of 10%	
Russia	5%	no change	no change		
Slovakia	3%[1]	5% for a party, 7% for alliances of 2–3 parties; 10% for 4 or more[1]	no change	5% (each party, whether allied or not)	5% (party), 7% (alliances of 2–3 parties), 10% (4 or more parties)
Slovenia	2.5%	3 seats for 2nd tier distribution	no change	4%	
Ukraine	n/a	4%	no change		

[1] Elections to National Council. [2] Post-independence elections with new laws.

party representative in their own constituency. Still, in theory thresholds should gradually reduce the number of contenders and the share of wasted votes, as parties withdraw from hopeless contests and voters withdraw from hopeless parties.

Therefore if one can see a decline in wasted votes as an indication of 'learning', the converse is not true: one cannot necessarily view the absence of decline as an indication that voters have not learned, especially where uncertainty remains high or recurs. Wasted votes are a function of the number of contenders, thresholds, district magnitude, formulae, the accuracy and availability of opinion polls, and election dynamics that voters cannot always accommodate.

We can generate a number of expectations regarding both founding and subsequent elections, but in both cases the number of contenders and the electoral system will play a part. In the regime-choice elections in Central Europe one might expect a lower wasted vote because of the polarisation of the electorate into those for and against the system, often with lower thresholds. Yet this could be counteracted by the novelty of competition, unfamiliarity with a new electoral system, and the sheer number of contenders. Subsequently uncertainty continued to reign, as umbrella movements split, electoral parties emerged with names different from their constituent elements, and other new parties appeared. So wasted votes would be expected to rise, particularly where thresholds were highest.

Thirdly, after a threshold is raised, the wasted vote may rise for the first subsequent election, as voters find it difficult to assess parties, especially at the threshold margin. Fourthly, wasted votes will decline roughly in line with a reduction in the number of contenders, including the disappearance of Independents in list systems where they are permitted. Fewer contenders present fewer costs to voters in gaining information about the choices offered, and voters learn that Independents have little political influence. Finally, the overall trend will be one of declining wasted votes – though this is a hypothesis that may require a longer-term perspective. The number of cases in each category is too small for useful statistical analysis, but a look at these cases offers some support for these propositions (see Table 4.7).

We see from Table 4.7 that Bulgaria's first election in 1990 had the lowest wasted vote of all elections save that in Slovenia in 2000. Bulgaria's was an archetypal regime-choice election. Despite the presence of 41 contenders and a 4 per cent threshold, the Socialists (BSP) and the Union of Democratic Forces (SDS) together gained 83.4 per cent of the list vote, and the total share for the four groupings entering parliament from the list element was 97.4 per cent. The next election occurred in the following year with a fully proportional system but greater uncertainty because of the state of the two main parties. The governing BSP was unpopular, and it lost almost 13 per cent of its vote. The SDS had split, and its fragments took some 13 per cent of the vote (but none crossed the threshold). The Agrarian Union fell

Table 4.7 Proportion of list votes cast for parties failing to gain parliamentary representation, 1990–2002 (%)

Country	Election 1	Election 2	Election 3	Election 4	Election 5
Bulgaria	3.64	24.96	15.6	8.05	14.48
Czech Republic	18.38[1]	26.78[1]	11.16	11.31	12.42
Estonia[2]	14.6	12.69	8.4		
Hungary	15.81	12.68	11.41	11.31	
Latvia[2]	10.69	12.03	11.37	15.78	
Lithuania[2]	16.19	32.59	23.42		
Poland	7.33	34.67	12.42	9.72	
Slovenia[2]	16.79	10.58	3.60		
Romania	4.57	18.49	18.21	19.64	
Russia	12.94	47.59	13.38		
Slovakia	7.61[1]	23.79[1]	13.01	5.78	18.09
Ukraine	n/a	31.03	18.79		

[1] Elections to National Councils of the constituent republics of Czechoslovakia. [2] Post-independence elections.

below the threshold, leaving three parties in parliament and one-quarter of voters without the representation of their choice.

Over the next two elections, however, the wasted vote fell. In December 1994 the original four contenders were again in parliament, and the Bulgarian Business Bloc also scraped across the threshold with 4.7 per cent of the vote. In 1997 alliance strategies reduced the number of contenders as the two largest parties sought to broaden their appeal and hitherto unrepresented smaller parties flocked into electoral coalitions: The SDS formed the United Democratic Forces (ODS) with the Agrarian National Union, the Democratic Party, and the Social Democratic Party. The BSP constituted the core of the Democratic Left with Ekoglasnost and the Stambolijski Agrarian Union. The Movement for Rights and Freedoms allied with the Greens and Union New Choice in the Alliance for National Salvation. However, disillusion with the BSP, which had led the country into its deepest economic crisis, massive street protests, and early elections, saw the Democratic Left garner only 22 per cent of the vote, while the United Democratic Forces gained a majority with 52 per cent. Along with the Alliance for National Salvation and the eccentric Business Bloc, the Euro-Left Alliance also entered parliament.

The reduction in the wasted vote was not maintained, however, as ex-tsar Simeon burst on to the political scene and parties adjusted their alliance strategies. The Party of Rights and Freedoms formed a new electoral coalition with the Liberal Union and EuroRoma. The moderate nationalists of the Internal Macedonian Revolutionary Organization (IMRO) left the Democratic Forces and allied themselves with the St George's Day Movement (*Gergiovden*), a self-styled young neo-conservative movement. Both IMRO-*Gergiovden*

(3.6 per cent) and the controversial *faux* Simeon II coalition came close to the threshold. We argued in Chapter 3 that the latter (3.4 per cent of the vote), along with the National Union for Tsar Simeon II (1.7 per cent), may well have caused confusion to some voters. Still, some 6 per cent cast their votes for 30 other parties and Independents that clearly stood no chance, from the Democratic Party of Justice with about 11,000 votes to the Union of the Nation-Movement of the Deprived with 39.

In most cases the second election saw the largest proportion of wasted votes, but Estonia, Hungary, and Slovenia showed a decline in the proportion of wasted votes at successive elections (as did the two Ukrainian elections using a list element). We have seen that Hungary was distinctive from the outset, with political parties in place for the founding election in 1990. Ken Benoit has argued that Hungarian voters not only learned more about their arcane electoral system at successive elections but engaged in a measure of strategic voting.[38]

Slovenia had also developed parties early, though unlike Hungary an opposition alliance had stood in 1990 and new parties continued to appear. Still, the Slovene threshold (three seats) at first remained low, with just over 3 per cent of the vote enough to win seats in 1992 and 1996. By 2000 long-established parties were still performing well, however, and a bigger gap had opened up between parties crossing and failing to cross the new 4 per cent threshold: the new Party of Slovene Youth got 4.3 per cent of the vote, followed by the Greens with 0.9 per cent.

Estonia's threshold applied only to the national list, but more seats than anticipated were in fact allocated by the national list (see below). Unusually, Estonia also used a modified d'Hondt formula for allocating national list seats; its divisors $1, 2^{0.9}, 3^{0.9}, 4^{0.9}, \ldots$ were intended to give a further advantage to larger parties.[39] Neither mechanism meant high wasted votes, which dropped slowly but surely. The poorest performers did tend to withdraw from the electoral contest, and the number of electoral contenders fell quite rapidly. Estonia also banned electoral alliances from 1998, though this did not appear to have an immediate effect (see Chapter 5).

All other countries showed a considerable rise in wasted votes in the second *fully free* election. In Lithuania, Latvia, Romania, Slovakia, and Poland this jump coincided with a rise in the threshold (see Table 4.6). In Poland the move was substantial, from no threshold in the constituencies to 5 (party) and 8 per cent (coalition). In Romania the threshold increased in 1992 by 1 per cent and then rose again for the 2000 election with differential party-coalition thresholds, and there was a slight increase in the proportion of voters who failed to see their parties enter parliament. In Latvia the 5 per cent threshold excluded one party in 1995 that would have won under the previous threshold of 4 per cent: the Labour and Justice Coalition received 4.6 per cent of the vote.

It is hard to disentangle the effect of thresholds and that of the number of contenders, both on wasted votes and on each other. There were many incentives to maintain a high number of contenders, including the publicity gained through free media access in most states and initially at least, ease of registration. Stricter rules of entry generally had some effect (see Chapter 5) and many early entrants subsequently disappeared altogether. But new ones also emerged to replace them. In most countries the number of contenders did fall over time, but this was not a linear trend (see Table 4.8). Again, there were also factors that varied from country to country.

In Russia the large increase in the proportion of wasted votes in 1995 may be attributed to the political circumstances of the first two elections. In 1993 the election was called in haste, and parties had little time to organise the collection of 100,000 signatures throughout the country. Only 13 succeeded. By 1995 the choice was greater: 43 'parties' (or blocs) had developed some measure of infrastructure or could purchase signatures from private collecting firms to secure registration of their lists.[40] This had dropped to 26 by 1999, but as we saw in Chapter 3, many were complex electoral parties.

In Romania minority organisations swelled the total; special provisions meant that they needed to stand even though they did not do so 'to win' (see Chapter 9). Still, even without the minorities the number of contenders remained high. In the Czech Lands and in independent Slovakia, parties sought to bypass high coalition thresholds. Already in 1992 the Liberal Social Union debated intensely whether it should stand as a new unified entity (with a 5 per cent threshold) or a three-party coalition (9 per cent). The Election Commission permitted it to stand as a party, though shortly

Table 4.8   Changing numbers of list contenders, 1990–2002

Country	Election 1	Election 2	Election 3	Election 4	Election 5
Bulgaria	41[1]	38	48	39	32
Czech Republic[2]	13	19	16	13	28
Estonia[3]	17	16	12		
Hungary	28	35	26	13	
Latvia[3]	23	19	21	20	
Lithuania[3]	17	24	15		
Poland	111	35	21	14	
Romania[4]	71	79	64	68	
Russia	13	43	26		
Slovenia[3]	26	22	16		
Slovakia[2]	16	23	18	17	25
Ukraine	n/a	30	33		

[1] Total list and smd elements. [2] Including elections to the Czechoslovak Federal Assembly. [3] Post-independence elections. [4] Including national minority lists.

after the election it broke up into its three constituent elements. Larger parties often made room for smaller ones on their party lists: in Slovakia the 18 parties and electoral coalitions which contested the 1994 elections embraced 31 'parties' and 'movements', while the seven that entered parliament represented some sixteen entities.[41] In 1998 the Slovak Democratic Coalition and the Hungarian parties registered as single parties to overcome new coalition thresholds requiring 5 per cent of the vote for each constituent party. In 2002 the Coalition had split up, the prime minister had a new party, and several previous contenders had also split. Two pairs of divided parties – SDL' and SDA, and SNS and PSNS accounted for over 10 per cent of the wastage. Ivan Gašparovič had left Mečiar's HZDS, and his new Movement for Democracy (HZD) also took 3.3 per cent of the vote.

Few countries demonstrated a consonance of factors discouraging wastage. Where the electoral system remained the same, voters had constant reference points. Where the number of contenders fell, choices were clearer. Where remaining contenders were the same as in previous elections, choices were clearer still. In no single country did all these factors pertain, but the three countries that came closest – Hungary, Estonia, and Slovenia – were also those with successive decline in wasted votes. In these three cases there were clear signs that voters 'learned' and adapted to the electoral system. Elsewhere the second elections constituted the highpoint of wasted votes (save in Romania), but there were substantial fluctuations thereafter. We can be less certain about the extent or ways in which voters understood the voting system, not least because of persistent uncertainties and changing institutional mechanisms. We now turn to a different aspect of the electoral process, namely those mechanisms enabling voters to exercise another means of choice.

Preference voting

We have seen that many politicians favoured single-member districts in order to provide clear voter linkage to a particular named individual as their parliamentary representative. Since political parties were in their infancy, a majoritarian system was also deemed appropriate to connect citizens more broadly to the political system itself. We saw that one defence of the mixed system was that it would both foster political parties and provide an individual representative. An alternative solution – party lists with the option for voters to express their preference – was used in six countries with proportional representation and also in one – Lithuania – with a mixed system. Poland and Estonia opted for the open list system where voters select an individual candidate from a party list. Czechoslovakia and its successor states chose semi-closed lists, where voters could express individual preferences if they wished. In Latvia (effectively an open list system) and in Lithuania from 1996 voters indicated their positive preferences with plus signs and negative preferences by deleting names. Slovenia was peculiar in that voters had no choice from a list, since they had only one candidate per party to choose from; the ballot resembled that used in most single-member districts. In each case the mechanisms were highly complex.

The open list seemed to provide a compromise that would not undermine political parties in the way that single-member districts were thought to do by encouraging popular individuals to stand as Independents. The debates surrounding the respective merits of open and closed lists did not make reference to the putative consequences of open lists in other countries, namely that they encourage intra-party competition among candidates, factionalism, atomised parties, or even government paralysis and structural corruption.[42] The central arguments here were the party-fostering capacities of closed lists and the voter-friendly nature of open lists and attempts to find a middle road between the two.

In Estonia (as in neighbouring Finland) voters write the code number of their preferred candidate on the ballot paper (unlike Finland, Independents may stand). 'Personal votes' are allocated first, and any candidate achieving a full (Hare) district quota of votes is elected. Only then are seats distributed to parties in a second stage of district allocation, followed by a third stage in which remainder votes are transferred to a national pool. But in 1992 only 17 out of 101 deputies were elected by personal votes, 15 in 1995 and 12 in 1999. Top of the list in 1992 with 16,904 votes was Jüri Toomepuu, the leader of the new Estonian Citizens' group (see Chapter 3). Arnold Rüütel, Secure Home's popular former communist president, secured the highest personal total in 1995, with over 17,000 votes. In 1999 the controversial former Prime Minister Edgar Savisaar gained more than 14,000 votes. The peculiarities of the system meant that voter satisfaction was undermined by the next stages of seat allocation.

After the allocation of 'personal' seats, the remainders were added up for each party. Those parties receiving a full quota/s received district seats for their leading vote-winners. But (in a departure from Finnish practice) the district remainders were then aggregated at national level (for parties exceeding the 5 per cent threshold) and allocated by party-list order with the modified d'Hondt formula. Because the large number of contenders reduced the likelihood of achieving full quotas at district level, few lists gained full quotas at the second stage of allocation. Indeed, 60 per cent of parliamentary seats in 1992 were allocated by closed lists at national level, often to candidates who had received low personal votes but were obviously valued by their party. 'As a result, many voters felt disenfranchised, and questioned the legitimacy of the rules... There appeared to be a high component of randomness in the sense of no clear relationship between voter (personal) preferences and electoral outcomes.'[43]

Awareness of this problem was indicated by subsequent tinkering with these mechanisms. In 1995, seats were awarded in districts only (a) to those parties that had crossed the 5 per cent national threshold and (b) to those candidates whose personal votes constituted at least 10 per cent of the Hare quota for his/her district. For 2003 parties receiving one full quota would receive seats at district level for each 0.75 additional quota. Moreover, to be elected at national level a candidate must receive at least 5 per cent of the quota for his/her district; otherwise the seat goes to the next candidate on the national list meeting the quota requirement.

More than electoral system tinkering, however, it appears to be habitude that governs adaptation to complex electoral systems. Certainly turnout rose slightly in Estonia in 1995, but it is hard to attribute this to minor electoral-system adjustments. In Poland a similar problem arose in 1991, when unpopular candidates were elected from the national list.[44] The media made great play of this, but it did not appear to have a lasting effect.

In Poland a more conventional open list system gave voters the opportunity to move candidates up or down the party list, and they did so with alacrity. In 1991 candidates placed first on their party's list received 40.6 per cent of valid votes cast, 38.8 per cent in 1993, 33 per cent in 1997, and 33.6 per cent in 2001. Table 4.9 shows how the voters moved winning candidates around the list, confounding the parties' own rankings of candidates.

However, until 2001 the national list element (69 seats) provided a mech-anism by which parties could place their own most favoured candidates. Jerzy Buzek entered parliament through this route in 1997 as an obscure academic and immediately became prime minister. Even with the national list providing this insurance policy, the parliamentary committee on electoral reform favoured closed lists in 1993; but as opinion polls consistently showed the public strongly opposed, they did not press the matter.[45] In 2001, however, the national list was abolished as part of a package of changes intended to disadvantage the Social Democrats (SLD) in the forthcoming elections.[46] Since this left (successful) parties with no way of securing the election of competent but little known (or even unpopular) leaders, the issue continued to rumble on the party agenda and support for closed lists made an appearance in debates on the proposed electoral law for elections to the European Parliament.

Slovenia's system is complex in a different way, with the same under-lying goal of personalising the vote. After 1992 the eight multi-member constituencies were divided into eleven districts ('units') in which each party fielded a single candidate. Allocation takes place first at constituency level, where the votes of candidates for each party in the eleven districts are added together and seats are allocated by Hare quota to parties and awarded to candidates according to their share in the total number of votes (a winning candidate requires at least 9.1 per cent of the vote). Remainder votes are then allocated by d'Hondt to the closed lists at national level for parties receiving at least three 'direct mandates' or from 2000 exceeding the 4 per cent threshold. So Slovenia created an impression of being

Table 4.9   Candidates winning in Polish constituency seats by list place

List place	Poland 1991		Poland 1993		Poland 1997		Poland 2001	
	Number	% Seats	Number	% Seats	Number	% Seats	Number	% Seats
1	277	70.8	178	45.5	138	35.3	195	42.4
2	64	16.4	66	16.9	65	16.6	67	14.6
3	19	4.9	34	8.7	56	14.3	47	10.2
4	8	2.0	31	7.9	21	5.4	22	4.8
5	8	2.0	28	7.2	29	7.4	29	6.3
6	5	1.3	17	4.3	17	4.3	20	4.3
7	5	1.3	11	2.8	8	2.0	14	3.0
8	1	0.3	5	1.3	8	2.0	9	2.0
9	0	0.0	5	1.3	5	1.3	8	1.7
10	0	0.0	1	0.3	9	2.3	12	2.6
11	1	0.3	2	0.5	5	1.3	5	1.1
12	2	0.5	3	0.8	7	1.8	5	1.1
13	1	0.3	2	0.5	4	1.0	2	0.4
14	–	–	1	0.3	3	0.8	5	1.1
15	–	–	2	0.5	2	0.5	2	0.4
16	–	–	3	0.8	3	0.8	3	0.7
17	–	–	0	0.0	1	0.3	1	0.2
18	–	–	1	0.3	1	0.3	1	0.2
19	–	–	1	0.3	0	0.0	1	0.2
20	–	–	–	–	2	0.5	1	0.2
21	–	–	–	–	1	0.3	2	0.4
22	–	–	–	–	0	0.0	1	0.2
23	–	–	–	–	0	0.0	0	–
24	–	–	–	–	1	0.3	3	0.7
25	–	–	–	–	0	0.0	0	–
26	–	–	–	–	1	0.3	0	–
27	–	–	–	–	1	0.0	2	0.4
28	–	–	–	–	1	0.0	0	–
29	–	–	–	–	0	0.0	0	–
30	–	–	–	–	0	0.0	0	–
31	–	–	–	–	0	0.0	0	0.2
32	–	–	–	–	0	0.0	1	0.2
33	–	–	–	–	1	0.3	1	0.2
34	–	–	–	–	1	0.3	0	–
35	–	–	–	–	–	–	0	–
36	–	–	–	–	–	–	0	–
37	–	–	–	–	–	–	0	–
38	–	–	–	–	–	–	1	0.2

majoritarian and candidate-centred, while in essence remaining proportional and party-centred.

This impression was not strong enough, however, for a group of
centre-right parties spearheaded by the (right-wing, see Chapter 6) Social

Democratic Party. Just before the 1996 election it began a prolonged campaign for a two-round majoritarian system. Although formally defended as a mechanism to increase accountability, self-interest could also be detected. The opposition at that time appeared far more capable of cooperation than the left-wing parties and hence of avoiding the fragmentation so lethal for parties in single-member districts. It gathered 43,710 signatures for a referendum on the issue. The protracted aftermath saw extensive battles in which the Constitutional Court played a highly political role and a complex referendum whose outcome remained uncertain for two years. The issue contributed to a political crisis that brought down the government.[47] But it is hard to judge the popular mood on this, save that it was not one of great excitement.

Although the referendum saw 44 per cent endorsing the two-round system, with 26 per cent favouring a slightly modified proportional system, and 14 per cent a German-style mixed system, the turnout was only 38 per cent. The situation was finally resolved when the People's Party changed sides in the argument. A constitutional amendment provided for PR with a 4 per cent threshold, and the electoral system was left virtually intact, save for the new threshold.

In Czechoslovakia in 1990 if at least 10 per cent of a party's voters in a constituency expressed a preference, then those votes would be taken into account. Then, candidates gaining the preferences of a majority of preference-expressing voters would secure seats in order of their vote: in theory, with voters expressing four preferences, then four candidates could have moved up each list. In 1990 in the Czech Lands 17 of 200 deputies were elected by preference votes and in the Slovak Republic 13 of 150.[48] The 1992 amendment retained the requirement that 10 per cent of voters for a party must indicate preferences, but a candidate would move to the top of the ballot in that district if just 3 per cent of that party's voters circled his or her number. It made some difference. In the Czech Republic 13 deputies owed their seats to voters' preferences in 1992. In the independent Czech Republic only one deputy was elected by preference votes in 1996 and two in 1998, but in 2002 preference votes elected 10 coalition deputies.

In the Slovak Republic in 1992 nine deputies won on preferences, and in 1994 in independent Slovakia ten. But the introduction of a single national constituency in 1998 made it extremely difficult for voters to influence candidate order, and no candidate was elected by preference votes. In 2002 only voters for the Hungarian Coalition elected a deputy out of list order, giving Árpád Duka-Zólyomi 36,422 preference votes and moving him from list place 23.

The revised Lithuanian electoral law of 1996 altered the previously closed-list system, and the voter could indicate any number of positive or negative judgements of the candidates. Voters there (and in Latvia) indicated a positive preference by putting a 'plus' sign next to the candidate's name. A negative opinion could be indicated by either crossing out the candidate's name or his/her number. However, a party could choose to retain a closed list, and in 1996 5 of the 19 lists remained closed. The final results still depended mostly on the order set by parties due to the method of calculation employed.[49] Although preferences changed the order in which many candidates were elected in 1996, they did not affect the actual results.

The electoral law was again modified before the 2000 election with the negative option removed and the number of list candidates for which the voter could express a preference limited to five. More importantly, the method for calculating the ratings of candidates was modified, increasing the weight of preference votes.[50] As a result, preference votes affected the election of 15 deputies out of 70 in 2000.

The Latvian system was far simpler with its highly permissive ballot. Voters must choose a party, but they may mark as many positive and negative preferences for its candidates as they wish. Seats won are allocated to the candidate with the highest net score of positive votes.

We then see that only in Poland and Latvia did voters' choices necessarily make a difference. Elsewhere the position often depended on other features of the system. The peculiarities of the Estonian system were most salient in 1992 simply because the high number of contenders meant that more seats than anticipated were allocated by the closed national list. The Czech and Slovak preference systems made a difference at the margin, but in Slovakia the national constituency undermined this provision, illustrating how different elements of the electoral system may pull in different directions. The Lithuanian case appears a distinct oddity, since the system already provided for individual choice in the single-member element, while the preference system proved complex and costly. At first it had virtually no effect on the outcome, but changes to the computations did make a difference.

Conclusion

The generally high turnout of the first competitive elections reflected the early political mobilisation of the population against the regime as well as the excitement and novelty of the opportunity for genuine choice. Where the first real choices were conducted within the framework of the old regime (as in Poland), where elections arose from élite pact (Hungary) and where they were delayed and consequently less clear cut (Russia and the Ukraine), the initial fervour was less and turnout was lower. With the exceptions of Russia and Hungary, turnout fell from this original benchmark and a pattern of decline set in.

This decline varied substantially. It was least evident in Latvia, with turnout very comparable over the last three elections (to 2002) and the Ukraine. But it was continuous over successive elections only in the Ukraine (where reductions were slight), Romania, and the Czech Republic. Elsewhere particular elections did bring some voters back to the polls, although it was not necessarily the closeness of the electoral race that (at least partly) re-engaged them. Clearly, however, if participation is valued, then there remained a problem, both for the political parties and for the quality of democracy itself. Low turnout could not be interpreted as signalling voters' contentment with the political process. On the contrary, it appeared to be a function of transition-related hardship and disillusion with the new political élites. How far the fluidity of party names and new alliance configurations made it difficult for people to orient themselves and encouraged abstention is unclear.

Voters did adapt to the mechanisms of democratic choice. Only in Romania was there a serious problem of spoiled ballots, with little indication that this was a deliberate act by voters. Despite the fact that all political parties formally endorsed the principle that a permanent electoral commission should be established to ensure (*inter alia*) conformity in decisions regarding the validity of a ballot, the politicians did not act. But in Poland, the Ukraine, and Slovenia there were also larger numbers than elsewhere, at least raising the question of a need for civic education.

The issue of wasted votes was more complex. Changes in electoral laws, the numbers and complexity of electoral contenders, and the appearance of new parties undermined assumptions that successive elections would lead to greater predictability. Instead electoral volatility remained high. Voters found it difficult to behave strategically. Only in Hungary (over four elections), Estonia (over three elections), and the Ukraine (over two elections) was there a decline in the proportion of wasted list votes over successive elections.

Preference voting gave voters personal options as well as party choices. Mixed electoral systems in Hungary, the Ukraine, Russia, and Lithuania provided individual choice through the single-member districts of their mixed systems. Of the PR systems only Bulgaria and Romania used closed lists. We shall see in Chapter 6 that there was no automatic link between closed lists and strong parties; and certainly in Romania there remained persistent demands for some system offering individual candidate choice.

The Czech Republic, Slovakia, Latvia, and (oddly) Lithuania provided opportunities for preference voting. Choice may have given voters an increased sense of efficacy, but preference voting made little difference to electoral outcomes except in Latvia, where voters' choices did determine the winners from each party. Estonia and Poland used open lists, requiring voters to select a particular candidate; the Slovene system provided a choice of candidate, but not for a choice of candidates from the same party. In Poland voters routinely overturned party list-order, and there were few signs of dysfunctional battles between candidates of the same party. This option was clearly popular with the electorate, but it did not enhance their enthusiasm

Table 4.10 Indices of representation in the most recent election, to 2002 (%)

Country	Not voting[1]	Invalid vote (list)[2]	Wasted vote (list)[3]	Against all (list)[3]	% Electorate without representation in list element
Bulgaria 2001	33.2	1.1	14.5	n/a	43.5
Czech Republic 2002	42.0	0.4	12.4	n/a	49.4
Estonia 1999	42.6	1.7	8.4	n/a	48.3
Hungary 2002[4]	49.5	1.2	11.3	n/a	55.7
Latvia 2002	27.5	0.8	15.8	n/a	39.4
Lithuania 2000	31.4	4.4	23.4	n/a	49.7
Poland 2001	53.8	4.0	9.7	n/a	59.9
Slovenia 2000	29.6	5.9	3.6	n/a	34.4
Romania 2000	34.7	6.2	19.6	n/a	50.8
Russia 1999	38.3	2.0	13.4	3.3	49.6
Slovakia 2002	30.0	1.2	18.1	n/a	43.3
Ukraine 2002	30.7	3.7	18.8	2.6	47.5

[1] Share of registered electorate. [2] Share of votes cast. [3] Share of valid votes cast. [4] First round determines list allocation.

for voting, since turnout in Poland consistently remained the lowest in the region.

Despite these variations across the region substantial numbers of voters still lacked the party representatives of their choice, not least through their own abstention. Table 4.10 brings together varied participation indices for the most recent election (to 2002). Turnout was low everywhere, and some countries also saw rather high levels of invalid and wasted votes. The proportion of voters without representation in the list element is very high, though in Poland this is mainly because over half the population did not vote. In Romania in 2000, a rather low turnout (65 per cent) was accompanied by high numbers of invalid ballots (6.2 per cent), while almost one-fifth of voters 'wasted' their votes. In Lithuania also in 2000 turnout was very low, only 53 per cent, while 4 per cent of those voting cast invalid ballots. At the same time, of those correctly casting their votes, 23 per cent saw their parties fail in the list element. With the mixed system, however, some of these voters may have seen their preferred party win in single-member districts, where victory added eight small parties to the total represented in parliament. In Hungary turnout rose sharply to over 70 per cent in the second round; this gave clear opportunities for voters unrepresented by their list choice to vote their second choice (or lesser evil) in the decisive single-member contests between the two major parties. (The Ukraine and Lithuania had abolished their second round by 2002).

The picture is not unremittingly negative. There was some evidence that voters did 'learn'. However, since electoral uncertainty remained high, strategic behaviour was complex and not always rewarding. Continuing discussions about electoral systems also raised the possibility of further changes. Yet the electorate retained its ultimate collective decision-making role, as we shall see in Chapter 5.

5

Voters and Electoral Outcomes

Elections convey the judgement of voters on the successes and failures of their governing and opposition parties. As we argued in Chapter 1 this feedback is ultimately what makes representative government 'democratic'. Élites accept the verdict of the electorate through yielding or reconstituting their power according to routine procedures and evolving conventions. This chapter reviews the electorate's verdicts on the performance of their politicians in the new era of competitive elections.

There is no instance in any Central and East European parliamentary system of a defeated incumbent refusing to accept the election results. Moreover, in most cases the leading party went on to form the government. Despite the continuing problem of wasted votes (see Chapter 4), the distribution of the vote for parliamentary parties determined the shape of government. This is the first point to be elaborated in this chapter, and it is not a trivial one. Yet governments – and the parties that composed them – did not retain the confidence of the voters.

Generally political parties were found wanting, as we indicated in Chapter 4. One persistent feature of voters' choice in post-communist elections was their propensity to switch parties from one election to another. Indeed, considerable attention has been paid to high levels of aggregate electoral volatility in Central and East European elections. Very few parties maintained a consistent share of the vote. The picture conformed to Pedersen's finding that the larger the number of parties, the lesser the distance will be on policy issues and the greater likelihood of vote switching between elections.[1]

Although there is agreement on measures of volatility,[2] far from generating an agreed set of figures, assessments varied widely.[3] This is primarily because of the sheer difficulty of determining precisely which parties are counted as successors or equivalents from one election to the next, with intervening splits and mergers, changes of name, wholly new parliamentary entrants, and new alliance configurations.[4]

The more sophisticated the analysis, the more such differences of judgement are likely to affect the calculations. However, there were serious attempts to measure not only total volatility but also that volatility derived from voters' choice, excluding that determined by changes in the parties, and volatility within and between ideological groupings or blocs. On this basis, for example, Radek Markowski argued that the Polish electorate developed fairly clear ideological perspectives, so that even though voters changed parties, they remained within the same ideological family.[5] But this was not much comfort to the parties losing voters. Nor, as we have seen, was ideology the sole basis of parties' electoral appeal. The 'family' of many parties was unclear or indeterminate.

None the less, there is no doubt that large aggregate shifts took place. They indicated that identification with a particular political party was slow to develop, and that voters were not developing the ingrained loyalty that provided a lasting basis for the stability of West European democracies.[6] In the most general sense it seems safe to judge that voters deserted parties they felt had not served them well. They sought parties that would better represent them. Of course, when 'their' party disappeared, they had no alternative but to look elsewhere.

Still, some parties proved highly successful in maintaining their basic share of the vote. Others successfully wooed voters from other parties. Some parties shot up like rockets from one election to the next; others fell back just as rapidly. In some cases parties regained or surpassed lost support; in others they disappeared into the political ether. In theory electoral volatility was expected to decline over time, just as we noted with wasted votes: the number of parties should fall, their profiles should become clearer, and gradually voters should come to associate their own preferences with a type of party or indeed a particular party.[7]

After a decade of post-communist politics voters were still searching, and few parties could assume more than a small loyal core electorate. Appearances of stability could also prove illusory, as the Polish Freedom Union (UW) showed. Throughout the 1990s it maintained its strength among the urban intelligentsia. It was universally regarded as a stable element of the Polish centre. In 2001, however, the party split and well-known leaders deserted it. In the autumn elections voters followed suit, abandoning the UW for new offerings or even for the social democrats, and its vote share fell to 3.1 per cent.

Government formation

Did most voters get governments of their choice? Clearly in some instances they did not, namely where wasted votes were very high (see Chapter 4), altering the relative positions of the victorious parties. Yet, in most cases where votes counted, the majority of voters saw their wishes embodied in government. Governments took office according to the rules of the game; defeated parties withdrew, if not always gracefully. In the parliamentary systems the largest party following the election was generally charged with the task of government formation. This is shown in Table 5.1, where we see that out of 42 elections, in 34 cases (81 per cent) the largest party led or at least participated in government. Even where minority administrations were formed, they needed the support or at least the sufferance of other parties.

Exceptions arose for two reasons. The first resulted from the considerable number of parliamentary parties, increasing the need for multi-party coalitions. In several cases the leading party was simply not strong enough. The Polish position in 1991 provided the most dramatic illustration, with winning contenders under 29 different labels. The largest party, the Democratic Union, had 13.5 per cent of parliamentary seats, and its association with shock therapy made others reluctant to join it in government. The second-largest grouping, the successor Alliance of the Democratic Left, was effectively ostracised by most of parliament. With an election in no group's interest, Jan Olszewski's minority government gained sufficient parliamentary support, but it lasted only six months.

Other cases illustrated the inability of leading parties to find partners or to prevent cooperation against them. We saw in Chapter 3 that hostility to Mečiar generated a new electoral party, the Slovak Democratic Coalition (SDK), in 1998. Not only did the SDK place second, but it also had potential coalition partners. With the Association of Slovak Workers failing to cross the threshold, Mečiar had only the Slovak National Party; this was not enough to form a government. In 2002 Mečiar's party continued its decline, and this time the nationalists also failed to cross the threshold.

Edgar Savisaar's Centre Party faced the same fate in Estonia; it was the largest party after the 1999 election, but not large enough in circumstances where the vote was so dispersed. He was a controversial figure, detested by the alternative three parties that proved (just) capable of forming a majority government. The newly founded Latvian People's Party (TP) came first in 1998, but a (short-lived) minority government, supported by the Social Democratic Alliance, proved preferable to party élites. In 2000 the broad social democratic coalition in Lithuania gained 36 per cent of the seats, not enough to ward off a concerted attempt to prevent it taking office.

The position in Hungary was rather different. In 1998 the Hungarian Socialist Party did well in both the list and single-member elements; but its hitherto and effectively sole coalition partner, the Free Democrats (SzDSz), had done much worse than before. Fidesz on the other hand was well able to find partners to add to its own also-considerable weight. In 2002 the tables were turned. Fidesz fielded joint candidates with the Forum, and although they won most seats, only two other parties, the Socialists and the Free Democrats, entered parliament. Both had effectively campaigned on an anti-Fidesz platform and their renewed coalition partnership was never in doubt.

Table 5.1 Election results and consequences for largest parties in parliamentary systems

	Largest winning contender	List vote share (%)	Formed government?	Prime Minister
Bulgaria				
1990	Bulgarian Socialist Party, BSP	47.15	yes, majority BSP	A. Lukanov, BSP
1991	Union of Democratic Forces, SDS	34.36	yes, + DPS	F. Dimitrov, SDS
1994	BSP Coalition	43.5	yes, BSP + electoral allies	Z. Videnov, BSP
1997	United Democratic Forces	52.02	yes, SDS + electoral allies	I. Kostov, SDS
2001	National Movement Simeon II, NDSII	42.74	yes, + DPS	S. Saxecoburggotski, NDSII
Czech Republic				
1992[1]	Civic Democratic Party–Christian Democratic Party, ODS–KDS	29.73	yes, + KDU–ČSL + ODA	V. Klaus, ODS
1996	Civic Democratic party, ODS	29.62	yes, + KDU–ČSL + ODA, minority govt	V. Klaus, ODS
1998	Czech Social Democratic Party, ČSSD	32.31	yes, minority government	M. Zeman, ČSSD
2002	Czech Social Democratic Party, ČSSD	30.2	yes, + KDU–ČSL, US–DEU	V. ³pidla, ČSSD
Estonia				
1990	Estonian Popular Front (Rahvarinne)	n/a	yes, supported by elements of Free Estonia	E. Savisaar, Rahvarinne
1992	Isamaa–Pro Patria	22.0	yes, + ERSP + Moderates + Liberals	M. Laar, Isamaa
1995	Coalition Party and Rural Union, KMÜ	32.23	yes, + Centre Party	T. Vähi, KMÜ
1999	Centre Party, EK	23.41	no, alternative coalition of IERSP + RE + M stronger	M. Laar, Pro Patria Union, IERSP
Hungary				
1990	Hungarian Democratic Forum, MDF	24.73	yes, + KDNP + FKgP	J. Antall, MDF
1994	Hungarian Socialist Party, MSzP	32.99	yes, + SzDSz	G. Horn, MSzP

Table 5.1   (Continued)

	Largest winning contender	List vote share (%)	Formed government?	Prime Minister
1998	Hungarian Socialist Party, MSzP	32.92[2]	no, opposition coalition stronger	V. Orbán, Fidesz
2002	Fidesz–MDF	41.07 + smd[2]	no, opposition coalition stronger	P. Medgyessy (MSzP/non-Party)
Latvia				
1990	Latvian Popular Front, LTF	n/a	yes, majority LTF	I. Godmanis, LTF
1993	Latvia's Way Alliance, LC	32.41	yes, +LZS, minority government	V. Birkavs, LC
1995	Democratic Party 'Saimnieks', DPS	15.22	yes, in broad coalition with LNNK + LC + TB + LVP + LZS	A. Šķēle, non-party
1998	People's Party, TP	21.3	no, LC + LNNK + JP minority government	V. Kristopans, LC
2002	New Era, JL	23.9	yes, + ZZS + LPP + TB/LNNK	E. Repše, JL
Lithuania				
1990	Sajūdis	n/a	yes, broad-based Sajūdis and communist party	K. Prunskienė, LKP
1992	Lithuanian Democratic Labour Party, LDDP	43.98	yes, majority	B. Lubys, LDDP
1996	Homeland Union – Lithuanian Conservatives, TS(LK)	31.34	yes, + LKDP + LCS	G. Vagnorius, TS(LK)
2000	Social-Democratic Coalition of Algirdas Brazauskas	31.08	no, minority coalition of Liberal Union–Social Union	R. Paksas, Liberal Union
Poland				
1991	Democratic Union, UD	12.32	no, failed to form government; minority government was PC + PL + ZChN	J. Olszewski, PC
1993	Alliance of the Democratic Left, SLD	20.41	yes, + PSL	W. Pawlak, PSL
1997	Solidarity Election Action, AWS	33.83	yes, + UW	J. Buzek, AWS
2001	Alliance of the Democratic Left – Labour Union, SLD–UP	41.04	yes, + PSL	L. Miller, SLD

Romania				
1990	National Salvation Front, FSN	66.31	yes, majority government	P. Roman, FSN
1992	Democratic National Salvation Front, DFSN	27.72	yes, minority government	N. Vacaroiu (non-party)
1996	Democratic Convention of Romania, CDR	30.17	yes, + UDMR + PD	V. Ciorbea, CDR/ PNȚCD
2000	Social Democratic Party (PDSR)	36.61	yes, minority government	A. Nastase, PDSR > PSD
Slovakia				
1992[1]	Movement for Democratic Slovakia, HZDS	37.26	yes, minority government	V. Mečiar, HZDS
1994	Movement for Democratic Slovakia, HZDS	34.96	yes, + ZRS + SNS	V. Mečiar, HZDS
1998	Movement for Democratic Slovakia, HZDS	27	no, opposition coalition stronger	M. Dzurinda, SDK
2002	Movement for Democratic Slovakia, HZDS	19.5	no, opposition coalition stronger	M. Dzurinda, SDKÚ
Slovenia				
1990	DEMOS coalition	54.9	yes, majority DEMOS coalition	L. Peterle, SKD
1992	Liberal Democracy of Slovenia, LDS	23.46	yes, + SDS + ZLSD + ZS + SKD	J. Drnovšek, LDS
1996	Liberal Democracy of Slovenia, LDS	27.01	yes, + SLS + DeSUS	J. Drnovšek, LDS
2000	Liberal Democracy of Slovenia, LDS	36.21	yes, + SLS + DeSUS	J. Drnovšek, LDS

[1] To National Council of the Republic. [2] In 1998 the MSzP had the largest list vote and the most seats; in 2002 the MSzP had the largest list vote, but Fidesz had more seats.

Several of these 'anti' coalitions proved unstable, and in Poland (1991), Latvia (1998), and Lithuania (2000), the largest party formed a new coalition following the fall of the first post-election government. But many other governments also found themselves in difficulties, and governments fell in Poland, Slovenia, the Czech Republic, Latvia, Slovakia, Estonia, and Lithuania after the erosion of a majority or a decision to withdraw support from a minority government. In some cases parties also reached for a non-partisan figure to divert attention from economic difficulties or intra-party squabbles, or to gain enhanced legitimacy or wider support for a minority government (see Table 5.2).

The non-party stance did not always endure: Andris Šķēle, for example, founded the Latvian People's Party in 1998 and in Romania Vacaroiu,

Table 5.2   Governments under non-partisan prime ministers in parliamentary systems

	Tenure	Prime Minister
Bulgaria	12/7/90–29/11/90	Dimitar Popov
	30/12/92–2/9/94	Lyuben Berov
	17/10/94–25/1/95	Reneta Indzhova
	13/2/97–21/5/97	Stefan Sofiyanski
Czech Republic	30/12/97–22/7/98	Josef Tosovský
Estonia	30/1/92–19/10/92	Tiit Vähi
	8/11/94–5/4/95	Andres Tarand
Latvia	21/12/95–20/1/97	Andris Šķēle
	13/2/97–28/7/97	Andris Šķēle
Romania	1/10/91–4/11/92	Theodor Stolojan
	4/11/92–6/3/94	Nicolae Vacaroiu
	6/3/94–3/9/96	Nicolae Vacaroiu
	22/12/99–28/12/00	Mugur Isarescu
Lithuania	21/7/92–26/11/92	Aleksandras Abisala

Isarescu, and Stolojan all shed their purported neutrality for party activity. But as a temporary expedient it proved quite effective, if only providing a caretaker until the subsequent election. In most subsequent elections, however, voters remained volatile. Incumbency was not an advantage in circumstances of profound change.

The burden of incumbency

If volatility generally remained high, then how did voters move in their search for effective representation? If movement is a broad indicator of dissatisfaction, then the converse is also true: staying with a party may be seen as a sign of approval. Of course we cannot establish individual preferences; but there is an implicit assumption that when a party's vote stays the same, it will be because many voters have chosen it again; when it increases, it has gained new supporters. So it makes sense to examine the records both of successful and unsuccessful parties. It also seems appropriate to look at the voters' judgements of their governments. Despite the occasional shocks of 'earthquake elections', in Western Europe incumbency was traditionally regarded as an advantage, especially with proportional electoral systems.[8] In postcommunist Europe, it was the super-presidentialism of Russia and the Ukraine, where election results did not determine the composition of government, which proved the greatest obstacle to 'getting the rascals out'. Elsewhere incumbent parties tended to do badly or even very badly (see Table 5.3). Kieran Williams calculated that in ten countries two-thirds of elections led

Table 5.3   Vote-share change of governing parties in Eastern Europe, 1990–2002

Country	Vote share going to parties that will sit in government	Vote share at next election of parties that have been in government	Difference between the two elections
Poland 1997–2001	47.20	8.70	−38.50
Slovakia 1990–1992	52.96	16.24	−36.72
Lithuania 1996–2000	50.44	14.55	−35.89
Latvia 1998–2002	61.53	26.98	−34.55
Lithuania 1992–1996	43.98	10.01	−33.97
Bulgaria 1997–2001	52.02	18.18	−33.84
Romania 1990–1992	77.17	45.78	−31.39
Estonia 1992–1995	40.52	13.85	−26.67
Latvia 1995–1998	61.81	37.26	−24.55
Romania 1996–2000	49.74	25.72	−24.02
Bulgaria 1994–1997	43.5	21.97	−21.53
Slovakia 1998–2002	58.14	38.95	−19.19
Poland 1991–1993	43.85	27.77	−16.08
Estonia 1995–1999	62.69	46.91	−15.78
Czech Republic 1990–1992	67.95	52.4	−15.55
Latvia 1993–1995	48.41	33.06	−15.35
Hungary 1990–1994	42.92	27.59	−15.33
Slovenia 1990–1992	86.6	74.31	−12.29
Hungary 1994–1998	52.73	40.49	−12.24
Bulgaria 1991–1994	36.21	24.23	−11.98
Romania 1992–1996	37.69	25.88	−11.81
Slovakia 1994–1998	47.72	37.37	−10.35
Slovenia 1996–2000	76.46	66.79	−9.67
Bulgaria 1990–1991	89.38	80.81	−8.57
Czech Republic 1996–1998	44.06	36.74	−7.32
Hungary 1998–2002	45.43	41.82	−3.61
Czech Republic 1998–2002	32.31	30.2	−2.11
Poland 1993–1997	35.81	34.44	−1.37
Slovakia 1992–1994	68.78	69.44	0.7
Slovenia 1992–1996	59.90	61.79	1.89
Czech Republic 1992–1996	41.94	44.06	2.12
Average	53.54	36.59	−16.95

Source: Kieran Williams, 'PR's First Decade in Eastern Europe', *Representation*, 2003 (forthcoming).

to a complete change of government. Of the 59 prime ministers in ten parliamentary states from the advent of free elections to 2002, only Janez Drnovšek of Slovenia (in 1992, 1996 and 2000), Václav Klaus of the Czech Republic (1996), and Mikuláš Dzurinda of Slovakia (2002) took office for a consecutive term.[9]

Utter defeat was not unknown: In Latvia the Popular Front had won a substantial victory in the (Soviet republican) elections of 1990 and governed through the difficult period of gaining and securing Latvian independence; in 1993 it won just 2.6 per cent of the vote. In Romania in 2000 the major element of the governing Democratic Convention won 5.4 per cent of the vote, below the coalition threshold. In Poland in 2001 neither of the previous governing partners entered parliament, with the largest vote loss of all.

There are several problems in disentangling voters' choices from electoral outcomes, of course. Electoral systems distort the translation of votes into seats, and losing power did not always signify voter disillusionment. Governing incumbents may be difficult to identify in a context of highly complex coalitions, especially when electoral alliances or umbrella formations collapsed. With non-partisan caretaker governments it is even more difficult to discern precisely what judgements voters (in aggregate) have made at the next election. But it is clear that many parties paid a high price for their governing role, though others bounced back to take centre stage once again.

If voters punished incumbents, they often had good reason to do so. Campaigns made promises that went unfulfilled and raised expectations that could not but be dashed. Time and again students of individual countries have pointed to disillusion with government performance. We have already observed how the Bulgarian Socialists suffered in 1997 for leading the country to the brink of economic collapse. In Romania after two terms in office the Social Democrats had delivered little in the way of economic reform, with high inflation, repeated corruption scandals, and falling living standards, so the Democratic Convention gained credibility in the 1996 campaign with its 'Contract with Romania'.[10] But the coalition made no attempt to develop a common strategy, notably for economic restructuring: Save for the Hungarians 'each of the coalition parties...was trying to impose *its plan* and...*its people*'.[11] Narrow party interests and personal bickering beset all three cabinets. Four years later the Convention, and particularly the National Peasant Christian Democrat Party (PNȚCD), had achieved little; it became 'the main culprit for the dismal situation of state, economy, and society'.[12]

These were not isolated examples. Transition dislocations remained acute everywhere. No country was free of corruption, scandal, and visible absence of public probity. Yet within this picture there is also another. Despite the emphasis on fluidity and change as crucial characteristics of the post-communist electoral process and political party development, a number of parties established themselves as apparently durable features of the political landscape.

Successful parties

We can see the fortunes of successful parties in Table 5.4, which includes those parties that (1) maintained a continuing presence and (2) gained a

Table 5.4 Successful parties, vote share (%), and effects

Country	Party	Election 1	Election 2	Election 3	Election 4	Election 5
Slovenia	LDS	14.5 (led 2nd government coalition after DEMOS split)	23.46 (led coalition)	27.01 (led coalition until 4/2000)	36.3 (led coalition)	
Czech Republic	ODS	in coalition as part of Civic Forum	29.73 (led coalition in new state)	29.62 (retained power in minority coalition government)	27.74 (lost power)	24.47 (still in opposition)
	ČSSD	not in first parliament	6.53 (opposition party)	26.44 (opposition party)	32.31 (formed minority government)	30.20 (retained power as coalition leader)
Hungary[1]	MSzP	10.89	32.99 (led super-majority coalition)	32.92 (lost power)	42.05 (gained power as dominant coalition leader)	
	Fidesz	8.95	7.02 (opposition party)	29.48 (gained power as dominant coalition leader)	41.07[2] (went into opposition)	
Lithuania	LDDP	43.98 (gained power as sole governing party)	10.01 (lost power)	31.08[3] (in opposition, then gained power after government unity crumbled)		
Poland	SLD	11.99	20.41 (led 2-party coalition)	27.13 (lost power)	41.04 (gained power as coalition leader)[4]	

Table 5.4 (Continued)

Country	Party	Election 1	Election 2	Election 3	Election 4	Election 5
Romania	FSN–FDSN–PDSR–PSD	66.31 (majority government)	27.72 (retained power, 1st as minority govt then in coalition)	21.52 (lost power)	36.61 (sole party in minority government)	
	UDMR	7.23	7.46	6.64 (in coalition)	6.8 (cooperation agreement with PSD)	
Russia	KPRF	List 12.4[5] Smd 3.5[5]	22.3[5] in opposition 12.78[5]	24.29[5] in opposition 13.73[5]		
Bulgaria	BSP	47.15[1] (majority government)	33.14 (lost power)	43.5[6] (returned to power)	21.97[7] (lost power)	17.15[8] (remained in opposition)
	SDS	36.21[1] (in opposition)	34.36 (led coalition government)	24.23 (lost power)	52.02 (majority government)	18.18 (lost power)
Estonia	Centre Party (Eesti Keskerakond)	12.25[9]	14.17 (junior coalition partner to scandal of 10/95)	23.41 (three years in opposition, then in governing coalition with Reform Party)		
Slovakia	HZDS	in power as part of Public against Violence	37.26 (led government in new state, later lost on confidence vote)	34.97 (returned to power from opposition to lead 3-party coalition)	27.00 (lost power)	19.05 (remained in opposition)
	SMK, Hungarian Coalition	8.66 (supported government but did not participate)	7.42 (in opposition)	10.19 (in opposition)	9.13 (member of 8-party coalition)	11.16 (junior coalition partner)

[1] List element. [2] Nominally all candidates were joint candidates with the Forum (MDF). [3] It formed the core of the Social-Democratic Coalition of Algirdas Brazauskas. [4] In electoral alliance with the Labour Union (UP). [5] In oppsition. [6] In BSP Coalition with smaller parties. [7] As Democratic Left. [8] As Coalition for Bulgaria. [9] As element of Popular Front.

large share of the vote. The Hungarian parties in Slovakia and Romania also proved notable in largely retaining the confidence of their more narrowly based electorates (they will be discussed more fully in Chapter 9); they also served as governing coalition parties. Both the Russian and Ukrainian Communist Parties performed well by comparison with their competitors, but they could not translate popular support into political power.

We have already discussed the development of the successor parties at some length in Chapter 3. The Social Democrats (SLD) in Poland and the Liberal Democrats (LDS) in Slovenia provided the most striking cases of parties that established themselves as pivotal players. They were the only parties in the region to increase their share of the vote at every successive election. The Hungarian Socialist Party (MSzP) was similar in consolidating a broad electorate, but in Fidesz it faced a similarly successful opposing party, providing the potential for the alternation in power of two large parties.

The SLD, LDS, and MSzP started from a low support base, making the Czech Civic Democrats (ODS) the most consistently strong party. But the ODS vote gradually declined. Fidesz and the Czech Social Democrats registered the largest rises (though not of all parties: in Bulgaria the new Simeon II Movement gained that distinction in 2001). The Romanian National Salvation Front lost the overwhelming preponderance it enjoyed after the first free elections, but in its subsequent social democratic incarnations the PSD remained the largest Romanian party by a considerable margin. The Lithuanian social democrats saw wild vote swings, from 44 per cent, taking a large share of the protest vote in 1992, to 10 per cent in 1996, when disillusioned voters moved elsewhere;[13] as the centre of a broad social democratic alliance their vote rose again to 31 per cent in 2000. Mečiar's Movement for Democratic Slovakia (HZDS) was more consistent and remained the largest of the Slovak parties, though its rate of erosion increased, while the decline of its allies and the unity of its opposition excluded it from power after 1998.

With the partial exceptions of the Hungarian ethnic parties and HZDS, the successful parties based their appeal to the electorate on ideological-programmatic grounds. This is consonant with von Beyme's observation that in Western Europe only ideologically based parties succeeded in establishing themselves in the long term.[14] Five of these interim success stories were social democratic parties of the left, four of them communist successor-parties. Fidesz evolved from a liberal party to a conservative one, while ODS remained liberal on economic matters but also became more conservative on social issues. The Slovene Liberal Democratic Party evolved from the former communist youth association into a staunch liberal party, but one which pursued a remarkably successful, cautious, gradualist programme of economic transformation.[15] Slovakia's HZDS, while making serious efforts to transform itself into a more conventional centre-right pro-European party at the end of the decade, none the less remained the captive of Vladimir Mečiar.

Mečiar was consistently the most popular Slovak politician and the most enduringly charismatic post-communist leader anywhere.[16] We argued earlier that HZDS remained extremely difficult to categorise on the basis of its electoral appeal. For many observers it remained a populist party, seeking to capitalise on anti-establishment sentiment even when itself part of that establishment, but also with strong elements of a leader-party.

The position in Estonia was somewhat different. The Centre Party established itself within the Popular Front in 1991 on a liberal platform of 'representing the emerging middle class' and its leader Edgar Savisaar served as prime minister until the subsequent election. It did well enough in 1995 to join the government as junior partner of the Coalition Party, but Savisaar was disgraced by a bugging scandal and his party left the coalition after a few months. As the party shifted centre-left, it was often accused of irresponsible populism. But Savisaar offered a more conciliatory approach to the Russian population and developed his political base in the capital Tallinn, where he became mayor. The Centre Party 'won' the 1999 elections but was excluded from government (see Table 5.1), but the failure of the three-party coalition of the right led to its return, and it looked confident for the elections of 2003.

Latvia, however, did not possess a successful party by these criteria. The liberal Latvia's Way would have been included before the 2002 election. It gained 32.4 per cent of the vote in 1993 and led a two-party coalition. In 1995 its vote fell to 14.7 per cent, but it remained a member of the subsequent six-party government. In 1998 its vote rose to 18.2 per cent; again it participated in government as a member and twice leader of coalition governments. But Latvia's Way was the punished incumbent in 2002; it won only 4.9 per cent, taking it below the threshold and out of parliament.

Indeed, the most dramatic cases of electoral punishment were precisely those in which governing parties subsequently failed to cross the threshold. It was rare for a party to restore its fortunes from outside parliament, though the Polish Labour Union did this through electoral alliance with the Social Democrats (SLD) in 2001. Other losing parties experienced spells of opposition before returning to government.

But losing an election did not necessarily result from a loss of confidence of the party's voters. We can illustrate some of the complexity of judging success by outcome with the Hungarian and Polish examples, both of which saw the successive alternation in power of right- and left-wing parties.

We recall that in Hungary the conservative Democratic Forum (MDF) won the first election in 1990, to be replaced by the Socialists in 1994. In 1998 Fidesz in turn displaced the Socialists, who returned to office after defeating Fidesz in 2002. Yet the picture was more complex than the mere fact of alternating governments. The defeat of the Forum in 1994 was indeed considerable. In 1994 its vote fell to 11.7 per cent in the list element and 12 per cent in the first-round single-member vote, suggesting a core of consistent voters.

The Socialists' (MSzP) vote rose from 10.9 to 33 per cent of the list vote and ultimately gained an absolute majority (54 per cent) of seats.[17] In 1998, however, the Socialists kept their vote largely intact, and they won more votes in both elements of the electoral system than did Fidesz; but in the event they received fewer single-member seats. Fidesz won by effective alliance-bargaining: 229 opposing candidates withdrew in a strategy that generated huge gains.[18] In this sense the socialists were the victims of the electoral system. Though the MSzP ran a poor campaign and surely 'could have done better',[19] its defeat was not a result of voters' defections, but a consequence of Fidesz's clever alliance strategy and the new-found unity of the centre-right. It is also difficult to see 2002 as a vote of no confidence in the existing Fidesz-dominated government. Of the three contenders entering parliament Fidesz won the largest number of seats. It was the failure of its allies that left it powerful but excluded.

The Polish case was rather similar, albeit without the complexity of the Hungarian electoral system and without the early development of clearly identifiable political parties. The semi-competitive 1989 election generated two successive Solidarity-led governments. Neither of the two major governing parties did particularly well in the first free election of October 1991,[20] but given the enormous fragmentation of the vote, they did not do badly: The Democratic Union was the largest party with but 12 per cent of the vote; the Liberals, totally unknown before Krzysztof Bielecki's premiership, gained 7.5 per cent.

The voters' judgement was also difficult to assess in 1993, after a particularly complex coalition had eroded and Suchocka's minority government had been narrowly defeated on a vote of confidence. Whether voters knew the party composition of her government is doubtful, and we shall see that coalition complexity also featured elsewhere. The Democratic Union had formed the core of the government and it was the only governing party to cross the new threshold – with some erosion of its support to 10.6 per cent of the vote. The coalition's small parties were defeated as much by the new electoral thresholds as by the voters. At the same time the victorious Social Democrats, the core of the Democratic Left Alliance (SLD), saw their vote rise by 8–20 per cent in 1993. The (successor) Polish Peasant Party (PSL) recaptured much of the peasant vote and almost doubled its vote share to 15.4 per cent. These two parties easily formed a strong coalition, benefiting from a huge seat-premium due to the exclusion of so many parties and groupings rather than to wide electoral support.

In 1997 Solidarity Electoral Action brought together a myriad of smaller parties and groupings as the electoral party AWS (see Chapter 3) and won a convincing victory. As with the Hungarian Socialists in 1998, the SLD did not lose votes; indeed its vote rose by a further 7 per cent. Despite its narrow class profile the PSL by contrast proved unable to retain its electorate; like the Free Democrats in Hungary (SzDSz) it lost support – in this case falling back to 7.3 per cent. It was not the leading governing parties but their smaller coalition partners who suffered electoral punishment. The PSL in particular was blamed for its irresponsible behaviour in government.[21]

The year 2001 saw a further boost to the SLD, now in alliance with the small Labour Union (UP); the two parties won 41 per cent of the vote, confirming the ability of the SLD to continue to gain votes. The 2001 election, however, was a disaster for both coalition partners with a clear electoral verdict that left both the AWS rump (AWSP) and the Freedom Union (UW) below the coalition (8 per cent) and party thresholds (5 per cent) respectively. The UW had withdrawn from coalition with AWS in June 2000 in the light of the government's growing unpopularity but to no avail, as the party split and its hitherto loyal core electorate deserted it, mostly for the new Civic Platform (PO) but also for Law and Justice (PiS) and for the SLD.

Of course, these are not the only examples of successful party-consolidation on the one hand and party-failure on the other. The Czech Republic provided the sole example of both a successful non-successor social democratic party (ČSSD), a successful liberal-conservative party (ODS), but also successive incumbent victories (see Table 5.4) for each of them. But in numerous cases parties paid dearly for electoral defeat. Such shifts increased the uncertainty of electoral outcomes and provided continuing openings for political entrepreneurs to establish new parties. Voters still appeared 'up for grabs'. Many new parties remained unknown and left no trace. Some were 'flash parties' that made a mark for one parliament and then vanished. But there were also some that survived and flourished.

New parties

New parties were new to varying degree, and many were formed from within parliament rather than from external challenges. A position in parliament provided material resources and the potential for media exposure. Some new parties were merely new 'electoral parties' combining existing elements in alliances or electoral coalitions (see Chapter 2). Solidarity Election Action in Poland and the Slovak Democratic Coalition provided examples of this format. Some 'parties of power' had this character, while others such as Unity in Russia could claim some genuine 'newness' and explicitly courted previous non-voters, including young people entering the electorate.

New parties arose for a variety of reasons. Some emerged when existing parties split because of genuine ideological or programmatic differences. This was the case with the Slovak Democratic Left (SDL'), which lost first an anti-reform wing (the Association of Slovak Workers) and then a liberal pro-reform wing (the Social Democratic Alternative). In Romania the origins of the Democratic Party (then still as the National Salvation Front) lay in disputes between President Ion Iliescu and Prime Minister Petre Roman over the nature and pace of economic reform. Roman's reform wing was much the smaller, but it retained a place in successive parliaments as a more liberal, EU-oriented form of social democracy.

Parties with strong leaders were particularly prone to erosion, with splits centring on the allegedly autocratic character of their leadership. In Slovakia HZDS suffered chronically from defections, most of which focused explicitly on the personal characteristics of Vladimír Mečiar. From the early 1990s well-known individuals such as former Foreign Ministers Josef Moravčik and Milan Kňažko fell out with Mečiar and left the party, later to form the Democratic Union. In 2001 Ivan Gaðparovič founded a counter-HZDS, the Movement for Democracy (HZD). Later other prominent members also left the party, criticising Mečiar's leadership following a disappointing perform-ance in the 2002 elections. In Hungary the Independent Smallholders suffered a series of splits from November 1991 onwards, and their leader József Torgyán remained a perennial source of controversy. Four different Smallholders' parties contested the 1994 election, and the unity of 1998 proved short-lived, as the party fractured again. In the Czech Republic corruption scandals centring on party finance split the Civic Democrats in 1997, but leaders of the new Freedom Union (US) were also alienated by Klaus's personal leadership style.

New parties also formed because popular individuals believed themselves capable of wooing disaffected members of other political parties and build-ing on a strong personal following. Andrzej Olechowski (Civic Platform, PO) and Lech Kaczyński (Law and Justice, PiS) in Poland, Mikuláš Dzurinda (SDKÚ) and Róbert Fico (Smer) in Slovakia, Kazimiera Prunskienė (the Women's Party) in Lithuania, and Yulia Tymoshenko (National Fatherland Forum, later the Yulia Tymoshenko bloc) in the Ukraine all took this route with some initial success. Dzurinda took advantage of his premiership, caus-ing consternation within the Slovak Democratic Coalition when after but few months in office, he announced the formation of a new party, the Slovak Democratic and Christian Union. With less success Slovene Prime Minister Andrej Bajuk split the Slovene People's Party to form New Slovenia–Christian People's Party.

Numerous new parties also formed outside parliament. We saw that the number of contenders remained high in most countries (see Table 4.8). But few succeeded, and those that entered parliament did so largely because of the individual reputations and extensive media exposure of their leading personalities. The most striking case of a successful 'outsider' was undoubt-edly that of ex-tsar Simeon, whose National Movement Simeon II took 43 per cent of the vote in the Bulgarian election of 2001. But there were other successes too. Siim Kallas, founder of the Estonian Reform Party in 1994, was then head of the National Bank. Andris Šķēle, who founded the neo-liberal Latvian People's Party in 1998, was both a former (non-party) prime minister and a highly successful businessman.[22] In 2002 another banker, former head of the Latvian Central Bank Einars Repše set up New Era

(*Jaunias laiks*), declaring war on corruption and calling for a new generation of political leaders. In Lithuania Arturas Paulauskas's New Union (Social Liberals) gained credibility because of his role as a former procurator under the 1990–2 Sajūdis government and his subsequent independent political stance. Despite having 'the most ideologically incoherent and eclectic platform of all the political parties...',[23] the New Union came second in the PR vote and third in the majoritarian vote in the elections of 2000. Estonia's Res Publica, founded in 2002, was the creature of former state auditor Juhan Parts, promising, like so many others, a moral revival coupled with a clampdown on corruption and crime.

Unusually the new Slovene Youth Party did not have a well-known leader. It was a genuine outsider party that attracted not only its own youth constituency but also older people with a vigorous campaign. Many of its candidates were active in civic associations in their communities, including sports associations and cultural organisations. In 2000 Slovenia became the only country to have both a youth party and a (long-standing) pensioners' party (DeSUS) represented in parliament.

Table 5.5 shows the frequency with which new parties entered parliament after the first free elections. It does not include parties that merged if the identity of the resulting merger remained widely known, as in the case of the Polish Freedom Union. It does not show those (few) parties that contested several elections before finally gaining a parliamentary presence, such as Self-Defence in Poland, Justice and Life in Hungary, or the Communist Party of Slovakia. Nor does it include new umbrella formations allying or reuniting existing groupings, as in Our Ukraine in 2002.

We can see that voters' inclination to support new political formations remained salient in a number of countries. Only in Hungary did new challengers, such as the Centre Party in 2002, consistently fail. The Czech Republic also proved inhospitable ground, and in Romania no new parties succeeded after 1992. Elsewhere wholly new groupings generally garnered more support than new parties arising from splits in existing ones.

The distinction is not a firm one, however, since in some cases elements of existing parties broke off to form distinctive new associations, such as the SDKÚ in Slovakia in 2002 or all three new parties in Poland in 2001. In Latvia in 1995 the Democratic Party-Saimnieks combined the Democratic Centre Party and Saimnieks (Master), a new grouping of directors of now-privatised enterprises and collective farms. In the Ukraine the core of the National Salvation Forum, later the Yulia Tymoshenko bloc, was Fatherland (Batkivshchyna), formed as a breakaway group from Hromada in 1999; other elements were new, but some were not.

Latvian voters proved particularly receptive to new parties. In 1995 the top two parties were both new, and in 1998 and 2002 the largest party was also a new one. The 1995 result has been attributed to the massive losses suffered when Latvia's major bank collapsed early in the year, leaving

Table 5.5   New parties entering parliament

	Election	Type	Vote (%)	Seats	Vote share at next election (%)
Bulgaria					
Euro-Left	1997	splinter	5.5	14	0.98 as part of alliance
National Movement Simeon II	2001	new	42.7	120	
Romania					
National Salvation Front[3]	1992	splinter	10.2	43	12.9
Party of Romanian National Unity (PUNR)	1992	new	7.7	30	4.4
Lithuania[1,4]					
Lithuanian Women's Party	1996	new	3.86	1 smd	in alliance for list[2]
Lithuanian Peasants' Party	1996	new	1.75	1 smd	4.1
New Union (Social Liberals)	2000	new	19.64	28	
Union of Moderate Conservatives (NKS)	2000	splinter	2.01	1	
Union of Modern Christian Democrats (MKDS)	2000	splinter	in alliance for list vote	3	
Poland					
BBWR	1993	new	5.4	16	did not contest
Labour Union (UP)	1993	merger	7.3	41	4.7
League of Polish Families (LPR)	2001	new	7.9	38	
Law and Justice (PiS)	2001	new	9.5	44	
Civic Platform (PO)	2001	new	12.7	65	
Czech Republic					
Freedom Union (US)	1998	splinter	8.6	19	in alliance
Slovakia					
Association of Slovak Workers (ZRS)	1994	splinter	7.3	13	1.3
Party of Civic Understanding (SOP)	1998	new	8.0	13	did not contest
Social Democratic and Christian Union (SDKÚ)	2002	new	15.1	28	

Table 5.5   (Continued)

	Election	Type	Vote (%)	Seats	Vote share at next election (%)
Smer	2002	new	13.5	25	
Alliance of New Citizens (ANO)	2002	new	8.0	15	
Slovenia					
Slovenian National Party (SNS)	1992	new	10.0	12	3.2
New Slovenia (NSi)	2000	splinter	8.8	8	
Slovene Youth Party (SMS)	2000	new	4.4	4	
Estonia[4]					
Reform Party (ER)	1995	new	16.2	19	15.9
Right-Wingers (Parempoolsed)	1995	splinter	5.0	5	did not contest
Rural People's Party (EME)	1999	merger	7.3	7	
Latvia[4]					
People's Movement for Latvia (Siegerist Party)	1995	splinter	15.0	16	1.7
People's Party (TP)	1998	new	21.3	24	16.6
New Party (Jaunā partija)	1998	new	7.3	8	did not contest
New Era (Jaunias laiks)	2002	new	23.9	26	
Latvia's First Party (LPP)	2002	new	9.5	10	
Russia[1]					
Our Home is Russia	1995	new	10.1	55	1.2
Unity (Medved)	1999	new	23.3	73	
Fatherland-All Russia	1999	new	13.3	68	
Ukraine[1]					
Popular Democratic Party (NDP)	1998	new	5.0	28	part of For a United Ukraine
Hromada	1998	new	4.7	24	
Progressive Socialist Party (PSPU)	1998	new	4.1	16	
Yulia Tymoshenko bloc	2001	splinter + new + old	7.5	22	

[1] Vote share is list element. [2] Changed name to New Democracy. [3] Although it retained the NSF label for the election (and later became the Democratic Party), this was by far the smaller of the two divided elements, and the larger Democratic National Salvation Front retained its clear association with President Iliescu. [4] After first post-independence elections.

'voters desperate for change' and susceptible to populist appeals.[24] This may help explain the success of the extreme-right Siegerist Party, whose attractions were short-lived. But Saimnieks was not notably populist, though parties with similar outlooks certainly tried to outbid one another in non-ideological arenas such as leadership, competence, and honesty. The People's Party (TP), the 1998 victor, was more explicitly ideological, with a clear neo-liberal stress on entrepreneurship and strengthening the market economy. Yet the New Era Party (JL) in 2002 was not substantially different from the People's Party or indeed the dominant Latvian orientation, 'pro-Europe and NATO; for economic expansion and steady but controlled privatisation; and pro-Latvian in citizenship and language issues but mindful of European imperatives in these areas'.[25] Repše tapped into the public mood with his 'almost messianic mission to clean up politics and government of the corruption and inefficiency... of the public sphere'.[26] This could also be said of the appeal of Law and Justice (PiS) in Poland in 2001.

The propensity for new parties to succeed was a function of perceived opportunities for new politicians in the context of low levels of attachment to political parties and disillusionment with the performance of existing parties, both governing and opposition. But this did not necessarily mean that the disenchanted moved out of the ambit of democratic politics. Some new electoral parties such as the Yulia Tymoshenko bloc, were attractive precisely because of their democratic, anti-presidential credentials. Many, such as the People's Party and the New Era Party (JL) in Latvia tried to combine a clear liberal pro-reform cast with leadership appeal based on proven competence. In Slovakia, Pavel Ruško's Alliance of New Citizens (ANO) also fell into this category. ANO served as a 'respectable' protest party for those unhappy with the (numerous) governing parties while sharing the government's anti-Mečiar sentiments. Many of these parties claimed to offer new faces and a new morality, but they were not anti-reform or anti-democratic. Many of them represented a distinctive liberal populism (see Chapter 2) and thus an alternative home for disillusioned pro-reform voters. Indeed, in Table 5.5 only the Romanian nationalist PUNR, the Siegerist Party, and the Association of Slovak Workers could be regarded as dubiously democratic. Of course, some early-established parties could also be regarded as antithetical to democracy. Although they often attracted substantial support, most radical parties failed to cross electoral thresholds.

Radical parties

Many early students of transition feared that democracy itself would suffer from the coupling of economic and political change in the 'dual transition'.[27] Not only would incumbent governments bear the brunt of popular dissatisfaction with the hardships and dislocation of economic and social transformation (as indeed we have seen), but more seriously, such dislocation would make the public susceptible to extremist appeals or populist dema-gogues offering anti-democratic solutions. In fact, in no new parliamentary democracy did we see a reversal of democracy or the installation of an anti-democratic regime through the electoral process. Only in Slovakia were there genuine grounds for seeing an increase in authoritarian practices under Vladimir Mečiar.[28] Radical parties made an appearance, and a number gained parliamentary representation. Their presence restricted coalition-formation options in some cases and forced strange coalition bedfellows in others, but it did not generally constitute a challenge to democratic procedures and processes.

Students of the region often disagreed about which parties could be regarded as 'radical' or 'extremist' or 'anti-democratic' or 'anti-system', as well as whether these parties were better placed as 'left' or 'right'. The term 'extremism' itself implies a kind of deviance, an existence beyond the norm. Its usage thus entails an implication that rules out self-ascription as a means of identifying the object of investigation: parties rarely regarded themselves as extremist or even anti-democratic. Moreover, parties were often diverse, and judging the role of extremist elements could also be difficult. In Poland the new Solidarity electoral party AWS (1996–2001) included some indubit-ably xenophobic and anti-democratic elements.[29] Not only conglomerates but also mainstream parties like the Party of Social Democracy in Romania or the Civic Democratic Party in the Czech Republic often appropriated nationalist themes.[30] In Romania the social democrats brought the stridently nationalist parties into government for a brief period.[31] From time to time open anti-minority sentiments surfaced in the SDL' in Slovakia, and both the Union of Democratic Forces and especially the Bulgarian Socialist Party incorporated nationalist elements[32] (see Chapter 9).

Most communist parties continued to style themselves as radical parties of the left, as opponents of the new inequalities of transition, if no longer as revolutionary parties. In the Baltic states communism was too closely associ-ated with Soviet domination to prove an attractive option. Indeed, Latvia banned all who had belonged to Soviet security services, as well as those affiliated to the Communist Party after 13 January 1991. Under this provi-sion the social democrats' leader and former KGB officer Juris Bojars could not stand for parliament.

In Central Europe, where the old ruling parties transformed themselves into European social democrats, communist splinter movements remained of little import. Exceptionally the Communist Party of Slovakia entered parliament in 2002 after contesting successive elections, while the Party of the Democratic Left (SDL') and the Social Democratic Alternative failed to do so. But this radical strand of Slovak politics was not new: in 1994 the Association of Slovak Workers (ZRS), a hard-line breakaway faction from SDL', had crossed the threshold to become a governing party alongside the Movement for Democratic Slovakia and the Slovak National Party. It had little impact on government policy[33] and in 1998 it gained a derisory share of the vote.

In the Czech Republic the Communist Party (KSČM) remained a radical party of the left (though asserting its commitment to multi-partism) with a durable parliamentary presence. Its association with the repression of the communist regime and its lack of repentance made it untouchable as a potential coalition partner even for its natural ally, the Social Democrats (ČSSD).[34] But in 2002 the KSČM's vote share rose considerably, as it accrued votes from the extreme-right Republicans and mobilised the protest vote against mainstream parties.

In Russia and the Ukraine the communist parties, still opposed to capitalism, were the largest and most institutionalised of all parties (see Chapter 3), though their programmes were far from clear. The Ukrainian Communist Party was not nationalist; rather its initial stance was strongly pro-Russian and pro-Soviet. The Russian KPRF flirted with nationalist allies, but its own bent was statist rather than nationalist.[35] Both parties may be regarded as radical, but in their respective political contexts they were also a 'normal' part of the political landscape. Many other left-splinter groups appeared and reappeared, but the 5 per cent threshold proved too great an obstacle. For example, although the Communists and Workers' Russia–For the Soviet Union gained 4.5 per cent of the vote in 1995, by 1999 they had split and their combined vote was less than 3 per cent.[36]

Radical parties of the right were easier to identify, if not always to categorise.[37] Ultra-nationalist parties placed their central emphasis on safeguarding the (organic) 'nation', though they did not lack other themes. Extreme-right parties were also usually virulent nationalists and their list of enemies was often similar to those of nationalist parties, but some favoured Pan-Slavism rather than the ethnically conceived nation.[38] The Romanian nationalist parties were exceptional in their failure to embrace anti-communism, a standard staple of right-wing discourse. But this is unsurprising given that their leaders were rooted in the previous regime, in the 'Communist Party, one or another fraction of the old/new Secret Police, members of the local police, and the henchmen of all these'.[39]

Unlike communist or radical left parties, extreme-right parties were overtly hostile to democracy and often prepared to countenance violent means of political action. Anatolii Shcherbatyuk of the Ukrainian National Assembly-Ukrainian People's Self-Defence, another Pan-Slav formation, called for the setting up of 'purification detachments' to cleanse the country of 'anti-Ukrainian parasitic material'.[40] The vitriol directed against the Roma in many countries also went well beyond the democratic pale. The dividing line between extreme-right parties and radical nationalist parties was often unclear, since nationalists often maintained a formal commitment to parliamentary democracy while endorsing exclusionist concepts of the polity, notably in their advocacy of anti-minority policies (see Chapter 9). Parties such as the Hungarian Justice and Life Party were usually viewed as ultra-nationalist, but some observers placed them firmly on the extreme right.[41] The Slovene National Party was – like Zhirinovskii's Liberal Democratic Party in Russia – also initially imperialist, seeking the annexation of Corinthia from Austria, Istria from Croatia, and Trieste from Italy to create an 'ethnically pure' Great Slovenia.[42] Corneliu Vadim Tudor's 2000 election campaign for the Greater Romania Party included promises to 'govern with a machine-gun on the table' and the elimination of Hungarians, Jews, and traitors of the nation.[43] Shafir's concept of the 'externalization of guilt',[44] offering absolution both for having failed to act as an individual and for collective responsibility for the fate of one's society, applies to both ultra-nationalist and right radical blame of Westerners, Jews, the IMF, the World Bank, ethnic minorities, and the like. Janez Janša of the Social Democratic Party of Slovenia overtly contested the legitimacy of democratic institutions, supporting proposals to deport Slovene immigrants and refugees and expressing a 'vengeful spite against everything "Yugoslav", communist and liberal...'.[45] Janša's was one of the few radical parties that later moderated its stance and gained a position of respectability – in Romania the PUNR essentially disintegrated when it pursued a strategy of more moderate nationalism. In Poland religion was an integral element of the nationalism of the Christian National Union (ZChN), the Movement for Rebuilding Poland (ROP), and the League of Polish Families (LPR), all of which included radical anti-democratic and anti-minority elements alongside nationalist democrats.

We argued in Chapter 3 that populist parties had few ideological underpinnings for their strong anti-establishment, 'pro-people' outlook. In some cases their democratic credentials were questioned, whether because their commitment to democracy was unclear or because their actions belied their words. This was so with Vladimir Mečiar, who engaged in authoritarian and flagrantly unconstitutional behaviour, though we noted earlier that HZDS was not uniformly classed as 'populist'. Like HZDS, Fico's Direction (Smer) was not averse to anti-minority rhetoric. The Confederation for Independent Poland (KPN) was sometimes viewed unpersuasively as a radical nationalist or even extreme-right party.[46] It gradually lost credibility through perennial infighting over the leadership of its founder Leszek Moczulski, who had established it as an illegal anti-communist grouping as early as 1979. Although fond of direct action and even paramilitary training in preparation for a new communist onslaught, and although the Germans were high on its list of the usual suspects, the KPN was not anti-minority or particularly xenophobic. It favoured a strong executive along with quintessentially populist appeals for high public expenditure. The KPN split irrevocably before the 1997 election, when one faction joined AWS and Moczulski's remaining group withdrew from contention at the last minute. Its successor, The Alternative, was an ill-digested mishmash of right-wing populism.

'Self-Defence' in Poland was more clearly a radical left-populist party, and its leader Andrzej Lepper coupled a penchant for direct action with a dubious commitment to democratic principles. Self-Defence had made little electoral impact until 2001, when its breakthrough into parliament was dramatic. It immediately proved uncooperative, sometimes downright obstructive, with little regard for the niceties of parliamentary procedure. Lepper was rapidly ejected from his new post as Deputy Speaker of the Sejm after abusing his position with a series of scurrilous attacks on fellow politicians.

Given these difficulties, Table 5.6 takes a broad view of political radicalism, including parties whose presence or categorisation could well be disputed. It includes parties that have been described as radical because of anti-minority or anti-democratic rhetoric or because of a willingness to resort to violence (nationalist, populist, and extreme right parties), as well as parties rejecting the dominant transition discourse (radical left parties).

Of the parties identified in Table 5.6, several won a substantial proportion of the vote. It is unlikely that voters always shared their chosen parties' programmatic outlook,[47] but their votes broadly reflected the frustration, difficulties, insecurity, and uncertainty associated with the processes of transformation. At times mainstream parties funnelled off such support with their own nationalist appeals or attractive leaders. In Poland the AWS umbrella absorbed religious fundamentalist and nationalist elements in 1997, substantially reducing the vote for more explicit radicalism. Religiosity found expression in votes for the League of Polish Families in 2001. In the Ukraine voters preoccupied with issues of Ukrainian nation-building chose Rukh or its offshoots, rather than radical nationalists.

Generally speaking the appeal of extreme-right and radical nationalist parties appeared to decline over time. In Latvia, Slovenia, and Slovakia their rationales eroded as issues of nation-building receded (see Chapter 9). Many leader-oriented radical nationalist parties split, such as the Slovak National Party, which lost its 'moderate' element, and the Slovene National Party, whose extremists were alienated by Jelinčič's shift to a more pragmatic nationalism.[48] Yet in 2000 the Greater Romania Party (PRM) did exceptionally well, coming second in the parliamentary elections and seeing its leader Corneliu Vadim Tudor go through to the second ballot in the presidentia[l] race. The PRM had emphasised the problems of poverty and corruption, and it served as the main 'party of protest', while also securing a near monopoly of the nationalist vote.[49]

In some cases the voters' choices were tested when their parties entered government. Mečiar's HZDS government brought the Slovak National Party (SNS) into coalition in October 1993, though a subsequent SNS split cost the government its majority and led to its fall. In 1994 Mečiar won again and both the SNS and the Association of Slovak Workers became his coalition partners.[50] The latter did not survive the following election, nor the SNS

Table 5.6 Vote share of radical parties in fully competitive elections, 1990–2002 (list vote, %)

	Election 1	Election 2	Election 3	Election 4	Election 5
Nationalist parties					
Slovak National Party (SNS)	*10.96*[1]	*9.39*[1]	*9.11*	*9.07*	3.32
Real Slovak National Party (PSNS)	–	–	–	–	3.65
Young Lithuania	3.55	4.01	1.15[2]		
Lithuanian Nationalist Union	no list	no list	0.88		
Movement for Rebuilding Poland (ROP)	–	2.7[3]	*5.56*	*stood with LPR*	
Christian National Union (ZChN)	*8.74*[4]	*6.37*[5]	*in AWS*	split, but formally in AWSP	
League of Polish Families (LPR)	–	–	–	*7.87*	
Greater Romania Party (PRM)	–	*3.89*	*4.46*	*19.48*	
Party of Romanian National Unity (PUNR)	2.12[6]	*7.72*	*4.36*	1.38[7]	
Bulgarian National Radical Party	–	1.13	0.54	?	0.07
National Front Bloc (Ukraine)		2.72			
Hungarian Party of Justice and Life (MIÉP)	–	1.59	*5.47*	4.37	
Congress of Russian Communities	–	4.31	0.61		
Derzhava (Russia)	–	*2.57*	–		
Republican Party (Russia)	–	1.6	–		
Slovene National Party		*10.02*	*3.22*	*4.4*	
For Fatherland & Freedom/Latvian National Independence Movement	*5.35*	*11.99*	*14.73*	*5.38*	
Estonian Citizen	*6.89*	3.61[8]	–		
Populist parties					
Movement for Democratic Slovakia (HZDS)	*32.54*[1]	*33.53*	*25.44*	*27.0*	*19.5*
Confederation for Independent Poland (KPN)	*7.45*	*5.77*	one faction in AWS	remnants in Alternatywa	

Party X (Poland)	0.47	2.74	–	–	
Self-Defence (SO, Poland)	0.03	0.08	2.78	***10.2***	
Alternatywa (Poland)	–	–	–	0.42	
Smer (Slovakia)	–	–	–	–	***13.46***
Extreme-right parties					
Peoples Movement for Latvia (Siegerist Party)	–	***14.97***	1.74	–	
Czech Republicans (SPR–RSC)	0.94[1]	***6.48[1]***	8.01	3.9	0.14[9]
Republicans of Miroslav Sladek	–	–	–	–	0.97
Polish National Commonwealth–Polish National Party	0.05	0.11	0.07	0.02	
Social Democratic Party of Slovenia	as part of DEMOS	***3.34***	***16.13***	***15.8***	
Ukrainian National Assembly		0.40	0.05		
Liberal Democratic Party of Russia	***22.9***	***11.18***	***5.98***		
Communist Parties					
Communist party of the Russian Federation (KPRF)	***12.4***	***22.3***	***24.29***		
Communist Party of the Ukraine (KPU)	***86 smd seats***	***24.65***	***20.76***		
Association of Slovak Workers (ZRS)	–	–	***7.34***	1.3	0.55
Hungarian Workers' Party (Munkáspárt)	3.68[10]	3.19	3.95	2.16	
Slovak Communist Party (KSS)	***13.81[1]***	0.76[1,11]	0.72	2.8	***6.33***
Czech Communist Party (KSČM)	***13.48[1]***	***14.26[1,12]***	***10.33***	***11.03***	***18.51***
Romanian Socialist Party of Labour (PSM)		***3.04***	2.15	0.71	

Note: **italic bold** indicates that the party won seats.
[1] To section of the Chamber of Peoples. [2] As Young Lithuania, New Nationalists (Tautininkai), and Political Prisoners. [3] As part of Coalition for the Republic; [4] As Catholic Election Action (WAK). [5] As Fatherland (Ojczyzna). [6] In the Romanian Unity Alliance. [7] As National Alliance. [8] With Better Estonia. [9] As Republikani. [10] As MSZMP- Hungarian Socialist Workers' Party. [11] Union of Communists. [12] As Levý blok.

that of 2002. In Poland the Christian National Union (ZChN) was a governing party in 1991 (under Jan Olszewski, who later formed ROP) and 1992–3 (under Suchocka). It played a significant role in the AWS coalition government after 1997 before dispersing into new formations. In Romania the nationalist parties also enjoyed a brief spell in government with the social democrats (then the Democratic National Salvation Front) after the second election in 1992.

For the most part radical parties remained on the fringe, whether because they were unnecessary to government formation or untouchable as coalition partners. This could complicate government formation, as in the Czech Republic, where the combined strength of the Republicans and Communists gave the victorious party little room for manoeuvre. The Civic Democrats (ODS) led a minority government in 1996, and the Social Democrats (ČSSD) formed a minority government in 1998. In Russia and the Ukraine the communists were not averse to bargains with the current 'party of power', but despite their strength, they played no part in government.

It is true that the combined vote of radical parties presents a picture of considerable voter appeal (see Table 5.7). They took between one-fifth and one-third of the vote in a number of countries, most notably in Russia, the Ukraine, Slovakia, and Poland. Indeed, Table 5.7 underestimates the total strength of such parties because it omits some of the very smallest formations failing to field candidates in all constituencies or gaining a truly minute share of the vote. But these parties were highly diverse in nature, they often competed against one another, and their electorates were neither stable nor wholly interchangeable. They were also prone to splits and erosion, and

Table 5.7 Total support for radical parties, 1990–2002 (% list vote)

	Election 1	Election 2	Election 3	Election 4	Election 5
Slovakia[1]	24.8	10.2	17.2	13.2	27.3
Lithuania[2]	3.6	4.0	2.0		
Poland	16.7	17.8	8.4	18.5	
Romania		14.7	11.0	21.6	
Hungary	3.7	4.8	9.4	6.5	
Bulgaria		1.1	0.5	?	0.17
Russia	35.3	42.4	30.9		
Slovenia	–	13.4	19.4	4.38[3]	
Latvia[2]	5.4	27.0	16.5	5.4	
Ukraine	c.89 smd seats	27.8	20.8		
Czech Republic	14.4[2]	20.7	18.3	14.9	19.6
Estonia[2]	6.9	3.6	–		

[1] Excluding HZDS. [2] Post-independence elections. [3] Excluding the Social Democratic Party, SDS.

electoral thresholds reduced their impact on the political process. In mixed systems new radical parties found it difficult to win seats in single-member districts. The Communist Parties of Russia and the Ukraine were distinctive: as parties of historical continuity they enjoyed a measure of loyal support, and they represented the most credible force offering a slowing of change, social protection and – in the case of Russia – national pride. The 'median voter' may not always congregate in the centre.[51]

Conclusion

Democratic progress was signalled by the use of formal institutional mechanisms of government succession. All losing parties accepted the democratic rules of the game, and with few exceptions the largest party generally went on to form the next government. Almost all countries also possessed at least one durable party that continued over successive elections to attract a considerable share of the vote. Some maintained a consistent voter appeal, and others demonstrated a capacity to recover from the adversity of defeat. Generally these were ideological/programmatic parties, although their appeal did not necessarily depend on ideological clarity or consistency. The Romanian Social Democrats demonstrated considerable ideological flexibility, along with attributes of a patronage party deriving from a lengthy early tenure. The same was true in Hungary of Fidesz, which marched to the right to create a broad-based party with a powerful conservative-nationalist appeal.

Yet one recurring theme of this book is that in the decade following the downfall of European communist regimes uncertainty remained a characteristic feature of many new political systems. Instead of gradual evolutionary processes of routinisation and stabilisation many new polities saw fluidity, uncertainty, and continuing change, even where apparently stable institutional frameworks had emerged. Voters moved in large numbers from parties they had previously voted for, and they showed little inclination to develop enduring loyalties. Voters usually punished incumbents severely, and a high proportion of parliamentary elections witnessed a transfer of power.

This context in turn created favourable conditions for political entrepreneurs to seek their political fortunes with new parties, to desert their existing ones, and to experiment with new alliance configurations. The success of new formations in turn fed the notion that other new parties could succeed. Russia and the Ukraine remained an exception in this regard, for governments depended more on the support of president than of parliament – even though 'parties of power' did not normally 'win' elections. But there too voters often showed a willingness to support 'parties' often founded just a few months before an election, with no social penetration, little organisation and no previous parliamentary record. By and large this was 'personality politics' writ large, and most of the new parties fit easily into the populist category as discussed in Chapter 2.

Yet despite early fears that disappointment and hardship would lead to alienation from the democratic process, most new parties entering parliament were by no means radical, and voters did not shift en masse to overtly anti-democratic alternatives. Generally successful new party leaders came from the existing establishment, and their populism was of the liberal-reformist ilk.

Radical parties were certainly present everywhere, and their total vote was often large; but their support varied with the nature of their opponents and their particular profile. They provided a needed safety valve rather than a signal of democratic reversal, and they were diverse in character. Some were extreme nationalists, some were radical left or right-wing populists, and some were radical left-wing egalitarians. In some cases small left-wing parties were essentially hard-line remnants of the communist parties. In others, communist parties remained 'unreformed' but maintained a strong presence as legitimate political actors. They may have tapped common reservoirs of discontent. Yet the presence of radical parties in parliament did not ensure their capacity to act together. The distinctive combinations of parties and the resulting party configurations in individual countries will form the basis of the next chapter.

6
Political Parties and Party Systems

Much of the study of post-communist politics carried with it assumptions that over time these political systems would manifest increasing stability and predictability. While 'transition' implied change, and with it the importance of élite actors, uncertainty, and 'windows of opportunity', consolidation implied that once institutions were in place they would themselves begin to shape élite behaviour. Though the 'consolidationists' were often careful to stress that democratic reversals remained possible, that developments were not linear, and that consolidation operated at different levels over a time span lasting up to a generation,[1] the very term 'consolidation' suggested that the complex elements and processes comprising a political system would some-how 'solidify', gradually becoming routine and institutionalised.

Many students of political parties also assumed that party development would form one aspect of this evolution.[2] Some observers went beyond parties *per se* in postulating conditions of democratic success. It was not just the development of political parties, even 'strong' parties, but *the institution-alisation of the party system* that was seen as a feature of democratic consoli-dation: '...democracy has generally thrived when party systems have been institutionalised'.[3] Conversely, 'institutionally weak party systems' constituted an obstacle to democratic consolidation.[4]

This was not viewed as a particular problem for the new European parlia-mentary systems. Parties would rapidly 'settle down'. There was reason to believe that after an initial period of chaos and fluidity, parties would see the advantages of unity for electoral purposes: 'Too much swinging, splitting, or name changing ends up becoming a liability.'[5] Moreover, insiders would behave as rational choice models suggested, altering the rules to make it more difficult for outsiders to break through. As economic changes progressed, clearer perceptions of 'interests' would emerge. Class in parti-cular would reappear as a basis of political division.[6] All this would simplify electoral choice, and both party identity and party identification would gradually strengthen. By extension the quality of representation would be enhanced, as voters would know what they were likely to get from their parties and parties would have incentives to act in accordance with voters' preferences.

Earlier chapters have already suggested that in many respects this picture does not reflect post-communist experience. This chapter investigates such expectations from the perspective of the 'party system'. It examines the concept of the party system and assesses the extent to which we may speak of party systems and their institutionalisation in post-communist Europe. It describes the interactions of political parties rather than the individual parties discussed in Chapter 3. All countries are mentioned, though Bulgaria receives little attention: the fate of its two major political parties was extensively reviewed in Chapter 3 (and its minority party will be discussed in Chapter 9).

In Giovanni Sartori's classic definition a party system 'results from, and consists of, the patterned interactions of its component parts' but is also greater than the sum of its parts.[7] It is thus by definition a stable configuration, since a pattern repeats itself; but it is not static, since polities always have dynamic aspects. Unlike political parties, which have a concrete existence in the form of physical gatherings of members, the party system is not the sum of the particular parties but an analytical abstraction characterising their interactions over time.

For Sartori the pattern of competition depended primarily on the number of relevant parties, their relative strengths, and their respective ideological distance; and this has been the commonest heuristic approach to the analysis of party systems.[8] Peter Mair emphasised the structure of competition as 'the most important aspect of party systems',[9] and for him the number of parties subsided to a relatively minor position. Structures of competition may be open (unpredictable) or closed (predictable), depending on patterns of alteration in government, persistence or novelty in government formation, and the access to or exclusion of parties from government. When over time, patterns of cooperation and opposition remain relatively stable, a proliferation or reduction in the number of parties does not necessarily make much difference to the party system. By implication, without this stability over time – as in new democracies – numbers can and do matter.

The number of parties

How should we try to characterise political parties at any given time and over a given period? The number of parliamentary parties is often seen as central to the characterisation of a party system, not least because their number determines their potential interaction streams. The more fragmented they are, the more interaction streams and (probably) the more open the structure of competition. Yet it should be clear from previous chapters that in some countries one can hardly speak of regular patterns of interaction. The nature of parliamentary parties often changed considerably from one election to another, even when the number of parties represented in parliament did not change much. Counting the parties represented in parliament is a start, and it can tell us something about the party configuration over a particular (short) time period. However, there are huge problems of deciding what, when, and how to count.

Generally there are three ways to count the number of parliamentary parties. All present problems. The first method is simply to count how many entities gained seats at an election. At first this seems straightforward. Yet we have noted that in post-communist elections not all competitors were necessarily political parties. This means that 'counting the entities that entered parliament following an election' may include local pressure groups or social organisations (permitted to stand for a time in Poland, the Ukraine, Lithuania, and Estonia for example). Even if we counted only registered political parties, this could be very misleading. For example, of the 29 labels that entered parliament in Poland in 1991, sixteen were registered as parties. Yet although conveying the messiness of the Sejm, it would be highly misleading to describe Poland as a 'sixteen-party system' in 1991.

Furthermore, many other electoral contenders were not 'parties' either but alliances; they were composite entities. Some were 'electoral parties' or new umbrella-coalitions, with the constituents rarely named on the ballot paper.[10] Others were pragmatic electoral alliances that often shifted from one election to the next. This means that it is very difficult to speak of electoral contenders as unified actors. In Estonia, for example, the total number of parties contesting the 1992 election was 38, making up the 17 contenders that presented lists; 29 of these participated in an electoral coalition. In 1995, 30 parties contested the election, forming 16 lists, with 21 parties in alliance.[11] In Lithuania in 1992, 17 contenders embraced 26 'parties'. In independent Slovakia larger parties often gave smaller ones room on their party lists: the 18 parties and electoral coalitions which contested the 1994 elections embraced 31 'parties' and 'movements', while there were 16 'parties' on the eight lists crossing the threshold.[12] In some countries the problem of independent candidates was also salient, for if they are treated as an aggregate, they collectively assume the character of a single 'party' and if they are treated separately, they assume the character of individual parties, which clearly they are not.

The second method, associated with Sartori's work on party systems, is to count only those parties deemed 'relevant'. This entails discounting parties that have neither coalition potential nor 'blackmail potential', while counting 'all the parties that have either a governmental relevance in the coalition-forming arena, or a competitive relevance in the oppositional arena'.[13] But, as Sartori acknowledges, these criteria are 'postdictive' and difficult to operationalise; moreover, they need to be analysed over time: 'A minor party can be *discounted as irrelevant* whenever it remains over time superfluous...'.[14] It is not impossible to use this method,[15] but it becomes extremely difficult with highly fluid parties, new combinations of parties and improbable inter-actions (see below).

The most widely used measure for tapping the dynamics of party develop-ment was developed by Taagepera and Laakso as the 'effective number of parties', which can deal both with parties contesting elections and with parliamentary parties.[16] They sought an operational definition that took into account the relative size of parties and would assist in detecting change in party numbers over time. 'The effective number of parties is the number of hypothetical equal-size parties that would have *the same total effect on fractionalization of the system* as have the actual parties of unequal size.'[17] In other words, the formula provides another mechanism for deciding how to count. 'Effective number' is said to indicate the degree of fragmentation, viability in government formation, and the process of institutionalisation. It is a measure that is now almost routinely applied to the study of post-communist systems.[18] Birch calculated the average number of effective parliamentary parties for 20 post-communist countries and for all of Western Europe as 4.08 in the former and 3.72 in the West. She concluded that after ten years Eastern European party systems were 'slightly larger than those of the West, but the overall patterns are similar...'.[19] However, this seems unwarranted. Despite its manifold uses the 'effective number' is not a real number, and its use for assessing new party configurations is problematic for several reasons.

Most importantly, it does not distinguish between individual parties and electoral alliances. It measures the effective number of parties 'for any system of *qualitatively similar components* which differ in size'.[20] But we saw above that these entities are not qualitatively similar. Moreover, not even all 'parties' could be regarded as 'qualitatively similar components'. This is not merely because they differed in terms of their electoral appeal, their structure, or their degree of penetration of society. That is true of parties in all demo-cracies. But in post-communist states many parties lacked entirely the structures needed to link together centre and region and to bind supporters, members, and leaders into a common project. To become part of a 'system of patterned interaction' requires some stability and coherence of the elements comprising the system. If these elements change rapidly, the effect is rather like a kaleidoscope; with one shake the component parts fall into new relationships.

The election of particular contenders certainly tells us how many competing entities began a particular parliamentary term. This is the figure used as the basis for all three calculations. In Poland in 1991 (excluding local interest groups, trades unions, and the like) my count is sixteen 'real' parties (whose party-ness was not uniform), eleven 'relevant' parties, and an 'effective number' of 9.04.[21] Obviously these are rather different. The message is that one must be extremely clear about the criteria for counting.

Moreover, these numbers do not tell us anything about what happened to electoral contenders once elected to parliament; yet treating parties as collective actors assumes at least some minimum level of cohesion, that is, a willingness to act together in pursuit of common goals. In fact we shall see in the next section that neither electoral parties, nor coalitions, nor *soi-disant* political parties necessarily behaved as coherent entities after election, though later many countries took steps to try to counter political fragmentation. Individual parties lost members through splits or individual defections. Electoral alliances did not automatically generate parliamentary cooperation. Even the pull of governmental office did not prevent governing coalitions from defections or lack of disciplined support in parliament.

Parties in parliament

Parties in the first parliaments were often more like fluid coteries of individuals than genuine collective entities.[22] Although this fluidity weakened, it did not disappear; it remained a feature of many polities. Moreover, it was not only shifting alliance-formations that complicated the process of stabilisation. Party electoral alliances broke down and 'party tourism' became a regional phenomenon as individual deputies moved from one 'party' to another or founded new ones. The parliamentary factions ceased to 'match' the parties the electors had chosen. This was not surprising at the early stages where umbrella groups were splintering; but self-styled parties also saw defections and no country was exempt from such migration.

The persistence of this mismatch belied the expectations of gradual consolidation. We have already noted the facility with which party leaders left their parties to establish new ones. Successful parties were less prone to internal division and serious splits, but we have also seen that they were not exempt (see Chapter 5). Only in Hungary did the period of initial shifting and realignment lead to a reduction in the number of parliamentary parties *and* a continuity of survivors, along with increased party cohesion.

The phenomenon of party tourism

Figures on party tourism are patchy but they leave no doubt as to its prevalence. Only in Bulgaria did the early dominance of two major political forces and the bitterness between them reduce the likelihood of wanderings between them. Only in Slovenia was the process of merger more important than the politics of division. After the first election in 1990, Left parties united in the United List, and the Peasant Party merged with the Christian Democrats. After 1992, the Greens and two members of the Democratic Party joined the Liberal Democrats, as did some smaller extra-parliamentary parties. With the exception of the Slovene National Party and the Christian People's Party in 2000 there were few party splits in Slovenia.

Elsewhere the picture was very different. Between the first and second elections 38 per cent of Estonian incumbents and 24 per cent of Latvian incumbents deserted their parties.[23] The Estonian Popular Front (in opposition after 1992) split before its dissolution in November 1993. The Centre Party developed as a faction within the Front, but some members in turn defected to a new Free Democrat faction; by summer 1994 the Centre Party's strength had plummeted from 15 to 5 members, below the faction minimum of six.[24] By 1995 the most popular candidate in 1992, Jüri Toomepuu, had lost *all* his parliamentary colleagues from Estonian Citizen.

The first freely elected Hungarian parliament also saw factional splits, expulsions, and individual defections, especially by deputies elected in single-member districts. Only the Christian Democratic and Socialist parliamentary factions did not lose members, and the number of Independents had increased from 7 to 35 by July 1993.[25] Fifty-six deputies (of 386) changed factions in the 1990–94 parliament.[26]

In Poland the twenty-nine groupings elected in 1991 settled into sixteen parliamentary clubs. By the end of that parliament there were still sixteen, but neither their names nor their composition remained the same. Only the two successor formations, the Alliance of the Democratic Left and the Polish Peasant Party remained virtually intact, losing one deputy each.

In Slovakia not only did Public against Violence split, but the Slovak National Party and the Christian Democratic Movement (KDH) lost members to a new parliamentary faction, the Slovak Christian Democratic Movement. Between 1990 and 1992, 44 of 150 deputies moved to a different parliamentary faction. As new parliamentary clubs emerged, each sought to establish itself as a political party for the next election.[27] Similarly, in the Czech section of the Federal Assembly the number of parliamentary clubs doubled to 18 by the 1992 elections, with a 'very open and fluid concept of membership'.[28]

Party tourism in the early stages of party development should not be regarded as surprising. Parties emerged without a clear identity, despite much historical baggage. As party identity began to take shape, not all deputies endorsed shifts in their party's profile. Parties had few sanctions with which to command discipline in the absence of underlying consensus. Yet this party-hopping did not necessarily lessen with successive elections. Many deputies were new, lacking the socialisation incumbency brings. In Latvia the proportion of deputies deserting their parties actually increased to 32 per cent between 1995 and 1998.[29] Small parties often fell below the numbers needed for a parliamentary club or caucus. By the 1998 elections Siegerist's TKL (which won no seats) had already lost seven of its eight members in parliament. In Romania eight parties entered parliament in 1992, but there were 13 by 1995, with 22 deputies sitting as Independents.

In the Czech National Council in 1992 (and then the independent Czech Republic) the rate of flux abated, but there were still substantial changes. The Liberal Social Union split into its three elements following the election. The Christian Democratic Party also formed its own parliamentary group after standing with the Civic Democrats (ODS), and in 1994 the Communists left the Left Bloc. Forty-nine deputies – almost one-quarter – changed their party between 1992 and 1996. In the 1996–8 parliament 38 deputies switched allegiance, most of them as a result of a split within the governing ODS (see below). However, from 1998 to 2002 not a single deputy left his/her parliamentary party grouping, and this was also the case in the six months following the 2002 election.[30]

In the Ukraine, deputies after 1998 'changed their faction membership more frequently than ever and the party spectrum in parliament became more fragmented'.[31] The amorphous centre was the least cohesive, with splits and reconfigurations closely linked to battles for access to the presidential administration. Within a year the number of factions had increased from eight to fifteen, and from 1999 faction membership was particularly fluid.

Apparent trends often proved illusory. In Slovakia, for example, defections fell between 1994 and 1998;[32] but that drop proved only temporary. Between 1998 and 2002 the victorious Slovak Democratic Coalition broke up; its ally SOP effectively disappeared; HZDS, SDL', and the nationalist SNS split; and Dzurinda and Fico attracted deputies to their new parties.

Governing parties

Perhaps more surprising than the phenomenon of party tourism itself was that it applied not just to opposition parties but also to parties in government. Power might be expected to serve as a strong glue, not least because of the massive patronage opportunities opened up by the reform process, especially privatisation. Yet governing parties could not always count on the support of their individual members or even their government colleagues, adding to the tensions between coalition partners.

Governing parties saw rebellions or even splits for four main, often overlapping reasons. Many of these factors applied also to opposition parties. First, there were often genuine policy or ideological differences as parties faced the multiple tasks of transformation. Secondly, there were intense personal quarrels centring on thwarted political ambitions or perceptions of high-handed leadership. In some cases individuals were expelled, particularly for alleged corruption or incompetence; in others they left of their own volition. Thirdly, as parliamentary terms progressed, the unpopularity of governments increased the attractions of leaving a foundering ship. Individual deputies wishing re-election looked for a safer home in another party or distanced themselves from their own governments by founding a new one. Finally, rebellions could be used as a bargaining lever in coalition politics, especially when tensions with coalition partners were high. All four factors operated in the specific conditions of post-communist transformation.

The broad-based Hungarian Democratic Forum and its allies barely retained their majority after 1990, though the government lasted its full term. The Forum responded to internal ideological and policy conflicts by expelling both its liberal wing and the extreme nationalist followers of István Csurka, later the leader of the Justice and Life Party. Following the death of Prime Minister Antall in December 1993 further tensions developed over his successor. The Forum continued to splinter in the new 1994 parliament. In the case of the schismatic Smallholders, ideological and personal divisions centred on issues (land restitution), tactics (to remain with or leave the coalition), and the controversial leadership of József Torgyán, both his autocratic ('paranoid megalomaniac'[33]) style and his extreme nationalism.

In Romania the National Salvation Front formed a government strong enough to retain its majority after its split in March 1992, a result of policy issues surrounding the pace of economic reform and personal tensions between Prime Minister Roman and President Iliescu. The PDSR (DFSN) maintained its unity in office, especially after losing its majority status in 1992; but in opposition after 1996 it split once again, when former Foreign Minister Theodor Meleşçanu founded the Alliance for Romania (APR).

After 1996 the new Romanian government – another coalition of coalitions – was chronically beset by internal squabbles. The Democratic Convention was a heterogeneous collection centred on the National Peasant Party–Christian Democratic Party (PNŢCD), and the Social Democratic Union was a party alliance, albeit with Roman's (old FSN) element the stronger member. Even the Hungarian UDMR was internally divided between a radical wing, strong advocating territorial autonomy, and a more pragmatic wing (but it did not suffer defections).

In Poland the 1991 minority governments were beset by inter- and intra-party tensions. The 1993–7 coalition of the social democrats and peasants suffered from disputes between the partners (in 1997 the Peasant Party laid before parliament a vote of no confidence in its own government); but the internal discipline and cohesion of the two parties remained solid. The SLD had 171 deputies at the start of the 1993–7 term and 168 at the end. The PSL had declined by 5 to 127.

This position was not maintained by the subsequent Solidarity – Freedom Union (AWS–UW) government after 1997. As an electoral party oriented to defeating the social democrats, AWS had succeeded. As a governing entity it was chronically divided, with a lack of ideological coherence reflected in serious parliamentary indiscipline that undermined its own government. It did not formally split until after the presidential election of 2000. But its parliamentary group had already eroded, especially with the departure in 1998–9 of a group of deputies stressing Catholic fundamentalism, a centralised state, concern with national identity, and negative attitudes to European integration – all of which found expression in the League of Polish Families (LPR) in 2001. When the UW withdrew in June 2000, AWS continued as an increasingly fractious minority government. It began to fragment in earnest after the presidential elections returned President Kwaśniewski for a second term. By the end of its tenure in office the number of AWS deputies had fallen from 201 to 134. The Buzek government's deep unpopularity and obvious incompetence made defections more likely, as deputies and ministers alike scurried to find new homes in the Civic Platform (PO, January 2001), Law and Justice (PiS, spring 2001), as well as the LPR.

With independence Vladimir Mečiar's government of the Slovak National Council took over as the government of independent Slovakia with two seats short of a majority. Already dependent for support on the Slovak National Party, the government's position deteriorated further when Mečiar dismissed Milan Kňažko as foreign minister: Kňažko and seven other deputies left the HZDS. In October 1993 HZDS entered a formal coalition with the nationalists, but within a few months both parties had split.

Mečiar lost another foreign minister, Jozef Moravčik, Deputy Prime Minister Roman Kováč, and six more deputies. Although Malová attributed these divisions to 'personal tensions', rather than programmatic differences or values,[34] the leading defectors were more committed to European integration, as well as to a more rapid and more open economic reform programme.

On returning to office after the 1994 election Mečiar took steps to improve internal party discipline, and party factions generally remained more stable (see above). But after 1998, government in the broad-based 'coalition of coalitions' was particularly turbulent, struck by internal struggles leading to Dzurinda's new party the SDKÚ and bitter infighting within the Democratic Left (SDL') and Christian Democratic quarrels.

In the Czech Republic, the 1996 minority government similarly saw increased tensions within the leading Civic Democrats (ODS), as well as with its coalition partners. Economic deterioration, party financing scandals, and Klaus' leadership style generated the breakaway Freedom Union (US). The coalition broke up in acrimony and a caretaker government took over. Changes in deputy allegiance between 1996 and 1998 were above all due to the departure of ODS deputies to the Freedom Union.

In Lithuania the (successor) social democrats (LDDP) won a spectacular victory with 75 seats (53 per cent) in the Seimas in 1992, and it captured the presidency the following year. But its parliamentary faction was neither cohesive nor disciplined. By mid-1995 it had effectively lost its majority, and by the next election it had only 65 deputies, though parliament served its full term – with three governments, often supported by some independents and the contingent of Polish deputies. Almost three-quarters of the faction's deputies voted against the government at least once in contentious roll-call votes.[35] Initially ideological differences over the economic reform programme (1993–4) – including land reform – were the major reason for defections. Later, following a banking scandal (over which the prime minister resigned) and a savage decline in the government's popularity, the deputy's personal calculus of his/her re-election prospects became the most important consideration. Some deputies resigned from the Seimas to take up jobs in the civil service or private sector while the government could still 'dole out favours', while others sought to distance themselves from their party.[36]

After 1996 the Homeland Union (Conservatives) and the Christian Demo-crats governed in an apparently ideologically compatible coalition. But flagrant leadership ambitions and internal disagreements caused a loss of credibility, which in turn led to increasing dissension within and between partners. Two groupings split from the Conservatives and initiated new parties, first the Homeland People's Party and then the Union of Moderate Conservatives. At the same time, dissatisfaction arose within the Christian Democrats over its satellite position in government, as well as more marked tensions between its traditionalist and more liberal wings. It withdrew from its coalition agreement in June 1999 and the liberal wing formed the Union of Modern Christian Democrats just before the 2000 elections.[37]

In Estonia governing parties did not maintain their unity either. The Estonian National Independence Party (ERSP), the first party in the USSR to oppose the ruling Communist Party (1988), suffered from 'life-threatening factionalisation and fragmentation as a governing party' after the 1992 elections.[38] The new Future's Estonia Party (*Tulevikupartei*) took two deputies from the ERSP in August 1993. Pleading for a new consensual unity, it aimed to benefit from dissatisfaction with the more established parties 'and the discordant tone they had set'.[39] In November the new National Progress Party (*Eesti Rahvuslik Eduerakond*, ERE) took two more deputies, including a former leader, Ants Erm. This time it was policy issues, particularly that of citizen-ship, where ERE saw the ERSP as too soft; it was also anti-EU. It fought the 1995 elections as part of the radical 'Better Estonia' alliance.

Slovenia, too, was not wholly exempt from such dissension. The merger of the People's Party and the Christian Democrats in June 2000 seemed to confirm a continuing trend. Yet the coalition government formed with the (right-wing) Social Democratic Party proved short-lived. Coalition tensions exacerbated tensions within the new party, whose Prime Minister Andrej Bajuk promptly announced the formation of his own party, New Slovenia (NSi), taking Foreign Minister (and former Christian democrat prime minister) Peterle with him.

Parliamentary factions in Russia and the Ukraine

In Russia and the Ukraine super-presidentialism continued to affect the development of parties. Following the first elections, factions had even less meaning than elsewhere; often they were merely labels of convenience. In 1993 in Russia the consequences of the election for the composition of the Duma were initially unclear. In the single-member districts candidates' affiliations were not listed on the ballot, and there was little reference to 'party' during the campaign. The Ukraine kept its majoritarian system for the 1994 election. The weak development of parties, along with onerous procedures for party registration[40] meant that only about half the deputies elected had party affiliations, and they were not enduring. The new mixed electoral system still provided strong incentives for local notables to stand as Independents. In 1998 Independents still won in more than half the single-member seats in the Ukraine, and in 2002, 94 of 225 single-member deputies were 'self-nominated'. The position was little different in Russia. In 1999 half (51.3 per cent) the candidates in single-member districts of the mixed system were Independents.

In both countries Independents joined factions of convenience and they and party deputies alike frequently switched allegiance. In Russia only Yabloko saw virtually no change in the first Duma – and new factions emerged with no clear links to the electoral contenders. Almost one-quarter of deputies changed their faction at least once.[41] Membership of a parliamentary faction did not ensure disciplined voting. Only the communists, Yabloko, Russia's Choice, and Zhirinovskii's group developed a measure of cohesion; other deputies did not generally follow the lead of their factions in voting.[42] The 1995 Duma became more faction-oriented, though deputies still frustrated decision-making by their highly individualistic behaviour and high levels of absenteeism.[43]

But presidential patronage was a powerful magnet for growing cohesion, especially in Russia after 1999. Putin had a liberal economic reform agenda, which he sought to achieve through legislation rather than by decree, as in Yeltsin's time. The executive generally found support in four pro-presidential factions, supplemented by bargaining around particularistic interests and the construction of ad hoc majorities.[44]

Factions whose members owed their seats to the Kremlin's favour tended 'to be attentive to the Kremlin's policy wishes in order to preserve the many material, career, and electoral benefits' provided by the presidential administration, and vote-buying and reciprocal trading of favours were 'commonplace'.[45] 'Unity' was distinctive for its disciplined support for the Kremlin, and it gained strength after its merger with Fatherland in 2001. Russia's Regions had few list deputies and was less cohesive, but it used its pro-presidential stance to bargain for selective benefits to the constituencies of its members.

We noted above continuing shifts within the Ukrainian Rada. In the Ukraine the president hindered the development of coherent parliamentary parties and manipulated parliament in a variety of ways, including coercion and bribery[46] and imposing successive vetoes on efforts to introduce a fully proportional electoral system. In the 2002 election the 33 list-contenders included large numbers of self-styled political parties gathered into electoral coalitions, several of which were clearly artificial creations associated with the president.[47] The pro-presidential For a United Ukraine won 111 seats (and only 12.23 per cent of the list vote), but it rapidly attracted self-nominated 'independents' and defectors from other groupings to its faction to make an initial total of 177 seats (39.3 per cent), rising for a time to 182 seats.[48] Once parliamentary positions had been allocated and several presidential candidates for office confirmed, For a United Ukraine split into seven factions.[49] Faction fluidity continued and the main opposition bloc 'Our Ukraine' lost some powerful supporters, as well as representatives of its trade union allies.

Clearly in this context of internal divisions, realignments, and new challengers, the (quasi-)established parties had an interest in mechanisms to try to discourage continuing fragmentation. A variety of rule changes, both of electoral laws and internal party regulations, aimed at promoting fewer, more cohesive parties. Of these, the most important were electoral thresholds.

Promoting party consolidation

Thresholds

In Chapter 4 we noted the tendency to introduce or to increase electoral thresholds. Thresholds were seen as a mechanism to discourage splits and to stimulate and sustain the merger of small groups, as well as preventing small parties from entering parliament. Parties were encouraged to form electoral alliances by the introduction of differential thresholds for parties and coalitions. Thresholds for coalitions (see Table 4.6) were introduced in Czechoslovakia and in its successor states, as well as in Lithuania, Poland, and Romania. Generally, small parties could do well by pooling their resources: two smaller parties might well meet a 7 per cent threshold together.

The position was clear in proportional systems, but mixed-parallel systems were rather more complex. There the threshold affected entrants under the list element, but many additional 'parties' (some merely the personal vehicle of an individual), incapable of meeting the threshold, entered parliament with one or two seats from single-member districts. In Russia only the communists were successful in both elements of the ballot. In Lithuania in 1992 three parties gained single-member seats but no list seats, in 1996 eight, and in 2000 seven. While the number of contenders fell in the proportional component, the number of parties remained high in the majoritarian component in 2000; small parties did not stand in the list element or formed alliances with larger ones.

Thresholds certainly achieved their primary purpose. Most of the smallest parties ceased to contest elections after one or two failures. Successive low votes signified acute difficulty in gaining the extra votes needed to cross the barrier. Indeed, of those parties which persisted, very few were rewarded with parliamentary success. The most important exceptions were the Czech Social Democrats' (ČSSD) in 1992, the Hungarian Justice and Life Party (MIÉP) in 1998, Self-Defence (SO) in Poland in 2001, and the Communist Party of Slovakia in 2002. No parliamentary party succeeded in making an electoral comeback under the same label after exclusion from parliament.

We saw in Chapter 4 (Table 4.8) that the numbers of contenders did not fall steadily or routinely, however. In general this was the result of new entrants, including splinter groups from existing parties, rather than the same groups trying their hand again. These new entrants also included new alliance configurations.

Thresholds could not prevent party splits, as we have seen above. Nor could coalition thresholds ensure the parliamentary cohesion of election allies, whether they stood as alliances subject to coalition thresholds or as electoral parties subject to lower thresholds. Only the 'parties of power' could exercise major centripetal influence through the use of presidential resources. The more disparate an electoral alliance or indeed an 'electoral party', the more likely it was to break up in parliament. If gaining entry to parliament was the aim of numerous coalitions, then the presumption that they would subsequently act together was unwarranted.[50] In Poland the savage impact of the new thresholds in 1993 reduced the number of parliamentary groups from sixteen to six; but between 1993 and 1997 fourteen different parliamentary 'circles' (*koło*) formed (requiring at least three members), while the number of non-affiliated deputies grew from one to sixteen.

In Slovakia Vladimir Mečiar's government introduced a highly contentious change when the 1998 electoral law required that *each* element of a coalition must receive 5 per cent of the vote to qualify for seats (the next government removed this provision). Designed to damage opposition moves to greater unity and to preclude representation for the Hungarian minority,[51] Mečiar's move backfired: five parties registered the Slovak Democratic Coalition (SDK) as a single entity with one list, and three Hungarian parties also coalesced into a single party. SDK unity was largely fictional; Prime Minister Dzurinda's new initiative, the Slovak Democratic and Christian Union, confirmed its ephemeral character.

Estonia did not raise its (national list) threshold. After the 1995 election new rules provided that those failing to win seats at successive elections would be stricken from the register of parties. Then in 1998 coalitions were prohibited altogether (only a political party or group of citizens could nominate candidates). In the 1999 elections the Moderates joined forces with the People's Party, and the Country People's Party (*Eesti Maarahva Erakond*) brought together the Rural People's Party and the Rural Union, both having defected from previous alliance with the unpopular governing Coalition Party.[52] Estonia saw increasing stability of its parliamentary groups, and the groups also 'matched' the political parties elected. The Centre Party, Isamaa, the Moderates, and the Rural People's Party did not lose deputies after 1999, and the Reform Party and the Coalition Party lost only one each. The trend towards mergers continued in 2000 with the formation of the People's Union from the main rural parties and smaller allies.

Thus the situation was certainly not one of unrelenting fluidity and reconfiguration. Particular parties, and parties in particular countries, did indeed witness fairly clear paths of development from less to more unity and cohesion. As anticipated by Sartori and others, many parties began to behave more like 'parties'. A variety of factors promoted greater 'party-ness'. Some were institutional. Increased thresholds did have an effect, as did new requirements for the increased size of parliamentary clubs, which were the basis of resource allocation, or stipulations of fewer financial resources for new factions. Many countries increased the required size of their parliamentary-group minimum: Hungary from ten to fifteen, the Czech Republic from five to ten, Slovakia from five to eight. Hungary required defecting deputies to sit as Independents for six months. The Romanians massively increased the minimum members needed for party registration from 251 to 10,000. In the Ukraine the move to a mixed electoral system in 1998 meant that now at least half the deputies owed their mandate to a political party (though the Constitutional Court's reversal of new rules regarding factions threw the Rada into a state of renewed flux[53]). But the general party-led preference for a PR system was effectively thwarted by the president, who exercised five vetoes as the 2002 election drew nearer.

We also need a diversion into the technicalities of Russian institutional developments here, for not all mechanisms aided development of a party 'system'. In Russia new electoral regulations continued to provide incentives for individual politicians to foster party fragmentation. In particular the Law on Political Parties (2001) increased the cost of electoral entry by an inordinately complex and lengthy party registration process and a virtual ban on regional parties. This gave existing parties a particular value as legal entities, thus encouraging politicians to protect their own status quo rather than seeking potentially risky mergers. It also meant that parties needed to contest elections, since failing to do so during a five-year period would entail party dissolution.

At the same time parties were displaying little capacity to act as the 'truly national parties' the law was intended to promote. Parties virtually disappeared in the Russian regional elections of 2002, and the regional structures of Yabloko, the Liberal Democratic Party, and the Union of Right Forces were 'effectively being destroyed or virtualized'. This decay of regional party networks was attributed to the 'general lessening of the authority of parties at the national level, and . . . the expansion of the authority of a non-party president alongside the erosion of influence of the State Duma'.[54]

In the parliamentary systems aside from new legal regulations, impetus to greater cohesion also came from the parties themselves. Once a party had split, its remaining members were less heterogeneous and more inclined to cohesive behaviour. Though not without internal tensions, ethnic parties seldom split. Patronage opportunities for incumbents (especially second-term incumbents) became more obvious. Some parties took measures to increase discipline within their ranks, including the central control of allocation of list placings or written declarations of loyalty. The social democratic successor parties, most of which had split in 1989–90, and the communist parties of Russia[55] and the Ukraine[56] and (after an early period of extreme turmoil[57]) the Czech Republic restored their traditions of stern party discipline. In Slovakia HZDS required candidates to pledge to pay a vast sum should they leave the parliamentary party (this did not prove a deterrent after 1998).

Yet only in Hungary, the Czech Republic, and Slovenia could one detect a process of gradual system-development from a nucleus of durable parties. Elsewhere there was some partial stabilisation, particularly where large successor parties overcame their legitimacy problems. In Poland and Romania the SLD and PSD commanded the centre-left space. Estonia possessed durable parties but also saw the breakthrough of new ones. Elsewhere the picture looked more uncertain. The next sections provide an overview of these different paths of party development.

Party systems in Hungary, the Czech Republic, and Slovenia

Hungary

Hungary was unusual in the early emergence of its political parties from the developing pluralism of the communist period and at the Round Table. Despite initial turbulence their parliamentary factions were becoming increasingly 'well-structured, well-organised and highly disciplined working units in the first parliamentary term'.[58] Only Round Table participants had won list seats in 1990, and they occupied all of the central ideological space, leaving only the extreme left and the extreme right vacant. New external challengers did not succeed, with the partial exception of the already well-known nationalist István Csurka in 1998. But the Hungarian party configuration did not harden after the first free election. The number of parties, their ideological positions, and their relative strengths shifted over successive elections. The weak socialists made an impressive comeback to dominate the centre-left, and Fidesz moved from centrist liberalism to right conservatism in a highly successful strategic shift that left it in the position originally occupied by the Forum.

By 2002 the Hungarian party system had coalesced around two major actors, the Hungarian Socialist Party and Fidesz, along with two smaller parties, the Free Democrats and the Forum. Eighty-three per cent of the vote went to the two largest electoral contenders, the Socialists and the Fidesz–Forum joint lists (the Forum was able to form its own parliamentary faction, thus increasing the pooled resources of the right). Of the six contenders winning in 1990, the Smallholders had split themselves into oblivion and the Christian Democrats were largely ensconced inside Fidesz's big tent, while the Forum was closely tied to Fidesz's apron strings. The Free Democrats saw their vote erode at successive elections, and they remained vulnerable with just 5.6 per cent in 2002. Of the extra-parliamentary parties Csurka's Justice and Life Party saw its vote hold, despite attempts by Fidesz to woo its supporters; but the relatively high turnout left it below the threshold.

Fidesz (initially the Young Democrats) began as a small, narrowly based 'generation party' of the young, stressing direct democracy, collective leadership, and minority rights. By April 1993 it had become 'a hierarchically organized election party with a professional administration' under the leadership of the charismatic Victor Orbán.[59] For a time it was the most popular party, but a real-estate scandal, a vote in parliament against increased pensions, and Orbán's open willingness to contemplate coalition with the Forum scuppered its chances in 1994. Anti-communism was an enduring feature of Orbán's political stance, and the idea of cooperation with the Socialists was anathema to him. But instead of offering a substitute for the now highly unpopular Forum, 'a vote for Fidesz appeared to many voters to be a vote for keeping the existing government in power'.[60] With only 7 per cent of the list vote and 20 seats, Fidesz was the smallest of the six recognised parliamentary factions.

But Fidesz was also viewed as a pragmatic party, with few negative overtones; it was 'the most popular "second choice" party ... (so) voters were more ready to overlook its ideological shifts and liberal past'.[61] Initially the Forum and the Christian Democrats rebuffed Orbán's proposals for a broad 'civic alliance'. Yet the Forum split again in 1996, leaving behind a more nationalist wing under its new President Sándor Lezsák (the new Hungarian Democratic People's Party made no lasting impression). With the Forum's support registering less than the 5 per cent threshold, it opted for agreement with Fidesz rather than with Csurka's Justice and Life. The Christian Democrats were in the throes of even greater internecine warfare between the parliamentary party and a new national party leadership over personal, policy and organisational issues.[62] When the parliamentary party group dissolved itself in July 1997, Christian Democratic 'moderates' joined the Fidesz group and Fidesz became the largest opposition grouping in parliament.

By 1998 Fidesz had fully embraced the conservative-nationalist agenda. In its election campaign it promised lower taxes and higher public expenditure, a restoration of law and order, respect for traditional values, greater support for Hungarian minorities abroad, and vigorous defence of Hungary's 'national interests'. It was a new-look Forum with a dynamic young leader. Indeed, the new Fidesz government 'looked as if a reunion of Antall's team (had) hired a new captain to restore chances to qualify for the Premier League. And it worked. Orbán and some other Fidesz politicians provided a fresh media face for more conservative social and political groups.'[63] Unlike the Forum, moreover, Fidesz remained intact through its period of government. It won the most seats in 2002, with fewer list votes but more single-member seats than the MSzP.

The mixed-linked electoral system certainly played a role in the development of Hungarian parties. The complex electoral law proved more party-friendly than its architects had perceived, and there were no victorious Independents by 2002. The law virtually compelled serious parties to maximise their candidates in the single-member districts and regional and national lists. Office-seekers could not submit regional lists without sufficient single-member candidacies, and they needed to maximise their regional lists to ensure passing the national electoral threshold. They could not submit national lists without sufficient regional ones. Moreover, losing-votes in both the single-member and proportional elements remained valuable, as together they constituted a party's national pool.

The two-round system for the majoritarian element also provided a clear incentive to form alliances. The Opposition had already won by-elections under the old system by fielding jointly supported candidates, though in 1990 this practice was not widespread; parties were testing their individual strengths in an atmosphere of high uncertainty with rapidly changing survey recordings of their popularity. Their mutual bargaining power was weak. Only Fidesz and the Free Democrats ran 16 joint candidates and agreed to withdraw after the first round in favour of the higher-ranking candidate, though the Forum, Smallholders, and Christian Democrats agreed to appeal to their voters to support the best-placed candidate of the three. The results did not match their expectations.[64] In 1994 the Socialists did so well in the first round that they proved virtually unchallengeable; they lost only eleven of the second-round seats they contested.

In 1998, however, alliances came into their own. Seventy-eight candidates were joint candidates of Fidesz and the Forum. Two-hundred and twenty-nine candidates withdrew from the second-round contest, including 71 Smallholders, 28 Christian Democrats, and 22 from the Forum in a strategy that generated huge gains for Fidesz.[65] Fidesz needed the Smallholders for its coalition, and it repaid its bargain with four ministers and the (unfulfilled) promise of support for the Smallholders' presidential candidate in 2000. In 2002 all Fidesz–Forum candidates ran as joint candidates. In the second round Fidesz had little option for alliance negotiation, but the Socialists withdrew seven candidates where Free Democrats led, while they in turn withdrew their remaining candidates and asked their supporters to support the socialists.[66]

Of course, the final decisions obviously rested with the voters. In 1990 although second-round turnout dropped radically, indicating that some voters probably withdrew after their parties had failed, remaining voters moved massively to support the Forum in the second round. In 1994 the Socialists maintained their position and emerged as decisive victors of the election. In 1998 voters switched to Fidesz as exhorted by its allies.[67] So voters did not always need to understand the more abstruse elements of the system to behave strategically. But both the single-member and proportional elements generated a bias to large parties, with thresholds, d'Hondt and a formula limit for regional allocations operating to the detriment of the smaller ones.

The pattern of competition in Hungary was increasingly closed. In 1994 the Socialists did not need a coalition partner, but they aimed to broaden their support base and hence their legitimacy by allying with the Free Democrats; no other party was prepared to cooperate with them. In 1998 Fidesz had no option but a coalition with the Smallholders; an alliance with Csurka's radical nationalist MIÉP was still unacceptable. In 2002 also the options were limited, with the Free Democrats prepared to serve in coalition with the Socialists, but not with Fidesz. In 2002 Fidesz 'won' the election; but having pooled its vote with that of the Forum in joint candidacies, it had no available coalition partner. Parties had become cohesive and disciplined. There was a 'pattern of interaction', in other words a party system.

The Czech Republic

Party development in the Czech Republic also appeared to present a picture of relative stabilisation and an increasingly clear spatial location of parties along a left–right spectrum. Unlike in Hungary, however, the ideological nature and relative distance of the parties made coalition-building extremely difficult. At first the largest party had close natural allies. We saw that the original disintegration of Civic Forum gave rise to one large element, the Civic Democratic Party (ODS) associated with the principles of economic liberalism under Václav Klaus. Of its two smaller offshoots, the Civic Democratic Alliance (ODA) remained in parliament and provided a junior coalition partner in 1992 and 1996. In 1992 the Czech National Council (later the Czech lower house), had one strong party of the liberal right (ODS), with almost 30 per cent of the vote. The centre-right included the Christian Democrats and the ODA. On the left were the historic Social Democratic Party, which also included elements from Civic Forum, and the short-lived tripartite Liberal Social Union (Agrarians, Greens, and the historic Czechoslovak Socialist Party, LSU). Communist and Republican deputies occupied the extreme left and right respectively. The Republicans were already prone to splits, losing 8 of 14 members by late 1994.[68] The Movement for Self-Governing Democracy was distinctive both in its regional base and its platform of greater autonomy for Moravia–Silesia. Neither it nor the LSU survived the next election in 1996.

After the 1996 election the number of parliamentary parties fell to six; all were more or less coherent political parties. The ODS remained the largest party, but the biggest change came from a huge shift in the relative strengths of the parties arising from the sudden upsurge of support for the Social Democrats (ČSSD) – from 6.5 per cent of the vote in 1992 to 26.4 per cent. Two large parties now dominated the chamber of deputies, with almost two-thirds of the seats, alongside four smaller ones. The smallest, the ODA, was a cadre party, resembling a 'think-tank' and largely unconcerned with structures or membership.[69] But the ideological polarisation of the parties meant the exclusion of 20 per cent of seats from coalition-building, as neither ODS nor the ČSSD would touch the communists or the Republicans. Since the ČSSD had campaigned on the basis of its opposition to the former government, no majority government was possible. Klaus and his former allies formed a minority coalition, later abandoned by the junior partners in circumstances of economic deterioration, party-finance scandals, and attacks on Klaus from his own party and his coalition partners.

The 1998 election followed a brief caretaker government under the Chair of the National Bank. The number of parliamentary parties fell from six to five, with the exclusion of the Republicans. But the victorious Social Democrats also found themselves incapable of forming a majority coalition. The ODS had split following Klaus's re-election as party leader, but the party had lost relatively few votes from its turmoil. The new Freedom Union (US) that replaced ODA as the smallest parliamentary party was no more sympathetic to the ČSSD than its parent. Although the Christian Democrat leader Josef Lux had carefully positioned his party as a potential pivot point for a centre-left or centre-right coalition, the arithmetic did not add up.

In the event the ideological hostility between the social and civic democrats did not prove unbridgeable, as neither wished an immediate fresh election: Their 'Opposition Agreement' promised the cooperation of the two major parties on issues of constitutional and electoral reform; it gave Milos Zeman the assurance that ODS would not bring his government down, while Klaus gained the speakership of the Chamber of Deputies and other key posts for ODS deputies. This did not inspire voters' confidence, for Klaus had campaigned forcefully against the 'leftist danger'. The Agreement appeared nothing more 'than a cynical power-sharing deal promoting corruption'.[70] Such allegations gained strength with investigations by the *Prague Business Journal*, which questioned how far the parties' public disagreements were merely a smokescreen to hide corrupt practices. There was 'too much opacity, too many clear conflicts of interest, and too much cooperation between the two in recent privatisations, procurement tenders, and other "political deals"...'.[71] In addition, the agreement left the Communist Party as the only serious option for those wishing to express their dissatisfaction with these signs of a party 'cartel'.

In 2002 both ODS and the Social Democrats lost votes and the communists indeed gained, though the Social Democrats remained the largest party. The latter finally achieved a bare minimum winning coalition with 'the Coalition', that is, the Christian Democrats and their electoral coalition partner, the merged Freedom Union–Democratic Union; but the Freedom Union lost its leader over the decision. Inter-party tensions characterised the government from the outset. The social democratic prime minister was in the uncomfortable position of being pulled to the right by his coalition partners, while facing a now far stronger Communist Party to his left. Ideologically the Czechs looked to have a coherent party system, but a natural alliance of left-wing parties was not natural in the post-communist context.

The party system in Slovenia

In Slovenia, as in Hungary, opposition parties had emerged early, and DEMOS was an electoral alliance of parties in 1990, not an umbrella movement. Most of these parties remained in existence, though with some mergers and realignment. The left remained 'respectable' in Slovenia, and decommunisation did not arouse much public passion. The successor parties had been closely associated with the struggle for Slovene independence, including both President Kučan and Janez Drnovšek. The economy benefited from ties developed with Austria and Italy under the old regime.

The centre-left embraced Drnovšek's solidly consistent Liberal Democrats (LDS), the United List of Social Democrats, and the Pensioners' Party (DeSUS). Despite a lengthy political crisis in 2000, Janez Drnovšek remained the most successful office-holder in the region, as long-serving prime minister and then as president. Both he and President Milan Kučan remained popular politicians, impervious to charges of neo-communism laid by their rivals. The LDS was the party of government, with only one short break in its tenure after 1992. It proved able to work effectively with parties of both right and left.

The Slovene right consisted of the Christian Democrats and the People's Party (united for the 2000 election); the (new for 2000) Christian People's Party New Slovenia; and the Social Democrats. The Social Democrats had originated as a moderate left party, but under the then Defence Minister Janez Janša it traversed an erratic road to the right. In the mid-1990s Janša was regarded as potentially 'the most potent force for populist authoritarianism'.[72] Although the party had gained only four seats in 1992, its strength rose to 16 with a strong anti-corruption and 'accountability' platform in 1996. In 2000 he was the main architect of right-wing cooperation in 'Coalition Slovenia', aiming to end the eight-year tenure of the LDS.

Though not demonstrating the demented reshuffles of the Poles or the bickering paralysis of the Romanians (see below), the right-wing parties found it difficult to cooperate, despite their pre-election agreement in 1996. The People's Party defected to join a left-wing coalition, then in April 2000 announced its merger with the Christian Democrats and left the government, provoking a protracted crisis of government formation in the evenly divided parliament. It took two months to construct a government of the newly merged People's Party and social democrats under Andrej Bajuk, and that government held together for about the same period before the departure of the social democrats. For Janša the issue of an electoral reform was central, but the People's Party (SLS) had been a rather reluctant supporter of majoritarianism. To avoid a continuing constitutional crisis the SLS threw its weight behind a constitutional amendment ensuring proportional representation.[73]

Janša's Social Democrats left government and Bajuk split the new Slovene People's Party (SLS + SDK). Indeed, the People's Party was back in government for a time after the 2000 elections, serving with the LDS, the United List, and the Pensioners to give Drnovšek an overwhelming parliamentary majority.

The extreme nationalist Slovene National Party found an early niche with its radical anti-Serb, anti-refugee stance and its claims to 'Greater Slovenia'. It split very early over allegations that its leader Zmago Jelincič had served as an agent of Yugoslav military counterintelligence. Its vote fell from 10 per cent in 1992 to 3.2 per cent in 1996, but it improved slightly in 2000 (4.4 per cent) and Jelincič gained 8.5 per cent of the vote in the presidential elections of November 2002. Its nationalism became less stridently anti-minority (the SNS opposed NATO's bombing of Yugoslavia) and focused more on attacking Slovenia's accession to NATO and the EU, coupled with an anti-clerical, anti-Vatican posture.

All three countries, then, could be regarded as having strong elements of systemness: clearly identifiable, durable parties with some predictable patterns of interaction both in parliament and in the electoral arena. Hungary had the strongest division between left and right, although much of it was based on symbolic politics rather than key programmatic differences. Secular–religious and cosmopolitan–nationalist dimensions were reflected by 1998 in two strong parties, the Hungarian Socialists and Fidesz. The Socialists adapted their structures to democratic practices, making good use of their organisational strengths and former *nomenklatura* networks, while retaining their discipline and cohesion. Fidesz built a strong, professional organisation, benefiting from its early lack of incumbency, strong leadership, and its ability to benefit from the intra-party warfare of its erstwhile smaller allies. It is difficult to know how much weight to attribute to Hungary's distinctive electoral system, but it provided strong party-building and alliance-building incentives and a bias to larger parties. Parties could not submit regional lists without sufficient single-member candidacies, and they needed to maximise their regional lists to ensure passing the electoral threshold. They could not submit national lists without sufficient regional ones. The MSzP and Fidesz responded effectively to electoral-system incentives, but many parties elsewhere did not.

The Czech and Slovene parties also fit rather neatly onto a left–right political spectrum, if with a larger number of parties and greater ideological distance. The Czech Republic had a large centre-right party, the Civic Democrats, and a divided left with strong Social Democrats and a smaller Communist Party. The Slovenes had a substantial party of the centre-left, Liberal Democracy, with smaller parties clustering to the right and left, and a nationalist party of waning extremism. These three saw the most highly institutionalised political parties and the most coherent party systems.

Partial stabilisation

If few countries appeared to be developing the measure of coherence and predictability of Hungary, the Czech Republic, and Slovenia, others also showed signs of some partial stabilisation. It would be rash to predict that the successful parties (see Chapter 5) could now be regarded as permanent fixtures of the political scene. None the less these parties had all displayed previous resilience in the face of adversity and provided a measure of predictability for the first decade of democratic politics. This was the case in Poland and Romania.

Stabilisation of the left in Romania and Poland

In Romania two parties remained durable features of the parliamentary scene, the Social Democratic Party (PSD after several changes of nomenclature from its inauguration as the National Salvation Front) and the Democratic Union of Hungarians in Romania (UDMR, to be discussed further in Chapter 9). Romania lacked 'new party syndrome', but the relative fortunes of parties changed dramatically from one election to another and unity 'against Iliescu' did not endure. The Social Democrats (PSD) retained their position as the strongest single party. As the FSN they formed a majority government in 1990, with almost two-thirds of seats in the lower house. The Front's initial control over and use of government resources had earned it popular credit for alleviating the severe hardships of the late Ceauşescu era, and its national-egalitarian rhetoric proved comforting to the electorate and the old élite alike. Although it suffered the erosion seen by most governing parties, it remained the largest party after 1992, when it formed a minority government, later bringing the nationalists into coalition along with the neo-communist Socialist Labour Party.

With its personnel and attitudes rooted in the old regime and lacking 'even the most fundamental social constituency for reform',[74] the Front's moves to change remained shaky and hesitating. Much of the European, modernising wing of the party left with Petre Roman in 1992, leaving the traditionalist nationalists as the strongest element of the now Democratic National Salvation Front. Indeed, save for the privatisation of agriculture and small retailing, not much changed in Romania before the mid-1990s. Pressure for continuing subsidies of outdated industries were strong for both electoral and clientelist reasons (the state remained the sole owner of 89 per cent of fixed assets[75]).

But as the FSN–DFSN–PDSR–PSD gradually moved to a more explicitly pro-European orientation seeking membership of NATO and the EU, its relationship with the Greater Romania Party (PRM) became more confrontational. Iliescu withstood attack from both the PRM and his own nationalist faction over the treaty with Hungary in August 1996. After 2000 the new PSD minority government relied on support from the Hungarian Democratic Federation, with a cooperation agreement renewed again in January 2002 (see Chapter 9). The PRM was the largest opposition party, and it was not slow to accuse Iliescu of national betrayal.

The reduction of the number of parliamentary parties to five and the support of the Hungarians for the PSD government left three disparate parties that found it difficult to function as a coherent opposition. The National Liberal Party was beset with internal dissension after Valeriu Stoica assumed the leadership, and he lost his position shortly after negotiating a merger with the extra-parliamentary Alliance for Romania in 2002. The Greater Romania Party maintained its steadfastly anti-Hungarian stance. The Democratic Party appeared to suffer an identity crisis after the removal of Petre Roman from the leadership and the return of several prominent members to the Social Democratic fold. Outside parliament the Christian Democratic National Peasant Party (PNŢCD) had split over a merger with the Christian Democratic National Alliance, leaving two PNŢCDs for a time. At the start of 2003 it was still rent by internal leadership battles and the absence of a coherent strategy.

In Poland the Alliance of the Democratic Left (SLD) developed as a broad-based alliance of the successor Social Democratic Party (SdRP) with the 'old' trade union and ancillary organisations, before becoming a united political party (SLD) in 1999. With the Hungarian MSzP it was distinctive not only in the success with which it established its legitimacy as a typical European social democratic party, but also in maintaining its unity. There were acute tensions between the party and the OPZZ (*Ogólno-Polski Związek Zawodowy*) trade union, and between the central party leadership and the provincial 'barons'; but there were no splits. In electoral alliance with the Labour Union (of Solidarity provenance), the SLD's monopoly of the left looked secure, if far from invulnerable.

The 2001 parliamentary elections and subsequent local elections raised the spectre of a serious left populist challenge. Self-Defence (SO) had visibly undermined the Peasant Party (PSL) in its rural heartland, but it also constituted a potential urban competitor for the SLD. Like many leader-oriented parties, Self-Defence lost parliamentary deputies, but its presence in local government provided some patronage opportunities. The SLD also experienced the usual decline in support for governing parties, particularly after excluding the PSL from government in march 2003. Unemployment continued to rise, growth was slow, investment was down, and a serious media scandal over a purported government bribe (Rywingate) focused public attention on internal machinations of party and government. Leszek Miller's minority government was weak, and open divisions emerged within the party. Yet no party compared to the SLD in the degree of its institutionalisation, its organisational skills, and its relatively large membership base.

The parties of the centre had already proved themselves vulnerable. The apparently durable Freedom Union (UW) and its predecessor the Democratic

Union had suffered a succession of splits and individual defections before its break-up in 2001. The UW's liberal economics made it 'too right' for some, while its secularism and strong 'compassionate' wing made it 'too left' for others. The Peasant Party did not split, but its 'nationalist' and 'pragmatic' wings were in constant struggle and the party had proved unable to mono-polise the peasant electorate. But the SLD, the UW (until 2001), and the PSL stood in marked contrast to the permanently fractious, fragmented, and quarrelsome *soi-disant* right-wing. The new parties that entered parliament in 2001 proved fragile. Nor did they cooperate effectively with one another. As in Romania a strong, coherent, conservative party remained notable by its absence.

Estonia

Estonia provided a greater contrast, with no single party as strong as either the Polish SLD or the Romanian PSD. But party durability was notable in Estonia in Pro Patria (Isamaa), the Centre Party, and the People's Union (from the two main rural parties). Parties such as the Independent Royalists disappeared early on, and by early 2003 the Reform Party – the major party of Soviet-era industrial interests – also appeared defunct. Extreme nationalism waned as a driving political force (we shall consider features of Estonian 'ethnocracy' in Chapter 9) and was absorbed into the Pro Patria Union by 1995. Isamaa lost votes in 1995, from 22 to 7.9 per cent, not merely because of the 'incumbency factor', but also because of persistent upheavals and divisions within its own ranks.

Estonia appeared highly susceptible to government reshuffles and prime ministers of relatively short terms in office. Mart Laar's first Isamaa-led government lost its incompetent economics minister within four months, followed by the scandal-beset ministers of defence and the interior. In June 1993 it suffered a deterioration in foreign relations and domestic fallout over the discriminatory dimensions of the proposed Law on Aliens. The coalition finally disintegrated in June 1994 after allegations that Laar had been involved in 1992 in the secret transfer of funds to the breakaway Russian republic of Chechenia. Yet Isamaa bounced back to a respectable 16 per cent of the vote in 1999.

Edgar Savisaar's Centre Party was in certain respects the analogue of the social-democratic left elsewhere, with the moderates challenging this ground from 2001. Savisaar survived his removal as prime minister for allegedly bugging his rivals to become mayor of Tallinn and achieve a creditable result of almost one-quarter of the vote in 1999. He did not form the government. His right-wing opponents maintained their earlier coalition with strong support from President Meri, whose hostility to Savisaar was undisguised. In 2002 Prime Minister Laar resigned, ostensibly because coalition infighting was threatening to derail Estonia's bid for EU and NATO membership.[76] The liberal Reform Party, an unlikely partner for Savisaar, reached agreement on local cooperation in

Tallinn and subsequently reproduced this at national level. The coalition government remained divided on many issues, including tax policy.

Savisaar provided an element of continuing unpredictability. So too did the growing role of Russian voters (see Chapter 9). A new party, Res Publica, did surprisingly well in local government elections shortly after its founding. Savisaar was a divisive politician, with Res Publica among his most bitter critics and a likely vote-winner in 2003. But the mechanisms promoting party mergers seemed to be working, and important elements of continuity persisted, despite the rapid emergence of Res Publica, which could best be seen as another variant of the liberal populist party. (In the event, Res Publica put up a strong performance in 2003, coming second with 24.6 per cent of the vote and as many seats (28) as the Centre Party.)

Conclusion

We began this chapter by averring that the implication of a party 'system' of interaction suggests at least minimum levels of cohesion, expressed in common voting patterns by members of a party (parliamentary faction). We noted enormous difficulties in counting political parties, given the phenomenon of party tourism and the prevalence of electoral alliances and electoral parties that could mean little in terms of parliamentary cooperation. The relative strengths of the electoral contenders were not necessarily reproduced in parliament, because of realignments of alliance partners and their internal divisions. The number of successful contenders was not necessarily a good guide to parliamentary politics.

Indeed, in many post-communist countries party configurations shifted rapidly from one election to another and fell into still different arrangements between elections. Only Hungary, the Czech Republic, and Slovenia developed clear patterns of party interaction and thus could be loosely described as having stable party systems offering a measure of predictability to their voters. Where a large party maintained its attraction, as in Poland and Romania, it provided a reference point for its opponents and thus an element of partial stabilisation. But in both countries the right remained highly fragmented and volatile. Estonia's politics also remained more highly personalised, and Estonia still lacked a clear social democratic party. Competition, as in Slovenia, remained rather open. But still there appeared to be some constants in the interaction of its political parties.

Elsewhere parties often remained fluid, and deputies' interests were not closely bound to those of their party. Considerable scope remained for new political entrepreneurs, and parties emerged as a result of splits and defections, as well as from external challengers. There was no single reason for these divisions. Some were principled, others stemmed from personal rivalries or individual assessments of self-interest.

Electoral choices became rather more clear-cut as voters gained knowledge and experience of surviving parties and adapted to threshold constraints. Yet this clarity suffered not only from new, untested offerings but also from the shifts in electoral alliances. Successful parties combined both organisational penetration and a measure of ideological clarity to secure their persistence, though these were not sufficient conditions of success. Edgar Savisaar (Estonian Centre Party) and Vladimir Mečiar (Movement for Democratic Slovakia) provided rare examples of enduring charismatic leaders, adored by their followers, if loathed by their opponents.

Yet some mechanisms for reducing party numbers and providing incentives for increased cohesion could also be identified. Thresholds served their primary purpose of reducing the numbers of parliamentary parties. They were rather less successful in promoting stable, effective mergers. The major exceptions, as so often in this study, were provided by the Ukraine and Russia. The distinctive features of super-presidentialism reinforced the proliferation incentives of the mixed-parallel electoral system where regional fiefdoms and a lack of truly national parties prevented the polarising effects of single-member districts and encouraged varieties of electoral parties in the list element. Few parties acted as coherent entities in parliament, and factions proved subject to the pull of presidential power and resources.

Elsewhere all countries save Latvia had at least one enduring party and sometimes several. But it seemed premature to speak of party systems. New parties disrupted the development of patterned relationships. They continued to enter parliament in Slovakia, Latvia, Lithuania, Bulgaria, Russia, and the Ukraine, as well as in Poland and Estonia. These new, mainly populist parties benefited from broad 'new face' anti-establishment platforms. Their success did not necessarily threaten the political establishment; we saw in Chapter 5 that many were non-political insiders seeking to enter politics. In part their success was a product of particular circumstances of electoral disillusionment: anti-corruption messages had a wide appeal, given the number of corruption scandals. But it was also a product of existing party relations. Quarrelsome governing coalitions and intra-party struggles were prevalent. Electoral parties in particular distorted patterns of political competition.

If disillusioned voters had 'somewhere to go', they usually went to existing parties. In Romania in 1996 the Democratic Convention served as the 'party of protest' against the social democrats. In 2000 those disappointed with the Convention *and* with the social democrats went to the nationalist Greater Romania Party, preaching a strong anti-corruption message. In the Czech Republic the Communist Party was also free of the taint of power and corruption, and its vote rose sharply in 2002. Slovak voters in contrast had fewer options in 2002. Those who had supported the Coalition in 1998 but were now disappointed with the government effectively lost the choice of some four parties. They could hardly shift their votes to its arch-enemy Mečiar or the splinter HZD, and both the social democrats and nationalists had split into warring elements. But new parties were available to attract the reform protesters (ANO), as well as the more deeply alienated (Smer), while the Communist Party now benefited from the absence of another radical left alternative. In Bulgaria the dominance of two hitherto strong parties also paved the way for ex-tsar Simeon. Union of Democratic Forces and Socialist Party votes were not interchangeable, and the smaller parties had made little impression. Their voters could move to Simeon, who offered a moral message and a new beginning, with exceptional personal resources.

This propensity to try something new was both a cause and consequence of the general disaffection from parties and the political process. Social divisions were not translated into political cleavages manifest in party competition. Rootless parties did not generate loyal electorates. Party volatility and electoral volatility provided reinforcing mechanisms for one another so that the relative strengths of parties altered dramatically and in many countries the political space remained relatively ill defined.

7
Standing for Office: Parties and their Candidates

Throughout Western Europe, parliaments are unrepresentative of their populations' social structure and this was also the case with post-communist parliaments, where striking change in the social composition of deputies was evident from the outset. We have noted that the Soviet concept of representation placed great stress on parliament as a reflection of the social character of the population. Although communist parliamentarians never provided a precise mirror image of their populations, their social composition was indeed wider than that characteristic of the West. Yet the composition of the new freely chosen legislatures was far narrower than that of their communist predecessors; generally, it became more so with successive elections. The speed with which the new parliaments came to resemble their Western counterparts was a feature of post-communist political transformation, though the resemblance was far from exact. There were also some considerable differences between countries.

The idea that the composition of parliament matters was not simply a Soviet construct. It was deeply rooted in the class politics of the nineteenth century, with both bourgeois and working-class demands for representation. We saw in Chapter 1 that philosophers like Jeremy Bentham pioneered views that a diverse parliamentary make-up would better represent the multitude of social interests. The first social democratic deputies were indeed drawn largely from working-class trade unionists and their entry broadened the representative basis of the early democratic parliaments. In Britain about three-quarters of Labour members of parliament were rank-and-file workers in the period 1918–31.[1] Yet their numbers diminished rapidly in the post-war period, and legislatures in Western Europe became increasingly unrepresentative of the societies they served. Everywhere both deputies and candidates were preponderantly of higher socio-economic status and more educated than the wider population.[2] How far this resulted from candidate-selection procedures is not clear. However, legislators' profiles are well documented: the law, business, and education provided the most numerous deputies in stable European democracies.[3]

As the concept of class representation waned in Western Europe and found little reflection in party practice, many scholars justified an élitist concept of parliament. Eric Nordlinger vigorously attacked the 'social theory of representation': If deputies 'typical of the class of people who elected the representative' sat in parliaments, this would lead to representation by 'men [*sic*] with typical minimal educational training and average intellectual abilities'.[4] He argued that the performance of government would suffer and thus its effectiveness and stability. Such intellectually impoverished representatives would be no match for clever civil servants, thereby reducing the 'authenticity' of democratic government.[5] Nordlinger's prejudice and élitism shine through the whole passage, with his assumption that the less educated are intellectually inferior (and that deputies would perforce be men). His views dovetail nicely with the élitist views of conservative parties, denying the salience of class and presenting themselves as best equipped to serve the public good.

Iain McLean has argued more neutrally that the microcosmic concept of representation is incompatible with a principal-agent view of representation: Either one favours a parliament reflective of society (composition) or one stresses the ability of parliament to act properly in the interests of its citizens (outcomes).[6] However, it is not clear why one should preclude the other. Certainly most proponents of 'improved' social composition argue that the characteristics of representatives matter to outcomes. Hanna Pitkin observed almost forty years ago that they '... are interested in what the legislature does; they care about its composition precisely because they expect the composition to determine the activities'.[7] In other words the interests of social groups are best expressed by representatives drawn from their particular milieu. Yet if this approach provided the basis for both women and minorities to pursue the cause of representation (see Chapters 8 and 9), class issues faded away apparently unnoticed and unmourned.

By contrast, in Soviet-dominated Central and Eastern Europe the microcosmic approach to representation reigned supreme, and part of the avowed purpose of the diversity of these part-time deputies was precisely to prevent social distance and élitism. Deputies would be 'like' their electors and they would retain their ties with the workplace. It is often argued that the composition of these 'communist parliaments' did not matter, since the parliaments themselves met infrequently, perhaps for a single week in the course of the year; they were seen as mere 'rubber stamps' in the context of Communist Party domination.[8]

This is somewhat misleading, since the role of parliaments in the legislative process was often of some worth, particularly the work done in committees to improve legislation.[9] However, although committee work became increasingly important, not all deputies sat on committees or parliamentary working parties. Moreover, the 'mirror image' of society was never precise. In the USSR about one-third of deputies were usually senior party or government officials, re-elected at each session. Despite the centrality of the working class to Soviet ideology, only about one-third were manual workers.[10]

Yet we saw in Chapter 2 that in the debates on electoral systems for the first free elections, there was little echo of this fundamental principle, though the idea of 'personal' representation and constituency service remained strong. The notion of the part-time deputy in constant touch with electors was implicitly rejected in favour of working bodies of full-time parliamentarians. Only in the Ukraine and to a lesser extent in Russia did the concept of social representation surface, both directly and indirectly through debates on the rights of social organisations to nominate candidates. The debate seemed more about local networks and power centres, however, than about the character of those who would stand. The profile of candidates and deputies in those countries was not more working class than elsewhere. Indeed, the reverse was true.

We cannot address the issue of class directly, but occupation stands as a relevant proxy. Occupational data are far from complete, but they provide an indication of the general profile of the candidates that stood in many post-communist elections, as well as the resulting composition of parliaments. In some countries candidates were required to provide information about their jobs, their age, and perhaps also their educational qualifications. This was not always the case, nor was it always compulsory.

The data presented here are based largely on the self-defined occupations listed by candidates themselves. Sometimes individuals reported changes in their occupation from one election to another, for example where deputies took up business opportunities or redefined themselves as politicians. To some extent we can also supplement these data with education as another broad indicator of class. Even where candidates were not required to provide details of their education, the practice of indicating one's academic titles was prevalent in Hungary, Slovakia, and the Czech Republic.

In our categories workers include both blue-collar (manual) and white-collar (non-manual) workers. State officials are those employed by the government at both national and local level (but not incumbent deputies). Professionals include lawyers, economists, teachers, academics, doctors and others such as psychologists employed in health care, scientists, engineers, and technology specialists, as well as journalists and writers. Those engaged in business activities could not be disaggregated into public and private sector employment by self-description, so this category embraces both old-style managers of state enterprises, as well as new entrepreneurs, both large and small.

Candidate selection

Because we lack information about the pool of aspiring candidates, we have no way of judging how far selectors sought particular qualities, nor indeed the size or nature of the pool from which they drew. Candidate-selection procedures were rather different in the first elections and perhaps also in the second, though data are sparse. Mixed electoral systems (Hungary, Lithuania, Russia, Bulgaria in 1990, and the Ukraine after 1998) required two sets of decisions: whether and whom to place in the single-member districts and the selection and ranking of candidates on party lists. In Hungary the complex linkages of the system meant that parties needed to maintain the same identity in each element. Elsewhere parties could decide whether or not a district campaign would promote their identity for the list element, while individuals could decide whether the party label would help or hinder their success in a particular district. Parties allied for the list element often stood separately in single-member districts.

At first new parties often struggled to find candidates, so that selection procedures were rather open. In Central Europe the communists generally pressed for speedy elections precisely to capitalise on the lack of organisational resources of their opponents. In Poland's semi-competitive election of 1989, Solidarity used networks of local personal contacts, including priests, to recommend prospective candidates. In Estonia in 1992 only Isamaa and the Popular Front were able to run virtually a full slate of candidates. Indeed, although initially large numbers of contenders took part in all countries, few proved able to mount national campaigns. In Poland's first free election 111 election committees fielded candidates, but only nine stood in all 37 constituencies.

Czechoslovakia lacked willing candidates in 1990 and 1992. Indeed in 1990 both Civic Forum and Public against Violence recruited well-known actors and artists to gain greater visibility, placing these popular figures low on party lists because they did not actually wish to become members of parliament. When a number were 'accidentally' elected through the use of preference votes, they resigned their seats.[11] But David Olson still found in interviews with Czechoslovak deputies that 'at least some members of the Federal Assembly had (had) neither the wish nor the expectation' of election.[12] In Hungary twelve parties, including the Young Democrats (Fidesz), met the conditions for submitting a national list in 1990. But Fidesz managed only 79 candidates in Hungary's 176 single-member districts.[13] In Russia's 1993 election it proved difficult to gain the required signatures both for single-member districts (1 per cent of the electorate) and for registering as an 'electoral association' (100,000 signatures), with allegations of official obstruction and malpractice.[14] Even the most significant parties were absent from a high proportion of the 225 single-member constituencies. Russia's Choice fielded the largest number with 101 candidates, while Yabloko was second with 82.

However, selection was not entirely an ad hoc process, even in Central Europe in 1990. Indeed, a sample of 1240 Hungarian candidates (of 3507) in 1990 perceived local community activities and prominence arising from their jobs as the key reasons for their selection. In the successor Socialist

Party (MSzP) almost two-thirds attributed their nomination to these factors. For the opposition parties an 'oppositionist past' was also important.[15] Many deputies had strong local roots, winning in the counties of their birth.[16]

Similarly in Czechoslovakia a core of dissidents were available for candidate selection in 1990. Jiri Pehe argued that subsequently a record of dissidence was not enough, especially for those unable to improve their skills and qualifications because of communist repression.[17] But it was also the case that a number of former dissidents opted for parties that subsequently failed to make an impression. The Civic Movement was crushed by Klaus's Civic Democratic Party in 1992, when it failed to reach the 5 per cent electoral hurdle.

We would certainly expect candidate-selection difficulties to be a short-term factor where parties maintained an existence over successive elections and began to develop their structures and procedures. In 1994 in Hungary none of the six major parties 'complained about a lack of candidates'.[18] Yet when parties split, they needed to find candidates to replace those who had departed, and new parties needed to find new candidates or poach them from others. Certainly in many countries by no means all candidates were necessarily party members. In 2002 the new Slovak Alliance of New Citizens was not untypical in fielding media and sports personalities in a list openly 'put together to attract the voters'.[19]

In Russia the problem of placing candidates persisted, especially in single-member districts. This reflected the size of the country, but also the weak organisational capacity of both new and existing parties. In 1995, 187 candidates stood for Zhirinovskii's Liberal Democrats, 104 candidates for Our Home is Russia, and 129 for the Communists. Large numbers of Independents still contested single-member districts. In 1999 the position was similar: the Communist Party led the field with 129 candidates, then Yabloko with 114, while the 'party of power' Unity could manage only 31. Unity's campaign experts in consultation with regional governors recruited candidates for the party list,[20] but even where Unity (and also Fatherland-All Russia) had the support of a regional governor, it did not manage to field candidates in all the single-member districts in that region.[21]

The composition of the first parliaments depended of course on the outcome of the election and thus on the recruitment practices of those winning seats. In the fully free regime-choice elections the number of first-time deputies was high. In Czechoslovakia just over 1 per cent of those elected to the Federal Assembly in 1990 had served in the last parliament. In Hungary only 5 per cent of deputies had previous parliamentary experience. Continuity in turn depended partly on the willingness of incumbents to stand again, as well as on their success when faced with new challengers.

Where parties dominate, as with PR list systems, the composition of parliament is a function of the candidate-selection processes of victorious parties. Losing parties may have quite different candidate profiles. Certainly a degree of fluidity was to be expected in subsequent elections, but whether parties would select different types of candidates remained unpredictable. In fact we shall see that there were considerable variations in the candidate profiles of different parties.

In the Czech Republic the Civic Democrats (ODS), the communists, and the Christian Democrats (KDU–ČSL) developed highly centralised selection procedures, as did the Movement for Democratic Slovakia (HZDS) and the Christian Democrats (KDH) in Slovakia. Most deputies were party activists before being selected to stand for office. But ODS yielded some control of nomination and list construction to local bodies, with the centre retaining a veto, precisely to promote deputies' communication with their constituencies.[22] In the Czech Republic parties saw an 'increase in the homogeneity of their representatives'. This, along with the fact that longer-established parties could distribute selective incentives to their members, whether in the form of patronage or for opposition parties 'in the increasingly routine and complex process of candidate selection', also enhanced party cohesion within parliament.[23] We saw earlier that no Czech deputies left their party after the 1998 elections.

Hungarian parties moved rapidly not only to develop pools of potential candidates but also to establish mechanisms for their recruitment and selection practices.[24] The liberal Free Democrats (SzDSz) administered central tests to potential candidates, and those receiving the required minimum score constituted the candidate pool for local party organisations.[25] Both Hungary and the Czech Republic began to reflect Western Europe practice, where local party activism and local government experience proved stepping stones to national politics.[26] By 1998 in Hungary 29 per cent of deputies had some background in local politics.[27] In Poland and Estonia there was less evidence of such institutionalisation.[28]

Where new parties emerged, much depended on their origins. In Bulgaria the Simeon II Movement was a genuinely new formation. Its need (for technical reasons of electoral registration) to form an electoral coalition with two small groupings also provided some ready candidates. In Russia and the Ukraine, where 'parties of power' were a characteristic feature, the situation was more akin to a shuffling of an old deck of cards. They chose prominent individuals to head their national lists (initially three top names appeared on federal lists in the Russian ballot).

We have already noted earlier that in Russia 'parties' were often simply shifting electoral alliances. In 1999 Unity had no institutional form; it held its own founding congress only ten weeks before the election. The new Union of Right Forces was associated with former Prime Minister Kirienko and former Deputy Prime Minister Yegor Gaidar of Russia's Choice (later Russia's Democratic Choice) and was also a supporter of Putin; it combined four associations under its new name. Fatherland-All Russia, created by the mayor of Moscow Yuri Luzhkov (Fatherland) and a group of regional governors (the All Russia Movement) combined five. Candidate selection was in part a process of negotiations among the notables of these associations. Luzhkov was also said to have used his group's (temporary) popularity 'to solicit additional backing from ambitious politicians, guaranteeing a seat in the Duma by offering a high place on the Fatherland list'.[29] This was not an isolated phenomenon: many Russian 'parties' received funding from powerful business interests, and these 'oligarchs' also influenced candidate selection.[30]

The occupational profile of candidates

What kind of profile did we expect to find among candidates and in the new parliaments? Unfortunately although one can generate hypotheses about the dynamics of change, we cannot test them satisfactorily. We lack candidate data for many early elections, and we have no occupational data for the interesting cases of Bulgaria and Romania and little for Hungary. Slovenia was not part of our original data sets, and although much information is available, we have lacked resources to code it. Even when supplemented by valuable research done within the region itself, we need to stress the implications of our patchy data and the lack of a sustained picture over time.

In a general sense however we anticipated some linking of the composition of both candidate pools and parliaments to the speed of political and economic transformation and the decisiveness of the break with communism. Where new élites came rapidly to the fore, we expected them to bear the marks of opposition-experience. Ágh referred to 'hopelessly élite parties', usually led by a small group of intellectuals and operating in a 'sociological vacuum'.[31] In the Czech Lands the core dissidents of Civic Forum were also intellectuals. However, the extensive mobilisation of Polish society, particularly through the Solidarity trade union, suggested a wider candidate pool than elsewhere.

The exclusionary citizenship policies of Latvia and Estonia (see Chapter 9) rapidly opened up new positions in the state administration and provided new opportunities for economic patronage. We noted the association of both the Estonian Coalition Party and the Reform Party with business élites (see Chapter 3), and we would expect some reflection of that in the parties' recruitment. The dominance of Lithuanians in Sajūdis suggested that this might also be a feature of politics there, as Russians were displaced from the bureaucracy, the police, the judiciary, and other state institutions. In Russia and the Ukraine, there was a blurring of 'new' (reformist) and old (conservative) élites and the continuing operation of widespread patronage networks.[32] So in the Baltic states and in Russia and the Ukraine we expected a higher proportion of government officials and those employed in the economy (from new entrepreneurs to enterprise directors seeking to gain or retain political capital) from winning parties, albeit for different reasons.

Thus we expected differences between the Central European countries and those of the former Soviet Union. Our anticipation of large numbers of highly educated professionals in the former stemmed from the greater openness of the new political process and the esteem in which such groups were held. Although professionals often earned less than skilled workers in the communist period, they still maintained their traditional high status.[33] In Poland academics and doctors were particularly prestigious, but engineers, journalists, lawyers, and teachers were also highly esteemed.[34]

Moreover in some countries the creative intelligentsia in particular – writers, historians, journalists – had a 'long tradition of political engagement', as well as a sense of historic mission.[35] In Czechoslovakia active dissidents were drawn largely from this stratum of society; it was they who provided the leadership of Civic Forum, effectively symbolised by the playwright-president Václav Havel. In Poland, Solidarity forged an effective alliance between workers and dissident intellectuals. Indeed, a 1984 report prepared for the Polish Communist Party's Politburo described the Academy of Science as a hotbed of opposition.[36] From the mid-1960s Hungary possessed a galaxy of critical intellectuals ranging from sociologists associated with the Budapest School, to popular literary figures and historians debating the nature of Hungarian nationhood.[37]

The communist parties increasingly came to value the importance of the new technical intelligentsia, and communist political élites had over time become better educated and more specialist.[38] Reformist elements came to dominate the Party in Hungary in the late 1980s, and they initiated the process of system-change from within. Indeed in Poland, Hungary, Czechoslovakia, and Bulgaria both sides of the Round Tables of 1989–90 were dominated by experts drawn from government ministries, universities, and specialist institutes.

In addition, many professionals had skills that were either directly or easily transferable to the new socio-economic environment. They faced fewer anxieties about job security. In addition to their expertise, they also possessed highly developed communication skills and subjective political confidence. This would suggest a substantial presence of doctors, academics, teachers, and lawyers. However, the communists' economic and political stress on industrial development gave technical specialists such as engineers a higher profile than in 'post-industrial' Western Europe. So although we expected a predominance of professionals, we also anticipated that many would come from a scientific or technical background.

We also expected candidates to differ depending on the type of party. It seemed likely that communist and successor parties with strong links to trades unions would have rather more workers than liberal parties appealing for radical economic transformation. Liberal parties would have increasing numbers of candidates drawn from the economic sector. At the same time we would clearly expect the 'parties of power' to maintain high proportions of state- and economy-based candidates. Radical populist and nationalist parties should also be less professional in their candidate corpus, if not necessarily in their leaders.[39]

Given vast opportunities for government patronage in both the state and the economic sphere, it seemed likely that successful parties would reflect this with changing candidate corpuses. This does not imply that parties would seek different types of candidates, since at a time of profound economic transformation and changing class structures, the same individuals often appeared later with a different occupational identification. However, according to this reasoning, parties contesting elections as incumbents should see more candidates drawn from the state sector, whether from jobs in national administration or local government. Parties that remained marginalised, either failing to cross electoral thresholds or entering parliament but with no prospect of holding office, would maintain more stable bodies of candidates.

The data we have on the first fully free elections are limited to three countries: Poland, Estonia, and Lithuania, along with some partial data for the Ukraine, Hungary, and Russia. In Poland (1991), the two Baltic states (1992 and 1993), Russia (1993), and the Ukraine (1994) these fully competitive elections came later than elsewhere, because of Poland's distinctive semi-competitive election in 1989 and because free post-Soviet elections awaited the break-up of the Soviet Union. Particularly in Poland, Estonia, and Lithuania former opposition elements were already represented in their respective parliaments and had assumed the role of incumbent governments – only in Hungary was the election a genuine 'new start' for political parties.

There were some striking differences (see Table 7.1) in these candidate profiles. Poland had a higher proportion of professional and working-class candidates, but a lower proportion of businesspersons, with state officials and the non-governmental sector largely absent. The Ukraine had the lowest proportion of professionals and the highest proportion drawn from the economy, providing another indirect confirmation of the continuing importance of old *nomenklatura* ties in both the economy and political life.[40] Other data from Russia indicated that there too nearly a quarter of all candidates in 1993 were involved in economic pursuits, including heads of large industrial enterprises, joint stock companies, funds, commercial banks, and the like.[41] Lithuania had as many state officials as professionals, along with the same low proportion of workers as in Estonia and the Ukraine.

Although different, the deputy profiles maintained these broad differences: Poland had a high proportion of professionals, with workers as the second-largest category. Reschová also reported that in Czechoslovakia's first federal parliament the number of political, state, and economic functionaries drastically fell and those from the technical and creative intelligentsia increased markedly.[42] In Estonia the largest group of deputies comprised state officials, with professionals in second place, followed by smaller proportions from

Table 7.1 Major occupational categories among candidates (C) and deputies (D) (%) in the first free elections

	Professional		State administrative officials		Business		Workers		Party & trade union officials	
	C	D	C	D	C	D	C	D	C	D
Hungary 1990[1]		67.0		4.4		8.0		3.6		1.6
Poland 1991	62.5	74.6	1.5	0.4	3.9	4.1	21.2	10.2	0.1	0.9
Estonia 1992	36.5	27.7	23.8	41.6	14.8	9.9	7.6	3.0	6.7	11.9
Lithuania 1992	41.4	47.5	41.4	47.5	13.1	14.9	7.3	4.3	3.9	7.8
Russia 1993[2]		15.5		18.0		10.6				17.3
Ukraine 1994[3]	27.9	22.3	20.8	33.7	21.9	26.7	6.3	4.0	1.1	1.8[4]

[1] Derived from G. Loewenburg, 'The New Political Leadership of Central Europe: The Example of the New Hungarian National Assembly', p. 37. [2] Dmitri Orlov, 'Portret dumy w tsifrakh', *Rossiiskie vesti*, 10 January 1994, cited in Peter Lentini, 'Elections and Political Order in Russia: The 1993 Elections to the State Duma', *The Journal of Communist Studies and Transition Politics*, vol. 10, no. 2, June 1994, p. 180. [3] Excludes 86 cases of missing data. [4] Party only.

business, and political parties or trades unions. Lithuania had as many state officials as professionals. This suggests that the displacement of Russian bureaucrats through the patronage opportunities of the new parties did indeed play a role.

In the Ukraine the largest group in the Rada was drawn from state officialdom, but the Ukraine had a higher proportion from the economy than any other country. We should remember, however, that many of these candidates stood as Independents: almost two-thirds of victorious state officials had no declared party affiliation, and over half the winning enterprise directors and administrators were also non-party.

Some of these apparent anomalies arise from the nature of the data themselves. In Poland (and surely not only in Poland) many candidates apparently preferred to define themselves by educational background or previous occupation. Even the social democrats' leader Aleksander Kwaśniewski described himself as a journalist, while the hardened apparatchik Leszek Miller was a 'political scientist' rather than a politician. Nor did those who stood for the Solidarity trade union define themselves as trade unionists. Yet Wojciech Arkuszewski and Stanisław Baran, an 'economist' and a 'machinist' in their election papers, were 'trade union activists' in their parliamentary profiles. Indeed, Włodzimierz Wesołowski calculated that in fact 13.9 per cent of deputies in the Polish 1991 Sejm were party politicians or trade union activists.[43] A close examination of Polish parliamentary profiles broadly confirmed Wesołowski's findings of more diversity than their candidate papers suggested. This draws attention to the problems both of interpreting data and of assuming that cross-national data are directly comparable.

Data on educational qualifications are limited, but it is clear from the occupations represented that they were generally very high. In Hungary a sample of 1240 candidates (of 3507) in 1990 reinforced the view that candidates were disproportionately well educated: 79.7 per cent had university or college degrees, with the largest group coming from the humanities, especially in the Hungarian Democratic Forum, the Hungarian Socialist Party, and the Alliance of Free Democrats. Among deputies 89.4 per cent had higher educational qualifications.[44] In Russia all but two deputies elected in 1993 had completed higher education.[45] In Poland in 1991, 77.4 per cent of deputies had at least a first degree, with 18.7 per cent a general or vocational secondary education and 3.9 per cent only primary schooling.

The relatively low proportion of workers in Poland (if high by comparison) may seem surprising, given the country's long history of worker activism. However, there was already a sense in 1989 that Solidarity had ceded politics to the intellectuals. Many noted worker-activists, including Solidarity's leader Lech Wałęsa, decided not to stand for parliament at the Round Table election. When Solidarity stood not as a party but as a trade union in 1991, about one-third of its candidates (36.9 per cent) were urban workers. Despite its own strong trade union links the Democratic Left

Table 7.2   Occupations of candidates and deputies in the second elections (%)

	Professionals		State officials		Business		Workers		Party/union	
	C	D	C	D	C	D	C	D	C	D
Poland 1993	62.2	78.3	1.4	0.4	4.7	2.6	18.0	9.0	0.3	1.1
Hungary 1994		23.0[1]				18.8			13.3	
Estonia 1995	34.0	16.8	23.0	63.4	17.8	10.9	2.2	0.0	4.8	4.0
Russia 1995[2]	25.4	13.1	17.7	21.8	25.5	19.6	2.1	2.0	8.1	5.3
Lithuania 1996	39.1	43.1	19.6	35.8	23.2	9.5	3.5	1.5	2.3	4.4
Ukraine 1998[3]	16.8	9.9	18.7	54.2	17.7	22.5	2.8	1.6	1.8[4]	3.3[4]

[1] Teachers, writers, journalists, and lawyers only. Hungarian data are from G. Ilonszki, 'Consolidation of Hungarian Democracy' in Dirk Berg-Schlosser and Raivo Vetik eds, *Perspectives on Democratic Consolidation in Central and Eastern Europe*, Boulder: East European Monographs, 2001, p. 99. [2] 5.2 per cent of candidates and 34 per cent of deputies were incumbents whose previous occupation is not known. [3] Includes missing 1008 (19.2 per cent) candidates. [4] Party only.

(SLD) fielded far fewer, with 19.6 per cent. We will discuss differing recruitment by party in Table 7.2.

With the second free elections professionals remained the largest single group of candidates, save in the Ukraine where recruits from the state and the economy were more numerous. The disparity between Poland and other states still appeared considerable – in Poland's large proportion of professionals, the greater involvement of industrial workers, and the very limited role of business and state officials (but with these latter categories assuredly understated). Estonia drew a greater proportion of its candidates from central and local government than was the case elsewhere.

The differences were even greater in the composition of parliaments than for the candidate corpus, with Estonia and Lithuania showing large increases in the proportion of deputies drawn from the state administration, whether at national or local level. We noted above that this is commensurate with the opportunity to restaff the administration caused by the displacement of Soviet officials. The Ukraine also had a very high proportion of deputies coming from the state administration. In Poland and Lithuania professionals formed the largest contingent of deputies. However, in the Russian Duma businesspersons constituted the largest group.

In the third elections Poland still provided the highest proportion of professionals among its candidates; but the Slovak figure was certainly comparable, while the Czech was far lower (see Table 7.3). Russia had the lowest, though not so low as the Ukraine in 1998. Lithuania retained the highest proportion of state officials. Both the Czech Republic and Slovakia had higher proportions of working-class candidates than Poland; but these three constituted an obvious contrast with Russia and the two Baltic states. The picture for the

Table 7.3 Occupations of candidates and deputies in the third elections (%)

	Professionals		State officials		Business		Workers		Party/union	
	C	D	C	D	C	D	C	D	C	D
Poland 1997	54.4	64.3	2.9	6.7	6.3	4.3	18.3	7.4	0.7	5.5
Estonia 1999	36.6	20.8	20.4	63.4	21.1	6.9	4.1	1.0	4.0	5.0
Russia 1999[1]	22.6	12.4	19.7	22.2	28.1	19.9	2.5	0.5	5.2	4.3
Lithuania 2000	29.8	28.4	24.9	24.1	31.3	36.9	2.4	0.7	2.0	7.8
Slovakia 1994	53.7	58.7	5.4	6.0	11.9	3.3	18.8	10.7	3.7	18.7
Czech R 1996[2]	37.0	27.0	10.5	14.5	15.4	8.0	23.3	5.5	2.1	8.5

[1] 6.7 per cent of candidates and 34.8 per cent of deputies were incumbents whose occupational background is unknown. [2] 2.3 per cent of candidates and 17 per cent of deputies were incumbents whose previous occupation is unknown. 1.1 per cent of candidates and 1.5 per cent of deputies were unspecified 'directors'; they could be businesspersons or directors of state bureaux.

fourth elections, however, does not enable much direct comparability, since Estonia and Lithuania had not had their fourth elections at the time of writing (see Table 7.4).

Where we can view changes over several elections there are some considerable differences. In Estonia the candidate corpus looked remarkably stable. The major change was the steady increase in candidates from the business sphere at successive elections. The composition of deputies changed far more, both in comparison to candidates and from election to election. We can note the particular success of state officials in standing for winning parties and the near absence of working-class deputies in the last two parliaments (see Table 7.5).

In Lithuania by contrast the proportion of state officials standing as candidates fluctuated, while the proportion represented in parliament actually decreased. Deputies coming from the economy, on the other hand, rose

Table 7.4 Candidates and deputies in the fourth free elections (% total candidates)

	Professionals		State officials		Business		Workers		Party/union	
	C	D	C	D	C	D	C	D	C	D
Poland 2001	57.0	73.0	2.6	2.8	6.3	4.1	20.3	7.3	0.3	1.5
Slovakia 1998	52.0	78.0	3.5	4.0	14.5	6.7	23.2	4.7	1.2	4.7
Czech R 1998[1]	33.8	57.0	11.5	14.5	17.4	7.5	21.3	2.5	1.7	8.5

[1] 1 per cent of candidates and 8 per cent of deputies were incumbents whose previous occupation is not known.

Table 7.5 Changes in the occupational composition of candidates (C) and deputies (D) (%) over successive elections

	Professionals		State officials		Business		Workers		Party/union	
	C	D	C	D	C	D	C	D	C	D
Estonia 1992	36.5	27.7	23.8	41.6	14.8	9.9	7.6	3.0	6.7	11.9
Estonia 1995	34.0	16.8	23.0	63.4	17.8	10.9	2.2	0.0	4.8	4.0
Estonia 1999	36.6	20.8	20.4	63.4	21.1	6.9	4.1	1.0	4.0	5.0
Lithuania 1992	41.4	47.5	41.4	47.5	13.1	14.9	7.3	4.3	3.9	7.8
Lithuania 1996	39.1	43.1	19.6	35.8	23.2	9.5	3.5	1.5	2.3	4.4
Lithuania 2000	29.8	28.4	24.9	24.1	31.3	36.9	2.4	0.7	2.0	7.8
Slovakia 1994	53.7	58.7	5.4	6.0	11.9	3.3	18.8	10.7	3.7	18.7
Slovakia 1998	52.0	78.0	4.0	4.0	14.5	6.7	23.2	4.7	1.2	4.7
Slovakia 2002	40.1	62.0	6.6	10.0	22.5	17.3	19.2	2.6	0.8	7.3
Poland 1991	62.5	74.6	1.5	0.4	3.9	4.1	21.2	10.2	0.1	0.9
Poland 1993	62.2	78.3	1.4	0.4	4.7	2.6	18.0	9.0	0.3	1.1
Poland 1997	54.5	64.3	2.9	6.7	6.3	4.3	18.3	7.4	0.7	5.5
Poland 2001	57.1	73.0	2.6	2.8	6.3	4.1	22.6	7.3	0.3	1.5

sharply in 2000. In Poland, as in Estonia, the candidate profile did not change much from election to election, even with the formation of new Polish parties in 2001. But unlike Estonia, the deputy profile also remained rather similar, though the proportion of professionals fell in 1997, then rose again; and the proportion of workers never reached its high of 1991. In Poland and Slovakia more professionals stood as candidates than in the two Baltic states, but the proportion dropped sharply in Slovakia in 2002.

Deputy profiles did change, but this appeared to have more to do with differences between parties than changes in candidate recruitment practices. 'Ironically, workers' interests have been openly and explicitly underrepresented even though Solidarity and its communist era trade union equivalent, OPZZ, have been part of every (Polish) government since 1989.'[46] But this was not because working-class candidates did not stand, it was because fewer of them won. Moreover, more workers sat as deputies in the Polish Sejm than in most other parliaments.

The professionals

Professionals played a clear role in political mobilisation and they were the largest single group of candidates in all Polish, Estonian, Czech, and Slovak elections, and in the Ukraine in 1994 and Lithuania in 1996. We do not know whether they were more prepared to stand as candidates, as seems likely (see above), or whether parties were eager to select them. The differences noted above between Central Europe and the former Soviet Union also apply to the type of professionals who sought a role in politics. Table 7.6 shows the kinds of professionals who stood as a proportion of the whole candidate corpus, while Table 7.7 shows these types as a proportion of candidate-professionals. They include only those countries for which we have complete data: Poland, Lithuania, Estonia, and independent Slovakia.

It was not unexpected to find that the candidate pool included fewer lawyers than in Western Europe or more scientists and engineers. But it was interesting to note that the Balts differed not only in having a smaller share of candidate-professionals but also in the type of occupations they represented. This could be linked to the lesser role of Estonians and Lithuanians in the industrial sector during the communist period. It could also result from scientists, technologists, and engineers rapidly redefining themselves as businesspeople.

Political parties and their candidates

We can begin to unravel some elements of the composition of parliament and candidate corpuses by examining the political parties themselves. Radical parties, whether of the left or right, were far more likely to field worker-candidates. They were also less likely to cross electoral thresholds, making parliaments less representative of their societies than was the candidate corpus. Of course radical parties achieved a parliamentary presence in many countries, if only fleetingly (see Chapter 5). It was often the fragmented nature of many extremist groups that led to their electoral defeat.

In Slovakia, for example, there was a clear association between left-wing ideology and worker-candidates. The break-up of the Czechoslovak Communist Party had resulted in a variety of splinter groups, as well as the small Communist Party of Slovakia (KSS) and the major successor party, the SDL'. The hard-line Association of Communist Workers split from the SDL' and stood in 1994 as defenders of the working class. In 1994 five avowedly workers' parties of various ilk contested the elections and accounted for 42 per cent of working-class candidates. Seventy-one per cent of candidates of the Association of Slovak Workers (ZRS) were urban workers (mostly manual workers), and 37 per cent of those of the Communist Party (but 9 per cent of Communist Party candidates were pensioners, who may well have been workers). The picture in the centre-left SDL' was rather different. Only 5.2 per cent of Common Choice candidates (the electoral alliance dominated by the SDL') were workers, but none of its 18 deputies. It was the success of the ZRS that led to a (relatively) high proportion of working-class deputies: more than half came from the ZRS.

In 1998 also, five workers' parties (having undergone some reshuffling and changes of name) accounted for almost half (48.6 per cent) of the worker-candidates, but four failed to reach parliament.[47] In addition to its

Table 7.6 Professional candidates (% candidates)

	Slovakia 1994	Slovakia 1998	Slovakia 2002	Poland 1991	Poland 1993	Poland 1997	Poland 2001	Lithuania 1992	Lithuania 1996	Lithuania 2000	Estonia 1992	Estonia 1995	Estonia 1999
Law	3.6	3.9	3.9	7.2	6.1	6.3	4.8	2.0	2.4	1.6	1.6	1.6	2.4
Economics	6.3	8.0	7.7	5.7	7.3	6.6	7.6	3.9	2.5	2.0	1.4	1.4	2.5
Education	7.4	9.7	9.4	10.2	9.4	11.2	10.8	5.3	7.4	7.0	3.7	3.7	7.4
Health	7.9	6.4	5.7	6.9	5.7	7.6	6.5	5.6	6.2	4.9	4.0	4.0	6.2
Academic	3.8	2.4	2.0	2.3	3.2	3.7	2.6	14.4	5.6	5.3	8.3	8.3	5.6
Arts	1.4	1.0	0.4	1.4	1.1	0.9	0.9	3.5	0.9	0.5	1.9	1.9	0.9
Writing & journalism	2.0	2.1	1.1	2.5	1.7	2.2	1.8	3.8	3.4	2.0	5.1	5.1	3.4
Science, engineering & technology	18.6	21.3	18.1	22.7	25.9	18.6	16.3	6.3	8.4	4.1	5.9	5.9	8.4
Other professions	2.5	2.9	6.2	5.3	4.9	4.3	5.5	1.6	3.4	2.0	7.2	7.2	3.4

Note: % is of total candidates whose occupation is known. Education excludes higher education.

Table 7.7 Candidates by type of profession (% professional candidates)

	Slovakia 1994	Slovakia 1998	Slovakia 2002	Poland 1991	Poland 1993	Poland 1997	Poland 2001	Lithuania 1992	Lithuania 1996	Lithuania 2000	Estonia 1992	Estonia 1995	Estonia 1999
Law	8.0	6.8	3.3	11.3	9.4	10.3	8.4	4.4	5.9	1.6	3.1	3.5	4.1
Economics	12.4	14.0	6.8	8.8	11.2	10.7	13.5	8.5	6.1	1.4	3.9	18.1	26.9
Education	19.1	16.6	8.1	15.9	14.3	18.3	19.1	11.4	18.5	3.7	10.0	13.4	19.7
Health	9.7	11.1	4.9	10.8	8.7	12.4	11.4	12.0	15.5	4.0	10.5	9.6	10.7
Academic	4.2	4.2	1.7	3.6	4.9	5.8	4.6	31.1	13.9	8.3	22.7	13.9	10.7
Arts	0.5	1.7	0.3	2.1	1.8	1.5	1.5	7.3	2.3	1.9	5.2	6.8	5.7
Writing & journalism	2.4	3.7	1.0	3.9	2.7	3.6	3.2	8.2	8.4	5.1	14.0	12.2	4.1
Science, engineering & technology	33.8	36.7	15.6	35.5	39.6	30.4	28.7	13.5	20.8	5.9	14.0	6.6	8.9
Other professions	9.9	4.9	5.3	8.2	7.5	7.0	9.6	3.5	8.6	7.2	16.6	15.8	9.3

[1] 0.3 per cent not known.

working-class candidates (27.8 per cent), the small, orthodox Communist Party also increased its pensioner-candidates (23.4 per cent). Seventeen per cent of SDL' candidates were workers, though again no SDL' worker won a seat. Of those offering full lists, the Association of Slovak Workers' (ZRS) fielded the highest proportion of workers (53.4 per cent), and the reduction in worker-deputies can be largely attributed to its failure to cross the electoral threshold. In 2002, eight left-wing contenders stood, but this time only the communists entered parliament. More than half the candidates of three parties were workers, but none of the three, including the ZRS, proved able to present a full slate of candidates. The Communist Party (KSS), with about one-third of its candidates drawn from the working class (but fewer pensioners – 6.7 per cent), elected eleven deputies, none of whom were workers.

The nationalist parties in Slovakia showed a rather different profile. Though dominated by professionals, their proportion of working-class candidates was greater than that of many left-wing parties. In 1994, 21.5 per cent of Slovak National Party (SNS) candidates were urban workers, falling slightly to 19.4 per cent in 1998. The 1998 candidate profile does not confirm the hypothesis that parties in office would see an increase in the number of state officials standing for election: under 1 per cent of SNS candidates defined themselves as working in national or local government posts. The ejection from office certainly had some effect: By 2002 the party had split, and it looked very different: the proportion of professionals had dropped to 46 per cent, and the proportion of workers fell to 12 per cent (see Table 7.10). Its counterpart the Real Slovak National Party (PSNS) bore a greater resemblance to its parent in the proportion of working-class candidates, but it too lost professionals and gained a stronger business presence. Neither of these two incarnations crossed the threshold. As with other non-mainstream parties the tiny Slovak National Community (*Slovenská národná jednota*) fielded just a handful of candidates in 1998, but 56 per cent were urban workers.

In the Czech Republic working-class candidates stood in some numbers for a variety of parties. Still, in 1996 the highest proportion was to be found among the radical right Republicans: 52 per cent of their candidates worked in manual or clerical occupations (about half and half). But one-third of candidates of the single-issue Pensioners' Party were workers, and it seems safe to assume that many pensioner-candidates were retired workers. One-quarter of candidates for the regional Czech–Moravian Union were workers. These figures were not dissimilar to those of the radical left-wing parties: 35 per cent of candidates of the Party of the Democratic Left and one-quarter of the Communist Party's were workers. However, only 17.9 per cent of the Social Democrats' team were workers. Neither the pensioners, the regionalists, nor the Democratic Left entered parliament. It was the Social Democrats, (four deputies) along with the Republicans (four) who provided most worker-parliamentarians: the Civic Democratic Party had two and the communists one.

In 1998 the Democratic Union had the highest proportion of worker-candidates (39.4 per cent), followed by the Republicans (36.6 per cent), and the Greens (27.4 per cent), with the National-Social Party (*Česka Strana Narodne Socialni*, 24.7 per cent) and the Communist Party about equal (24.8 per cent), and the Pensioners just below (23.3 per cent). Of these parties, only the Communists crossed the threshold. The victorious Social Democrats recruited more professionals this time (53.4 per cent) and fewer workers (14.9 per cent). Even the emphatically liberal Civic Democrats (ODS), with only 7.3 per cent of its candidates drawn from among urban workers, managed to elect as many worker-deputies (3 of 63) as did the ČSSD – now with only 3 out of 74 seats. The highest list place of a winning worker was second (the KSČM). But the Communists improved their performance in 2002 and though their worker-candidates fell slightly, the number of communist worker-deputies rose to five.

In Poland also it was the case that worker-candidates were more common in populist and extremist parties. However, the position there was somewhat different for two main reasons. First, the radical left disappeared rapidly, almost without trace. Although the Polish Socialist Party remained active after its withdrawal from the Solidarity movement, it proved unable to mount national election campaigns, while the old communist Polish United Workers' Party (PZPR) did not generate a hard-line left party submitting itself to electoral competition. Secondly, whereas urban workers predominated elsewhere, in Poland there were also peasant parties recruiting candidates from rural areas. Although the Polish Peasant Party's longevity had seen the growth of a strong technical professional element, other rural parties, including the Peasant Alliance (PL) in 1991 and also Self-Defence (SO) from 1993 onwards, numbered peasants and farmers among their candidates.

Of the 'parties' fielding candidates in most constituencies in 1991, the populist Confederation for Independent Poland (KPN) had both the highest number (143) and the highest proportion of worker-candidates (38.6 per cent). We have noted that Solidarity itself – standing as a trade union – had rather fewer workers (36.9 per cent). Yet Polish workers were not inactive politically: they made up 27.6 per cent of candidates standing for the 'non-parties' – the myriad local groupings, trades unions, and pressure groups that also contested the election – while another 6 per cent came from the rural sector (farmers, peasants and agricultural workers). They were also a clear presence among the entities that could be at least vaguely described as 'parties': 17.3 per cent of their candidates came from the urban working class and 8.7 per cent from the agrarian sector. Despite its strong trade union links, the SLD was not notably worker-oriented in its candidate pool, though by the standards of the region's other social democratic parties it was initially quite favourable to worker-candidates (19.6 per cent), as Table 7.8

Table 7.8 Candidates of left-wing parties by type of occupation (%)

	Urban workers	Business	State officials, local and national	Party/union leaders and officials	Professionals
ZRS, Slovakia 1994	69.1	6.4	0.0	0.0	16.0
ZRS, Slovakia 2002	66.3	2.7	0.0	0.0	8.4
ZRS, Slovakia 1998	56.6	2.7	2.7	0.0	35.1
KSS, Slovakia 1994	37.7	7.4	4.1	0.0	33.6
KSS, Slovakia 2002	37.3	15.7	6.7	0.7	33.3
KPRF, Russia 1993[1]	36.0				31.0[2]
KSS, Slovakia 1998	27.8	15.3	7.3	1.5	20.4
KSČM, Czech R 1996	25.2	13.1	4.7	8.4	37.6
KSČM, Czech R 1998	24.8	13.8	6.4	6.7	36.6
KSČM, Czech R 2002	22.2	15.8	8.8	10.5	37.1
SLD, Poland 1991	19.6	1.0	0.5	0.0	71.2
ČSSD, Czech R 1996	17.9	19.6	13.5	7.8	32.1
SDL', Slovakia 1998	17.3	7.3	1.3	2.7	64.0
ČSSD, Czech R 1998	14.9	11.1	10.8	2.7	53.4
SLD, Poland 1993	14.6	2.1	1.0	0.0	75.9
SLD, Poland 1997	14.3	6.2	11.3	3.3	55.0
SDA, Slovakia 2002	13.3	19.3	12.0	0.7	46.0
Munkáspárt, Hungary 2002[3]	13.1	37.7	6.6	3.3	13.1
SLD–UP, Poland 2001	12.2	2.1	2.3	0.3	77.2
KPU, Ukraine 1994	11.8	24.1	13.1	0.3	28.3
SDL', Slovakia 2002	9.3	18.0	23.3	1.3	47.3
SDL', Slovakia 1994[4]	5.2	8.6	8.6	13.8	55.2
LDDP, Lithuania 1992	2.4	19.2	12.0	10.8	41.0
KPRF, Russia 1995	2.0	15.4	13.4	1.3	16.1
LDDP, Lithuania 1996	1.9	15.9	48.6	5.6	27.1
LDDP, Lithuania 2001	1.7	37.9	25.9	3.4	29.3

Note: Russia 1995 16 per cent of incumbents not known; Russia 1999 42 per cent of candidates not known. *Italics* designate social democratic parties, including successor social democrats.
[1] From Richard Sakwa, 'The Russian Elections of December 1993', *Europe-Asia Studies*, vol. 47, no. 2, March 1995, p. 206. [2] Academics only. [3] Proportion of total candidates providing personal data. [4] Stood as element of Common Choice.

shows. This candidate share dropped slowly but steadily in 1993, 1997, and 2001.

In 1993 the KPN again fielded the highest number (230) of worker-candidates (33 per cent), though Solidarity, with 209, had the highest proportion (38 per cent). The Populist Party X and Self-Defence (SO) had

29 per cent and 17 per cent urban workers respectively, but SO's peasant orientation was reflected in its high proportion of farmers, peasants, and agricultural workers (37 per cent). The tiny fascistoid Polish National Commonwealth (PWN) could not find candidates to stand in all constituencies, but it drew 42 per cent of its candidates from urban workers.

This pattern was broadly maintained in 1997, though KPN was largely defunct, with one main wing incorporated into AWS and the second withdrawing from the election at the last minute. Despite the fact that AWS depended very heavily on its trade union base, workers were squeezed out by leaders of the small but numerous constituent parties: only 13.7 per cent of AWS candidates were workers. Self-Defence (SO) increased the proportion of urban workers in 1997, broadly maintaining it in 2001, when it made its national breakthrough and entered parliament.

Almost one-third of candidates who stood for the League of Polish Families in 2001 were workers, including 7.6 per cent from agriculture. About 35 per cent of SO's candidates came from the rural economy, but another 25 per cent were urban workers. The Polish Peasant Party (PSL) drew just 13.7 per cent of its candidates from peasants, farmers, and agricultural workers. Its largest contingent by far (24.5 per cent) came from scientific and technical experts, especially agricultural engineers. The idiosyncratic populist Alternative – in some measure the descendant of the KPN – saw the highest proportion of urban workers, with almost 53.5 per cent, while another 3.5 per cent were rural workers or peasants. Over half the candidates of the (still tiny) PWN were manual workers.

Candidates of left-wing parties

Table 7.8 shows that radical left-wing parties drew heavily on urban workers for their candidates, and workers were also a presence in many communist parties. Social democrats (including transformed successor parties) had fewer workers, and the share of worker-candidates declined over time. We cannot account for the extraordinary decline in working-class candidacies in Russia; it may simply reflect different reporting bases of the data.

The most solid workers' party was the Association of Slovak Workers. It fielded more professionals in 1998 after its spell in power, but this did not endure, and by 2002 it was a shadow of its former self. The Hungarian Workers' party Munkáspárt, the orthodox offshoot of the former ruling party, looks out of place so low in the table. But workers may have been less inclined to provide electors with the voluntary personal statements that are the source of these data, and it also fielded large numbers (24.6 per cent) of pensioners, many of whom were probably retired workers.

Populist and extreme-right parties

Comparative data are sparse for the rather murky categories of populist and extreme-right parties (see Table 7.9). We saw in Chapter 3 that the populist

Table 7.9 Populist and extreme-right parties by candidate composition (%)

	Urban workers	Peasants, farmers & rural workers	Business	State officials	Professionals
Alternatywa, Poland 2001	53.3	3.5	5.2	1.4	32.3
Republicans, Czech R 1996	51.9	1.2	14.2	0.7	10.0
PWN, Poland 1993	42.1	9.5	2.1	3.2	40.0
Republicans, Czech R 1998	41.6	1.9	17.9	4.2	13.0
KPN, Poland 1991	38.6	4.5	2.1	0.8	49.5
PWN, Poland 1997	37.1	3.1	5.2	0.0	45.4
KPN, Poland 1993	33.0	4.7	7.5	1.9	44.7
Party X, Poland 1993	28.6	7.8	12.3	2.3	42.9
SO, Poland 1997	27.6	30.3	3.9	1.3	31.6
SO, Poland 2001	24.8	34.8	7.7	0.2	22.0
SO, Poland 1993	17.4	37.4	3.7	1.1	38.0
Smer, Slovakia 2002	4.0	0.0	34.7	4.7	54.0
HZDS, Slovakia 1994[1]	*6.1*	*0.5*	*5.2*	*8.2*	*70.6*
HZDS, Slovakia 1998	*6.0*	*1.3*	*3.3*	*5.3*	*82.7*
HZDS, Slovakia 2002	*6.0*	*0.0*	*25.3*	*11.3*	*48.0*

[1] With Agrarian Party.

category is a particularly controversial one, including disputes over how to categorise the Movement for Democratic Slovakia (HZDS). HZDS is included in italics in Table 7.9, and 'liberal populists' such as the Slovak Alliance of New Citizens have been excluded. While the profiles of most of these parties were rather similar, not only for the varied Polish parties but also for the Czech Republicans (data are not available for the Republican splinter groups for 2002), in Slovakia both Smer and HZDS were distinctive. The other populist and extreme-right parties attracted more urban workers than other parties and, save for Self-Defence (SO), which originated in the countryside, they recruited few candidates from the agrarian sector. They were not dominated by professionals as were other political parties, and there was a virtual absence of state functionaries.

We do not know the types of business with which candidates were associated, but they appeared to be drawn from small private-sector businesses. Most of these candidates designated themselves in a general sense as 'entrepreneurs' or 'traders' rather than 'directors' or 'managers'. In the Czech case this picture is confirmed by the absence of formal qualifications: In 1996 only 1.6 per cent of Republican candidates indicated the possession of academic qualifications (10 per cent claimed professional status); though this rose sharply to 8.8 per cent in 1998, the proportion was still very low compared to other parties in the Czech Republic. These parties were more similar to extreme-left parties than to any other. Both types looked far more like the 'ordinary folk' to whom they sought to appeal.

Nationalist parties

Radical nationalist parties, however, were less worker-based and (with sketchy data) apparently more highly educated than other radical parties (see Table 7.10). The League of Polish Families in 2002 fielded most workers – one-quarter – but half of its candidates came from the professions. Indeed, the Russian parties fielded almost no candidates who could be described as 'working class', while candidates working in the state administration and the business sector constituted relatively high proportions. Zhirinovskii's Liberal-Democratic Party [*sic*] rapidly lost or replaced the large number of academics who had stood in 1993, as well as its then worker-candidates. But the Russian parties fielded a highly qualified team: 82.5 per cent of Zhirinovskii bloc candidates and 94.9 per cent of Russian Community candidates had higher educational qualifications in the 1999 elections. There were other major changes from one election to another: the Lithuanian Nationalist Union first increased the share of candidates working for the state administration, then they dropped to only a small presence.

Liberal parties

We have seen that there were relatively few unambiguously liberal parties in the post-communist world. Although the 'liberal consensus' was widespread in Central Europe, many parties espoused the cause of free market reforms and the need for massive privatisation programmes without necessarily adopting the philosophical underpinnings of individualism or a limited state. Of those that identified themselves unambiguously as 'liberal', some like the Civic Democratic Party (ODS) in the Czech Republic stressed the economic dimensions of liberalism, including strict financial discipline and measures to encourage foreign investment. The Estonian Reform Party (*Reformierakond*) was from a similar mould. Established in November 1994 by the then head of the National Bank, Siim Kallas, it held pro-business views close to those of Klaus, and Kallas had extensive networks of personal contacts within the state apparatus and in successful enterprises. Kallas (acquitted of corruption charges just prior to the 1999 elections) became prime minister when the Reform Party entered government in January 2002.

Other liberals, like the Democratic Union in Poland between 1991 and 1994 or the Alliance of Free Democrats in Hungary, stressed their concerns with civil liberties and the development of a 'humane capitalism'. The Democratic Union merged with the Liberal Democratic Congress to form the Freedom Union (UW) in 1994; it acquired a harder monetarist profile under the leadership of Leszek Balcerowicz, leading ultimately to a profound identity crisis and exclusion from parliamentary politics in 2001. Although the liberalism

Table 7.10 Candidates of radical nationalist parties by type of occupation (%)

	Urban workers	Peasants, farmers & rural workers	Business	State officials	Party & trade union leaders	Professionals
LPR, Poland 2001	25.3	7.6	6.1	1.1	0.4	50.5
Zdrowa Polska, Poland 1991	22.5	7.5	6.3	0.3	0.0	59.7
PSNS, Slovakia 2002	21.3	0.0	25.3	6.0	0.0	38.0
SNS, Slovakia 1994	21.5	1.2	2.9	1.2	0.6	69.8
SNS, Slovakia 1998	19.4	0.7	4.0	0.7	0.0	76.7
Liberty League, Lithuania 1992	19.1	0.0	19.0	14.3	0.0	14.3
ROP, Poland 1997	18.7	7.5	8.1	1.8	0.0	52.5
LDPR, Russia 1993[1]	16.0	nk	10.0	8.0[2]	nk	51.0[3]
Ojczyzna, Poland 1993	13.3	9.3	4.2	1.0	0.1	69.5
SNS, Slovakia 2002	12.0	0.0	22.7	9.3	0.7	46.0
Young Lithuania 1996	11.4	2.9	28.6	11.4	2.9	28.6
Lithuanian Nationalist Union, 1992	10.0	0.0	10.0	17.5	15.0	40.0
Lithuanian Democratic Party, 1992[4]	8.7	0.0	4.3	13.0	0.0	47.8
Lithuanian Democratic Party, 1996	6.7	0.0	20.0	3.3	0.0	56.7
Young Lithuania 2000[5]	6.7	2.2	17.8	13.3	4.4	35.6
Lithuanian Nationalist Union 1996	6.5	3.9	9.1	23.4	3.9	45.5
PRM, Romania 1992[6]	6.2			6.2[7]		73.8
Estonian Citizen 1995	6.0	3.0	6.0	14.9	0.0	43.3
Justice and Life, Hungary 2002[8]	3.5[9]	nk	25.7	15.2	nk	36.8
Liberty League, Lithuania 1996	4.3	0.0	26.1	4.3	0.0	52.2

Table 7.10 (Continued)

	Urban workers	Peasants, farmers & rural workers	Business	State officials	Party & trade union leaders	Professionals
Lithuanian Nationalist Union 2000	3.1	6.3	21.9	6.3	3.1	37.5
Lithuanian National Democratic Party 1996	1.7	0.0	54.2	1.7	3.4	33.9
Derzhava, Russia 1995	0.0	0.0	28.0	25.0	25.0	20.0
Congress of Russian Communities, 1999	1.1	0.0	29.7	20.6	2.2	26.3
LDPR, Russia 1999[10]	0.6	0.0	22.1	38.0	3.1	13.5
LDPR, Russia 1995	0.5	0.0	20.2	18.3	24.5	14.9
Estonian Citizen 1992	0.0	3.8	15.4	7.7	3.8	61.5

[1] *Source:* Sakwa, as Table 7.8. [2] Military candidates only. [3] Academics only. [4] 21.7 per cent not known. [5] 'Young Lithuania': insufficient data for 1992; in 2000 in alliance as Union of 'Young Lithuania', New Nationalists and Political Prisoners, with some candidates drawn from LDP. [6] *Source:* Francisco Veiga, cited in Michael Shafir, 'Radical Politics in East-Central Europe Part VIII: Radical Continuity in Romania: The Greater Romania Party (A)', *East European Perspectives*, vol. 2, no. 16, 16 August 2000. [7] Candidates drawn from the military. [8] MIéP figures are the share of candidates providing optional personal statements. [9] Blue- and white-collar workers and peasants. [10] Zhirinovskii Bloc in 1999.

of UW's new chief rival in 2002, the Civic Platform (PO), was somewhat weakened by the inclusion of Christian conservatives, economic policy and Euro-enthusiasm remained at the heart of its platform. The Czech Freedom Union was often regarded simply as 'the OSD without Klaus'; and it maintained a strong free market orientation. The Hungarian Young Democrats (Fidesz) differed little from the Free Democrats in 1990 (though appealing explicitly to a constituency of young people); but within a few years had shifted to commandeer the conservative-nationalist space of the weakened Hungarian Democratic Forum. Klaus appeared to many to be pursuing a Fidesz-strategy, with the ODS seen in 2002 as 'a mix of conservative, nationalist, and populist ideas' leavened with increasingly open anti-EU rhetoric.[48]

Table 7.11 shows that the Alliance of New Citizens (ANO) in Slovakia in 2002 and the Lithuanian Liberal Union in 2000 had the highest proportion of candidates drawn from the economy. ANO was a new party, created by the entrepreneur-publisher Pavol Ruško. The Liberal Union had been a minor party until 2000, when it benefited from the defection of Rolandas Paksas from the Conservatives. The party improved its performance under Paksas's leadership, and it was a member of the governing coalition from October 2000 to June 2001. The main liberal party arising out of the dissident opposition, the Polish Democratic Union, was the least business-oriented. Its merger as the Freedom Union with the Liberal Democratic Congress in 1994 made some difference to the overall composition of its candidates; the Liberals were known as a party of entrepreneurs.

Data for other parties are sketchy, especially list data for Russian parties. In 1993 Russia's Choice (which was also the 'party of power') drew many candidates from the state administration and politics (42 per cent) and from amongst academics (26 per cent).[49] In 1995 over one-third of single-member district candidates of Russia's Democratic Choice were incumbent deputies; of the remainder 30 per cent were drawn from the business sector, 33 per cent were professionals, and – no longer a 'party of power' – 12.5 per cent worked in the state administration. Its successor, the Union of Right Forces, maintained this strong role for candidates drawn from the economy (see Table 7.11).

There appears to be some basis for postulating a division between liberal parties in the former Soviet Union, where business sought directly to assume positions of political influence, and liberals in Central Europe, where intellectuals espoused the entrepreneurial cause.[50] Clearly liberal parties did not provide the only avenue for economic interests to seek parliamentary representation. In Russia the parties of power and independent candidacy also offered such a route. Although the parties of power showed high concentrations of state officials, as their origin and nature would suggest, they were also business-friendly, with correspondingly lower numbers of candidates from the professions (see Table 7.12).

Table 7.11 Liberal parties' candidates by type of occupation (%)

	Business	Professionals	State officials	Urban workers
New Citizens, Slovakia 2002	48.7	38.0	4.0	7.3
Lithuanian Liberal Union, 2000	47.3	30.5	17.6	0.8
Democratic Party, Slovakia 1994	44.6	44.1	2.7	5.4
Lithuanian Liberal Union, 1996	41.5	34.1	19.5	0.0
Union of Right Forces, Russia 1999	29.7	23.2	16.8	1.3
Reform Party, Estonia 1995	28.2	34.0	30.1	1.9
Reform Party, Estonia 1999	27.4	34.4	29.2	1.9
Lithuanian Liberal Union, 1992	27.3	47.7	4.5	4.5
Democratic Union, Slovakia 1994	22.8	42.6	14.2	7.4
Freedom Union, Czech R 1998	21.9	47.8	11.1	8.1
ODS, Czech Republic 1998	15.8	37.9	27.9	8.4
ODS, Czech Republic 1996	13.8	31.5	25.5	9.4
Civic Platform, Poland 2001	12.0	70.3	1.8	8.3
Liberal Democratic Congress (KLD), Poland 1991	11.6	68.0	1.2	11.9
SDKU, Slovakia 2002	10.6	75.9	5.7	4.2
Liberal Democratic Congress, Poland (KLD), 1993	10.4	72.5	2.5	8.5
Freedom Union, Poland 2001	7.1	71.9	3.1	9.9
Freedom Union, 1997	6.2	72.2	1.8	7.6
Democratic Union, Poland 1993	3.0	85.3	0.6	6.6
Democratic Union, Poland 1991	1.9	85.4	0.8	8.2

Table 7.12 Candidates of parties of power and Independents in Russia (%)

	Business	Professionals	State officials	Party/trade union
Russia's Choice, 1993[1]	nk	26.0[2]	42.0	nk
PRES, Russia 1993[1]	31.0	19.0	40.0	nk
Our Home is Russia, 1995	25.5	21.8	41.2	3.7
PRES, Russia 1995	36.3	20.9	19.8	2.2
Unity, 1999	34.6	12.4	28.8	9.7
Independents, 1999	33.4	20.2	21.5	4.4
Independents, 1995	28.7	21.6	28.7	1.8

[1] Sakwa, as Table 7.8, p. 206. [2] Academics only.

Conclusion

The social composition of parliaments in Central Europe was heavily dom-inated by the professions. Scientists and engineers were the main group, but there was a visible presence of academics, teachers, health workers, academics, lawyers, and economists. Workers played a small role in the new parliaments, even in Poland with its record of worker-activism. The economy itself initially provided few deputies, whether from state enterprises or the new private sector, but the number of deputy-entrepreneurs increased, if somewhat erratically. Again Poland provided an exception, with very few deputies defining themselves as directors, managers, or entrepreneurs.

In the former Soviet Union deputies included higher proportions of state functionaries and those engaged in the economy. This was not only the case when parties of power mobilised from within the state sector in Russia and the Ukraine. Other parties also took advantage of such linkages. Estonia's Reform Party provides a good example: Its leader Siim Kallas was able to mobilise his substantial contacts inside the state apparatus and among successful enterprises to provide a large share of the party's candidates on a platform of wholesale liberalisation of the economy. Estonia and Lithuania had a higher proportion of deputies drawn from posts in the state administration or local government than the Ukraine or Russia in the first post-independence elections. In the second elections the Ukrainian figure rose sharply to over 50 per cent, but it remained lower than Estonia's massive share in 1995.

It was also the case that where parties appealed to a particular constituency, they often drew on that constituency for candidates. This was well illustrated by the Polish radical populist Self-Defence, which began as a rural party and continued to draw on the agricultural sector for its candidate pool. When it broke through into parliament in 2001 farmers, peasants, and agricultural workers not only made up 35 per cent of its candidates but also 51 per cent of its deputies. Radical left-wing parties had more urban workers, and the parties of power more candidates from business and the state administration.

Candidate profiles differed from those of deputies, but deputies' profiles also shifted from one election to another. As parties differed in the type of candidates they selected, so changes in a party's seat shares often changed the deputy profile of parliament. We cannot say whether parties changed their candidates or whether some of the same candidates had different occupations by the next election, but parties' candidate pools were not stable. We lack good incumbency data to help judge whether or not party activists redefined themselves as politicians. However, the parties whose candidates reflected a rather broad social profile tended to be those who did not often win (many) seats. This was positive in terms of participation, but advocates of social representation can find little comfort in the data presented here. Deputies came largely from existing, if dynamic élite strata.

8
The Representation of Women

The position of women is of little consequence to those who deny the significance of the role of women in the political process or in the composition of parliaments. The underlying assumptions of this chapter accept many of the arguments on women's representation noted in Chapter 2, namely that social representation does matter. Unfortunately we cannot address all facets of those arguments. Our focus is on the numbers, nature, and characteristics of women candidates and deputies. We thus ignore the issue of women's behaviour as deputies, and in particular the important question of whether gender matters to decision-making.[1] Instead we concentrate on aspects of the input side of the electoral process.

The social composition of parliaments in the new democracies: gender

One striking feature of the new post-communist parliaments was the precipitous decline in the number of women deputies. In Soviet-type systems 'socialist' representation required deputies reflective of society (under the benign guidance of the Communist Party), if not a complete mirror image. Women never constituted a majority of deputies in 'socialist' parliaments; but for many years women were far more numerous in communist legislatures than in their Western European counterparts. In the 1980 elections to the parliaments of the union republics and autonomous republics of the USSR 49.5 per cent of deputies were women, and in 1984 women comprised 32.8 per cent of deputies to the Supreme Soviet.[2] In 1985 the Ukrainian (republican) Supreme Soviet had 38.5 per cent women,[3] and the Lithuanian 35.7 per cent.[4] In 1986 the Romanian parliament had 34.4 per cent women and the Czechoslovak 25.4 per cent.[5] We noted earlier a tendency to dismiss as irrelevant the social composition of the communist parliaments. Yet however ritualistic the formal sessions, women gained a degree of experience in the public domain. Setting a high official value on women's participation added a symbolic dimension, even given the palpable domination of communist politics by men.

It is however the case that the first multi-candidate elections already signalled a decline in the number of women deputies. The Polish and Hungarian elections of 1985 were both (limited) multi-candidate elections along with a national list, and in Hungary, Barany reported that 'if there was a choice between a male and female candidate, the male usually won'.[6] The resulting proportions of women in these parliaments were 21 and 20.2 per cent respectively. Similarly, in all-Union Soviet multi-candidate elections in 1989 women's representation fell by half, to 17.1 per cent.[7] The proportion of women deputies elected to the Congress of People's Deputies from the Ukraine in 1989 was 9.7 per cent, and in the Ukrainian 1990 republican elections a mere 3 per cent.[8] In Lithuania 9.9 per cent of deputies in the 1990 republican Supreme Soviet (later the Constituent Seimas) were women.[9] In the Polish semi-competitive elections of 1989, the proportion of women dropped to 13.2 per cent.

These figures suggest that the decline is not specifically a phenomenon of the dislocations of democratic transition, since in some cases there was actually an increase in women's representation in the first *fully* free elections. Broadly speaking, however, women's representation remained low, especially by previous standards. New democracy became (in the words of a Polish feminist) 'masculine democracy'.[10] Of course great disparities emerged between Western Europe and Central and Eastern Europe, although France, Ireland, and Italy stood out in the former group and Bulgaria, Latvia, and Poland in the latter (see Table 8.1).

Table 8.2 shows some changes in Central and Eastern European (CEE) parliaments over time. These are not unidirectional and we cannot speak of trends. Nor do we have full data for all countries. In Poland, the Czech

Table 8.1   Women elected to some European parliaments (latest election to lower chamber, %)

Sweden 2002	45.3	Bulgaria 2001	26.3
Denmark 2001	38.0	Latvia 2002	23.0
Netherlands 2003	36.7	Poland 2001	20.2
Norway 2001	35.8	Czech R 2002	17.0
Austria 2002	33.9	Slovakia 2002	14.7
Germany 2002	32.2	Slovenia 2000	12.2
Belgium 1999	23.3	Lithuania 2000	10.6
UK 2001	17.9	Romania 2000	10.0
Ireland 2002	13.3	Hungary 2002	9.1
France 2002	12.2	Russia 1999	7.9
Italy 2001	9.8	Ukraine 2002	5.1

Sources: Parline http:www.ipu.org (Western Europe): current deputies as at 7 March 2003; http:\\www.essex.ac.uk/elections (Central and Eastern Europe): deputies at time of election.

Table 8.2 Candidates elected by gender in post-communist elections

Country	Women deputies (%)	Number of women	Number of men	Total deputies
Poland				
1991	9.6	44	416	460
1993	13.0	60	400	460
1997	13.7	63	397	460
2001	20.2	93	367	460
Czech Republic				
1996	14.5	29	171	200
1998	15.0	30	170	200
2002	17.0	34	166	200
Lithuania				
1992	7.1	10	131	141
1996	16.8	23	114	137[2]
2000	10.6	15	126	141
Estonia				
1992	12.9	13	88	101
1995	11.9	12	89	101
1999	17.8	18	83	101
Latvia				
2002	23.0	23	77	100
Russia				
1993	13.7	60	390	450
1995	9.8	44	406	450
1999	7.9	35	407	442[2]
Slovakia				
1994	14.7	22	128	150
1998	10.7	16	134	150
2002	14.7	22	128	150
Romania				
1992	3.5[1]	12	329	341
1996	7.3[1]	25	318	343
2000	10.0[1]	38	307	345
Hungary				
1990	7.3	28	358	386
1994	11.1	43	343	386
1998	8.3	32	354	386
2002	9.1	35	351	386
Bulgaria				
1991[3]	13.3	32	208	240

Ukraine				
1994	3.5	11	327	338[2]
1998	7.8	35	410	445[2]
2002	5.1	23	424	447[2]

[1] Including minority deputies. [2] Not all seats were filled at the election. [3] Petya Pachkova, 'Electoral Behavior During Political Transition' in Georgi Karasimeonov, ed., *The Bulgarian Grand National Assembly and the 1991 Election to the Bulgarian National Assembly. Analyses, Documents and Data*, Berlin: Sigma, 1997, p. 57.

Republic, and Romania more women entered parliament at successive elections, and in Russia fewer. In 1993 more than one-third of women deputies came from Women of Russia which had 22 seats, but in 1995 it failed to cross the threshold. In Hungary, Slovakia, Lithuania, and the Ukraine numbers rose, then fell, but rose again in Slovakia and Hungary in 2002. It does seem however that the initial changes in the composition of parliaments were not due to some isolated or ephemeral factors.

Approaches to the representation of women

So if there is a 'problem' in Central and Eastern Europe, how best can we explore the factors that hinder or enhance the representation of women? The major approaches, drawn largely from the study of Western Europe and the US, focus on structural, political-cultural, and institutional factors. For worldwide comparisons the structural approach has proved useful: there is a clear relationship between the representation of women in parliament and a country's level of socio-economic development.[11] Of course, women's participation in paid work, their increased education, and the articulation of demands look highly relevant factors. It may well be that 'more affluent nations are the most (gender-) egalitarian',[12] though the linkages of affluence to (gender-) egalitarianism are not clearly spelt out. Moreover, there are serious problems with measuring socio-economic development by per capita income, as many do.[13] Above all the economic argument does not help to differentiate between countries nor to explain variations within a given region. In many Western European countries levels of socio-economic development are comparable, but there are big differences in the proportion of women in parliaments.

Norris and Inglehart argue that culture is the 'missing factor'. They found strong correlations between positive attitudes towards women leaders and the proportion of women elected to national parliaments.[14] (Gender-)egalitarian attitudes were most prevalent in 'post-industrial' societies, especially among the young. Norris and Inglehart see such values as persuading more women to seek office and as influencing the 'political gatekeepers' evaluations of suitable candidates'. Moreover, changes in values generate a climate of change more conducive to policy reforms.[15]

However, political-cultural arguments are subject to criticism similar to that made of structural arguments. Few doubt that the broad attitudes, values, and symbols present in society affect the political process. Yet there are serious problems in assessing political culture, in determining how political culture is itself shaped (structural factors affect political culture, but not in a straightforward or automatic fashion), and in extracting its effects on the political process. Nor are underlying values easy to measure or to tap with survey data, as Norris and Inglehart do with their index of 'rational' vs. traditional values.[16] A political culture is not merely the sum of individual preferences.[17] Moreover social institutions such as pressure groups and political parties link society to the political system, but they are not simply passive transmitters of its values. They may reflect political culture (or sub-cultures), and they may also influence it. Culture does not feed automatically into the political process: someone – some individual, body, or institution – must act as its agency, whether to promote alternatives to traditional views of women or to promote policies favourable to women's representation.

Institutional approaches thus need to be added to the tools of investigation, and some scholars have argued that institutions are vital. First, we can stress the importance of organisations promoting women, including feminist groups. Most discussions of women's representation in Western Europe begin with the socio-cultural arena and the increasing mobilisation of women from the 1970s. This was also the case in those Latin American states where active women's organisations successfully promoted gender quotas despite the persistence of *macho* political culture.[18] Active women place women's issues on the political agenda, and active women's organisations bring pressure to bear on other actors, including political parties.

Secondly, some institutional approaches centre on political parties themselves. Parties are clearly important as the main agencies of political recruitment in European democracies. Moreover, if parties expect to win seats, they cannot be too out of line with public opinion, but they can also help to educate and socialise it. Caul's work suggests that certain party characteristics, including institutionalisation, ideology, the presence of women activists, and candidate-selection rules may promote women.[19] Clearly ideology is an obvious factor, with left-wing parties proving the trendsetters in this regard[20] because of their openness to social movements and their egalitarian attitudes. Right-wing parties with traditionalist ideologies are often linked to conservative Catholicism in Western Europe, and they have been viewed as at best indifferent to promoting women's participation. The gender dimension of right-wing radicalism also received attention, with emphasis on the particular appeal of extreme-right parties to young blue-collar males.[21] In this regard we can note the contrast between the masculine variant of national identity, in which national communities are conceived as 'fraternities' of males experiencing a sense of 'deep, horizontal comradeship' and the patriarchal variant, in which national communities are seen as a family of families with a patriarchal leader at its head.[22] The former would apply to extreme-right parties, the latter to Christian, conservative, and nationalist parties. Populist parties have no obvious 'philosophical' gender dimension, though when prone to direct action, they may attract more men.

Candidate selection has also received considerable treatment in the Western European and general comparative literature.[23] A primary focus here has been the social composition of candidate and legislative corpuses and on the different pathways followed by different groups, including women.[24] Stress is often placed on a 'lengthy series of incremental steps up the political ladder',[25] with a party track record and local roots serving as key selection criteria.[26] Successful women are most likely to be professionals, managers, or high-level administrators – jobs that 'commonly provide the flexibility, financial resources, experience and social networks that facilitate running for elected office'.[27]

Candidate-selection rules are also important: bureaucratic rules are better for women than informal procedures; and quotas are the most effective means of all for increasing women's representation. Many Northern European parties introduced gender quotas in the 1970s, followed by social democratic parties, for example, in Germany, the Netherlands, Spain, Austria, and Portugal.[28] In 1997 the British Labour Party introduced women-only short-lists for some of its (single-member) constituencies. The OSCE imposed gender quotas in Bosnia following the Dayton Agreement of 1995. The introduction of practices in one party also gives rise to the possibility of contagion,[29] spreading the practice to other parties.

Finally, there are explanations centring on the nature of the electoral system. The electoral system has been deemed 'the most important variable affecting women's share of legislative seats'.[30] Norris claims that 'the effect of the electoral system on the representation of women is well established'.[31] In a nutshell proportional representation is more conducive to women's representation than majoritarian systems. Women's relative success with PR systems has been linked to the opportunities they provide for ticket-balancing[32] and in particular to party expectations of success in certain seats.

There is also a pervasive view that political parties in majoritarian systems do not select women in winnable seats because they perceive voters as reluctant to support women (an argument that takes us back to political culture). Of course, such perceptions are not necessarily correct: Converse and Pierce observed that in 1967 in France it was 24 times more likely that a man would be nominated than a woman, though once nominated women's chances of being elected were virtually no different.[33] But they may be powerful never the less. Interests also come into play, as high incumbency rates in majoritarian systems make the displacement of men more difficult.[34]

Within the realm of PR one also finds the contention that closed lists are 'better' for women,[35] since voters choosing a party are forced to be gender-blind.

Women also do better when district magnitude is high[36] because larger constituencies provide more opportunities for a more broadly based group of deputies. A highly fragmented party system is not beneficial, however, since smaller parties are likely to be dominated by male leaders. Party magnitude is thus another factor identified as facilitating women's representation.

Thus a range of general factors and specific variables have been identified as relevant to issues of women's representation. They may be roughly summarised as follows:

- Affluent societies are more conducive to women's representation, especially where there is a pool of educated women professionals, managers, and administrators.
- Traditional political culture is not conducive to women's representation, while secular, 'post-modern' values are beneficial.
- The presence of women's organisations in society is advantageous in raising women's issues, and may feed back into the political culture and into political parties. Women party activists promote women's representation.
- Left-wing parties are most favourable to women. Conservative parties are not very favourable to women. Right-wing extremist parties are least favourable to women. However, once reform has begun, contagion effects may occur and practices such as quotas may extend to other parties.
- Institutionalised parties are better for women, and large parties are better than small ones.
- A strong women's presence in local government may provide a career ladder for women.
- Single-member districts are less conducive to women's representation than PR systems. Once women are recruited, high district magnitude increases their chances of success so long as there is not a very large number of parties. Closed lists are better for women than open lists.

Testing theories in Central and Eastern Europe

We are not concerned here to develop or refine approaches based on structural or cultural factors, but a few comments are in order. All Central and Eastern European countries were highly industrialised (if with a strong agricultural sector), and they could hardly be regarded as 'backward'. These were educated societies; often women were more highly educated than men. In this sense there is no reason to doubt the availability of a 'pool' of women capable of political action.

However, post-communist political culture appeared inhospitable indeed. Despite the egalitarian ideology of official communism, there was little sign of partnership in gender relations under the old regime. The 'double burden' was ubiquitous, with women fully active in the labour force but also occupying traditional gender roles within the home. It would be surprising if the ambiguities of cultural attitudes to women in the communist period did not persist. With the post-communist liberation of the churches, ecclesiastical hierarchies turned to these issues, and all post-communist countries saw some explicit articulation of an ethos of traditional home-centred roles as the appropriate ones for women.[37] Yet it is hard on the surface at least to see political culture as a *distinguishing* factor for countries within the region.

Supply-side factors

In part at least, political culture may account for the absence of strong women's groups in civil society, and the resulting lack of articulation of gender-egalitarian values and feed-in of demands to the political parties. Of course, women's groups emerged, but few were strong or nationally based, and the term 'feminism' was viewed everywhere with deep scepticism. Despite some ephemeral successes such as that of 'Women of Russia' in 1993,[38] the gaining of a seat by Women against Life's Hardships in Poland in 1991, the presence of small women's parties in Bulgaria and Lithuania (later New Democracy), women's mobilisation was notable for its weakness.[39] Few collective voices spoke for women on the national stage.

More specific arguments focused on the 'triple burden' of job, family, and politics, exacerbated by the nature of the economic and psychological impact of transition-dislocation on women, including loss of benefits, high unemployment, and low pay.[40] Poverty increased everywhere without exception, and previous coping strategies became less relevant in new-capitalism. This could indeed have generated a potential 'supply-side' problem, that is, the availability of women for activism.[41] Women were seen as less interested in politics than men and except for voting, unwilling to participate, at least not through the vehicle of political parties. Wolchik and Szalai have argued that this was so in Slovakia and Hungary.[42] Opinion polls in Slovakia in the mid-1990s gave some credence to the view that women neither understood nor cared much about politics.[43] In Hungary women eschewed public activism in favour of 'individual survival strategies'.[44]

If these broad cultural assessments are correct, then we would expect to see low levels of women members of political parties, and hence a smaller pool of potential parliamentary recruits. However, much depends on age and education, and the situation is not everywhere identical. Enterprise child care and health provision declined at different rates in different countries. Women's unemployment tended to be higher than men's. But in Poland women with higher education were not generally unemployed,[45] yet in the Ukraine in the mid-1990s women made up 70 per cent of the jobless, and two-thirds of these women had higher education.[46] In Hungary the proportion of economically active women fell from 80 to 50 per cent in the 1990s; female employment dropped by 40 per cent from 1985 to 1997 (male employment fell by 29.8 per cent).[47]

Unfortunately, party membership figures were mostly non-existent or notoriously unreliable. Nor then was there much evidence of parties' gender composition. There were a few exceptions, and these did not indicate particularly low proportions of women members. Some 31 per cent of members of the Hungarian Socialist Party were women around 1999.[48] In Slovakia the official membership figures indicate a surprising disjuncture with the general findings on Slovak political culture. In 2000 women comprised 42 per cent of HZDS's membership, an extraordinary 56 per cent (perhaps) of that of the Christian Democratic Movement, about 40 per cent of that of the SDL', and one-quarter of the Slovak National Party's.[49] But the Greater Romania Party was decidedly male dominated: 83 per cent of its members were men in 1998.[50]

Nor was it the case that women 'role models' were absent. In most countries (though not in Russia or Romania) there were popular, highly visible, and experienced women in parliament. Lithuania, Poland, and Bulgaria had women prime ministers – Kazimiera Prunskienė, Hanna Suchocka, and Reneta Inzhova. Vaira Vike-Freiberga was President of Latvia. Lithuania and Slovakia had women ministers of finance, Poland and the Czech Republic women leaders of the Senate. In the Ukraine former Deputy Premier Yuliya Tymoshenko led the opposition election bloc under her name to win seats in 2002. In the Czech Lands, Dagmar Burešová served as Chair of the Czech National Council in 1990, Vlasta Parkanová became the Czech Republic's Minister of Justice in December 1996. In the 1998 parliament Petra Buzková was described as the most popular social democratic politician. Hana Marvanová led the Czech Freedom Union. Slovakia's largest and most successful party, the Movement for Democratic Slovakia, included Ol'ga Keltšová and Katarína Tótova among its leaders, with Zdenka Kramplová as foreign minister in 1997–8. Nadezhda Mihailova was highly respected as Bulgaria's foreign minister after 1997. In Hungary in 2002 there was a sudden influx of women into key posts in parliament, with Ibolya David leading the opposition Hungarian Democratic Forum. Monika Lamperth became Minister of the Interior. However, the lack of data about parties creates a huge gap in identifying women activists and in reconstructing the 'ladder' of their recruitment process. It perforce shifts attention directly to the arena of candidate selection.

Candidate selection

Political parties rapidly became the primary mechanism of candidate selection in Central and Eastern Europe, though not in Russia and the Ukraine, where single-member districts encouraged popular individuals to stand locally and Independents remained a major force. Of the candidates who stood in the Ukraine in 1994, only 643 (11.0 per cent) were nominated by political parties, 72.8 per cent of women candidates stood as Independents. Half the deputies had no party affiliation (eleven women were elected, seven Independents and four from the Communist Party). In 1998 with the new mixed system, Independents still won in more than half the single-member seats and 42 per cent in 2002. In 2002 only eight women (3.6 per cent) won in single-member districts, three of them Independents. The position was little different in Russia. In 1999 half (51.3 per cent) the candidates in single-member districts were Independents, of whom 9.6 per cent were women. Independents won 105 of the 225 seats (46.67 per cent, including three women).

Where parties were significant, we cannot judge how far women were reluctant to come forth as candidates and how far the parties failed to select them. Very little is known about this aspect or indeed the candidate recruitment processes of particular parties. We do know that parties often recruited 'attractive' candidates from outside their own membership. Much of the 'problem' may indeed arise from the reluctance of women to become active in political parties, as political culture approaches stress. We cannot rule this out. Yet where quotas were established, there appeared little difficulty in finding women willing to stand.

At the outset relatively few women stood for parliament, but the proportion of women candidates was already substantial in Latvia, in Slovakia in 2002, in Poland in 2001, and in Estonia in 1999. Hungary virtually doubled its share of women candidates over four elections. However, it was also the case that with one exception fewer women were elected (see Tables 8.3 and 8.4) than stood for election. This could be because winning parties fielded fewer women, though some of the differences in Table 8.3 are very small. In Poland in 1993 more women actually stood for winning parties than non-winning parties. But winning parties may also have placed women less often in winnable seats (see below).

The occupational profile of women candidates

Who were these women who stood for parliament? The occupational composition of the candidate corpus is laid out in Table 8.5. It is not surprising to see a large percentage of women professionals standing as candidates, though again, Russia and the Ukraine display rather different candidate characteristics. The arguments why this should be the case were rehearsed in Chapter 7, and they are no different for men and women. In the communist period health and education were heavily feminised, and we would expect that to be reflected more strongly in the profile of women candidates. Professional women were indeed the largest single group, except in Russia, and they were a smaller proportion in the Ukraine than elsewhere. This was because of the greater presence of businesspersons, state officials, and the NGO sector (including parties). Russia had the highest proportion of women from the NGO sector – in 1999 about half consisted of trade unionists and political party workers, but the figure remains puzzlingly high.

Table 8.3 Legislative recruitment of women (% of total)

Country	Women standing	Women elected	Difference
Czechoslovakia			
1990[1]	13.1	10.0	−3.1
Poland			
1991	12.9	9.6	−3.3
1993	13.1	13.0	−0.1
1997	15.7	13.7	−1.8
2001	22.8	20.2	−2.6
Slovakia			
1994	15.5	14.7	−0.8
1998	16.7	10.7	−6.0
2002	23.6	14.7	−8.9
Czech Republic			
1996	20.4	14.5	−5.9
1998	21.1	15.0	−6.1
2002	26.3	19.0	−9.3
Lithuania			
1992	11.7	7.1	−4.6
1996	20.3	16.8	−3.5
2000	18.4	10.6	−7.8
Estonia			
1992	14.0	12.9	−1.1
1995	17.3	11.9	−5.4
1999	26.8	17.8	−9.0
Latvia			
2002	28.9	23.0	−5.9
Ukraine			
1994	7.4	3.5	−3.9
1998	8.7	7.8	−0.9
Russia			
1995	13.4	9.8	−3.6
1999	14.7	7.9	−6.8
Hungary			
1990[2]	8.5	7.3	−1.2
1994	10.0	11.1	+1.1
1998	12.5	8.3	−4.2
2002	17.8	9.1	−8.7

[1] Candidates for the Federal Assembly in V. Rak, 'Candidates in Czechoslovakian Parliamentary Elections in June 1990' in Ivan Gabal, ed., *The 1990 Election to the Czechoslovakian Federal Assembly*, Berlin: Sigma, 1996, p. 75.
[2] E. János Farkas and Agnes Vajda, 'Candidates for Parliament' in Gábor Tóka, ed., *The 1990 Election to the Hungarian National Assembly. Analyses, Documents and Data*, Berlin: Sigma, 1995, p. 73.

Table 8.4 Candidates for parliament by gender

Country	Women (%)	Women	Men	Total
Poland				
1991	12.9	898	6082	6980
1993	13.1	1151	7636	8787
1997	15.7	1008	5425	6433
2001	22.8	1708	5800	7508
Slovakia				
1994	15.5	301	1641	1942
1998	16.7	270	1348	1618
2002	23.6	618	2001	2619
Czech Republic				
1996	20.4	798	3111	3909
1998	21.1	703	2635	3338
2002	26.3	1593	4471	6064
Lithuania				
1992	11.7	97	730	827
1996	20.3	274	1077	1351
2000	18.4	233	1034	1267
Latvia				
1998[1]	26.6	288	793	1081
2002[1]	28.9	294	725	1019
Estonia				
1992	14.0	88	542	630
1995	17.3	215	1039	1256
1999	26.8	505	1379	1884
Ukraine				
1994	7.4	412[2]	5172[2]	5597
1998	8.7	460[3]	4672[3]	5261
Russia				
1995	13.4	978[4]	6301[4]	7310
1999	14.7	761	4407	5168
Hungary				
1990	9.0	316	3191	3507
1994[5]	10.0			
1998[5]	12.5	272	1910	2182
2002	17.8	600	2779	3379
Slovenia				
1996[6]	18.6	242	1058	1300

[1] Data from www.cvk.lv. [2] 13 missing from total. [3] 129 missing from total. [4] 31 missing from total. [5] Data from Központi Stastisztikai Hivatal, *Pártok, Képviselöltek Az 1998, Èvi Parlamenti Választásokon*, Budapest, 1999. [6] From www.sigov.si:90/elections.

Table 8.5 Occupational profile of women candidates (% women candidates)

Occupation	Slovakia			Estonia			Lithuania			Poland				Czech Republic		Russia		Ukraine	
	1994	1998	2002	1992	1995	1999	1992	1996	2000	1991	1993	1997	2001	1996	1998	1995	1999	1994	1998
Not known	2.7	0.0	0.0	0.0	0.0	0.2	4.2	0.7	0.0	0.4	1.2	4.9	0.3	3.5	2.2	11.3	7.4		
State officials	6.3	2.2	5.2	22.7	18.0	12.9	13.5	14.6	21.5	0.7	0.6	2.1	2.3	11.8	11.5	17.7	19.7	18.2	17.4
Business/ Enterprise	7.3	8.1	15.7	9.1	13.4	15.2	4.2	13.9	19.3	3.7	3.4	3.6	4.0	16.7	17.4	25.5	28.1	12.4	12.4
Professionals	61.5	57.0	41.6	37.5	43.8	49.5	55.2	53.6	43.8	73.7	73.2	64.6	69.1	28.9	33.8	25.4	22.6	39.3	29.1
NGO sector[1]	2.7	0.7	0.8	13.6	7.8	5.5	9.4	3.3	5.2	0.3	0.3	0.2	0.4	3.9	2.7	14.4	11.5	10.7	8.3
Workers[2]	15.0	28.1	29.6	11.4	5.1	5.1	5.2	5.5	3.0	17.6	18.3	16.6	17.2	25.7	22.6	2.4	2.6	2.2	2.1

[1] Including political party leaders and officials. [2] Manual and non-manual, including peasants, farmers, and agricultural workers.

However, there were more businesswomen than anticipated, given the male-dominated character of the old state enterprises and women's lack of capital and other resources needed for entrepreneurship. Businesswomen stood not only in Russia and the Ukraine. Their share increased in Lithuania, and they were not insignificant in the Czech Republic. Of course men still overwhelmingly dominated this category, as we see from Table 8.6, which shows the dominant elements of these profiles for these four countries.

Women workers were of little import in the countries of the former USSR but they stood in some numbers in Poland, Slovakia, and the Czech Republic. Of the latter, Poland with strong trade union ties to political parties and general traditions of worker activism (including large numbers of women Solidarity activists in the 1980s, although without leadership roles)[51] in fact had fewer women-worker candidates (and fewer worker candidates as we saw in Chapter 7). Radical left parties were most worker-oriented, and there was effectively no radical left party in Poland.

The candidate profile diverged sharply from that of deputies (see Table 8.7). Poland remained distinctive in the large proportion of professional women and the relative absence of state administrative officials. In 2001 the Peasant Party fielded more than half the candidates drawn from local government, but it did not return even one woman to the Sejm. The presence of many state officials elsewhere perhaps indicates that patronage and local politics were beginning to have an effect. In the Czech Republic in 1998 six of the eight women deputies in this category worked in local or regional government. In Estonia in 1995 all seven came from the central state administration; in 1999 seven came from the centre and three more from the sub-national level. In Lithuania in 2000 two came from national government and two from local/regional government. In Hungary in 2002 just over half the women deputies had some background in local politics.[52] The strikingly

Table 8.6 The candidate corpus by gender (%)

	State officials		Business/enterprise		Professionals	
	Women	Men	Women	Men	Women	Men
Lithuania 1992	11.1	88.9	3.7	96.3	15.5	84.5
Lithuania 1996	15.1	84.9	12.1	87.9	27.8	72.2
Lithuania 2000	15.8	84.2	11.4	88.6	27.1	72.9
Czech Republic 1996	10.9	89.1	13.6	86.4	27.4	72.6
Czech Republic 1998	17.8	82.2	12.6	87.4	27.7	72.3
Ukraine 1994	6.2	93.8	4.2	95.8	10.4	89.6
Ukraine 1998	8.3	91.7	6.3	93.7	15.6	84.4
Russia 1995	13.1	86.9	7.8	92.2	18.0	82.0
Russia 1999	14.9	85.1	9.0	91.0	21.6	78.4

Table 8.7 Occupational profile of women candidates (C) and women deputies (D) (%)

	Slovakia						Czech Republic				Poland							
	1994		1998		2002		1996		1998		1991		1993		1997		2001	
	C	D	C	D	C	D	C	D[1]	C	D	C	D	C	D	C	D	C	D
State officials	6.3	7.0	2.2	–	5.2	22.7	11.8	15.2	11.5	12.4	0.7	–	0.6	1.7	2.1	7.9	2.3	2.2
Business	7.3	1.6	8.1	7.4	15.7	9.1	16.7	8.8	17.4	7.1	3.7	–	3.4	1.7	3.6	1.6	4.0	2.2
Professional	61.5	48.4	57.0	59.3	41.6	63.6	28.9	32.2	33.8	58.2	73.7	90.9	73.2	90.0	64.6	81.0	69.1	82.8
NGO sector	2.7	7.8	0.7	–	0.8	4.5	3.9	14.0	2.7	9.4	0.3	–	0.3	3.3	0.2	1.6	0.4	1.1
Workers	15.0	12.5	28.1	33.3	29.6	–	25.9	5.8	22.6	4.1	17.6	9.1	18.3	1.7	16.6	3.2	17.2	10.8

	Lithuania						Estonia						Russia				Ukraine			
	1992		1996		2000		1992		1995		1999		1995		1999		1994		1998	
	C	D	C	D[2]	C	D	C	D	C	D[3]	C	D	C	D[4]	C	D[5]	C	D	C	D
State officials	13.5	20.0	14.6	39.1	21.5	26.7	22.7	38.5	18.0	58.3	12.9	55.6	11.3	31.1	7.4	28.6	18.2	31.6	17.4	57.1
Business	4.2	–	13.9	13.0	19.3	20.0	9.1	15.4	13.4	–	15.2	38.9	17.7	4.4	19.7	11.4	12.4	21.1	12.4	19.0
Professional	55.2	80.0	53.6	34.8	43.8	33.3	37.5	15.4	43.8	33.3	49.5	–	25.5	22.2	28.1	22.9	39.3	31.6	29.1	23.8
NGO sector	9.4	–	3.3	8.7	5.2	20.0	13.6	30.8	7.8	–	5.5	5.6	25.4	5.6	22.6	5.7	10.7	5.3	8.3	4.7
Workers	5.2	–	5.5	3.0	–	–	11.4	–	5.1	–	5.1	–	14.4	–	11.5	–	2.2	0.0	2.1	0.0

[1] Plus 32 incumbents. [2] 4.2 per cent were students. [3] Plus one pensioner. [4] Plus 16 incumbents (35.6 per cent) and one student. [5] Plus 11 incumbents.

narrower occupational profile of deputies compared to candidates draws attention to the nature of the contenders, especially the political parties.

Political parties are obviously a major key to the issue of women's representation. We noted in Chapter 7 that the composition of parliaments may vary from one election to another simply because the same parties do not always win. Golosov's study of regional elections in Russia found that parties were good for women, especially when party organisations were relatively strong.[53] However, we lack the data to evaluate the institutionalisation of parties or to compare party structures. The situation is further complicated by the fluidity of parties and the complexity of electoral alliances. Still we can examine parties' candidate profiles, as well as distinguish between parties in a number of respects, particularly that of ideology.

Of course, we have stressed that not all post-communist parties were ideological. In addition, ideological positioning is always contextual. Further, most 'ideological' parties contained elements pulling 'rightwards' or 'leftwards' or both, and few remained static. In some complex electoral parties, such as AWS in Poland (1997) and the Slovak Democratic Coalition[54] (1998) a variety of orientations co-existed. We would expect these complex formations, including the 'parties of power' and the large electoral blocs, to be less woman-friendly on the assumption that allocation of list places to (male) leaders would have priority.

Political parties and their candidates

Communist and social democratic successor parties

We noted earlier that in many stable democracies left-wing parties were more responsive to pressures for increased women's representation. The egalitarian ideological basis of such parties facilitated such responsiveness, including the adoption of quotas. Historically the communist parties also had highly developed women's ancillary organisations. On the other hand, the upper echelons of the ruling communist parties were always male preserves, and many successor parties remained closely linked to male-dominated trades unions. Indeed, we can see (Table 8.8) that at the outset communist and ex-communist parties had fewer women than parties taken as a whole. The Central Europeans saw greater change than the East Europeans. But this was not just a difference between hard-line parties with fewer women and soft social democrats with more, as the Czech communists, the Slovak ZRS, and Hungarian Munkáspárt show. Still, there were striking increases for two successor parties that introduced quotas for the most recent elections, the Polish Social Democrats and the Hungarian Socialist Party (see below).

The position of other left parties (Table 8.9) was highly variable. Many were tiny and politically irrelevant. Only in the Czech Republic and Lithuania did a

Table 8.8   Women candidates in communist and successor parties

Election/Party	% Women candidates	% Women, all parties
Poland		
1991 (SLD)	12.9	12.9
1993 (SLD)	13.4	13.1
1997 (SLD)	15.5	15.7
2001 (SLD–UP)	35.8	22.8
Czech Republic		
1996 (KSČM)	18.5	20.4
1998 (KSČM)	20.1	21.1
2002 (KSČM)	20.8	
Lithuania		
1992 (LDDP)	4.8	11.7
1996 (LDDP)	14.1	20.3
2000 (LDDP)[1]	13.8	18.4
Russia		
1993 (KPRF)[2]	10.0	
1995 (KPRF)	10.9	13.4
1999 (KPRF)	13.1	14.7
Slovakia		
1994 (SDL')[3]	13.2	15.5
1998 (SDL')	16.0	16.7
2002 (SDL')	20.7	23.6
1994 (ZRS)	13.8	15.5
1998 (ZRS)[4]	15.5	16.7
2002 (ZRS)	42.2	23.6
2002 (SDA)	32.0	23.6
The Ukraine		
1994 (KPU)	9.6	7.4
Romania		
1992 (DFSN)[5]	8.8	
1996 (PDSR)[5]	13.0	
Hungary		
1990 (MSzP)	10.0	8.5
1994 (MSzP)	10.8	10.0
1998 (MSzP)	8.9	12.5
2002 (MSzP)	23.4	17.8
1990 (MSzMP) (communists)[1]	9.5	8.5
1994 (Munkáspárt)[4]	17.7	10.0
1998 (Munkáspárt)[4]	17.0	12.5
2002 (Munkáspárt)[4]	24.1	17.8

[1] In coalition for list element. [2] From R. Sakwa, 'The Russian Elections of December 1993', *Europe-Asia Studies*, vol. 47, no. 2, 1995, p. 204. [3] In coalition. [4] Did not win seats. [5] Change of name.

Table 8.9 Women candidates in non-successor left-wing parties

Party/Election	% Women candidates
Czech Social Democrats (ČSSD) 1996	14.9
Czech Social Democrats 1998	17.2
Czech Social Democrats 2002	25.1
Lithuanian Socialist Party, 1996[1]	30.0
Lithuanian Socialist Party, 2000[1]	25.0
Lithuanian Social Democratic Party, 1992	8.6
Lithuanian Social Democratic Party, 1996	23.5
Lithuanian Social Democratic Party, 2000	24.1
Labour Solidarity (SP), Poland 1991	16.8
Democratic-Social Mvmt (RDS), Poland 1991	25.8
Labour Union (SP + RDS), Poland 1993	17.2
Labour Union, Poland 1997[1]	24.7
Social Democracy, Slovakia 1994[2]	13.0
Hungarian Social Democratic Party, (MSzDP), 1990[1]	13.2
Hungarian Social Democratic Party, 1994[1]	7.6
Hungarian Social Democratic Party, 1998 [1]	8.3
Hungarian Social Democratic Party, 2002	14.3
Romanian Social Democratic Party (PSDR), 1996	18.4
Romanian Social Democratic Union (PSDR + PD), 1996	13.6

[1] Did not win seats; stood with SLD in 2001. [2] Did not win seats; stood with Slovak Democratic Coalition in 1998.

non-successor social democratic party prove successful. In Poland the Solidarity-derived Labour Union did well in 1993, but failed to cross the threshold in 1997; in 2001 it stood in alliance with the SLD. However both the Labour Union and the Lithuanian Social Democrats (merged with the LDDP in 2001) could be seen as sources of 'contagion' in their early commitment to quotas. Although the difference between those parties linked to the ruling communist parties and those that were not was small, what was particularly striking was the amount of movement. In almost all cases the number of women candidates standing for left-wing parties increased with successive elections.

Parties of the right

We argued above that right-wing parties associated with traditional religious values might be expected to want their women back in the home, rather than encouraging them into the political arena. There were few conservative parties in Central and Eastern Europe, and fewer still with any national scope or impact. Exceptions were the Lithuanian Homeland Union, Isamaa in Estonia, and Fidesz in Hungary, whose conservative credentials were clear by the 1998 election. We saw earlier that Fidesz moved from its earlier liberal stance, taking over the space occupied by the declining Hungarian Democratic

Forum. The Forum had only 5.9 per cent women candidates in 1990, 8.3 per cent in 1994, and 6.1 per cent in 1998. Fidesz did not favour women either, with 7.9 per cent women in 1994, 9.1 per cent in 1998, and 8.7 per cent (jointly with the Forum) in 2002, placing it at the lower end of parties overall. Yet Isamaa had 17.4 per cent women candidates in 1995 and 21.3 per cent in 1999. Neither was the Lithuanian Homeland Union (18.5 per cent in 1996 and 18.4 per cent in 2000) as inhospitable to women as Fidesz; indeed it placed women candidates to help secure women's votes, though it had no 'programme' concerning women.[55] But there were numerous Christian and Christian democratic parties (see Table 8.10) that did not generally reach these Baltic figures.

Indeed, overall religious parties did field fewer women candidates, albeit with some clear exceptions. There were also considerable country variations,

Table 8.10   Women candidates in some Christian and Christian Democratic parties

Party	% Women
Christian Democratic Party, Lithuania 1992	16.1
Christian Democratic Party, Lithuania 1996	20.9
Christian Democratic Party, Lithuania 2000	17.2
Christian Democratic Union, Lithuania 1992	2.6
Christian Democratic Union, Lithuania 1996	8.0
Christian Democratic Union, Lithuania 2000	16.3
Christian National Union (ZChN), Poland 1991[1]	12.4
Christian Democracy, Poland 1991	9.0
Christian National Union (ZChN), Poland 1993[2]	10.1
Centre Accord (PC), Poland 1993	13.6
Solidarity Election Action (AWS), Poland 1997	10.6
Solidarity Election Action – the Right (AWSP), Poland 2001	14.9
League of Polish Families (LPR), Poland 2001	24.6
Christian Democrats, Czech Republic 1996	13.4
Christian Democrats, Czech Republic 1998[3]	14.4
Christian Democratic Movement, Slovakia 1994[4]	6.7
Christian Democratic Movement, Slovakia 2002	16.7
Ukrainian Christian Democratic Party 1994	0.0
Christian Democratic Party of Ukraine 1994	6.1
Christian Democratic Union-Christians of Russia 1995	19.8
Christian Democrats (PNȚCD), Romania 1992	8.4
Christian Democrats (PNȚCD), Romania 1996	11.4
Christian Democratic Party (KDNP), Hungary 1990	6.4
Christian Democratic Party (KDNP), Hungary 1994	9.1
Christian Democratic Party (KDNP), Hungary 1998	19.2

[1] Stood as WAK (Catholic Election Action). [2] In coalition with Conservatives. [3] In coalition with Democratic Union-Freedom Union in 2002. [4] In Slovak Democratic Coalition in 1998.

though cross-country comparisons are problematic because of the parties' different size and nature. For example, the Russian Christians fielded only 81 candidates in 1995 and did not stand in 1999. The Hungarian Christian Democrats increased their women candidates in 1998, but they were defunct by 2002. In Lithuania the Christian Democratic Party maintained a stronger record, while the Christian Democratic Union moved upwards from its very low base (they later merged). Polish and Czech religious parties were not very hospitable to women, but the League of Polish Families fielded more women candidates in 2001 than many 'left-wing' parties in our survey. Generally, the Ukraine's Christian parties had fewer women than others, but they were also insignificant parties.

There are some reasons for judging liberal parties sympathetic to women's candidacies. Liberal parties were the most favourable of all to rapid change, and their ideology stressed individualism and equal opportunity. Urban professionals provided a major source of electoral support for liberal parties, and there is no obvious reason why women should constitute an exception. Liberal parties may well attract a core of and seek the electoral support of women professionals. However, we saw in Chapter 8 that these pro-business parties often had relatively high proportions of candidates drawn from that sphere. We surmised that such candidates were less likely to be women.

Indeed, liberal parties proved less supportive of women than one might have anticipated, though again, with major variations. In Poland the sharp jump for the Freedom Union in 2001 was a product of quotas, which the Lithuanian Liberals strongly opposed. The two Latvian liberal parties in 2002 recruited high proportions of women by regional standards, but they were below the total Latvian figure of 28.9 per cent. In Hungary the Free Democrats gradually increased women candidates at successive elections to match the Czech liberals. Romania was at the bottom of the list (see Table 8.11). In Slovakia in 2002 the new ANO had a surprising proportion of women, given its lack of a developed ideological basis (60 men and 12 women were drawn from business). The Union of Right Forces had far more women than its predecessor Russia's Democratic Choice (though the two were not identical). Again, however, we need to stress that the data are very patchy.

Populist, radical nationalist and extreme-right parties fielded few women in the first free elections (the unweighted average for all our parties was 11.8 per cent), but many parties increased the proportion of women candidates. They were male-dominated as expected, though the Russian and Romanian parties had decidedly lower numbers of women (see Table 8.12). In Poland the radical direct-action Self-Defence and tiny off-the-wall extremist PSN–PWN found a place for women candidates. The populist parties had candidate profiles comparable to those of other parties. Indeed, the controversial Movement for Democratic Slovakia fielded more women than Slovakia's successor parties.

If ideology does not govern candidate selection in predictable ways in circumstances of such dynamism, it clearly cannot be ignored. There were

Table 8.11   Women candidates in liberal parties (%)

Party	% Women
Democratic Union, Poland 1991	15.2
Democratic Union, Poland 1993	18.1
Freedom Union (UW), Poland 1997[1]	18.1
Freedom Union (UW), Poland 2001	31.4
Civic Platform (PO), Poland 2001	15.4
Civic Democratic Party (ODS), Czech Republic 1996	15.1
Civic Democratic Party (ODS), Czech Republic 1998	17.8
Civic Democratic Party, Czech Republic 2002	19.0
Freedom Union (US), Czech Republic, 1998[2]	18.2
Democratic Party, Slovakia 1994	12.9
Democratic Union, Slovakia 1994	14.2
Alliance of New Citizens (ANO), Slovakia 2002	21.3
Liberal Union, Lithuania 1992	2.3
Liberal Union, Lithuania 1996	9.8
Liberal Union, Lithuania 2000	13.0
Latvia's Way, Latvia 2002[3]	21.4
People's Party, Latvia 2002[3]	25.5
Young Democrats (Fidesz), Hungary 1990	12.3
Free Democrats (SzDS), Hungary 1990	11.9
Free Democrats (SzDS), Hungary 1994	12.0
Free Democrats (SzDS), Hungary 1998	14.1
Free Democrats (SzDS), Hungary 2002	19.1
Reform Party, Estonia 1995	19.4
Reform Party, Estonia 1999	19.3
Liberal Party, the Ukraine 1994	7.6
Liberal Party (PNL), Romania 1996	6.6
Liberal Party–Democratic Convention, Romania 1996	0.0
Russia's Choice, 1993[4]	7.0
Russia's Democratic Choice, Russia 1995	10.3
Union of Right Forces, Russia 1999	22.9
Yabloko, Russia 1995	12.9
Yabloko, Russia 1999	11.0

[1] Merger of Democratic Union & Liberal Democratic Congress, 1994. [2] Split from ODS. [3] From http://www.cvk.lv/cgi-bin/wdbcgiw/base/base.cvkand.otra. [4] From R. Sakwa, 'The Russian Elections of December 1993', *Europe-Asia Studies*, vol. 47, no. 2, 1995, p. 199.

Table 8.12 Women candidates in selected nationalist, populist, and extreme-right parties (%)

Parties	% Women candidates
Nationalist parties	
Slovak National Party (SNS)1994	13.4
Slovak National Party 1998	18.7
Slovak National Party 2002	12.0
Real Slovak National Party (PSNS) 2002	20.7
Party of Romanian National Unity (PUNR), 1992	5.6
Party of Romanian National Unity (PUNR), 1996	8.4
Greater Romania Party (PRM), 1992	11.5
Greater Romania Party (PRM), 1996	13.6
Organisation of Ukrainian Nationalists 1994	27.3
Justice and Life (MIÉP), Hungary 1994	10.2
MIÉP, Hungary 1998	11.4
MIÉP, Hungary 2002	16.9
Lithuanian Democratic Party 1992	13.0
Lithuanian Democratic Party 1996	23.3
Liberty League, Lithuania 1992	4.8
Liberty League, Lithuania 1996	21.7
Lithuanian Nationalist Union 1992	12.5
Lithuanian Nationalist Union 1996	15.6
Lithuanian Nationalist Union 2000	9.4
Young Lithuania 1996	20.0
Young Lithuania 2000	26.7
Latvian Fatherland and Freedom 2002[1]	16.9
Estonian Citizen 1992	19.2
Estonian Citizen 1995[2]	14.9
Liberal Democratic Party of Russia 1993[3]	6.0
Liberal Democratic Party of Russia 1995	5.8
Zhirinovskii Bloc 1999	7.8
Derzhava, Russia 1995	8.3
Congress of Russian Communities 1999	12.6
Populist parties	
KPN (Confederation for Independent Poland) 1991	9.3
KPN, Poland 1993	14.8
Alternatywa, Poland 2001	21.3
Self-Defence (SamoObrona), Poland 1991[4]	0.0
Self-Defence (SamoObrona), Poland 1993	16.6
Self-Defence, Poland 1997	17.1
Self-Defence, Poland 2001	19.7
Smer, Slovakia 2002	19.7
Movement for Democratic Slovakia 1994[5]	*21.5*
Movement for Democratic Slovakia 1998	*19.3*
Movement for Democratic Slovakia 2002	*33.3*
Extreme-right parties	
Polish Nat'l Comm'wealth-Polish National Party (PSN–PWN), 1991	14.3

Table 8.12   (Continued)

Parties	% Women candidates
PSN–PWN, 1993	19.5
PSN–PWN, 2001	29.3
Czech Republicans 1996	15.8
Czech Republicans 1998	15.3

[1] From http://www.cvk.lv/cgi-bin/wdbcgiw/base/sae8dev.cvkand.otra.   [2] Better Estonia.   [3] From R. Sakwa, 'The Russian Elections of December 1993', *Europe-Asia Studies*, vol. 47, no. 2, 1995, p. 205.   [4] 3 candidates only.   [5] With Agrarian Party; ***bold italics indicates controversy of classification***.

important variations between countries and within countries across time, but gradually the numbers of women have crept up in most parties. Left-wing parties were not notably more favourable to women candidates at the start of transition, but after several elections there appeared to be a clear shift in favour of more women, especially with the introduction of quotas. The religious parties generally had few women but also showed some variation. Extremist parties were not notably more male-dominated than other parties.

Electoral parties

The broad electoral-party format such as AWS in Poland, the Democratic Convention in Romania in 1996, the Slovak Democratic Coalition in 1998, and many electoral 'blocs' of Russia and the Ukraine did indeed appear markedly less women-friendly (see Table 8.13). We also saw some evidence of this in Chapter 7. These groupings had strong male leaders. The 'parties of power' in particular had undeveloped internal structures and informal candidate-selection procedures. When they negotiated candidacies with

Table 8.13   Women candidates in electoral parties (%)

New umbrellas	% Women Candidates
AWS, Poland 1997	10.6
Democratic Convention, Romania 1996	10.0
Slovak Democratic Coalition 1998	12.0
Our Ukraine 2002[1]	9.9
Parties of power	
Party of Russian Unity and Concord (PRES) 1993[2]	3.0
Our Home is Russia 1995	14.5
Party of Russian Unity and Concord (PRES)	12.1
Unity, Russia 1999	11.8
For a United Ukraine 2002[1]	7.7

[1] List candidates only.   [2] *Source*: R. Sakwa, 'The Russian Elections of December 1993', *Europe-Asia Studies*, vol. 47, no. 2, 1995, p. 201.

other leaders from the separate constituent 'parties', they cumulated the male dominance of party leaderships.

The use of quotas

Where parties attended to their own internal structures and procedures, formal rules governing candidate selection created an opening to challenge them and the idea of quotas gained ground. We have already suggested that some contagion may be at work, with smaller parties initiating new mechanisms to promote women. The origins of early initiatives remain unclear, but the Labour Union (UP) was the first Polish party with such a strategy. Poland had a strong parliamentary women's group, though its cross-party membership was limited to secular parties. In 2001 the Social Democrats (SLD) and the Freedom Union unsuccessfully promoted the inclusion of women's quotas in the electoral law, but they applied quotas to their own candidate lists in the September elections. The Freedom Union made the issue of increasing women's representation central to its television advertising strategy (we draw no conclusions from its ignominious defeat). The substantial victory of the SLD–UP alliance, however, was not the only reason for the considerable increase in women deputies. Women elected from the new clerical nationalist League of Polish Families also swelled their numbers.

In Lithuania Kazimiera Prunskienė's Women's Party (later New Democracy) brought the issue of quotas to the agenda. The Social Democrats introduced a quota for women candidates of 20 per cent in 1996, later raised to 30 per cent; and its merger with the successor LDDP in 2001 maintained the quota system for the new Social Democratic Party. The issue was then debated in all Lithuanian parties, as the use of quotas forced other parties to develop 'convincing arguments' against them.[56] In 2002 the Hungarian Socialists increased the proportion of women candidates substantially with a quota system. In Slovakia both HZDS and the Party of the Democratic Left introduced quotas for the 2002 elections.

Choosing women candidates is but one dimension of the process. Standing as a candidate may give personal satisfaction, and candidate recruitment tells us something about the general sphere of political participation. Whether a candidate can win or not depends on two other dimensions, whether the party itself gains seats and whether parties place women in winnable seats.

The electoral system

We have seen that while Bulgaria (in 1990), Russia, Lithuania, and the Ukraine (in 1998) adopted mixed-parallel electoral systems, PR was more common (Hungary had a distinctive mixed-linked system). The mixed-parallel systems constituted a new type of electoral system, and the interactive

Table 8.14   Women candidates in single-member districts[1]

	Number of women standing for parties in smd's	Women as % of party smd candidates	Women as % of list candidates	Smds without women candidates, number and %	Smds where no winning party fielded a woman, no. and %
Lithuania					
1992	93	11.3	11.7	41 (57.7)	48 (67.6)
1996	166	19.6	20.7	4 (5.6)	20 (28.2)
2000	101	15.6	17.7	17 (23.9)	22 (31.0)
Hungary					
1990	97	6.0		79 (44.5)	123 (69.9)
1994	158	8.4		21 (11.9)	84 (47.7)
1998	181	10.9		55 (31.3)	97 (55.1)
2002	164	13.2	18.2	65 (36.9)	119 (67.6)
Russia					
1995	202	12.9	15.2	69 (30.7)	115 (51.1)
1999	158	14.6	16.5	73 (32.4)	134 (59.6)

[1] Excludes Independents, but includes other 'non-parties'.

effects of the two elements were not entirely clear. However, Table 8.14 shows that parties were somewhat more reluctant to place women in single-member districts, though the difference was not great. Moreover, many single-member constituencies offered no choice of a woman candidate, and even more gave voters no chance to vote for a woman from a popular (winning) party.

Because mixed systems give parties a choice of recruitment strategy, parties made different choices (see Table 8.15) and changed between elections. In many cases candidates in single-member constituencies also stood on their party's list, though this also varied. In Russia in 1995 of the 202 women candidates who stood for a party in a single-member district, 70 (34 per cent) did not stand on their party's list in the proportional element; in 1999 it was 70 out of 158 (44 per cent). In Lithuania in 2000 of 101 women party candidates in single-member districts, 23 (22.8 per cent) did not stand on their party list.

Table 8.14 shows that popular parties (those that won seats) fielded women in fewer constituencies than did electoral contenders as a whole. Robert Moser noted that women did better in Russia's single-member districts than on party lists.[57] But generally this was not the case. Lists looked kinder to women. More women won in list seats than in single-member districts, *except* in Russia, where the disparity was less in 1999 than in 1995 (see Table 8.16).

Table 8.15   Women in SMD's and on party lists (%) of selected parties in Lithuania and Russia

Party	Lithuania 1996		Lithuania 2000	
	SMD	List	SMD	List
Lithuanian Liberal Union	8.6	9.8	12.7	12.9
Christian Democratic Union	0.0	8.0	17.4	16.3
Lithuanian Socialist Party	30.0	37.5		
Lithuanian Social-Democratic Party	22.5	24.2	12.1	in alliance
Lithuanian Democratic Labour Party	14.9	14.3	15.2	25.0[1]
Homeland Union (Conservatives)	19.4	16.7	24.4	17.1
Lithuanian Christian Democratic Party	18.5	20.9	15.4	17.2
	Russia 1995		Russia 1999	
Our Home is Russia	20.2	13.0	10.8	11.8
Yabloko	14.5	12.9	15.5	11.0
Union of Right Forces	n/a		13.5	17.4
Communist Party of the Russian Federation	11.6	10.9	13.2	10.8
Zhirinovskii Bloc/Liberal Democratic Party	4.8	5.8	13.5	1.4
Russia's Democratic Choice	13.9	9.7		

[1] Brazauskas Social Democratic Coalition (including New Democracy, formerly the Women's Party).

Table 8.16   Women deputies by element of electoral system in mixed systems

Election	Elected in SMDs	Elected from list	
Lithuania			
1992	5	5	
1996	9	14	
2000	6	9	
Ukraine			
1998	15	19	
2002	8	15	
Russia			
1995	30	13	
1999	19	16	
		Regional	National
Hungary			
1990	6	9	14
1994	13	16	12
1998	12	13	7
2002	13	16	6

Indeed, the underdeveloped nature of Russian parties was the source of many anomalies. In part this was a product of its sheer size and diversity. The multiplicity of factors affecting electoral outcomes makes it difficult to identify a significant role for the electoral system in explaining the position of women (who in any case remained severely underrepresented). Of the 30 women who won in Russia's 225 single-member districts in 1995, nine were Independents, while three came from Women of Russia and one from the 'non-partisan voters' movement' Common Cause; the largest single contingent (8) came from the Communist Party. In 1999 the number of women elected in single-member districts dropped substantially – to 19. Of these, three were Independents, while seven came from the Communist Party. Only 12 per cent of single-member district candidates were women, but they constituted 16.5 per cent of list candidates.

Moreover, when candidates stand in both elements, some candidates may also be placed high on their party's list. In the Ukraine in 1998 four women winners would have won from their party's list (two were placed first) even if they had been defeated in their individual constituency battles. This was also the case with one woman in Lithuania in 1996, placed second on her party's list. This party, the Homeland Union, fielded only 19 women candidates, but thirteen became deputies, seven from single-member districts. In 2000 the party's vote plummeted, and it lost all but one of its single-member seats.

Proportional representation

With no enduring examples of majoritarianism we obviously cannot compare proportional and majoritarian systems with reference to the putative advantages to women of PR. However, we saw above that that it did appear to make a difference whether a system was 'pure' PR, mixed-linked, or mixed-parallel. Party-strengthening and party continuity appeared beneficial to women's representation, and these were better served by PR or (the Hungarian) mixed-linked system, where Independents rapidly vanished from the political landscape. But PR by itself cannot generate women's representation. Party behaviour is the key. It is not sufficient for parties to field women candidates. If women sit bunched at the bottom of the list, they will never win.

With closed-list systems the decision about how many deputies rests largely with the voters, but who they shall be rests with the party. Closed lists can only be beneficial when there are women in winnable list places. Open lists are often said to disadvantage women (see above), but this is based on the controversial assumption that voters prefer a man to a woman. With opportunities to express a personal preference, do post-communist voters shy away from women candidates?

Table 8.17 shows that few parties chose to put women in the most visible and most winnable seats of all, the top two places. Table 8.18 also shows

Table 8.17 Party list placings of women candidates (% within list place, all contenders)

Election	Total women list candidates (%)	Women in 1st place	Women in 2nd place	Top two places	Top four of list	Top ten of list
Poland						
2001	22.8	11.2	17.6	14.4	16.6	21.4
1997	12.9	8.8	15.6	12.2	14.1	15.5
1993	13.1	11.2	13.6	12.4	12.9	13.0
1991	15.7	11.3	12.8	12.1	12.7	15.1
Lithuania						
2000	17.7	0.0	0.0	0.0	10.0	10.0
1996	20.4	4.2	12.5	8.5	9.4	16.3
1992	11.6	0.0	11.8	14.7	4.8	10.0
Russia federal						
1999	20.7	16.0	12.0	14.0	18.4	19.6
Russia regional						
1999	16.2	18.4	19.4	18.9	16.3	16.3
Slovakia						
2002	23.6	12.0	16.0	14.0	19.0	16.8
1998	16.7	11.8	17.6	14.7	10.4	13.0
1994	15.5	5.8	14.7	10.3	13.9	15.5
Czech Republic						
1998	21.1	15.5	17.5	16.5	18.4	17.6
1996	20.4	14.7	20.4	17.6	19.8	18.2
Hungary						
2002	18.2	11.0	12.4	11.7	13.3	14.5
1998[1]	13.7	11.1	13.3	12.2		

Note: Excludes independents.
[1] % of 1st and 2nd placed candidates respectively, not from the total of 3777 candidates.

Table 8.18 List placing of women candidates by political parties winning seats (%)

Election	Women list candidates	Winning women (party-list candidates)	Women in 1st list place	Women in 2nd list place	Average 1st/2nd placing	Women in top four list places	Women in top ten list places
Poland							
2001	22.8	20.2	12.7[1]	17.1[1]	14.9[1]	15.7[1]	20.8[1]
1997	12.9[1]	13.8	6.5[1]	16.2[1]	11.4[1]	11.9[1]	13.5[1]
1993	13.1	13.0[1]	12.2[1]	14.4[1]	13.3[1]	13.5[1]	13.6[1]
1991	15.7	9.6[2]	10.9[2]	10.3[2]	10.6[2]	11.0	11.1
Lithuania							
2000	18.4	12.9	0.0	0.0	0.0	28.6	13.0
1996	20.4	20.0	0.0	13.3	6.7	9.1	17.1
1992	11.7	7.1	0.0	15.4	7.7	8.3	11.1
Russia federal							
1999	20.7		0.0	0.0	0.0		
Russia regional							
1999	16.2		10.4	12.7	11.6		

Slovakia							
2002	23.6	14.7	0.0	28.6	14.3	10.7	8.6
1998	16.7	10.7	0.0	33.3	16.7	8.3	8.3
1994	15.5	14.7	3.6	10.7	7.2	11.6	14.7
Czech Republic							
1998	21.1	15.0	10.0	17.5	13.8	16.5	20.4
1996	20.4	14.5	14.6	17.4	16.0	19.3	17.7
Hungary							
1998	13.7	11.1	13.3	12.2	13.3	7.0	
2002	18.2	17.1	11.7	14.8			13.2

Note: these are regional list placings.

[1] Excluding German minority. [2] Excluding all social organisations, including Solidarity; local and regional groups, and minority organisations.

that often the parties that actually won seats were more reluctant than the total of all electoral contenders to place women at the highest reaches of their lists. Slovakia in 2002 illustrates this – of those in the top four list places, 19 per cent were women, but for winning parties this figure was less than 11 per cent. However, parties did not simply dump women at the bottom of their lists. Generally in bivariate regressions we found that gender was not significantly correlated with list place (Poland in 2001 and Lithuania in 2000 were exceptions). Indeed, this is also apparent in Tables 8.17 and 8.18.

Of course, the notion of 'winnable seats' may be highly problematic in conditions of high voter volatility. Parties often had little idea of which seats they might win, especially new parties testing the electoral waters. Opinion polls showed their national aggregate appeal, not constituency support. Some parties developed apparent strongholds over successive elections, but the imponderables of new challengers still remained high. But when a party was genuinely committed to increasing the share of women's representation, it produced results.

We can illustrate this with the Polish case. In Poland in 2001 both elements of the SLD–UP alliance had seriously addressed the issue of women's representation. In principle every three list places should have had a woman candidate. In the case of the SLD the party had to use the weight of its central apparatus against its provincial parties during the recruitment process, but that commitment was still not fully met. The abolition of the national list prevented the parties from attempting to shape the final composition of their parliamentary deputies. In addition, of course, the open list created uncertainties about outcomes. But the alliance had the huge advantage of strength in every constituency. About six seats was its realistic limit; in the event its maximum was eight seats and its minimum two. Table 8.19 shows the allocation of the top eight list places, accounting for almost 80 per cent of women deputies from the SLD–UP. In the 2001 parliament 25 per cent of

Table 8.19   Gender and list place in the SLD–UP, 2001

List place	No. of men	% Men	No. of women	% Women	Women winning from list place	% SLD–UP women winning
1	34	82.9	7	17.1	7	12.7
2	36	87.8	5	12.2	5	9.1
3	30	73.2	11	26.8	7	12.7
4	32	78.0	9	22.0	8	14.5
5	27	65.9	14	34.1	6	10.9
6	29	70.7	12	29.3	5	9.1
7	25	61.0	16	39.0	3	5.5
8	30	73.2	11	26.8	2	3.6

Table 8.20 Gender and list place in the SLD, 1997

List place	No. of men	% Men	No. of women	% Women	Women winning from list place	% SLD–UP women winning
1	46	88.5	6	11.5	6	19.4
2	43	82.7	9	17.3	4	12.9
3	45	86.5	7	13.5	5	16.1
4	45	86.5	7	13.5	2	6.5
5	44	86.3	7	13.7	3	9.7
6	39	78.0	11	22.0	3	9.7
7	33	76.7	10	23.3	2	6.5
8	31	86.1	5	13.9	1	3.2

its deputies were women. Quotas made a difference. Yet the increase was far from dramatic.

In 1997 the SLD increased its vote from the previous election, but it faced a united opposition in AWS, and it lost seats. It fielded fewer women candidates and placed fewer in top list places than in 2001 (see Table 8.20). Twenty-two per cent of its winning list candidates were women, but the SLD did not 'top up' its women: of 23 candidates elected from the national list, only 3 were women, making the proportion of its women deputies 20.7 per cent.

District magnitude

We did not systematically attempt to test the impact of district magnitude, not least because it changed in several countries along with other changes in the electoral system. However, we can see from the Lithuanian and Slovak examples that large district magnitude does not necessarily help women. The logic of the argument assumes that since men are more likely to occupy the highest list places, then small district magnitude will see men elected. Conversely, with larger district magnitudes, successful parties will see more candidates elected from lower down the list and more will likely be women. But this appears to depend in some measure on having large parties. If lots of small parties win seats, their deputies will still come from the highest list places. The formula is also an issue here, since it can have a great impact on which seats go to which parties. Trying to extract such factors was not only beyond our scope, but seemed largely irrelevant given the attitude of so many parties to women. If actors do not respond, then apparent incentives will not operate. But it is worth reinforcing in passing that this is not a facile or automatic causal factor.

Both Lithuania and Slovakia (in 1998 and 2002) used national constituencies, that is, their district magnitudes were the highest possible. In 1992 only 7 per cent of Lithuania's deputies were women. This figure rose to 16.8 per cent in 1996, but it fell back again to 10.6 per cent in 2000. In Lithuania the mixed system made it difficult to correlate list places with seats won; the largest parties fielded long lists – well over the number of seats – so that candidates could move up when other list members won in single-member districts. In 2000 the largest number of list seats was 28 (of 70), won by the Social Democrats; but of its five winning women candidates two won from list places 30 and 47. In the 2004 election the Social Democrats will operate a quota system, and that may indeed make a difference if they do well.

In Slovakia 14.7 per cent of deputies were women in 1994, but this figure dropped to 10.7 per cent when the single national constituency was introduced, rising again to 14.7 per cent in 2002. In Slovakia winning parties did not field as many women: the proportion of women candidates for winning parties in 1998 was 14.2 and in 2002 14.7 per cent. For non-winning parties the proportions were 19.8 and 24.1 per cent respectively. In Tables 8.17 and 8.18 we saw that this difference also applied to list placings. With a quota system and even though *one-third* of HZDS candidates were women, there were only three women in the top 30 list places and ten in the top 50 (women won 5 of its 36 seats or 13.8 per cent). Yet we should also note that the incompatibility rules of the Slovak parliament had an effect on its final composition. In 2002 after 18 male deputies resigned their seats to assume government posts, seven of their substitutes were women, increasing the proportion of women deputies from 14.7 per cent to 19.3 per cent.

It is also true that both countries used preference systems. We noted above that these have been deemed less beneficial to women than closed lists (so long as parties place women on their closed lists). But this finding was not borne out by the cases examined here. Voters did not systematically shy away from women candidates.

Preference voting

Earlier we looked at the general principles of preference and open-list voting (see Chapter 5), so here we shall move directly to address the question of preference voting and women's representation. Preference voting made little difference. In Slovakia in 1994, when 13 deputies (of 150) owed their seats to the voters, there was a net gain of one woman: Two women gained from preference votes and one woman lost. In 1998 the preference system was effectively irrelevant because of the single national constituency and made no difference at all. In 2002 one male candidate superseded another.

In the Czech Republic the impact of preference voting on women's representation was also limited; in 1998 only two candidates (of 200) were elected who would not have been victorious with a closed-list system; one was a woman. In 2002 two women displaced male candidates. In Lithuania in 2000, 15 deputies were elected out of party list-order: two women gained and two lost.

Poland's open-list system gave more scope for moving candidates. Judging by the battles over list placings within the political parties, they certainly regarded list place as the key to getting their favoured candidates elected; and many parties advocated closed lists. Voters did move candidates. In 1991 first-placed candidates received 70.8 per cent of votes, 45.5 per cent in 1993, 33 per cent in 1997 and 33.5 per cent in 2001. Table 8.21 shows how the voters could confound the parties' own rankings.

To better assess these relationships Marina Popescu ran a logistic regression equation in each of the four post-communist Polish elections with the dummy for 'elected or not elected in the constituency' as the dependent variable. The aim was twofold: First we aimed to see whether voters tinkered with their party lists and chose candidates placed on the list *below* the number of seats gained by the candidate's party in the respective constituency. Second we asked whether gender made a difference, namely – once list place and party affiliation are controlled for – whether female or male candidates were more likely to be selected by voters and thus elected.

We first created a variable that takes into account the number of seats that each party gained in each constituency. This was introduced into the equation as a control for party and constituency, and it fulfils the role of dummies for parties and possible interaction terms party*constituency, while avoiding multi-collinearity problems. Derived from it are two variables that give a positive or negative score respectively for the candidate that ranked above or below the number of seats his/her party received in the constituency. The higher the positive score of the candidate ranking above the 'electiveness threshold', the higher the candidate's place on the list, while the lower the negative score, the further the placement of the candidate from this threshold. The regression equation assumes that parties place their 'preferred' candidates in eligible places, and that they have a rough idea of how many seats they can win in each constituency. It does not assume that voters have information about how many candidates their party will elect in that constituency.

As Table 8.22 shows, both scores regarding list placement had a positive effect on the chances of being elected, which means that the closer to the top position a candidate was on the party list, the more likely he/she was to be elected; conversely, the lower a candidate on the list, the lower the probability of election.

The most significant trend that can be observed is the decrease in relevance of list placement over time, with a slight increase in 2001. This was especially the case regarding the chances of election for a candidate placed in the lower part of the list. The decrease of the coefficients from 1.38 in 1991 to 0.98 in 1993 and 0.66 in 1997 suggests that how much lower below the 'electiveness threshold' a candidate was placed on the party list mattered less for his/her chances of election in post-1991 elections compared to 1991. The lower values of the R^2 over time (with a slight increase in 2002, still

Table 8.21 Poland: victorious women candidates by list place

List place	Poland 1991		Poland 1993		Poland 1997		Poland 2001	
	Number	% Women winners	Number	% Women winners	Number	% Women winners	Number	% Women winners
1	28	63.6	19	31.7	14	22.2	28	30.2
2	5	11.4	11	18.3	9	14.3	10	10.8
3	4	9.1	6	10.0	10	15.9	7	7.5
4	4	9.1	7	11.7	5	7.9	10	10.8
5	1	2.3	4	6.7	4	6.3	8	8.6
6	1	2.3	–	–	4	6.3	7	7.5
7	–	–	5	8.3	2	3.2	4	4.3
8	–	–	1	1.7	1	1.6	3	3.2
9	–	–	1	1.7	1	1.6	3	3.2
10	–	–	1	1.7	2	3.2	4	4.3
11	–	–	2	3.3	1	1.6	2	2.2
12	–	–	1	1.7	3	4.7	2	2.2
13	–	–	–	–	1	1.6	1	1.1
14	–	–	–	–	–	–	2	2.2
15	–	–	1	1.7	–	–	–	–
16	–	–	–	–	1	1.6	1	1.1
17	1	2.3	1	1.7	–	–	–	–

18	–	–	1.6	1	–	–	–	–
19	1.1	1	–	–	–	–	–	–
20	–	–	1.6	1	–	–	–	–
21	–	–	–	–	–	–	–	–
22	–	–	–	–	–	–	–	–
23	–	–	–	–	–	–	–	–
24	–	–	–	–	–	–	–	–
25	–	–	1.6	1	–	–	–	–
26	–	–	1.6	1	–	–	–	–
27	–	–	–	–	–	–	–	–
28	–	–	–	–	–	–	–	–
29	–	–	–	–	–	–	–	–
30	–	–	–	–	–	–	–	–
31	–	–	–	–	–	–	–	–
32	–	–	1.6	–	–	–	–	–
33	–	–	–	1	–	–	–	–
34	–	–	–	–	–	–	–	–

Table 8.22   The role of list placing in Poland

Variable	B (S.E)			
	1991	1993	1997	2001
Placement in the top part of the party list	1.358 (0.425)	0.985 (0.153)	0.662 (0.100)	0.744 (0.155)
Placement in the bottom part of the party list	1.396 (0.080)	0.552 (0.040)	0.307 (0.026)	0.401 (0.036)
No. of seats won by respective party in constituency	0.170 (0.158)	0.143 (0.055)	0.143 (0.041)	0.143 (0.050)
Gender (0 male, 1 female)	−0.246 (0.241)	0.235 (0.203)	0.294 (0.190)	−0.188 (0.236)
Constant	0.296 (0.214)	−0.634 (0.158)	−1.034 (0.149)	−0.897 (0.174)
Nagelkerke R squared	0.597	0.517	0.399	0.505

Source: Marina Popescu.
Note: Logistic regression analysis. Dependent variable candidate elected or losing in a constituency.
B coefficients, standard errors in brackets.

much below the 1991 level) indicate the same trend, that is, a decrease in relevance of list placing, other explanatory factors being at work. Given that there were no significant changes in ballot format this may suggest a change in voters' behaviour, namely more frequent use of the possibilities of the open list.

Thus it can be said that a learning process took place in respect of the functioning of the electoral system and that the relevance of individual candidates in vote choice increased. Given that the impact of the relevance of party size (as measured by number of seats gained in each constituency) increased in 1993 to 0.14 (SE 0.05), from statistical insignificance in 1991, and remained at the same level over time, we are inclined to say that the increased salience given to candidates is not to the detriment of the party. It rather indicates better knowledge of party candidates and thus more familiarity with the parties themselves.

By introducing gender into the equation we sought to establish whether gender has a significant effect on the candidate's chances of being elected once placement on the list, size of the party, and constituency are controlled for. The statistically insignificant and inconsistent results of the four logistic regressions suggest that gender did not have a bearing once other conditions are accounted for. In other words, a similar place on the list of winning parties offers similar chances of election, whatever the candidate's gender. This is an indication that personal preference voting neither improves nor hinders the chances of female candidates, which stem simply from their party affiliation and list ranking.

However, it should also be noted that much depends on the skill the parties display in compiling their lists to accord with the voters' views. In 1997 AWS used a complex highly centralised system based on weightings of its component parties; high list places went mainly to party and trade union leaders, but the voters had their own preferences. AWS voters moved Halina Nowina-Konopka from sixteenth to first place in her constituency and Maria Smereczyńska from thirty-third place to third. They moved sixteen women upwards into winning places and reduced only two to lower (but still winning) rankings. AWS voters were more likely to move women candidates to winning places than voters for the Freedom Union. The women winners from the latter were already high on their lists and/or had high national list places.

Moreover in 2001 when the SLD–UP alliance introduced quotas, women gained further from voters' choices. Nine women lost because of this; but thirteen women won, making a net gain of four who would not have been elected with a closed list. This casts some light on the reasons why gender does not have a significant impact: effects in one direction for one party are likely to be cancelled out by effects in the opposite direction for another party. Since the AWS was a significant player in 1997, the changes in the rankings of its women candidates may be the reason why the positive relationship between gender and winning a seat just fails to reach statistical significance.

So are closed lists better for women? They cannot be unless women are placed in winning positions. Are open lists worse? This was not the case in Poland, but further analysis should try to account for the distinct dynamics of particular parties.

Conclusion

We have explored rather than tested some elements of theoretical propositions derived from Western European political systems. Clearly this is a very preliminary survey, and it would be inappropriate to reach dogmatic conclusions. We can summarise our findings as follows.

Communist economic development included women and bequeathed a pool of highly educated women. However, the prevalence of working women proved compatible with a political culture stressing traditional women's roles. Despite small enclaves or subcultures, and participation of women in 'local' civil society, political culture was inimical and no demands from below emerged for increasing the political role of women. Few women stood as candidates, and somewhat fewer were elected.

Of those who stood, women working in the professions played a substantial role. They were the largest group of candidates everywhere save Russia.

However, women candidates drawn from the business world played a greater role than expected, especially in the former Soviet Union. Workers maintained a presence in Poland, the Czech Republic, and Slovakia. Elsewhere they all but disappeared. But the profile of deputies was far narrower than that of candidates, and few workers were actually elected.

The type of party did not initially appear significantly to affect the proportion or nature of women candidates, though the success of Women of Russia made a difference to the proportion of women deputies in 1993. However, some evidence of 'contagion' became apparent. Several small left-wing parties introduced quotas for women, and large social democratic successor parties followed suit in Poland, Hungary, Slovakia, and Lithuania. In Hungary in 2002 about two-thirds of women deputies came from the Socialist Party. In Central Europe (but not in Russia or the Ukraine) the differentiation between types of party became apparent: being left-wing appeared to have an impact over time. Christian and Christian democratic parties fielded fewer women candidates, but not without exceptions. Radical parties were not as male-dominated as their image might suggest, but they had fewer women professionals than other parties. At the same time, electoral parties did indeed prove less favourable to women's representation. In Romania the Democratic Convention was particularly male (but so too were the Romanian social democrats and nationalists).

Electoral system characteristics do not explain similarities and differences. Parties are the key. Women candidates and deputies were more numerous in 'pure' PR systems, but we cannot attribute this simply to the electoral system. In mixed systems differences in the proportions of women contesting the two elements were not significant. However, more women won in list seats than in single-member districts, except in Russia. In PR systems parties did not put women in the lowest list places, though they did not put them in the highest places either. There was no significant correlation between gender and list place. Preference voting made little or no difference to outcomes. But closed lists cannot benefit women unless women are placed in winnable positions. In Poland there was no clear disadvantage to women from open lists.

The evidence for a country division between Russia, the Ukraine, and Romania and the others is admittedly thin. Yet their overall low levels of women's participation and analysis of their individual parties do show lower figures than the others: country may be more important than ideology, taking us back to structural/cultural features and historical legacies, as well as the super-presidentialism of Russia and the Ukraine. But the division also raises the question of physical proximity to Western Europe and links to Western European parties.

Deeply embedded clientelistic relationships appear particularly inimical to progress. The still partial democracy of Russia and the Ukraine in particular appeared to be reflected in this area too. However, the spread of the language of gender-egalitarianism could already be detected in Central Europe after the first post-communist decade. Some progress was undoubted, though reversals in particular party fortunes may be sudden. Yet exposure to the gender-egalitarian values and practices of many West European states will become greater with the accession of new members to the European Union and their participation in the European Parliament.

9
The Political Representation of National Minorities

Democracy and minority rights

National minorities have provided a thorny area for theorists of liberal democracy, for its underlying liberal individualism sits uneasily with concepts of group or collective rights. Liberal representative democracy is conceived as providing expression of the majority will, while simultaneously safeguarding the rights of minorities. Traditionally this entailed the protection of *individual* civil liberties, including the right to act collectively as with the freedom of association. But as democracy itself took root, rights' discourse changed and evolved from the late nineteenth century onward, as nationalism and socialism both offered collectivist perspectives on rights. Even the liberal Woodrow Wilson embraced the right of national self-determination as the key principle of the post-war peace settlement in 1918. At the same time the fears engendered among European élites by the Russian Revolution led to the establishment of the International Labour Organisation to develop standards for the protection and treatment of industrial workers, later acknowledged as 'workers' rights'.

Wilson's promotion of self-determination as the basis for unravelling empires revealed his ignorance of the patchwork of settlement of diverse ethnic groups throughout eastern and southern Europe. Of the newly created states only Hungary was ethnically homogeneous following the dismantling of its part of the Habsburg empire. The Treaty of Trianon was punitive, leaving large Hungarian minorities in every neighbouring state. More generally, numerous revisionist-irredentist territorial disputes in inter-war Eastern Europe were ethnic at base, and 'ethnic tensions constituted East Central Europe's most vivid and sensitive political problem...'.[1] In belated recognition of the impossibility of drawing 'ethnic' borders, especially when strategic and economic interests provided an additional criterion for boundary-making, the peacemakers sought to ensure national minority protection. They concluded specific minorities protection treaties with Poland, Czechoslovakia, Romania, and Greece, as well as offering an early instance of 'conditionality', when declarations concerning the protection of minorities served as a condition of entry to the League of Nations for Finland, the three Baltic states, Albania, and Iraq.

Neither the treaties nor the declarations made much practical difference[2] – though Estonia had a distinctive model of minority cultural autonomy[3] – and it was not until after the traumatic cataclysm of the Second World War that international human rights law began to develop. Western Europe led the way in the provision of supranational institutions to adjudicate on issues of human rights. The European Convention on Human Rights and Fundamental Freedoms (1950) provided a catalogue of rights to be enjoyed without discrimination, including discrimination on grounds of belonging to a national minority. The European Commission of Human Rights and the European Court of Human Rights would ensure the implementation of the human rights regime.

Gradually the concept of minority rights as collective rights developed – not always explicitly – in the International Covenant of Civil and Political Rights (Article 27) and in forums of the Council of Europe. But it was not until the 1990s that minority rights shot to the top of the European political agenda, spurred by ethnic conflicts in (ex)Yugoslavia and the former Soviet Union. Academic debates on the nature of minority rights,[4] the deficiencies of liberalism,[5] and mechanisms of conflict resolution[6] drew attention to minorities in parallel with practical concerns about political stability, human rights, and refugee flows in the Council of Europe, the Conference on Security and Cooperation in Europe (CSCE, later OSCE), NATO, and the European Communities.

These concerns found expression in various international instruments, such as the 1992 Charter on Regional and Minority Languages and the 1995 Framework Convention for the Protection of National Minorities, ratified by most European states under the auspices of the Council of Europe. The Framework Convention was the first legally binding international instrument dedicated to the protection of minorities.

In its 'pre-accession process' the European Union made minority rights central to the Copenhagen accession criteria in June 1993: 'Membership requires that the candidate country has achieved stability of institutions guaranteeing democracy, the rule of law, human rights and respect for and protection of minorities.' However, the Council of Europe's controversial Recommendation 1201, a new protocol on minority rights for the ECHR, was rejected, not least because of its acknowledgement of collective rights for minorities.[7]

So there was far from universal agreement on precisely which minorities should be recognised, whether and what rights should be accorded to them, or how these rights should be safeguarded. Even the very definition of a minority remained contentious, and some European states such as France and Greece denied the existence of minorities whose presence to others was palpably real. For those countries aspiring to EU membership, however, the notion of 'minority protection' began at last to be taken seriously. For the EU such protection had two dimensions: first, anti-discrimination measures 'to ensure that individuals are not treated differently from others for unjustifiable reasons' and second, rights protection 'to allow individuals and communities to preserve their differences so as to avoid forced assimilation into a majority culture'.[8] Political representation falls within this brief, but in contrast to language and education, it received little explicit attention.

This chapter examines the mechanisms for providing ethnic minority representation at national level, as well as the ethnic parties that emerged and their strategies. Its brief is simple and largely descriptive. It will not probe the challenges of collective-rights approaches to liberal democracy, though it will take cognisance of them. Clearly there is no 'theory of minority representation', nor indeed are there international norms or standards beyond the general provisions noted above. Special arrangements for minority representation remain rare, and there is a measure of *ad hocery* in this area of institutional design.

We take as given that certain groups possess a distinctive cultural identity, described as ethnic or national, that differs from that of their co-citizens. The terms ethnic or national minority are used interchangeably, although some minorities prefer to describe themselves as co-nations or partner-nations. Almost all countries accept the notion of minority self-identification. There is often merit in semantic distinctions, but this is an area where terminological refinement does not necessarily enlighten.

Of course, some minorities, especially small ones lacking political resources, may limit their aspirations to the cultural sphere, as with the Polish Tatars, who stress their 'Polishness' and identification with the Polish state but also their cultural and religious difference.[9] Paul Brass has argued that when an ethnic group succeeds in attaining national status and recognition, it becomes a nationality or a nation. 'A nation is...an ethnic community politicised, with recognised group rights in the political system.'[10] Yet few states recognise the existence of 'group rights', and groups differ widely in their degree of politicisation. So we shall stick to ethnicity and minorities, while concentrating on minority groups that have a degree of national-level political organisation or recognition.

Minorities in Central and Eastern Europe

Every post-communist country has pockets of minorities. They are the legacy of empire, conquest, and upheaval and resulting historical legacies ripe for rediscovery and revision. The largest minorities in post-communist Europe are the Russians, some 25 million strong, followed by the Roma and about 3.5 million Hungarians. Turks are concentrated in Bulgaria. The Ukraine has a mixed Ukrainian and Russian population, also with numerous other small minorities.

Yet ethnic mix does not automatically signify a high degree of ethnic consciousness. Neither language nor ethnicity proved a good guide to attitudes to the Ukrainian state. Linguistic and ethnic boundaries remained remarkably fluid: the three main groups, the Ukrainophone Ukrainians, Russophone Ukrainians, and ethnic Russians, were 'highly amorphous entities for which clear-cut bounded identities and even agreed definitions do not yet exist'.[11] The concept of a 'Soviet' identity persisted in parts of eastern and southern Ukraine, and regional identities also remained strong. In 2002 'reformers' still dominated western and central Ukraine and the oligarchic 'parties of power' the east and the south.

The Roma are particularly distinctive because they are non-territorial and have no 'homeland', many do not acknowledge a Roma identity (a 'Roma ethnic identity' is even more problematic); and they are often dispersed within a country. Their numbers are controversial but according to Zoltan Barany's careful study, an estimated 4.5 million Roma lived in the region in the 1990s, with Bulgaria, Slovakia, and Romania having the highest proportions.[12]

Hungarians form substantial minorities in Romania, Slovakia, and in the Serbian province of Vojvodina, and there are also Hungarians in the Ukraine. They constitute some 7 per cent of the population of Romania and some 10 per cent of the population of Slovakia. The Turks in Bulgaria are a direct legacy of Ottoman rule, constituting about 10 per cent of the population. They are largely concentrated in agricultural areas in two pockets of the north and the south, each with four 'subprovinces' with a Turkish majority.[13] Of the other countries examined here Estonia and Latvia have large Russian minorities and many other smaller ones. Inside the Russian Federation, a highly variegated ethnic mix, the largest minority are the so-called 'ethnic Muslims': they were some 12 million (8 per cent of the population) in 1989 and perhaps as many as 20 million (14 per cent) in 2001.[14]

The constitutional framework

Constitutional mechanisms establish the framework for minority politics, not least because the Constitution defines the basic political community that forms the foundation of the polity[15] on a given territory, as well as the degree of centralisation of institutions. Federal systems adopt a division of power that can accommodate distinct group identities within the polity, but so too can devolution and various provisions for local autonomy.[16] Politically, territory remains the principal basis for mobilisation and normatively, territory remains the basis for most systems of accountability and political representation.[17] However, territorial devolution cannot resolve problems of internal minorities or minorities-within-minorities.[18] Moreover, central government and nationalist forces may resist territorial devolution, making access to central government institutions of key importance.

Russian federalism

Of the countries studied here only Russia has a federal arrangement, with twenty-one ethnically defined republics accounting for about 18 per cent of the population.[19] All are ethnically mixed and the titular nationality is by no means always the majority. Yet of all the myriad troubles and traumas that beset the Russian Federation (RF) after 1992, minorities problems were well down the list. Only the desperately tragic issue of Chechenia and its surrounding overspill intruded into politics at the central state level. The continuing pursuit of separatism by the Chechens from their declaration of independence in 1991 effectively meant their long-term political exclusion from Russia, though legally Chechenia remained a constituent republic; from June 2000 it was formally under direct presidential rule.

In the 1993 Constitution each subject of the federation (republics, autonomous units, and non-ethnic regions) gained two seats in the upper chamber, the Council of the Federation. This benefited the élites of the titular nationalities. Yet the latter were well outnumbered. They were also restrained in playing on ethnic sentiments, for they could not ignore the Russians, who made up sizeable proportions of the population in many republics; while in many cases their demands for increased autonomy generated common interests of Russians and non-Russians vis-à-vis the centre.[20] However, the Federation Council is a distinctive body, chosen by three different procedures after 1993. Its members are not directly elected but (1996–9) were regional governors and legislative chairs, with no party groupings permitted.

Russia's institutional designers were anxious to ensure that federalism did not become a disintegrative factor. Federalism may be the best device for accommodating dual identities and loyalties, but to succeed it also needs mechanisms of integration and accommodation.[21] The new system included mechanisms designed to discourage ethnic and regional parties. The 1993 electoral law established a single electoral district for PR seat allocation in the Duma and required parties to gather signatures across the regions. This was intended to force parties to operate countrywide, as a party system based on regional divisions could engender ethnic unrest or even separatist potential. In 1995 parties were permitted to subdivide their candidate lists by region, with only the top 12 names being 'national', so that voters would feel a stronger connection to deputies chosen under PR. However, the process of party registration for list voting was also tightened, with the requirement that parties collect 200,000 signatures, only 7 per cent of which could come from a single region. In the 2001 law to qualify for the list element of the ballot a party or bloc must have at least 10,000 members and branches with at least 100 members each in at least half the country's 89 regions.

Neither the Constitution nor subsequent legislation included alternative means for ensuring national political representation of minorities outside the Federation Council. In the Soviet Union the Soviet of Nationalities had provided such an avenue, while the Central Committee and the Politburo also routinely included representatives of key ethnic groups. In Russia until its abolition in December 1993, heads of the constituent republics were also *ex officio* members of the federal government.

After 1993 several republics and regions carved out considerable autonomy through bilateral negotiations that left different parts of the country in different relations with the centre. The denial of mechanisms of minority representation at the federal level largely left inter-ethnic relations to the sub-federal level.[22] These varied enormously, as politics took different forms in the republics. Regional and republican élites varied considerably (including various manifestations of 'the old nomenklatura, ethnocracy, clan, family, or business networks'[23]), ranging from neo-authoritarian regimes to a wide variety of partially democratic regimes.[24]

Often the political opposition was totally unrepresented in local assemblies. Kynev argued that 'even in cases where the opposition has the support of 10–15 percent (and sometimes 30–40 percent) of the population, an unpopular governor can put forward for election local 'heavyweights'..., all of whom are wholly dependent on the administration. These are people who are guaranteed to win'.[25] It was difficult to see democratic practices as flowing upward; indeed regional and national politics largely operated in separate spheres.

Although Putin took centralising measures to curb this asymmetric federalism, enhancing democracy was not part of his brief. His new federal plenipotentiaries were drawn mainly from the military and security services, and they rapidly established security councils in each of the new federal districts. Minority voices remained largely unheard. Although new proposals for a mixed electoral system in the republics might make a difference, they were also a way of forcing regional élites to create party structures 'capable of becoming the basis for projecting the center's power into the regions'.[26]

Dmitri Glinski argued eloquently that as parliamentary representation had no impact on government formation, so the struggle for Duma seats made little sense for ethnic and religious minorities, and their only avenue of influence was through pro-government factions. In the Muslim regions, where electoral support for pro-government forces was consistently low, this situation offered 'a perverse incentive for the candidates from those regions...to seek positions on (pro-government) electoral lists or join them once elected to the Duma'.[27]

There were no explicitly minority-oriented contenders in the 1993 elections. In 1995 the All-Russian Muslim Public Movement 'Nur' gained 393,513 list votes (0.57 per cent) and just under 50,000 votes in a single-member seat. In 1999 there were again no minority contenders. Indeed, governors were particularly active in electoral blocs. Mintimer Shaimiev, President of Tatarstan, spearheaded All Russia (*Vsya Rossiya*), later allied to Fatherland, which in turn subsequently joined the pro-presidential Unity. All Russia also included Murtaz Rakhimov of Bashkiria and Ruslan Aushev of Ingushetia. Unity itself arose on the basis of a letter by thirty-nine regional leaders who warned of 'threats of destabilization in the pre-election period' and called for the election of 'honest and responsible people'.[28] Putin's endorsement was the making of Unity but also undermined its regional bias: 'Paradoxically, what began as a "governors' party" became the core of a centralist, anti-governor coalition in the Duma.'[29]

Minorities in unitary states

Aside from the Russian Federation, federalism did not survive in post-communist Europe, and ethnicity (national self-determination) became the recognised principle of state organisation. Arrangements such as consociationalism, designed to enshrine minority representation, did not reach the agenda.[30] However, we can also note that neither federalism nor particular arrangements designed to promote ethnic harmony saved Yugoslavia or Czechoslovakia from dissolution. In Czechoslovakia the complex arrangements to ensure fair representation of both Czechs and Slovaks entailed an effective Slovak veto so that the majority could not impose its will; but at the same time it frustrated the decision-making process. Indeed in both cases institutional factors designed to promote ethnic coexistence have been adduced as contributing to the break-up of the federation.[31]

In Slovakia and Romania the Constitution remained a source of contention for the minority populations, not least because of the determination of the institution-builders to maintain a unitary nation-state. The opening phrase of the Slovak Constitution 'We the Slovak nation...(having struggled) for our national existence and our own statehood...' appeared to relegate the minorities to secondary status. The phrase 'together with members of national minorities and ethnic groups living on the territory of the Slovak Republic' did not satisfy the Hungarian minority. Article 6 enhanced such perceptions by declaring Slovak the state language. Further, the protections of the Czechoslovak Charter of Fundamental Rights were undermined by the caveat that minority rights could not be exercised if they threatened 'the sovereignty and territorial integrity' of the state or entailed 'discrimination against its other inhabitants'. Indeed, Prime Minister Vladimir Mečiar was subsequently to claim that any greater recognition of Hungarian claims would undermine the principle of equality of citizens and would threaten the rights of Slovaks living in Hungarian areas.[32]

In Romania too similar constitutional principles caused concern: Hungarian deputies voted against the 1991 Constitution because it defined Romania as a 'national state', founded 'on the unity of the Romanian people'. Despite the existence of provisions protecting national minorities, constitutional experts initially propounded interpretations that did not seem to accommodate minority rights.[33] Arguments about the validity of collective rights, enthusiastically propounded by the Hungarian government as well as the Hungarian minorities, fell on stony ground.

In several countries minority populations faced more explicit obstacles to representation, especially in regard to citizenship rights. All the newly independent states of the former Soviet Union, as well as the Czech Republic and Slovakia, needed their own citizenship laws, and many were openly discriminatory, notably against the Roma and the Russian-speaking populations of Latvia and Estonia. Ethnic representation was bound up not only with the symbolism of 'identity politics', but it also had an instrumental dimension: discrimination can be a powerful means of securing or safeguarding access to political power, material benefits, and status.[34]

The 'ground zero' approach, granting citizenship to residents at the time of independence, was applied by Lithuania (with Polish and Russian minorities of some 15 per cent) and the Ukraine. In 2002 the Ukraine also alleviated the distinctive problem of Crimean Tatars, still returning in a steady trickle to their homeland from Central Asia, whence they had been deported by Stalin in 1944: A new simplified law permitted anyone with at least one grandparent born on current Ukrainian territory to apply for citizenship.

Latvia, however, reaffirmed its inter-war Constitution, and both Latvia and Estonia remained restrictive in terms of citizenship and naturalisation requirements, linking citizenship in 1991 to citizenship in 1940.[35] By stressing their restoration of the states illegally annexed by the USSR they blurred the differences between historical and contemporary statehood, while accentuating differences between the 'core nation' and the diaspora. In the rhetoric of post-communist national restoration Soviet-era settlers were often represented as alien colonisers and potential fifth columnists, threatening the homeland.[36] The results were highly exclusionary: Latvia's Russian minority was some 29.4 per cent of the population, of whom 44 per cent (17.6 per cent of the total population) were citizens.[37] Smaller minorities included Belorussians, Poles, Lithuanians, and others. Estonians comprised 65.3 per cent of the population of Estonia in 2000, with 28 per cent Russians, 2.5 per cent Ukrainians, and 4 per cent 'others'; in 1999, 14 per cent of citizens were Russian speakers.[38]

Pressure exerted by the European Union and the OSCE proved effective in ameliorating many restrictive laws on language, education, and naturalisation in both countries. However, by the end of the twentieth century about 21 per cent of Estonia's population, mostly Russians, remained without citizenship.[39] Protective legislation and entitlements, including the Framework Convention for the Protection of National Minorities, applied to citizens only (indeed, technically non-citizens are not regarded as part of a 'national minority').[40] Although the vote was extended to non-citizens for local government elections, candidates had to be citizens, and until November 2001 they could not stand for election without a fluent command of Estonian. Russian parties were active at local level (for example, the Estonian United People's Party, the Russian Party in Estonia, the Union of Estonia Party, and the Russian Unity Party) and gradually showed some capacity to cooperate. However the denial of citizenship precluded effective national representation, though it did not wholly exclude Russian candidates or parties (see below).

As of June 2001, 23 per cent of the Latvian population were 'non-citizens',[41] a distinctive legal status granted to permanent residents in 1995.[42] In Latvia only citizens enjoyed the right to vote and to form political parties. Latvia also proved more reluctant to rescind the requirement that minority representatives needed to demonstrate fluency in Latvian in order to stand for election. The OSCE[43] and NATO[44] criticised this provision, and President Vaira Vike-Freiberga urged that it be revoked. The EU's monitors judged that 'a debilitating effect of lack of access to citizenship' was the lack of influence of the Russian-speaking minority on the composition of decision-making bodies, and its 'powerlessness' in legislative and policy developments.[45]

Citizenship for the Roma also encountered many obstructions, not merely formal (the Czech Republic amended part of its controversial citizenship law of 1993[46]) but also administrative: Members of the Roma often lacked facility in the state language or the proper documentation to support their claims, and they encountered bureaucratic obstructionism and discriminatory attitudes from public officials. Obstacles to Roma citizenship characterised Lithuania, the Czech Republic, Slovakia, and Slovenia. But the problems of the Roma were far wider and pervasive: social deprivation and exclusion, deep-seated cultural stereotypes, overt and covert discrimination.[47]

Provisions for minority representation

Proportional representation is usually regarded as essential to minority representation,[48] since it provides a better reflection of the varied divisions within society than majoritarian electoral systems. Indeed, ethnic and religious tensions were one reason for the adoption of PR in many Western European countries, beginning in Belgium in 1899.[49] Minorities may seek representation directly through their own forms of political organisation, or they may work through other political organisations, pressing for recognition of their regional or local appeal in candidate-selection processes in ticket-balancing. However, PR of itself cannot ensure the representation of minorities. Much depends on their size and dispersal. Devising a PR system requires making choices about districting, formula, tiers, thresholds, and preferences for candidates. Because of the bias against small groups inherent in all electoral systems, minorities may not directly achieve effective representation.

We have seen that with the Ukraine's shift to a mixed system for the 1998 elections all of our countries included elements of PR in their electoral systems. Where minorities were reasonably large and/or concentrated, as with the Hungarians in Slovakia and Romania, and the Turks in Bulgaria (see below), this proved sufficient for them to gain national political representation. Without special arrangements very small minorities effectively had two complementary choices; they could restrict themselves to local representation or they could try to work through existing parties of the majority.

Some countries did make specific provisions to facilitate minority representation for very small groups at national level. From the outset Romania had the most developed arrangements for minorities that could not normally hope to win seats (i.e. all save the Hungarians). A duly registered ethnic minority organisation contesting an election would receive a seat in the Assembly with (a) at least one-tenth of the minimum number of votes that a political party needed to win at least one seat and (b) more votes than any other organisation referring in its name to the same ethnic group.[50]

Opponents considered this special representation to compromise proportionality and over-emphasise ethnic cleavages, but it remained a feature of Romanian elections. In 1990 (with no threshold) the Hungarian Democratic Union won 29 seats and the German Democratic Forum and the Democratic Union of Roma one each. Nine others gained seats under the special provisions. From 1992 (with a 3 per cent threshold) new rules gave minority organisations a seat with just 5 per cent of the average vote needed by parties to elect a representative and more votes than any other similar list. In 1992, 13 minorities gained a seat under the special provisions; in 1996, 15; and in 2000, 18.

Slovenia's arrangements took the form of separate single-member districts for Italians and Hungarians. The Chair of the Romanian Minorities Parliamentary Commission V. Pamianchan, though positive about Romania's minority provisions, expressed his own personal preference for a 'Slovene model'.[51] But many groups in Slovenia, notably the Roma, Croats, Serbs, and Bosnians, did not enjoy recognised minority status.

In Lithuania the 1992 electoral law included provisions exempting minorities from national threshold requirements, but these were later removed. The Lithuanian Poles gained four seats in 1992, but only one in 1996 and two in 2000; their concentration helped them in single-member districts (see Table 9.3). The Russians are more dispersed throughout the country, and they had no national representation until they gained three seats from their list alliance in the Brazauskas social democratic coalition in 2000.

The Polish electoral law of 1993 included a similar exemption (there was no threshold for the constituencies in 1991). A vocal minority of nationalist deputies and some from the Polish Peasant Party maintained that this undermined the equality of the electoral process,[52] but it remained in subsequent laws. In practice, however, this meant a reduction in minority representation, for only the German minority gained representation from 1993 onwards and its deputies fell to only two. A number of parties were sympathetic to minority rights issues, however, and there was a visible Belorussian contingent in the Democratic Left Alliance.

Only the 1998 Ukrainian election law included specific provisions regarding district boundaries. No seats were reserved for minorities, but 'areas of dense residence of national minorities shall not deviate from the boundaries of one election constituency' (Article 2.2). If a minority is larger than the number of voters in one constituency, then it must be ensured that at least in one constituency the respective ethnic minority constitutes more than 50 per cent of the number of registered voters. Deputies of minority background in the Rada valued the provisions, but in discussions of the 2001 amendments they complained that implementation could not be effective because of outdated demographic information. According to an ethnic Romanian deputy, the 2001 census was deliberately scheduled too late to be of use in redistricting, and questions on national/ethnic identity in the census were confusingly phrased in order to artificially create more but smaller ethnic groups.[53] Yet little discussion had been stirred by this topic in debates on previous election laws and no judicial complaints were made in 1997–8, probably because regional divisions were far more important in Ukrainian voting patterns than ethnicity.

Given the limited nature of the special provisions most minority groups effectively had two options in seeking the representation of their particular interests. Both have been alluded to above. The first method, in practice available only to larger groups, was to establish a political party designed to woo the support of a particular ethnic minority. The second was to use cooperation with another political party as a vehicle of minority representation – in particular by placing minority spokespersons on a hospitable party list.

The ethno-party strategy

Parties organised on the basis of ethnicity (ethnoparties[54]) in Central and Eastern Europe were diverse in nature. In some cases minority socio-cultural organisations were also permitted to contest elections. The minorities' diverse strategies were a function of factors such as size, unity, and their perceptions of threat. Larger minorities like the Hungarians in Slovakia and Romania, and the Turks in Bulgaria were capable of acting directly through their own political parties with some considerable success.

These large minority groups sought to contest elections to gain a voice for their constituents and influence on the political process. The nature of their parties depended on the context in which they operated, and in particular whether they faced the opposition of anti-minority nationalist, populist, or extreme-right parties purporting to represent the majority. The relationship between nationalist-majority parties and minority parties was an interactive, dialectical one: perceptions of threat often generated a spiral of mutual fear and anxiety. Nor was the process solely a domestic one. Because of the close proximity of the Hungarian 'host' state, charges of irredentism and separatism often fuelled the fires of nationalist protest in Romania and Slovakia.

However, it was not always the case that powerful nationalist parties led minority parties to adopt extremist demands, as sometimes postulated.[55] Indeed, ethnoparties were distinct from nationalist parties: they did not necessarily regard the 'nation' as the supreme focus of their loyalty, nor necessarily seek to constitute or become part of a 'nation-state' of their own. They were also distinctive (and distinguished from interest groups) in their concern with both material and symbolic interests. The culture and boundaries of an ethnic group are nearly always problematic in one sense or another... 'issues of control over the community and its central values and symbolic expressions are...a matter of recurring concern'.[56] Although their appeal was largely to particular groups – and using their own language of communication restricted wider access to their views – ethnic parties normally did not restrict their membership to their own ethnicity.[57]

In the post-communist context ethnic parties often emerged early as vehicles for seeking redress of particular grievances generated by communist minorities policy. Bulgaria provides a good example of this process. Despite the general picture of the Balkans as a cauldron of ethnic tensions, Bulgaria evinced a degree of tolerance of ethnic minorities, though it could easily have been otherwise. Periodic communist assimilationist campaigns against purported ethnic nationalism and religious fanaticism took a huge toll, with the first wave of repression against Bulgarian Turks in the early 1950s, linked in part to their resistance to agricultural collectivisation. In 1972–4 the government's notorious forced-renaming process began, first with the Pomaks (who are Muslim Slavs), then in 1984–5 the ethnic Turks, followed by attempts to prohibit all manifestations of cultural difference. The requirement that each Muslim citizen adopt a 'Bulgarian' name was of particular social and religious significance because a person's 'proper' name is necessary for the introduction to Allah after death.[58]

Relations between the Bulgarian and Turkish communities deteriorated badly, with renewed government repression right up to the eve of the 'palace coup' against Todor Zhivkov's leadership in November 1989. During the spring and summer of 1989 Bulgarian Turks embarked on a series of mass protests aimed at the restoration of their names. The brutal government response provoked a new exodus of some 350,000 to Turkey, of whom about one-third subsequently returned.

The Movement for Rights and Freedoms (DPS) was founded in 1990 by a former dissident, Ahmed Dogan. It grew rapidly to some 140,000 members by 1991.[59] Its early programme stressed the restoration of full rights for minorities, including religious freedom for Islam, Turkish language demands, and rights to form cultural associations, as well as redress for injury suffered under the communist regime. It rapidly moved to broaden its goals to further the freedoms of all minorities. These included measures to alleviate their particular economic problems, with declining agriculture and high levels of unemployment – the Turks in particular suffered from the loss of traditional tobacco markets.[60]

Supporting redress of minority grievances was one way of affirming both the new communist leadership's break with Zhivkov and its own democratic credentials. Dissident intellectuals had supported Turkish demands in summer 1989, and despite the presence within it of some strongly nationalist elements, the Union of Democratic Forces (SDS) also endorsed the rescinding of anti-Muslim and anti-Turk legislation. On 29 December the government issued a decree restoring the original names of Bulgarian Muslims, with subsequent laws to permit the exercise of religious freedoms, provide amnesty for political prisoners, and restore property of returning citizens. The ethnic 'backlash' that ensued, with a two-week period of widespread Bulgarian protests, proved short-lived,[61] though local protests in some ethnically mixed areas greeted the reintroduction of Turkish-language programmes in schools in spring 1991. The Bulgarian population generally opposed the principle of schooling in one's own language (only 18 per cent supported it in spring 1991)[62]; but it was quickly enshrined in the new Constitution.

The status of the DPS, effectively the party of Bulgarian Turks (some 9.4 per cent of the population), was earlier called into question because Article 11.4 of the new Constitution (July 1991) banned parties formed on the basis of ethnicity or religion. Surveys conducted at the time of the election appeared to confirm that this debate had spilled over into public consciousness: only 44 per cent of respondents supported the view that minority groups should have their own representation in parliament.[63] The Constitutional Court's strict interpretation of this clause affirmed the legality of the DPS, resolving the issue in a highly pragmatic fashion. The court decided that a party that did not restrict its membership to one ethnic group was not an 'ethnic party'.

Initially – despite their acceptance of some early remedial measures – neither the Socialists nor the SDS was averse to enhancing its own support by mobilising anti-Turkish feelings. The DPS remained uneasily poised between the two large parties, holding the BSP responsible for communist assimilationist policies and wary of its conversion to democracy. Indeed, throughout 1991 the BSP organ *Duma* attacked the DPS as divisive and antithetical to the principles of democracy.[64] The DPS was also suspicious of vocal nationalist voices within a section of the broad-based Union of Democratic Forces. However, explicitly nationalist parties remained small and politically irrelevant in Bulgaria. Strong pro-American sentiments and the radical improvement of relations with Turkey further undermined their limited appeal.

Moreover the practical demands of coalition partnership in a context of closer relations with Western Europe and the need for Western aid shifted the stances of both major parties. The Constitutional Court decision gave the DPS an effective monopoly on the representation of the Turkish population.

In 1990 it gained 6.5 per cent of the vote and in 1991, 7.6 per cent – partly as a defensive reaction to the BSP's allegations of a Turkish 'threat'.[65] It later experimented with a variety of electoral alliances, none of which had a substantial impact (see Table 9.1). Yet the DPS remained a major player in Bulgarian politics.

After 1991, beginning with the establishment of a minority government of the SDS, the DPS often found itself in a pivotal position. In 1991 its support for the SDS appeared to yield little, especially over issues of land restitution, which had a detrimental effect on its own rural constituency. By autumn 1992 the DPS's disenchantment led it to sponsor a successful no-confidence vote that brought down the Dmitrov government. It then helped to broker a new government under non-party Prime Minister Lyuben Berov, supported by the DPS, most of the BSP, and elements of the fractious SDS. The DPS gained further legitimacy through its subsequent participation in governing coalitions.

The DPS's role in government gave it a voice at the centre of power. It remained a force of moderation, denying its characterisation as an 'ethnic' party and stressing its open membership and concerns with the rights of all Bulgarian minorities. Its leadership included Bulgarians and Pomaks. However, tensions within the party surfaced over Dogan's leadership style, and the about-face of 1992 provoked serious opposition to collaboration with the hated BSP, with bitter recriminations and the departure of several deputies. The Party paid the price with lost support in the 1994 election, when it shifted its attentions back to SDS, whose candidate Stoyanov won the presidency in 1996. For the 1997 election the DPS led an improbable partnership with a group of monarchists endorsing the restoration of ex-tsar Simeon. Not only did it succeed in recouping previous electoral losses, but it unwittingly paved the way for a return to government after Simeon's victory in 2001. In 2001, allied with the Liberal Union and EuroRoma, it again became a junior partner in government with Simeon's Movement.

Table 9.1 Vote for the Movement for Rights and Freedoms[1]

Election	Stood as	Share of list vote (%)	Seats
1990	DPS	8.03	11 + 12 smd
1991	DPS	7.55	24
1994	DPS	5.44	15
1997	ONS[2]	7.57	19
2001	DPS – Liberal Union – EuroRoma	7.45	21

[1] Movement for Rights and Freedoms (DPS, Dvijenie za Prava i Svobodi). [2] Alliance for National Salvation (Obedinenie za Natsionalno Spasenie).

Surveys showed a high degree of tolerance of ethnic minorities, a reduction in the persistence of negative stereotypes, and little perception of ethnic tension in Bulgaria.[66] Intolerance[67] did not disappear overnight. There were instances of heightened local tension, as in a disputed mayoral election in Kardzhali in 1995. There was also some sign of a (not unusual elsewhere) gap between abstract recognition of rights and support for their practical embodiment.[68] But most observers agreed that traditional patterns of peaceful coexistence between Bulgars and Turks gradually reasserted themselves in Bulgarian political culture.

In Romania and Slovakia the Hungarian position also bore some resemblance to that of the Turks in Bulgaria, for in both cases the minority remained united and commanded the ethnic vote (see Table 9.2) and in both their representatives played a role in national governing coalitions. The major difference lay in the presence and role of nationalist parties with a strongly anti-minority discourse.

The manifestations of Romanian–Hungarian unity that characterised the December 1989 upheavals proved short-lived. Like the Turks, the Hungarians in Romania pressed for the redress of grievances suffered under the communist

Table 9.2   Vote for Hungarian parties in Romania and Slovakia

Election	Stood as	Share of list vote	Seats
Romania			
1990	UDMR[1]	7.23	29
1992	UDMR	7.46	27
1996	UDMR	6.64	25
2000	UDMR	6.80	27
Slovakia			
1990[2]	ESWS–MKDM[3]	8.66	14
1992[2]	MKM–EGYU[4]	7.42	14
	MPP–MOS[5]	2.29	0
1994	MK[6]	10.19	17
1998	SMK–MKP[7]	9.13	15
	MLHZP[8]	0.2	0
2002	SMK–MKP[7]	11.17	20

[1] UDMR/RMDSZ – Democratic Alliance of Hungarians in Romania (Uniunea Democrata a Maghiarilor din Romania). In 1990 the Independent Hungarian Party (Partidul Independent Maghiar) gained 0.02 per cent of the vote. [2] Slovak National Council. [3] Coexistence and the Hungarian Christian Democratic Movement (Spoluzitie a Maïarské krest'ansko-demokratické hnutie). [4] MKM-EGYU – Coalition of the Hungarian Christian Democratic Movement and Coexistence (Koalicia Mad'arské krest'ansko-demokratické hnutie a Együttéles). [5] Hungarian Civil Party (Magyar Polgári Párt – Mad'arská obcanská strana). [6] Hungarian Coalition (Mad'arská koalícia). [7] Party of the Hungarian Coalition (Strana mad'arskej koalície - Magyar Koalíció Pártja). [8] Hungarian Movement for Reconciliation and Prosperity (Mad'arské l'udové hnutie za zmierenie a prosperitu – Magyar Népi Mozgalom a Megbékélésért és a Jólétért).

regime. The well-organised, articulate Democratic Alliance of Hungarians in Romania (UDMR) presented its demands within days of Ceauşescu's demise and secured immediate gains; some of these, such as the reorganisation of schools, were undoubtedly disruptive to Romanian families, and others threatened local élites. In response, nationalist organisations such as *Vatra Românească* (Romanian Hearth) emerged to defend the Romanians against a perceived Hungarian threat to their vital interests.[69]

Though there was little violence after the bitter confrontations in Tîrgu Mureş in March 1990, Vatra's associated Party of National Unity of Romanians in Transylvania (later the Party of Romanian National Unity, PUNR) played on local fears and did well in the June elections in Transylvania, if not nationally. As Katherine Verdery noted, where a minority votes as a bloc, politicians from that region can win by persuading all voters of their own nationality 'that their group is under terrible threat'.[70] In May 1991 Vadim Tudor's Greater Romania Party emerged, using similar anti-minority rhetoric and charges of Hungarian state irredentism. These forms of virulent nationalism were seen as archetypal manifestations of identity-politics, evoking a strong psychological response from dislocated, traumatised elements of the population.[71]

The fact that the Romanian Hungarians faced the spectre of hostile nationalism undoubtedly aided their own cohesion, but it also meant that their influence depended on attitudes of other parties and the need for coalition partners. At first the Hungarians could rely only on an alliance with the centre-right, itself somewhat ambivalent about issues of minority rights. This shifted with a change in the social democrats' posture: after 1992 the social democrats preferred an association with nationalist parties, but on returning to power in 2000 their new European orientation pushed them towards the Hungarians.

Following the 1992 elections the then minority government of Iliescu's Democratic National Salvation Front gained support from both Romanian nationalist parties. After Gheorghe Funar of the PUNR won the mayoralty in Cluj in February, he stepped up his anti-Hungarian rhetoric, including the demand that the UDMR be banned and its leaders imprisoned for threatening Romania's territorial integrity; and he introduced numerous anti-minority measures of dubious legality.[72] The government's reluctance to intervene was seen as part of the price for PUNR support in parliament. Yet the social democrats' subsequent formal coalition with the nationalists (1994–6) was a difficult one, for they were constantly embarrassed by the intense anti-Hungarian rhetoric of their partners, especially that of Funar.[73] For its part the UDMR found itself isolated, as its allies in the Democratic Convention failed to support it on key legislation, especially the new law on education, seen as decisive for the preservation of the minority's right to a separate national identity.[74] It came under pressure from its radical wing to increase its demands, notably for full territorial autonomy.

Yet in 1996 the UDMR did enter the 'coalition of coalitions' (see Chapter 3). This was 'the first ever attempt by a Romanian government to apply "civic-inclusionary" strategies',[75] and prospects for genuine accommodation increased with the government's unambiguous and highly popular pro-EU and pro-NATO stance.[76] The now dominant nationalist force, the Greater Romania Party, proved quiescent in the face of the resulting Romanian–Hungarian détente. But the government's chronic infighting and general ineptitude soon saw a re-mobilisation of nationalist rhetoric by the mainstream press. This was eagerly embraced from within the government by some Christian Democratic politicians and also Petre Roman's Democratic Party, which refused to endorse government ordinances for the use of the Hungarian language in public institutions.[77]

When Vadim Tudor's Greater Romania Party came second in the 2000 elections, the social democrats (now called the PDSR, later the PSD) again found themselves as the largest party but still a minority government in need of support. Their overtures to the Hungarians gave them several advantages. First, they gave credibility to the Nastase government's pro-European stance, rewarded by an invitation to join NATO and an EU entry timetable for 2007. Secondly, it also divided the opposition, since any cooperation of the Democratic Party or the Liberals with the PRM risked guilt by association. It was still the case, however, that elements of both supported the PRM at times, even on minority issues. In March 2002 some senators supported the PRM's 'Abandonment of Transylvania' motion,[78] once again declaring the government's betrayal of Romania's territorial integrity.

Nastase's minority government reached a cooperation agreement with the Hungarians, pledging to meet a number of their key demands on the restitution of church properties, Hungarian-language university faculties, and Hungarian-language broadcasts. Although its renewal in February 2002 aroused strong criticism from their radical faction led by László Tőkés,[79] the Hungarians saw some real gains, including a new ordinance permitting the display of the Magyar flag and singing of their own anthem. Béla Markó saw his leadership overwhelmingly endorsed at the party's seventh congress in March 2003.

In Slovakia after 1989 several Hungarian parties sought to represent the Hungarian minority and, in the case of Coexistence (*Együttélés-Spolužitie-Wspólnota-Souižití*) other Slovak minorities too. The Hungarian parties were uniformly pro-federal, fearing (rightly) increased vulnerability in independent Slovakia. The Slovak position was complicated not only by the existence of anti-minority parties, but also by the broad perception that there was electoral mileage to be gained from an anti-Hungarian stance.

In the early phase of Czechoslovak political development the Hungarians provided an example of the classic dilemma of ethnic parties: working together to defend the interests of Hungarians meant sacrificing some of their ideological and programmatic concerns. Slovak independence required some redefinition of their priorities, especially in view of Prime Minister Mečiar's willingness to cooperate with the Slovak National Party, and also the higher 5 per cent threshold. Coexistence and the Hungarian Christian Movement formed an alliance for the 1994 elections, and some members of the Hungarian People's Party stood on their list. However, they remained distinct entities until Mečiar's change in the electoral system before the 1998 elections: there was no remote possibility that the Hungarian parties could meet new thresholds for electoral coalitions.

The dangers of division were illustrated by the Hungarian Civic Party. In 1990 the Hungarian Initiative (FMK), associated with long-standing dissidents and professionals, stood in alliance with Public against Violence (VPN). It won six seats in the Slovak National Council on a platform that can be broadly described as 'democratization first, then minority rights (but not autonomy)', and in February 1991 it briefly became a member of the Slovak governing coalition. After VPN split in 1991 it reconstituted itself as the Hungarian Civic Party (*Mad'arská Občanska Strana*, MOS); but VPN [after Vladimir Mečiar had taken the bulk of it into the Movement for Democratic Slovakia (HZDS)] believed that their association with FMK had cost them 20,000 Slovak votes in 1990 and they rejected a new alliance.[80] The MOS stood alone in 1992 but gained no seats (see Table 9.2).

The larger parties, Coexistence and the Hungarian Christian Democratic Movement (MKDM), stood together in 1990 and 1992 despite tensions arising from Coexistence's insistence on group rights of internal self-determination and Hungarian status as a 'partner-nation'.[81] They won 12 seats in the Federal Assembly in 1990 and 14 in the Slovak National Council, taking about 80 per cent of the Hungarian vote.[82] In 1992 they also elected 12 and 14 deputies respectively, with some members of the smaller Hungarian People's Party (MNP) on their list.

Despite initial differences the programmes of the two allies grew closer as more Slovak parties adopted nationalist rhetoric in their pursuit of maximum decentralisation of the Czechoslovak Federation or – in the case of the Slovak National Party (SNS) – independence. This emphasis on cooperation gained new impetus after Slovakia became an independent state. When Mečiar was in power (June 1992–March 1994 and October 1994–September 1998), the Hungarian parties were impotent. When his opponents governed, the Hungarians gained a voice at the centre of power, whether as government supporters (March–October 1994) or formal coalition partners (after 1998).

There is reason to see Vladimir Mečiar, the undisputed charismatic leader of the HZDS, as an 'expedient nationalist', rather than a nationalist by conviction. Mečiar had begun his post-communist career as prime minister of the Slovak Republic and a committed federalist, and his rhetoric shifted with changing circumstances. By 1992 most Slovak parties were advocating a radical renegotiation of the federation, though only the SNS fought the election on an explicit independence platform, winning 7.9 per cent of the vote for the Slovak National Council. Mečiar, in opposition following his removal as prime minister of the Slovak Republic by his own VPN colleagues in April 1991, 'took the nationalist card into his eclectic, populist pack'.[83] His election victory in 1992 was substantial; and despite protestations about the importance of the federation, he and Klaus promptly negotiated the break-up of Czechoslovakia.

Yet Mečiar was clearly unprepared to deal with the deteriorating economic situation that followed independence. As a succession of individual defectors and splinter groups detached themselves from HZDS, he became increasingly dependent on support from the anti-minority nationalists of the SNS, and his own rhetoric became increasingly anti-Hungarian. This was reflected in measures of special concern to the Hungarians. Hungarian groups gathered in Komarno in September 1993 called for a 'self-administering Hungarian province' – and this led to a further escalation of tensions.

In November the nationalists entered a formal coalition partnership, with Mečiar handing over the sensitive education portfolio; but the prime minister could not prevent further defections. In March 1994 Hungarian deputies supported the successful vote of no confidence that brought Mečiar down and installed a disparate coalition under Jozef Moravčik.

The Hungarians supported (but did not join) the new coalition. Inter-ethnic tensions declined appreciably, not least because of legislation of direct concern to the Hungarians on the use of Hungarian names and the provision of bilingual signs. Mečiar's continuing popularity compelled a still uneasy Hungarian unity, and the Hungarian Christian Democrats and Coexistence agreed to alternate list place positions in the 1994 elections, also finding room for a few MOS joint candidates. With 10.7 per cent of the vote overall and 17 seats, the Hungarian Coalition won 20.7 per cent (12 seats) in its stronghold of Western Slovakia. The main parties fielded their candidates in roughly alternate list places and won 6 and 5 seats respectively, along with Laszlo Nagy, leader of MOS, in eleventh place. In Central Slovakia Coexistence won two seats with the Coalition and in Eastern Slovakia three seats.

However, the elections saw Mečiar return to power in a new coalition with the nationalists, now led by the radical Ján Slota, and the Association of Slovak Workers. This was the most testing period for the Hungarian minority, as it faced a barrage of sustained anti-Hungarian government rhetoric coupled with new policies in the areas of language, culture, education, local administration, and the electoral system that undermined existing minority rights. In turn the mobilisation of Hungarian protest, along with the language of collective rights and ambiguous demands for greater Hungarian autonomy, fuelled Slovak fears of Hungarian irredentism and possible future border changes.

The response of international bodies such as the European Union, the OSCE, and the USA in its annual human rights' reports placed the pro-integration, anti-Mečiar opposition firmly on the Hungarian side so far as minorities issues were concerned. The Hungarians were also realistic enough to recognise that the new 1998 electoral law (with a 5 per cent threshold for each partner) required a united approach. Though protracted and difficult,[84] the process of unification seemed irreversible.

In 1998 Hungarian unity was rewarded when Mečiar's HZDS remained strong enough for the second-placed Slovak Democratic Coalition to require additional coalition partners to construct a government. Henderson observed that 'When the Dzurinda government took office, the symbolic importance of appointing a Hungarian as deputy prime minister for human rights and minorities...was as important as the concrete legislative steps that followed.'[85] Yet intra-government relations did not prove easy for the fractious, complex coalition of coalitions. The Democratic Left (SDL') had opposed Hungarian membership of the coalition and remained a thorny companion. Although their interests were by no means confined to minority rights, Hungarian conflicts within the government tended to centre on such issues. Indeed, they opposed the government's proposals for the law on minority languages, and the 1999 law passed without the support of Hungarian deputies. For much of 2001 the new Hungarian Status Law, providing benefits for Hungarians living abroad, aroused anxieties in both Slovakia and Romania.[86]

When Dzurinda proved successful in 2002, the Hungarians also saw significant gains. The return of the Socialist Party to power in Hungary had offered the prospect that the Status Law would be amended, and the Slovak Hungarians appeared more secure at home. The new government was a more manageable coalition, and the SMK were unquestioned partners. The Slovak National Party and the Democratic Left (SDL') had failed to enter parliament. Although Smer was not averse to expedient anti-Hungarianism, Mečiar was anxious to demonstrate his own European credentials and he was preoccupied with intra-party turmoil and further defections.

These three ethnic parties thus proved highly successful as vehicles for their respective minority groups, though with important differences. In Bulgaria and Romania the main minority party occupied a pivotal position because of its ability to join coalitions with both left and right. The Hungarians in Slovakia had only the right-wing option, given that so many Slovak parties retained an anti-Hungarian overlay, however shallow. Issues of state-building and the insecurity of the titular nation had a powerful medium-term effect on Slovak politics. However, the most ardent pro-European politicians responded to European concerns and proved sensitive to minority issues, whether from conviction or expediency. Participation in government enhanced Hungarian legitimacy as a co-nation.

The changing strategies of the Russian Balts

The Russian-speaking minorities of the Baltic states saw great obstacles to the achievement of effective representation in national parliaments, and their strategies evolved slowly. This was not merely a consequence of the lack of citizenship status for many, but also of their internal disunity and lack of support from their own communities. The results of minority parties and parties supporting the minorities are shown in Table 9.3. The minority voice was not absent, but the minority remained isolated for much of the decade. This appeared a greater problem in Estonia,[87] where the Russians were more concentrated than in Latvia (though Russians dominated the largest Latvian cities, Riga and Daugavpils). Non-citizens had to rely on citizens to express their grievances and press for resources.

Yet once basic nationalist aims were met with the securing of independence and declining perceptions of minorities as a threat to the integrity of the state, hostile nationalist rhetoric subsided and the most xenophobic of majority parties lost support. Gradually accommodative, partner-seeking strategies became possible. We noted earlier that in Lithuania, the Russian minority failed to gain seats until its partnership with the social democrats in 2000 (see Table 9.3).

In both Latvia and Estonia divisions between citizens and non-citizens, monolingual and bilingual speakers, those professing religious and secular belief-systems, and between adaptive and Soviet-nostalgic attitudes divided the Russian minority and weakened the basis for common political action. Moreover, the Russians lacked 'a substantive political or cultural élite... willing and able to champion ethnic grievances'.[88]

In Latvia one group of former communists, by no means all of them pro-Soviet, formed a group of small left-wing parties committed to improving conditions for the Russian population. The Harmony for Latvia-Rebirth of the Economy coalition and (ex-communist) Equal Rights Movement gained 13 seats in 1993 and 11 in 1995 (separately as the Harmony Party and the Socialist Party). Described as 'loose groupings of personalities',[89] they defined themselves parties capable of bridging differences, but their main appeal was indeed to the Russians and also smaller Slav minorities. None of these parties succeeded initially in mobilising the minority vote, and parliament remained unresponsive to their concerns. Harmony was very briefly in government in 1994, but the 'Russian voice' was excluded following the election of a polarised parliament and the formation of a broad-based government under the non-party Andris Šķēle.

Harmony had only six seats after 1995, and its split in 1996 left a group below the minimum for parliamentary recognition. But the Russian Citizens' Party, founded in January 1995 to oppose the accommodative strategy whereby 'Latvian deputies arrive with the help of Russian voters' and to speak directly for the Russian-language population,[90] gained a meagre 1.25 per cent of the vote. Tensions increased over excessive police enthusiasm for controlling a Russophone pensioners' demonstration in March 1998, and relations between Riga and Moscow worsened further after a bomb damaged the Russian Embassy.[91]

Table 9.3 Votes for minority parties[1] in the Baltic states

Election	Stood as	List vote (%)	Seats
Lithuania			
1992	Union of Lithuanian Poles[2]	2.14	2 list
			2 smd
1996	Electoral Action	3.13	0 list
	of Lithuanian Poles[3]		1 smd
	Alliance of Lithuanian	2.55	0
	National Minorities[4]		
	Union of Russians	1.71	0
	in Lithuania[5]		
2000	Electoral Action	1.95	0 list 0
	of Lithuanian Poles[3]		2 smd
	Union of Russians	part of Social	3 list
	in Lithuania[5]	Democratic Coalition	
Latvia			
1993	Harmony for Latvia-Rebirth	12.01	13
	of the Economy[6]		
	Equal Rights Movement[7]	5.76	7
	Russian Citizens of Latvia[8]	1.16	0
1995	Harmony Party[9]	5.58	6
	Latvian Socialist Party	5.61	5
	Russian Citizens of Latvia	1.25	0
1998	Harmony Party	14.2	16
2002	PCTVL[10]	19.04	25
Estonia			
1995	Our Home is Estonia![11]	5.87	6
1999	United People's Party[12]	6.13	6
	Russian Party in Estonia[13]	2.03	0

[1] Includes pro-minority parties. [2] Lietuvos lenku sajunga. [3] Lietuvos lenku rinkimu akcija. [4] Lietuvos tautiniu mazumu aljansas. [5] Lietuvos rusu sajunga. [6] Saskana Latvijai – Atdzimsana Tautsaimniecîbai. [7] Lidztiesîba. [8] Latvijas Krievu pilsonu partija. [9] Tautas saskanas partija. [10] Alliance For Human Rights in a United Latvia (Apvienîba Par cilvçka tiesîbám vienotá Latvijâ). [11] Meie kodu on Eestimaa!. [12] Eestimaa Ühendatud Rahvapartei. [13] Vene Erakond Eestis.

In 1999 the conservatives retained power, but Harmony was now a much stronger presence (16 seats) and the extreme-right anti-Russian Siegerist party had vanished almost as rapidly as it had arisen. President Vaira Vike-Freiberga proved sympathetic to the minorities and receptive to the views of the OSCE. In one view the easing of the sense of threat posed by such a large Russian population saw the Latvian nationalists gradually moderate the rhetoric of ethnic protectionism and engage in less 'nationalistic outbidding'.[92] Russian citizenship applications increased, and the government introduced new mechanisms such as a 'society integration programme' and a new National-ities' Consultative Council. Latvia was set to join both the European Union and NATO.

Yet the Russophone parties remained suspect, for several leaders were linked strongly with the old regime, including the understandably unpopular Alfreds Rubiks, who had received a prison sentence for supporting the attempted *coup* in Moscow in August 1991. Even the sober People's Party described the leaders of Harmony's successor, the Alliance for Human Rights, as 'wasps and hornets living on the edge of fear, hatred, cynicism and laziness while feeding off the benefits brought by others'.[93]

In the 2002 elections, however, Human Rights came second to the new New Era Party and increased its parliamentary presence to 25 seats, while the main nationalist party, Fatherland and Freedom, saw its vote fall to just 7 per cent. One of Human Rights' central policies was the demand for the withdrawal of the new education law, requiring secondary and vocational education solely in Latvian from 2004. With reports that the schools would not be capable of such provision until 2008, the issue served to mobilise minority voters.[94] Although there was no question of including Human Rights in the new governing coalition (among other things it was pro-EU, but anti-NATO), the minority voice now had strong representation. Sections of Harmony, one of the three elements of the Human Rights' Alliance, declared themselves in favour of forming a European social democratic party as a genuine centre-left alternative representing both Latvians and the minorities.

Estonia had some distinctive features stemming from historical patterns of non-indigenous population growth. The Russians tended to concentrate in urban areas, especially Tallinn, and the northeastern region abutting Russia. The Russian language was dominant there, and Russian military bases and industrial enterprises had formed 'the backbone of the economy' and an 'organic Russian society'. Indeed, Estonians were denied the right to live in most strategically important areas... 'the indigenous population was compressed between alien "palisades"'.[95] However, it would be wrong to attribute homogeneity to the Russian-speaking population or to assume its common interests. It was highly diverse and proved far from easy to mobilise.

The Estonian Communist Party sought accommodation with the Popular Front in the late-Soviet period. By autumn 1988 'proreform political actors held all the key positions within Estonian society, including those within the Communist Party itself... the fundamental institutions of the Soviet system... had been transformed into the agents for the dismantling of the existing sociopolitical system and the advancing of the cause of national liberation'.[96] Yet by the end of 1989 ethnic divisions were palpable. The 'Russian question' became the central problem, seen as threatening the cohesion and integrity of Estonian society.[97]

The first Estonian parliament was entirely Estonian in its ethnic composition. Soviet-era settlers could not meet the naturalisation requirements by that time, and there was no contending minority party in 1992. The young Prime Minister Mart Laar came from Homeland (Isamaa), which had promised thorough de-Sovietisation along with liberal economic reform. He governed with the radical nationalist Independence Party – still attacking Russian 'colonisers' – as his chief coalition partner. The soil was not fertile for sensitive minority politics, and there were substantial fears of political crisis or even secessionist threat when Russian council leaders in Narva and Sillamae called a local referendum on autonomy for the northeast region.

The government however was being pulled in two directions from its domestic nationalists and from 'Europe', which was concerned about the Russian speakers, citizenship, and restrictive language laws. Pressure from the CSCE and its minorities commissioner Max van der Stoel led to changes in the so-called 1993 Aliens' Law, and the seriousness of both the CSCE and the EU gave some hopes on the language issue, though not on the key issue of citizenship for all long-term Russian residents.

In 1995 Our Home is Estonia! (*Meie kodu on Eestimaa!*), a coalition of the United People's Party and the Russian Party of Estonia, fielded 73 candidates and won six seats in the Riigikogu with 5.9 per cent of the vote. As in the early Latvian elections, Russian citizens did not vote primarily on ethnic lines. The coalition rapidly broke up, and its deputies then sat as Independents, though they spoke vocally against new proposals centred on language testing for state officials, election candidates, and even entrepreneurs (ultimately this new law was declared unconstitutional). The two parties contested the 1999 elections separately, the United People's Party (*Eestimaa Ühendatud Rahvapartei*) again winning six seats but the Russian Party failing, with 2 per cent of the vote.

Yet Estonian parties proved less intractable than their Latvian colleagues. In December 2001 parliament amended the electoral law to abolish the language requirement for candidates to parliament and local councils. The Moderates and most Isamaa and Reform Party deputies joined Russian deputies in supporting the proposal. One argument adduced in favour of the new provisions was that it would help convince the OSCE to end its ten-year-long mission to Estonia (and this did occur).[98]

Despite anxiety about the status of the Estonian language, nationalist rhetoric eased somewhat. The Russians did not go 'home' to Russia, but they appeared to have accommodated themselves to their minority status and the need to learn Estonian. They wanted to join the European Union. These changes, coupled with the availability of possible partners no longer risking the alienation of their voters, made possible a shift on both sides to accommodation mode. First the (left-wing) Centre Party approved a cooperation agreement with the United People's Party (as prime minister of the Popular Front government, Edgar Savisaar had supported citizenship rights for all residents). Then the Reform Party and the Russian Baltic Party announced their intention to merge. Sergei Ivanov of the RBP said that efforts to unite the various Russian parties in Estonia had failed, and they had been unable to defend the interests of the Russian-speaking population.[99] When parties announced their candidate lists in February 2003, Ivanov was twelfth on the Reform Party's list for the forthcoming elections (in fact, the Reform Party won 19 seats and the Estonian People's Union 13 seats in the March 2003 elections).

The Baltic Russians, then, travelled a different political path from their more southern minority counterparts. Their position was initially defined by their large numbers of non-citizens and thus their lack of a potential electorate. Although this gradually changed as naturalisation increased, more important was the easing of nation-building tensions and a greater security of international relations. As the electoral advantage of Russian support increased and the electoral disadvantage diminished, accommodative relations with other parties became both a more realistic and a more fruitful strategy.

The Roma

We have already indicated that the position of the Roma provided another, very different sort of minority politics. Regarding the Roma as an ethnic group remains highly problematic, and they may be better categorised as a distinctive social group rather than a national minority. However, the Roma certainly encountered common problems and similar deep-seated cultural stereotypes throughout the region. No country was free of anti-Roma prejudice. Despite the mutual tolerance of Bulgars and Turks, Zhelyazkova saw anti-Roma prejudice in Bulgaria as increasing rapidly, acquiring 'a xenophobic nature' by 2001.[100] National politicians of mainstream parties such as the 'liberal' Civic Democrats (ODS) in the Czech Republic did not hesitate to openly express anti-Roma sentiments;[101] and this was certainly true of nationalist and populist politicians everywhere. It was only the 'discovery' of the Roma by the EU that led to national government action and a degree of Roma mobilisation.

Yet the political influence of the Roma remained insignificant. Romany integration depended less on negotiations between the Romany community and the majority than on each society's democratic development and the attitude of mainstream parties. External pressure and the development of civic organisations for human and minority rights were the main driving forces behind the progress thus far achieved towards undermining Romany exclusion.[102]

Never the less change was apparent. Unsurprisingly, given the distribution of the population, it proved easier for the Roma to organise at local level; indeed, several Roma mayors were elected in Slovakia and Bulgaria. Hungary had Europe's most highly developed system of minority self-government, providing the Roma with opportunities for gaining electoral and political experience though chronically beset by lack of resources.[103] In May 2002 in Slovenia new local government provisions guaranteed Roma representation on some 20 local councils.

The Roma became increasingly active, but they still suffered from extreme marginalisation, lack of resources, and acute internal divisions. At national level Roma parties were often numerous in theory, but they were seldom able to field candidates, still less form a united bloc, and they did not bring out Roma voters (see Table 9.4). Roma parties stood in every Hungarian and Slovak election, gathering but a handful of votes. The Hungarian Roma Party gained 745 votes for its sole regional list and the Democratic Roma Party attracted 171 votes in a single-member district in 2002. The Romanies stood in Slovakia in 1990 and the Romany Civic Initiative in 1992 and 1994, but when 13 Romany parties registered before the 1998 elections, not one put up candidates. The Romany Civic Initiative signed an agreement with the HZDS, while the Romany Intelligentsia for Coexistence reached agreement with the Slovak Democratic Coalition. 'Thus, the two most prominent Romani political groups became involved in the conflict between two incompatible concepts of public policy, two versions of Slovakia..., and two diverse approaches to minority issues.'[104] There were no Roma deputies in that parliament. Two groupings stood in 2002, when their combined vote was 0.5 per cent. The Romany Civic Initiative in the Czech Republic stood in 1992 but not again until 2002, when it gained 523 votes.

As mainstream parties sought votes, however, there were some signs of accommodative strategies emerging, despite acute divisions within Romany élites and their inability to command Roma votes. In Bulgaria after 1989 a number of Roma deputies were elected on the lists of mainstream parties. Gypsy political organisations received funding from the Bulgarian Socialists

Table 9.4 Votes for Roma parties and organisations

Party/election	% Vote
Romanies, Slovak National Council 1990	0.73
Roma Civic Initiative, Slovak National Council 1992	0.60
Roma Civic Initiative, Slovakia 1994	0.67
Roma Civic Initiative, Slovakia 2002	0.29
Political Movement of the Roma, Slovakia 2002	0.22
Roma Civic Initiative, Czech National Council 1992	0.26
Roma Civic Initiative, Czech Republic 2002	0.01
Hungarian Gypsy Social Democratic Party, 1990 (one smd)	0.01
Gypsy Solidarity Party, Hungary 1994 (one smd)	0.06
Hungarian Democratic Roma Party, 1998 (one smd)	0.01
Hungarian Roma Party, 2002 (list)	0.01
Democratic Roma Party, Hungary 2002 (one smd)	0.0 (171 votes)

and the HZDS in Slovakia in return for campaigning on their behalf in Romany communities.[105] In 1996 the Social Democrats (PDSR) in Romania used the Gypsy King Ion Cioabă to get out the Romany vote in Sibiu, and by the 2000 elections they (now the PSD) had reached agreement with the Romany Party (*Partida Romilor*) to bring its leaders into the heart of government. In Hungary in 2002 Florian Farkas, chairman of the Roma organisation Lungo Drom, reached a cooperation agreement with Fidesz, and Farkas later won a seat from the Fidesz national list.

One must remain sceptical as to how far these agreements gave the Roma any real collective voice. In Bulgaria it was reported that the government made little progress with its Roma integration programme (1999), and that Roma MPs seldom dared 'push for Roma political interests'.[106] Securing genuine political representation for the Roma appeared a complex, long-term issue clearly linked to the development of the civic capacity of the Roma communities themselves.

The smaller minorities

Governments continued to support cultural organisations rooted in the previous regime and small (non-Roma) minorities were easily accommodated in Poland, Hungary, and the Czech Republic. Hungary developed its local minority self-governments from an early stage, and though it did not meet its constitutional promise of securing national minority representation, there was little evidence of minority discontent. Estonia too had a strong Union of National Minorities, with numerous cultural associations representing a rainbow of Jews, Swedes, Ukrainians, Belorussians, and many other minorities. Local tensions were not uncommon, but they rarely achieved national resonance. The greater ease of border crossings made it easier for divided families to visit their kin, as well as providing new opportunities for trade.

Initially ethnic groups were permitted to contest elections as socio-cultural organisations and some did so, whether to gain visibility or to try to mobilise their own communities. Their number gradually fell, except where there were special reasons. The German Minority in Poland gained seven seats in 1991 and the Orthodox Believers one, but the Belorussian Election Committee and the Minorities Bloc won none. The Belorussian Union contested the 1993 election, but thereafter only German groups stood, winning two seats in that and every subsequent election. In Slovenia the Italians and Hungarians elected one deputy each in their single-member districts.

In Romania the number of minority organisations contesting elections actually increased, and so too did the number of minorities gaining special representation. Generally one organisation received most government cultural funding, and that organisation also usually gained the minority seat.[107] But only the smallest minorities needed to woo most of their potential supporters because the number needed for a seat was not large: In 1996 the Union of

Poles in Romania gained a seat with 1842 votes. Indeed, the system appeared to encourage intra-ethnic competition: *inter alia*, in 2000 two Greek, Romany, Italian, and Polish organisations stood, along with four Bulgarian, and three Croat. Stephen Deets noted that in 1996 six Italian parties gained 25,000 votes, though under 2000 individuals declared themselves Italian in the census: this suggested that political entrepreneurs were seeking an easy route to parliament.[108] In 2000 the two Italian organisations attracted 37,529 votes, strengthening the likelihood that the low barrier was encouraging contestation for reasons other than ethnic minority representation. So although providing some formal stake in the system and legitimising the minority presence, even carefully designed mechanisms could work in unexpected ways.

Conclusion

Although ethnicity was often seen as constituting a bitter and enduring dividing line in post-communist societies, this view needs serious qualification. All the new democracies set to join the European Union saw low levels of ethnic social conflict and violence was rare. It is true that the majority populations often tolerated attacks from violent subcultures on individual members of the most excluded group of all, the Roma; but these were the product of deep-seated patterns of social exclusion, not ethnic conflict. The Roma themselves remained poorly organised and Roma parties mobilised few voters in their cause.

The translation of ethnicity into enduring political cleavages was not common. Aside from the three major ethnic parties in Slovakia, Romania, and Bulgaria there were relatively few elsewhere, and they met with little success. And even there the cleavage was at best partial: countries did not divide on majority–minority lines in their politics, and all the major ethnic parties proved capable of political cooperation with their majority colleagues. In the Ukraine ethnicity was of cultural importance for the small minorities, but parties there did not organise on ethnic lines. Russia's federalism shifted ethnic relations to republican and regional structures, while regional notables sought a role in the 'parties of power'.

The Hungarians in Romania and the Turks in Bulgaria mobilised to seek redress for injustices wreaked by the communist regime. In Romania and Slovakia the Hungarians also mobilised defensively against the erosion of existing rights threatened by nationalist politicians, while their mobilisation in turn intensified the rhetoric of threat to the majority population, including that of insidious irredentism. Nationalist politicians competed against one another in their xenophobia, and many mainstream politicians shamelessly joined in the bidding. Times were hard, people were anxious, and playing the nationalist card all too often proved irresistible.

Yet minority participation in government and new measures to assuage minority grievances did not provoke a popular backlash anywhere. At the time of writing in early 2003 the Movement for Rights and Freedoms, the Democratic Alliance of Hungarians of Romania, and the Hungarian Coalition Party were all members or supporters of governing coalitions. This was only partly a result of the internalisation of values of multi-culturalism and mutual tolerance. It was also a matter of simple political expedience and political learning, as patterns of party competition made ethnic parties crucial to coalition arithmetic and they earned a reputation as responsible partners. In addition, it was a consequence of sustained pressure from institutions such as the Council of Europe and above all the European Union, which made national minorities an issue for post-communist democracy-building.

It was this factor too that saw a gradual shift away from the model of ethnic democracy [*sic*] originally claimed as necessary by the two Baltic states with large Russian populations. Estonia and Latvia dealt with their nation-building agenda through measures to exclude the large Russian populations from political power. As new élites gained experience and confidence, so did the international environment grow more secure. The Russian government toned down its rhetoric of protecting Russians in the Near Abroad and membership of NATO and the European Union loomed. Economic issues gradually took precedence over national ones. Zake suggested that in Latvia nationalism was transformed by exposure to free market and international economic and political networks.[109] The Russian-citizen minorities grew in line with easier opportunities for language-learning and naturalisation, but they did not behave as a cohesive entity. The nationalist vote declined and parties based on ethnic accommodation grew stronger.

Divisive issues remained, especially surrounding language and education. It would be premature to assume that ethnicity would cease to be a relevant political factor (whether in the Baltic or elsewhere). The short-term consequences of EU membership were unclear, and Russia's trajectory remained imponderable. Ethnic tensions can surface suddenly and with improbable triggers. We have observed continuing patterns of intra-party tension that could affect ethnic relations within parties, and we have seen the successful challenge of new political parties. At the start of 2003, however, there appeared reason for cautious optimism.

The innovative Romanian system of offering very small minorities opportunities for national representation successfully mobilised ethnic communities and their special representation increased with successive parliaments. Despite potential opportunities for abuse, the system acquired a positive symbolic significance. The German minority in Poland (with exemption from thresholds) and the Polish minority in Lithuania (which lost its 1992 exemption) were large enough and sufficiently concentrated to gain separate representation. Indeed, even their small number of votes was also occasionally needed by governments constructing ad hoc legislative coalitions in the absence of a governing majority. Ethnicity is clearly not an automatic recipe for conflict.

10
Conclusion: Elections, Parties, and Representation

The broad context of political change in post-communist countries was unique. In Western Europe, the process of democratisation was lengthy, organic, and largely evolutionary. It was effectively a process of gradual extension of the franchise and the opening up of the system to new election contenders. Underlying economic and social changes, arising from the spread of industrialisation and urbanisation, were undoubtedly both cause and consequence of this political process. But there was no notion of an advance blueprint guiding the direction of change and there was no single point at which the achievement of 'democracy' was proclaimed. The concept of representative democracy evolved as a part of the process itself. But at some ill-defined point in this evolution political parties emerged as the central actors of the democratic drama. In the communist states the starting point was quite different, both in context and in the *dramatis personae*. A single-party monopoly directed society on the basis of its claim to command the precepts of scientific socialism in order to construct an egalitarian society free from exploitation and alienation. Under communist party auspices economic development was substantial, if skewed to the industrial sector. Urbanisation was extensive. Levels of education were high. The franchise was universal, and efficient mechanisms of electoral administration were in place. The dysfunctions of the political-economic system, however, were acute, and attempts to reform the system gathered pace, triggering three different sorts of regime change. The 'modes of exit' from communism were crucial because they reflected the balance of political forces that determined the nature of the initial post-communist élites; this in turn affected the decisiveness of the break with the old regime and established the initial reform trajectory.

Regime change in post-communist Europe

In the first type of regime change élites with rather varied transformative agendas took over existing states through the electoral process. This was the case in those independent states of Eastern Europe that had comprised the former 'Soviet bloc'. There was a clear turning point, namely the acceptance by existing power holders of the principle of holding competitive elections to parliament. Once these elections were held, the new parliamentarians enjoyed the legitimacy of popular support and the authority their roles conveyed. State capacity was not in question, despite the fragility of the economies.

Circumstances in the Soviet Baltic republics and Slovenia provided an intermediate category. The key difference was the calling into question of the nature of the state itself. In the USSR the reform process snowballed into an avalanche of demands from the small republics of the periphery – notably the Balts, Moldova, Armenia, and Georgia. Demands for independence escalated and these republics enjoyed considerable de facto independence before the formal de jure dissolution of the Soviet Union, after new élites took over as a consequence of republican-level elections. The tasks of these élites included a wider agenda, namely that of state-building. Slovenia also belongs in this category, though with reform pressures coming from the Yugoslav republics, rather than from the centre. But similarly, de facto independence preceded international recognition and new élites came to power as a result of competitive elections. State-building, while having a strong foundation in the extensive autonomy of the Yugoslav federal model, none the less posed specific challenges to the new Slovene élites. In all four cases those elected to parliament had popular support for a platform of transformation.

Russia and the Ukraine were quite distinctive in the absence of popular nationalist movements. Independence came as a by-product of élite actions, with the death of the USSR pronounced by the leaders of the Russian and Ukrainian (and Belorussian) republics on 12 December 1991. The existing parliaments remained in place with small opposition factions, though support for Ukrainian independence was confirmed in the December referendum and the election of a new president. There were significant differences to be sure. Boris Yeltsin had been elected in June 1991 as the first directly elected Russian president. His commitment to radical economic transformation led rapidly to acute tensions between the executive and the Russian parliament. In the Ukraine, President Kravchuk effectively coopted the nationalist opposition for the primacy of the state-building project. In both cases the new states were weaker than their progenitor suggested, and in Russia in particular the centre could not ensure its remit in the new republics and regions. In neither case, moreover, were there mechanisms for the popular articulation of political views. There were no organised political opposition movements nor viable political parties. The communist parties were (temporarily) banned, but the *nomenklatura* remained effectively entrenched, poised to take advantage of the redistribution of assets. Despite the pervasive rhetoric of democratic commitment, free elections were delayed for some years. There was no inclination to follow even the vaguest

West European 'model'. Despite an initially strongly pro-Western Russian foreign policy, Russian institutions emerged from the domestic power struggle between president and parliament. In the Ukraine the issue remained that of the 'Soviet model' or a 'national model' right up to the passage of the new Constitution in 1996.

All these cases, with or without founding elections, were instances of regime change. Regime change was inherent in the dismantling of the communist party's monopoly of power and the unravelling of the planned economy. In Poland, Hungary, Czechoslovakia, Slovenia, Latvia, Estonia, and Lithuania the new élites had a vision of the future, based on emulation of Western European democratic capitalism. Precisely what kind of democracy or what kind of capitalism was far from clear. But their wholesale rejection of the communist system suggested a sweeping away of the old order that required a multi-faceted transformation: of the polity, the economy, society, and culture, as well as in the sphere of international relations. Most of these élites probably had little understanding of the complex interactions of the various elements of the communist system or the ways in which unravelling one strand had implications for other policy areas. They also lacked experience of public office, including effective communication with their citizens. But they had an electoral mandate for change.

The immediate priorities of the new political élites varied from state to state. In Poland and Czechoslovakia the economy came centre stage with strong finance ministers in the persons of Leszek Balcerowicz and Václav Klaus, both of whom were converts to Anglo-American economic liberalism's minimal state. In Czechoslovakia Klaus's economic strategy not only proved more painful to the Slovaks, but it also meant the subordination of their own priority, namely to redefine the terms of Czechoslovak federalism. In Slovenia, Latvia, Lithuania, and Estonia the highest priority after 1990 was that of securing independence. From 1992 they, and soon independent Slovakia too, sought to define and shape the state in order to ensure conditions in which their nations would flourish.

Yet despite these differences, a broad élite consensus emerged in these states for a 'return to Europe'. It ranged from the social democrats on the left (including communist-successor parties in Poland, Hungary, Lithuania, and Slovenia) to conservative-liberals on the right. Only in Slovakia did the new élites remain bitterly divided, with Prime Minister Mečiar propounding an incoherent but politically effective 'nationally-flavoured centrist economics, political illiberalism, and cultural essentialism'[1] that set him at odds both with his domestic political foes and with the European Union. Although Czechoslovak policies had seen Slovakia firmly on the capitalist road, Mečiar discontinued the process of voucher privatisation, relying instead on insider privatisation to benefit existing directors, along with continuing subsidies of uncompetitive enterprises. This placed Slovakia in a position more similar to that of Romania and Bulgaria.

Romanian and Bulgarian circumstances were a product of the initial retention of power by communist élites. Whether in the guise of Romania's National Salvation Front or a rechristened Bulgarian Socialist Party, sections of the former *nomenklatura* won the first free elections. In both cases they offered an ambivalent and opaque picture of the future. Iliescu used the language of the 'third way' and an 'original' Romanian democracy, overlaid with nationalism, to secure election victory for the National Salvation Front in 1990 and the Democratic National Salvation Front in 1992. The Bulgarian socialists were uncertain about capitalism, about a break with Russia, and about just how to transform themselves into a 'modern Marxist party of democratic socialism'. The Socialist government elected in 1990 rapidly succumbed to massive demonstrations as the economy went into free fall, yielding to a government of experts and then losing narrowly to the opposition Union of Democratic Forces (SDS) in the 1991 elections. But the SDS had no clear reform strategy either, preferring 'restitution first'; the restoration of property to former pre-communist owners delayed fundamental economic reform and permitted the 'hidden privatization' that emerged from the interstices of the public, private, and illegal economic sectors.

Thus the 'mode of exit' generated broad differences in the strategic actors who controlled the early stages of development, their legitimacy, their commitment to change, and their priorities. Despite the ubiquity of small-scale privatisation, their immediate task was to manage a state-owned industrial economy whose enterprises were notorious for their inefficiency and obsolescence. At the same time while one group of élites sought to 'rebuild the boat in the open sea',[2] another was more concerned to patch, mend, and bail their existing craft. What seems beyond doubt is that most passengers expected things to get rapidly and radically better.

The dislocations of transition

One surprising feature of post-communist development was the severity and intensity of economic decline. It made little difference *in the short term* whether economic strategies were based on radical 'shock therapy' or gradualism or whether there was a detectable economic strategy at all. In the medium and longer term it mattered hugely. At the outset, however, a grim and traumatising economic reality confounded high social expectations of economic prosperity. Every country experienced deep economic recession, coupled with high inflation and accompanying insecurity and anxiety.

Those countries that reformed quickly and those that failed to do so faced similar problems of falling output, lack of investment, and declining productivity. The shrinking tax base faced competing demands for supporting entrepreneurial initiatives alongside rising social demands for ameliorative action to cushion the economic downturn. The standard of living fell and unemployment rose. Those on fixed incomes reeled from the shock of their first experience of rapid inflation. Public services deteriorated. With poverty and unemployment came new social problems such as crime, drug abuse, homelessness, and poor health. Conspicuous consumption by the small but growing stratum of the very rich gave potent visibility to increasing social inequalities.

The intensity, the timing, and the duration of economic depression varied with such factors as the size, location, and economic structure of a country, as well as the impact of exogenous factors such as the Gulf crisis and the disruption of trade arising from the break-up of the Soviet Union. Only in the Czech Lands did rising income from tourism and an influx of German investment provide some counterweight to industrial decline, but pockets of high deprivation emerged there too. Central Europe never witnessed the partial re-emergence of a non-money economy, with workers and pensioners remaining unpaid for months on end, as in Russia and the Ukraine.

There are several points to be made in this connection. First, we want to emphasise the atmosphere of socio-psychological upheaval and disappointment. This found expression in the large reactive vote against the first post-communist governments regardless of the nature of the incumbents (see below). Secondly, a return to economic growth did not signify the end of structural dislocation. It took some considerable time before the advanced economies exceeded their 1989–90 levels of GDP. It also needs to be stressed that although vast differences emerged between countries, nowhere could socio-economic transformation be regarded as 'complete' by 2003. Even in countries with the highest rates of privatisation and the highest contribution to the economy of private enterprise, key sectors or major industries remained under state control and reforms in social policy (health, pensions, education) remained incomplete or inadequate.

Thirdly, the notion that transition hardships form a crucial dimension of any discussion of post-communist representation should not be taken to suggest an economic determinism. Transition dislocation embraced not only the socio-economic but also the socio-psychological dimension of change, including issues of identity and belonging. Finally, the role of the new political élites is crucial. They were the factor linking the mode of exit to the processes of transformation. They themselves embodied elements that need to be understood as part of the communist legacy, but they were also shaped by the imperatives of transformation, not least by the democratic imperative of competing for the confidence of the electorate.

The new political actors

Scholars have rightly placed considerable emphasis on the 'top-down' nature of post-communist political party formation, in contrast to Western Europe where existing parliamentary élites faced new challengers for political representation. The mass-membership party emerged throughout Western

Europe, based on the mobilisation of previously excluded groups of citizens, and was thus deeply rooted in society, with ideological bases and overt sociali- sation functions that helped develop and strengthen affective party attach- ment. Increasingly parties became seen as the key vehicles of representation, with functions of aggregating interests, political recruitment, and integration ensuring linkage between society and the state. Mass parties, if not all parties, served as agents for representing particular sections of the community.

The extent to which Central and Eastern Europe might replicate this broad pattern of development was far from clear. For some the development of post-communist mass parties was seen as unlikely because of the lack of strong cleavages in society, leading new parties to remain low-membership formations with very loose electoral constituencies.[3] For others, mass parties would need to await the stabilisation of new social structures and the crys- tallisation of interests, including class interests.[4] Thus far the former appears a more accurate forecast, though social structures remained rather fluid. The communist parties and the successor parties, however, constituted a modern variant of the mass party. Members deserted in droves as regimes toppled, but these parties retained larger memberships than most others. They varied in the extent to which they essayed a 'catch-all' appeal; but they devoted consider- able attention to organisational nurture. The representation of particular milieux was limited: only ethnic parties and some Christian democratic parties found a stable electoral niche.

It is certainly true that the social context was inhospitable to party pene- tration. There was a negative association of 'party' with the old regime in the minds of many. The willingness to take sides in a communist–anti-communist divide was not matched by an eagerness to undertake the obligations of party membership. Where civil society had been activated, its most prominent leaders had been siphoned off into parliament. 'Interests' were indeed fluid and life chances became unpredictable. The shift to a money economy, coupled with a fall in the standard of living, created new family pressures and diverted attention back to the private sphere.

There was, as we have seen, ample cause for disappointment with the performance of the new politicians. They could not be held totally culpable for inheriting a poisoned chalice or for their lack of expertise, but they proved incapable of communicating to the public either the nature of the tasks or the objective problems they faced. With lamentably few exceptions their quarrelsome behaviour, inability to compromise, and near-naked pursuit of self-interest rendered hollow their claims to public spiritedness and civic responsibility. Opportunities for patronage were legion, encouraging the persistence of behaviour that relied on informal contacts and social networks. The 'culture of connections' was a powerful communist legacy where the rule of law was far from entrenched. Undeveloped legal procedures blurred the boundaries of corrupt practice. Much remained hidden, but periodic scandals laid bare some intricate linkages of politics and business.

In these circumstances the public proved remarkably patient. Despite numerous signs of disenchantment (see below), most of the electorate remained firmly within the democratic political process. They expressed dissatisfaction with their current rulers by maintaining high levels of electoral volatility, switching their support to different parties at successive elections. Party development was a function of two dimensions. On the one hand party volatility was high – with splits and defections more common within parliament than party mergers and the emergence of new extra-parliamentary parties. On the other hand electoral volatility also remained high, as electors searched for effective representation of their interests, values, and concerns.

Party formation

We have noted that the balance of political forces differed considerably in the first proto-democratic period leading up to free parliamentary elections. Solidarity gained a clear moral victory in the semi-competitive elections of 1989, leading to a central role in government. The opposition won in Hungary, Czechoslovakia, Slovenia, and the Baltic republics in 1990. It remained too weak to triumph in Romania and Bulgaria. The second Bulgarian elections coincided with Poland's first fully free election in 1991, followed rapidly by elections in Czechoslovakia, Slovenia, Lithuania, Estonia, and Romania in 1992. Latvia had its second competitive but first post-independence elections in 1993, and Poland also had its second election. Russia, where the aftermath of the October crisis cast its shadow, had its first, along with the constitutional referendum on the new presidential system. Hungary had its second election in 1994, and the Ukraine its first. Only the Hungarian parliament served a full four-year term. The sequencing of elections depended largely on institutional factors, particularly on developments within parliament. Poland's first fully free election (October 1991) was delayed by a clash between president and parliament over the shape of the new electoral system. Where opposition movements fractured within parliament, governing majorities could erode or vanish altogether, sparking fresh elections, as in Lithuania, Estonia, and Slovenia. In Czechoslovakia and Romania the first parliaments were defined as provisional, with early second elections defined in advance.

The central electoral issues depended largely on the progress of economic reform. It is not much exaggeration to say that market reformers gained from a lack of reform in Bulgaria and Romania, while elsewhere campaigners focused largely on the scope and pace of change and ameliorative welfare. The new 1991 Polish parliament was so fragmented that a victor was hard to discern, and many votes went to local or regional groupings rather than to the many aspiring new political parties of Solidarity provenance. Perhaps some 20 per cent of voters endorsed the existing reform strategy, though this should not imply an anti-market stance. Indeed, no serious grouping rejected capitalist reform altogether: most offered a less painful route to the same destination. In the four newly independent states economic issues superseded (but did not totally displace) national ones.

The second elections (like Poland's first) saw a large number of contenders as opposition movements broke up and new (quasi-)parties took advantage of easy entry conditions. Many contenders were thus newly branded, although the media exposure of government ministers and leading parliamentarians gave them some opportunity to communicate their new allegiances. The defeat of incumbents was marked, if not universal, in the context of economic depression.

In Bulgaria in 1991 the main wing of the Union of Democratic Forces (SDS) defeated the Socialists. SDS benefited from growing economic chaos. The Socialists lost over one million votes, but SDS splits weakened the force of its success, and only four seats separated the two major opponents. The polarisation of Bulgarian politics into 'communist' and 'anti-communist' forces was also that of reluctant versus avid reformers. In Lithuania in 1992, most of the 26 contending 'parties' came from within the opposition move- ment Sajūdis, which had been splintering and losing support since 1991 and which had lost its majority by mid-1992. Anti-communism proved an insufficient vote winner for Sajūdis. In the new mixed electoral system the successor Democratic Labour Party gained 44 per cent of the PR vote and 54 per cent of seats in the Seimas, as well as the now directly elected presidency in February 1993. Parties were more clearly defined in Slovenia and after the break-up of the DEMOS coalition they made strenuous attempts to establish clearer identities. The Slovene Liberal Democrats, originating in socialist youth organisations, also triumphed with a pragmatic reform emphasis. Neither Lithuania nor Slovenia had much cause to fear the loss of independence and in both cases the communists had also endorsed the national cause; in both cases pro-reform successor parties were the main beneficiaries.

In Estonia, Pro Patria (Isamaa) won the largest share of the vote on a platform of radical economic reform after the erosion of the Popular Front. In Latvia too the Popular Front had split; by 1993 it retained only 53 deputies of the 132 elected in March 1990. More than half the deputies now sat as Independents, alongside five parliamentary factions with ten 'parties'. The liberal Latvia's Way, formed a few months before the election from an alliance of *nomenklatura* deputies, new businesspeople, and émigrés, became the largest party in 1993. Election observers from the British Helsinki Group commented on the Electoral Commission's openly biased information pack, describing Latvia's Way as the moderately right-wing and reformist dream ticket of the election[5] (its programme suggested a radical economic liberalism).

The elections of June 1992 proved decisive for the future of the Czechoslovak state, although only the Slovak nationalists advocated its dissolution. The anti-communist opposition had taken different forms in the two republics, Civic Forum (OF) in the Czech Lands and Public against Violence (VPN) in Slovakia. Each gave rise to republican-based parties, along with others that were also distinctively Czech or Slovak. The Czechs remained supportive of Klaus's economic strategy, with his Civic Democratic Party (ODS) proving the strongest of the Civic Forum offshoots. In Slovakia the Movement for Democratic Slovakia was the largest party, on a platform of more cautious economic reform and radical decentralisation of the federal state. The two victors proved incompatible governing partners, and they formed a temporary coalition designed to oversee the terms of the 'velvet divorce'.

In Romania in 1992 the split within the National Salvation Front (FSN) and new-found opposition unity in the Democratic Convention (CDR) led to a dramatic fall in the (now Democratic) FSN's support. The combined vote of the pro-reform CDR and (Petre Roman's) National Salvation Front was greater than that of the DFSN. Only seven of the 62 (non-minority) contenders gained seats, and the DFSN remained the largest party with 28 per cent of the vote; but it now formed a minority government.

Poland's premature election in the autumn of 1993 and Hungary's 1994 election, both won by social democratic communist-successor parties, meant that within four years all the parliamentary systems of Central and Eastern Europe had experienced two fully competitive elections. Some, if by no means all, uncertainties had been dispelled. This brief period had seen the international recognition of six new independent states; the adoption of new constitutions in all but Hungary and Poland; five new electoral laws; changes in government composition everywhere save the Czech Republic; and in all cases the structuring of government and parliament by political parties. Four countries had a large, successful party established from within anti-communist opposition movements: the Civic Democrats in the Czech Republic, the Movement for Democratic Slovakia, the Homeland Union in Lithuania, and the Union of Democratic Forces in Bulgaria. Five countries – Slovenia, Lithuania, Bulgaria, Poland, and Hungary – had strong, legitimate communist-successor parties of the left or centre-left.

Delayed democratic development in Russia and the Ukraine

The early period of democratic development in Central and Eastern Europe was not matched in Russia and the Ukraine. If anything, democratisation appeared to have taken a backward step, displaced by institutional crisis. In both countries post-Soviet institutional solutions proved inimical to political party formation, within a context of dubious élite commitment to democracy and serious flaws in the rule of law. In Russia the crisis took the form of intensified conflict between parliament and president over proposed constitutional arrangements and over further economic deterior-ation in the wake of a dose of shock therapy. Yeltsin favoured a presidential constitution but parliament a strongly parliamentary one; Yeltsin argued for continued radicalism in the move to a market economy but parliament for a gradualist approach, with continuing state control of strategic sectors. For all that parliament could be seen as an anachronistic holdover from the late-Soviet period, including deep suspicion of capitalist ownership, the Russian deputies' preference for gradualism was also in some measure a reflection of the pain suffered by their constituents. In this they were vindicated by the combined strength of nationalists and communists in the December 1993 elections.

Yet these elections were deeply flawed, not only because the president resolved the conflict by violence, including extensive restrictions of civil liberties, but also because of the haste with which they were organised. Changes to the electoral law in the few weeks prior to the election, last-minute decisions about who could stand, huge disproportions in financial resources and in access to the media, as well as deep disquiet at the turnout figures all undermined the electoral process. The weakening of parliament in the new Constitution, above all in the lack of government accountability, had enduring consequences for the representative functions of the Duma.

In the Ukraine, parliament remained the centre for institutional debate. The period 1992–3 was one of failed attempts at constitutional reform and failure to introduce significant changes to the Soviet-era election law. Without elections, nascent parties withered and the opposition movement Rukh fragmented. Most 'parties' remained little more than coteries of élites. The printing of money as a response to economic crisis merely served to fuel hyperinflation and with it, manifestations of social unrest, while massive subsidies of enterprises encouraged rent-seeking and preserved the power of the economic élite.

Many Socialists, the (newly legalized) Communists, and most unaffiliated deputies favoured maintaining a majoritarian system based on single-member districts. The old guard of the *nomenklatura* who had not linked themselves with political parties also had an interest in promoting electoral institutions that would allow them to capitalise on the local social networks that were their main political resource. Local power brokers found it especially easy to get out the rural vote. Indeed, only half those elected in 1994 were party members. The elections did not even generate a full complement of parliamentary deputies: largely because of careless drafting of the electoral law,[6] one-quarter of seats were not filled following the first two rounds of voting in March and April 1994. The election of the increasingly confrontational President Kuchma with extensive decree powers, deep divisions over the proposed constitutional settlement, and the difficulties of both shaping government and passing legislation with shifting parties and a large number of independent deputies deepened the 'sense of political nihilism across Ukraine' and strengthened popular anti-party sentiments. Only 6 per cent of the population believed that parties provided 'support for the people'.[7]

Types of political party

Processes of party formation developed with some broad, often unarticulated, acceptance of the idea that parties were the appropriate vehicle of representation in a modern democracy. This involved implicit acceptance of a 'responsible party' model of representation, coupled in mixed systems with the potential for independent individual representation. When Hungarian Minister of the Interior defended the proposed new electoral system before the Hungarian parliament in 1989, he stressed that democratic multi-party competition would not only alter the process of government formation, but also the nature of representation, with the role of the individual deputy now mediated by political parties. The issue would no longer be that of a particular individualistic relation of the deputy to his/her electors; rather parties as a whole would seek to ensure the responsiveness of their deputies.[8] But parties based their electoral appeal on rather different messages. In many cases new parties were not responding to a particular electorate or its interests but trying to shape and structure a political agenda to which they hoped the widest possible electorate would respond.

Ideological parties

Some parties sought to provide ideologically based programmes. They fit quite neatly into the 'party families' identified in Western Europe, and most of those 'families' were well represented. At the early stages crucial issues of macro-democratic and macro-economic strategy dominated political debate; but values, including attitudes to history, also played an important role in differentiating parties from many other competitors with similar outlooks. Macro-democratic issues included continuing constitutional issues (presidential powers, the mode of presidential election, citizenship laws); broad foreign policy orientations (for, against or cautious on European or CIS integration). Macro-economic issues included the nature, scope, and speed of privatisation; restitution of property to owners expropriated by the communist regime; schedules for freeing prices; the introduction of new tax regimes; and public spending priorities, albeit often with little specificity. Value conflicts reflected underlying divisions between egalitarianism and hierarchy, religion and secularism, individualism and collectivism, ethnic and multi-ethnic visions of the political community, national and cosmopolitan views of 'identity', antipathy towards and nostalgia for the communist order.

Not surprisingly, party stances on these various dimensions achieved different overall ideological mixes. There were individualist liberal parties, social liberal parties, liberal-conservative parties, alongside radical and moderate nationalists, social democrats, and communists. Generally the parties of the right were more prone to fracture than those of the left or centre-left. Parties attempting to appropriate the centre ground were more diffuse, less enduring, and easily squeezed. Large right-wing parties characterised the Czech Republic (the Civic Democrats, ODS), Hungary (Fidesz from 1998), and Bulgaria (the Union of Democratic Forces to 2001, SDS). But strong left parties developed in Poland (the Alliance of the Democratic Left, SLD), Hungary (the Hungarian Socialist Party, MSzP), the Czech Republic (the Social Democrats, ČSSD), Lithuania (the Democratic Labour Party, LDDP), Slovenia (the Liberal Democratic Party, LDS), Estonia (the Centre Party, EK), Romania (from the National Salvation Front to the Party of Social Democracy, PSD), and Bulgaria (the Bulgarian Socialist Party, BSP). The strongest parties in Russia and the Ukraine were the communists (KPRF, KPU).

This category of ideological parties also included a group of sectional parties, seeking to mobilise a specific electoral constituency. These included the ethnic parties of various minority groups, aiming to protect and promote the status, security, and values of their own communities. We charted the considerable successes of the Hungarians in Romania and Slovakia and the Turks in Bulgaria in Chapter 9. But these were rare examples. Many minority groups were too small for realistic hopes of parliamentary representation. Others, such as the Roma and the Russian Balts, lacked communal cohesion and effective leaders. Ethnicity did not serve as the basis for mobilisation in the multi-ethnic Ukraine nor in the diverse Russian Federation.

Some religious parties also did well. Christian parties made at least a brief appearance in every country except Bulgaria. However, they proved durable only in the Czech Republic, Slovakia, Lithuania, and Slovenia, where their electoral success was also matched by periods in government. The Czech Christian Democrats merged rapidly with the People's Party (KDU–ČSL); their vote over successive elections was 8.7 (1990), 6.0 (1992), 8.1 (1996), and 9.0 (1998). In 2002 their electoral alliance with the Freedom Union–Democratic Union won 14.3 per cent. Not only did they appear to have a respectable 'niche vote'; but they remained a pivotal force in government formation. In Slovakia the Christian Democratic Movement (KDH) was less consistent. Its vote in 1990 to the Slovak section of the Chamber of the People was an impressive 19 per cent. In 1992 its vote and its seat share had fallen by more than half (9 per cent), and it did little better in 1994 (10 per cent). In 1998 it stood as an element of the Slovak Democratic Coalition, but its vote share fell again (8.3 per cent) in 2002, eroded by Dzurinda's Slovak Democratic and Christian Union (SDKÚ).

In Lithuania the Christian Democratic Party (LKDP) and the Christian Democratic Union (KDS) competed against one another and selected different alliance partners for the list element. The KDS never gained list seats, but it retained its one single-member seat in successive elections. Even the stronger Lithuanian Christian Democratic Party, which had 9 seats in the Seimas in 1992 and 16 in 1996, remained in parliament in 2000 only by virtue of a single constituency win after losing its 'modern' element to the Modern Christian Democrats, who also picked up a seat in the single-member element. This poor performance stimulated a merger of the Party and the Union in 2001.

The Slovene Christian Democrats were the most successful element of the victorious DEMOS opposition in 1990 (13 per cent), and they provided the first prime minister. They did even better (14.5 per cent) in 1992. In 2000 they sacrificed their name for a merger with the People's Party (SLS + SKD); but with 9.5 per cent of the vote they failed to improve on their own 1996 performance (9.6 per cent) after losing part of their leadership to and facing competition from New Slovenia (the 'Christian People's Party').

Agrarian parties also emerged, notably in Hungary, Latvia, Bulgaria, and Poland, where they could claim historic links to powerful parties of the inter-war period; but they failed to carve out a stable niche with a loyal electorate. The Agrarian Union (BZNS) was represented in the Bulgarian parliament of 1990 (6 per cent of the vote), but two competing agrarian unions failed to cross the threshold in 1991. Their vote total was little better in 1994, in alliance with the small Democratic Party; but unity yielded 18 seats. They failed to capitalise on this foothold. In Hungary the Smallholders (FKgP) got off to a better start, with almost 12 per cent of the list vote and victory in 11 single-member seats in 1990 and a role in the governing coalition. Their vote dropped in 1994 but recovered to its previous level in 1998, again joining the government; but by 2002 they were effectively defunct. The Latvian Farmers' Union won almost 11 per cent of the vote in 1993, but in 1995, in alliance with the Christian democrats, it gained only 6 per cent, and in 1998 it could muster the support of fewer than 3 per cent of the electorate. The only survivor, the Polish Peasant Party, appeared to beat off a challenge from Solidarity-peasant parties when it performed strongly in 1993. It was the largest Polish party in terms of membership, and it had highly developed rural structures, including networks of ancillary organ-isations. Its vote share rose from 8.7 per cent to 15.4 per cent, and it provided the prime minister for the social democratic–peasant coalition. But it lost votes in 1997 (7.3 per cent) and did not recoup its clientele in 2001 (9 per cent) in the face of strong competition for the rural vote from the radical populist Self-Defence (SO).

Ideological parties were not always coherent or consistent, and their priorities and programmatic concerns differed substantially from their Western European counterparts. Many parliamentary parties proved poorly equipped to establish clear, detailed policies. Even governing parties found legislative drafting an arduous task. Yet these were the parties that came closest to fulfilling the broad aggregation functions necessary for the acting 'on behalf of' that lies at the heart of the idea of representative democracy.

Electoral parties

We identified two types of electoral parties in Central and Eastern Europe. They were similar in their office-seeking instrumental character, the weakness of their ideological profiles, and their lack of durability. They differed in the contexts in which they operated and in the basis of their unity. The first type arose to challenge the current incumbents by recreating the unity of the broad umbrella movements mobilised to challenge the communist regime. The Democratic Convention in Romania (CDR), Solidarity Election Action in Poland (AWS), and the Slovak Democratic Coalition (SDK) came together to counter ruling social democrats in Romania and Poland and Mečiar's Movement for Democratic Slovakia. In the Ukraine in 2002 the formation of Our Ukraine by former Prime Minister Yushchenko arose from general dissatisfaction with the 'reform process', including democratic reform; although not explicitly anti-presidential, Our Ukraine was associated with the opposition movement that arose after the murder of journalist Heorhiy Gongadze and the resulting 'Kuchmagate' scandal. But reluctance to campaign against Kuchma divided this movement, as Yulia Tymoshenko's own electoral party provided a more radical anti-presidentialism.

Unity brought temporary electoral success in the three parliamentary systems, but gaining power did not cement unity from such disparate groupings. The basis on which they came together was a negative one, there was little programmatic coherence, and the constituent entities were unwilling to sink their own putative identities into a single political party. They lasted through one election and a single term in office. Their effects were not uniform, however. In Poland and Romania the resulting (re-) fragmentation of the political right cemented (perhaps temporarily) the unity and dominance of the Social Democrats (SLD and PSD). In Slovakia the creation of the Coalition gave the country a Europe-oriented reform focus and generated a new party, the Democratic and Christian Union (SDKÚ), which provided the core of the next government in 2002. But in Poland and Slovakia new parties also achieved electoral success, compounding uncertainty and retarding the development of coherent party systems. Our Ukraine won a victory of sorts. It did well in the list element, but ultimately failed to overcome the strong regional divisions of Ukrainian politics. The defection of deputies put paid to a coherent anti-Kuchma parliamentary majority.

The second type of electoral parties were the 'parties of power' in the strong presidential systems of Russia (*de jure*) and the Ukraine (*de facto*). These were the alliances of groupings within the central and regional state administration that first emerged with Russia's Choice in 1993. These 'parties' were shifting coteries of élites with no ideological underpinning, seeking to retain power by appealing on broad 'trust us' platforms of continuity and stability. They simply needed a common label on which to contest the list element of the mixed system. They had no formal links with their presidents, although they utilised lavish presidential resources.

Such parties did rather badly, with the exception of Unity in Russia in 1999; but they did win seats that assisted them as individuals in maintaining local power bases. After entering parliament they lacked any foundation for cohesive action and any way of guaranteeing a continuing collective role separate from their relations with the presidential administration. But Unity proved useful to Putin's legislative programme and its merger with Fatherland-All Russia (as United Russia) strengthened the president's capacity to get his policies through the Duma. The division between the pro-Kuchma and anti-Kuchma factions in the Ukrainian Rada reflected only partially articulated but incompatible visions of the Ukraine's future, and it also gave For a United Ukraine leverage after 2002.

Populist parties

Populist parties emerged in the course of the reactive backlash against the dislocations of transition. They were absent in Russia and the Ukraine and they generally proved weak in countries which rapidly saw a fully occupied and clearly ordered ideological space. They were essentially non-ideological opportunists lacking clear-cut programmes, but they shared an approach based on offers of salvation to the (ordinary) people, who had been cruelly betrayed first by both the old regime and now by the emerging political class. Most were the creation of a single prominent individual and could be aptly described as leader-parties. Populism reflected another form of 'trust us' politics, and as such its platforms varied considerably. Allegations of corruption and moral decline and the need for a new broom were all but universal, but the broader diagnosis of society's ills varied from too much economic change to change that was too little or too slow. Most populist parties were new and many disappeared as rapidly as they had emerged. Self-Defence (SO) in Poland was an exception. Andrzej Lepper slowly built a grass-roots direct action movement that gave him considerable media attention for his brand of left-populism, while his remade media image gave him a new respectability that bore fruit in 2001.

Many of the populist parties initiated outside parliament still came from within the establishment. Their instigators gained attention because of their record of success in other spheres, such as banking (such as Latvia's New Era Party, JL) or business (such as Slovakia's Alliance of New Citizens, ANO). Generally they combined anti-corruption crusading with broad platforms of liberal economic reform. Those formed by defection from an existing parliamentary party (such as Slovakia's Direction, *Smer*) bore some hallmarks of their parent, in Smer's case the Party of the Democratic Left (SDL').

The scope for challenge by new populist parties varied, depending partly on developments in established parties and the existence of other new parties. New parties arising within parliament from splits and mergers tended to maintain (more or less) their existing programmatic outlook, while seeking to distinguish themselves from their parent or papering over differences between new allies. Perhaps unsurprisingly, larger parties weathered splits better than small ones. This was the case with the Czech Civic Democrats, the Homeland Union in Lithuania, the Romanian Social Democrats – both as the National Salvation Front and then as the Party of Social Democracy – and the Bulgarian Socialist Party. Neither the Czech Republic nor Romania provided fruitful ground for new populist challengers.

At successive elections different parties served as protest vehicles and the political marketplace remained open. In Romania and the Czech Republic existing ideological parties mobilised votes of the disenchanted. In 2000 and 2001 nationalists and Communists respectively added the anti-establishment vote to their core voters. But voters did not treat political parties as wholly interchangeable packets of soap power. The salience of anti-communism, issues of nation-building and identity, religious values, and impulses to egalitarianism varied from country to country. Perceived leadership competence was also extremely important. The condition of a party also mattered. Where party divisions were acute, they not only divided potentially loyal voters but weakened a party's attraction. New parties filled different types of gap. As the electoral cycle continued voters also gained practical experience of how different parties behaved in government.

In Bulgaria the socialists and the Union of Democratic Forces alternated in government over the first four elections. Economic crisis was protracted and corruption endemic. Simeon Saxecoburg could – and did – take disillusioned voters from both sides in 2001 on a platform of studied neutrality between the two and his personal commitment to moral renewal. In Poland disaffected Solidarity voters had the choice of three new parties in 2001 – liberal (Civic Platform), statist and anti-corruption (Law and Justice), and religious nationalist (the League of Polish Families) – and these voters were most hostile to the social democrats, but also to the left-populist Self-Defence.[9]

In Slovakia, where anti-communism was less salient, the division between Vladimír Mečiar and his opponents had drawn all the latter into the 1998 governing coalition, so that by 2002 all parliamentary parties had served in government. By 2002 the two major elements of the Mečiar camp – the Movement for Democratic Slovakia and the nationalists – had split. On the government side the Democratic Left had split, the Party of Civic Understanding had vanished, and the Slovak Democratic Coalition had broken up. In no case did the sum of the vote for the parent party and its splinters reach the previous vote of the united party. Instead voters turned to the liberal populism of ANO, the leftish-nationalist populism of Fico's Smer, and the radical left Communist Party.

Voters' response to the electoral offerings of would-be élites reflected a search for effective political representation. Parties in turn searched for effective ways to maintain and enhance their electoral appeal. Only the successor parties, ethnic parties, and a few Christian democratic parties could claim a core of loyal voters. But even these parties could not take their voters for granted. Electoral parties sought temporary tactical advantage rather than the development of loyalty, and there was no instance where an electoral party persisted, nor where a constituent element was not ultimately damaged by the experiment. Populist parties proved largely ephemeral.

Representation and the electoral process

We have argued throughout that a representative democracy is not merely one in which voters' preferences are roughly translated into a contingent of parliamentary deputies at a single election. It requires a continual process of choice, perceived responsiveness, accountability, and renewed choice. This process in turn is a product of the electoral sequence. This embraces eligibility requirements, voter registration, candidate selection and registration, the campaign itself, the casting of votes, the counting of votes, the translation of votes into parliamentary seats, the composition of parliament, the formation of government, the actions of government, political parties and individual deputies, and the calling to account through the renewal of the same process. Although the rules governing the process may change and the actors may also change, democracy requires the routinisation of elections. At the same time it requires a broader set of preconditions in which the rule of law is upheld and civil liberties are respected, including the freedom of association and the right of candidates and parties to disseminate their views. It also necessitates a result that *matters*. Those elected must influence the decision-making process. Otherwise they cannot be responsive to their electors, and they cannot be held accountable for decisions in which they played little or no role.

We have not reviewed these factors systematically, though we have made reference to all of them. We begin first with the question of the institutional framework, the nature of the political system itself. The parliamentary systems generated governments in consequence of the electoral process. The presidential systems in Russia and the Ukraine did not. In the parliamentary systems parliament was the crucial decision-making forum for determining the shape of legislation. In the presidential systems parliament's legislative role remained weak. This was not simply a product of constitutional arrangements providing for strong presidents, although such arrangements played a part, especially in Russia. It also arose because the presidential administration emerged as the key centre of power, with ample resources to buy off or discredit particular politicians.[10] Moreover, in these two countries the president could by-pass parliament using executive decree powers or ordinances. The lack of incentive for developing cohesive programmatic parties also undermined the capacity to develop cross-party alliances to override presidential vetoes. These factors were not static. Vladimir Putin made far greater use of parliament for translating his policies into law than Boris Yeltsin. Leonid Kuchma's bid for a Russian-style presidency came partly unstuck in the aftermath of the murder of the opposition journalist Heorhiy Gongadze. Nor were these the only factors inhibiting the development of political parties and undermining democracy as a process embodying representation, responsiveness, and accountability. In virtually every dimension of this study we found a divide between Russia and the Ukraine on the one hand and the remaining countries on the other.

The regulation of elections

The initial stage of the electoral process did not differ greatly in the mechanisms and procedures for contestation. Initially entry regulations were designed to facilitate the opening up of the electoral process. Political parties, party alliances, Independents, and in many cases social organisations were permitted to stand. Registration was generally easy, except in the Ukraine, where conditions for party registration were exceptionally onerous. In Bulgaria any registered political party could stand in 1990, with only 50 members needed to register as a party. In Romania a mere 251 signatures were sufficient for a party to contest the first election. In the two Czechoslovak republics it was 10,000. In Hungary it was easy to stand in the single-member element but less so to be a national contender across both elements: while 750 signatures were needed to stand in a single-member district, a party needed to have candidates in at least one-quarter of the single-member districts (a minimum of two) to field a list in the corresponding multi-member regional constituency. Moreover, fielding a national list required a list in at least seven of Hungary's 20 regions. This proved a valuable party-strengthening mechanism. Only in Hungary and Slovakia did entry requirements remain unchanged. Only in Poland were they actually reduced, with a signature requirement of 5000 reduced to 3000 in 2001. Elsewhere they were strengthened or substituted by a monetary deposit to deter frivolous candidacies.

Such changes appeared to have no discernible effect on the numbers of electoral contenders, however, save for the decline in Independents in single-member districts in Hungary and Lithuania (but not in Russia and the Ukraine). As new provisions banned social organisations from contention, the character of contenders changed somewhat, but their numbers remained high, while these single labels also embraced election alliances and large blocs. The rules of contention did not appear unduly restrictive.

Most countries were also rapidly able to ensure efficient electoral administration. Only Romania experienced four elections without a permanent state electoral commission, in other words without a core of increasingly experienced election administrators. Voter registration was rarely an issue, except in Romania and the Ukraine. In its report on the Romanian elections of 1996 the OSCE noted that inaccurate and incomplete voter lists, with fragmented arrangements for compiling them, were an urgent major area of concern.[11] In 2002 its Ukrainian report criticised voter lists as outdated and unreliable.[12] In contrast the report on the 1999 Russian election recorded approbation of a system that 'provided an exceptional basis for transparency, accountability and accuracy'.[13]

Candidate selection

With candidate selection our interest shifts once again to the political parties, the primary bodies responsible for candidates in systems of proportional representation. In the Ukraine and Russia the mixed-parallel systems provided incentives for individuals with local power bases to stand as Independents. In both Russia in 1999 and the Ukraine in 2002 about half the single-member candidates still stood without party affiliation. In the two other mixed systems, Hungary and Lithuania, Independents were insignificant by the third election.

Candidate selection began as a largely ad hoc process carried out through informal procedures. Increasingly, successful parties began to develop internal structures, strategies, and more routinised mechanisms for candidate choice. They continued to mobilise candidates largely from highly educated strata of the population, creating parliamentary profiles that were less socially representative than candidates taken as a whole. New parties often tried to attract 'social notables' to their lists, including well-known businesspeople and sports personalities.

Professionals were generally the largest single occupational category among both candidates and deputies. Their role was greatest where they gained early incumbency because of their leading role in opposition movements. The prevalence of science and engineering reflected the educational profile fostered by the communist system; but there was no shortage of teachers, doctors, and lawyers. Increasingly deputies came also from national and local government administration and from those engaged in entrepreneurial activity. While deputies in the communist period were drawn from a much broader cross section of the population, there were few workers and still fewer peasants in the post-communist parliaments.

The composition of parliament varied by country and over time, as different parties won successive elections. Professionals remained overwhelmingly dominant in Poland. In the former Soviet Union, deputies included higher proportions of state functionaries and those engaged in the economy. In Russia and the Ukraine this fit the pattern of 'nomenklatura democratization'. In Estonia and Lithuania this probably reflected the replacement of Russian officials in the state apparatus by Estonians and Lithuanians. In 1992 the Estonian Popular Front fielded more candidates from the state administration than any other party.

Parties differed in their candidate profiles. Their candidate-selection procedures reflected their ideological profiles or, in the case of populist parties, the constituency to which they sought to appeal. New liberal parties drew heavily on the economy for their candidates. The Lithuanian Liberal Union steadily increased its proportion of candidates drawn from business; by 2000 almost half its candidates came from this sector. Parties of power also drew their candidates from business, as well as from the state administration. The social democratic parties, whether successor parties or not, were more likely to recruit qualified engineers than members of the working class. Workers stood for radical left parties that rarely gained entry into parliament. Populist parties also fielded more representative candidates. Of all non-winning parties in Slovakia in 1998, 38.6 per cent of candidates were industrial or agricultural workers, and this was the largest category of their candidates. Only 12.5 per cent of candidates of winning parties were workers. However, it was also the case that the composition of the candidate corpus did not remain static.

Politics remained largely a male province, however, and the political culture remained largely traditional, while women experienced rather particular transformation adjustments. Yet over the period there was change in the gender balance of both candidates and deputies. In almost every case the proportion of women candidates increased at successive elections; in virtually every case the proportion of women deputies was lower than the proportion of women candidates. Commensurate with the Nordic lead on this issue in Western Europe, Estonia in 1999 and Latvia in 2002 had the highest proportion of women candidates. Latvia was second to Bulgaria, where the Simeon II Movement needed the Women's Party to provide candidates for their common slate, in the proportion of women deputies (35 per cent of NDSII candidates were women[14]). Women politicians were also becoming increasingly visible in key government and parliamentary posts.

Quotas began to affect candidate selection, but women stood in increasing numbers also in countries where quotas were not a subject of debate. Left-wing parties were more receptive to the idea of increasing women's representation through quotas. Of non-left-wing parties only the Movement for Democratic Slovakia introduced quotas and indeed then fielded a substantial proportion of women candidates; but its women were placed in low-list places, not in winnable seats. However, left-wing parties were not uniformly more sympathetic to women nor right-wing parties more inhospitable, though this was broadly the case. In Poland the proportion of women deputies rose from 13.9 per cent in the previous parliament to 20 per cent in 2001.

Of the women elected in 2001 the ten from the radical Catholic League of Polish Families constituted 26.3 per cent of the League's parliamentary contingent. The 55 women elected from the Social Democrat–Labour Union alliance constituted 25.5 per cent of the total deputies from the SLD–UP. Of the thirty-five women deputies in Hungary in the 2002 parliament, twenty-three came from the Socialist Party, two from the liberal Free Democrats, and ten from the conservative Fidesz–Forum alliance. In many countries parties were placing the issue on the agenda, and there were some early indications of a contagion process at work, both from within from competing parties, and from without, including from the European Union's concern with issues of gender equality.

Election campaigns

We have said little about the nature of electoral campaigns in the course of our discussion. Still, some comment is in order here. Yet in two cases, Russia and the Ukraine, international observers expressed reservations from the outset that worsened with successive elections. These centred on the linked factors of media bias and the use of incumbents' so-called 'administrative resources'. The report on Russia's 1999 election included a substantial discussion of the distorting role of the media and its biased, often scurrilous reporting, pressure on journalists, and promotion of an 'aggressive and bitterly negative campaign'. It also noted with concern instances where 'officials combined political and official functions in violation of law', while 'government forces were willing to exert undue influence to denigrate opponents and manipulate the political landscape...'.[15]

In 2002 OSCE observers in the Ukraine detected a grave atmosphere of mistrust and uncertainty prior to the election. They too found media bias, with disproportionate coverage of pro-presidential blocs, and they proposed the establishment of an independent media commission with election monitoring and enforcement powers. They observed 'illegal interference by public authorities and abuse of administrative resources', with failings reflecting 'a political tradition that fails to adequately distinguish between State and party activities, and uses incumbency to gain undue campaign advantage', as well as instances of obstruction of the opposition.[16] Although the financially well-endowed *parties faux* or clone parties established by pro-presidential forces made little impact,[17] they too should be noted as another attempt to manipulate the election outcome.

Elsewhere election campaigns became more professional as parties gained experience. Election contenders enjoyed free access to the public media and the initial amateur quality of their presentations gave way to slicker, glossier advertisements. Almost universally, incumbents were accused of abusing their media access, but increasingly voters had alternative sources of information, including choice from a highly partisan press. Negative attacks and mud-slinging were commonplace, including allegations of dubious activities during the communist regime or more recent corrupt practices. Head-to-head debates among party leaders were rather rare (Hungary was an exception in 1998, when considerable influence was attributed to the Horn-Orbán debate). Activities such as canvassing, holding public meetings, or distributing leaflets were not very widespread. The vast electoral mobilisation of the communist period was nowhere in evidence. Yet campaigns were judged free and fair, if often tepid and unexciting.

The vote

Indeed, voters displayed little enthusiasm for elections. Survey evidence confirmed their failure to embrace political parties with responses affirming that 'no party represents the interests of people like me'.[18] In a recent survey at the time of writing 62 per cent of Polish respondents had no party for whom they could vote confidently in a parliamentary election. Almost half – 46 per cent – believed that the Polish Sejm 'represented only the interests of certain social groups'.[19]

Election turnout, the key index of political participation, began to decline. This was not a steady, linear trend, and there were numerous instances of sudden upsurge in voter involvement. Many countries saw a fluctuating turnout rate in response to the circumstances of a particular election, though none returned to their high point of the early 1990s. This decline was marked above all in the Czech Republic, with a steady fall from 96.8 per cent in the federal Czechoslovak elections of 1990 to just under 58 per cent in 2002. It was most savage in Lithuania, with a single drop of over 22 per cent in 1996, the second post-independence election. Poland, with a long history of social activism under the communists, never came close to its 62 per cent turnout in the semi-competitive elections of 1989. The first fully free election saw only 43 per cent of the electorate attending the polls in 1991; over four free elections the average turnout was 47.3 per cent. Clearly the political élites had failed abysmally to engage the population in the democratic political process.

The failure of political parties to generate loyalty – in circumstances where citizens had few other structural linkages to the political process – was expressed in and provides a partial explanation for this declining turnout. It was also manifest in the large shifts in votes for political parties between one election and another. Some shift was natural, given radical changes in the parties themselves, including their disappearance. Yet even taking account of this party volatility, electoral volatility was substantial. Whatever the differences in precise estimates, average volatility for the region, and particularly for the former Soviet Union, remained far higher than that in Western Europe and higher in some cases than that of Latin America.[20]

A volatile electorate fed party volatility and party volatility encouraged a volatile electorate. The willingness of voters to choose new political parties was both a measure of their frustration and an invitation to still more political entrepreneurs. The success of new formations in turn fed the notion that other new parties could succeed. Despite the gradual increase in barriers to entry, such as through thresholds and changes in party registration requirements across the region, the most recent elections saw newly created parties entering parliament in Bulgaria, Poland, Slovakia, Slovenia, and Latvia, and Russia (and Estonia in 2003).

When voters went to the polls, few had difficulties with the actual ballot mechanism. In many countries invalid votes constituted only a tiny fraction of the total. In early elections one might expect some confusion or inconsistency, especially with inexperienced election commissions, complex ballots, and lists of unfamiliar and often similar sounding parties. The highest levels of invalid votes did indeed occur in the first and second elections. Over 12 per cent of Romanian voters cast invalid ballots in 1992. But they remained high in Romania even in 2000 (6.2 per cent), and in Slovenia, Poland, the Ukraine, and Lithuania they did not fall below 3 per cent.

Voters also had difficulties in assessing how their vote might matter. In some cases they were denied access to late opinion polls indicating campaign shifts in voters' preferences. But it was the combined effects of party volatility and electoral volatility that made election outcomes so hard to judge. Parties changed their names, stood in electoral alliances under different labels, and merged or split. The number of new contenders also remained high, with significant reductions only in Poland and Hungary.

Changes in the electoral system also made calculations more complex. Though we have assumed that voters were ill-equipped to deal with changes in district magnitude or the formulae for vote-seat calculation, the impact of electoral thresholds was clear to see, if not necessarily to judge in advance. Electoral thresholds rose most sharply in Poland in 1993 with a new threshold of 5 per cent for a party to win constituency seats; and in Romania, with 3 per cent in 1992 and 5 per cent in 2000, now with higher thresholds for electoral coalitions. But even slight rises made strategic voting more difficult.

So wasted votes remained at high levels: many voters did not gain representatives of their choice. The highest level was in Russia in 1995, where a staggering 48 per cent of list voters chose parties that did not cross the electoral threshold (a 4 per cent threshold would have added three parties and reduced wastage to 35 per cent). Only in Hungary, Estonia, and Slovenia did wasted votes decline at successive elections – in Slovenia they were only 3.6 per cent in 2000. Elsewhere non-participation and high proportions of wasted votes may not necessarily have undermined the legitimacy of the new democratic system, but they certainly did not enhance it.

Electoral outcomes

In the parliamentary systems of Central and Eastern Europe elections provided a means of orderly succession. Elections were by no means the sole mechanisms for changing governments. Votes of confidence and inter-party conflicts resulted in the reshaping or reconstitution of governments between elections. But elections set the broad parameters within which changes in government took place, and governments remained accountable to those chosen by the electorate.

Elections not only provided the means of choosing representatives, they also provided sanction for inadequate performance. Elections require politicians to give an *account* of themselves. Governments must also account for those for whom they were responsible, including the smooth running of the government machine by the bureaucracy. Elections provide a post hoc check on whether governments have fulfilled the promises made during the previous election campaign – or their reasons why not. Oppositions cannot be held responsible for unfulfilled commitments, but they can be judged in terms of their credibility in opposing, as well as for providing constructive alternatives to government policies. Elections are a blunt instrument of accountability, requiring packaged judgements on a range of policies or behaviour.

In Western Europe incumbency was seen as an advantage; it was common for parties to return to office, perhaps with a somewhat different array of coalition partners. In Central and Eastern European parliamentary systems the vast majority of elections led to a *complete* change of governing parties. Despite often protracted negotiations for the formation of coalition governments, governments changed routinely as voters demonstrated their displeasure. In no case did a losing governing party refuse to accept the outcome of the next election. In this respect the accountability built in to the electoral process operated as an integral feature of the democratic mechanism. Governments were found wanting, while those voting for new parties displayed their lack of confidence not only in the incumbent government but also in their parliamentary opposition parties.

The (almost) routine defeat of incumbents provided another reflection of a widespread popular disappointment in the ways in which those holding political office met, or failed to meet, the expectations of the electorate. Not only did incumbents risk loss of office, they also risked exclusion from the parliamentary arena. The most recent instances were the defeat of the Democratic Convention in Romania in 2000 and of the two governing parties in Poland in 2001. The Romanian Democratic Convention won 30 per cent of the vote in 1996 and 5 per cent in 2000. The broad-based electoral party Solidarity Election Action (AWS) went from 34 per cent of the vote in 1997 to 5.6 per cent for its remaining core in 2001. In both cases their governments suffered from acute intra-party tensions within government and an unreliable body of deputies to support them.

Yet most countries had at least one successful political party, characterised by organisational continuity and a substantial vote share. Moreover, most new parties entering parliament were by no means radical, and voters did not shift en masse to overtly anti-democratic alternatives. Many new parties, and a number of radical parties, struck a chord with their pleas for moral leadership and the need to tackle corruption. If they appeared to have some credentials – as in the perception of Simeon Saxe-Coburggotski – voters were prepared to try them. Latvian voters in particular had a high propensity to support new faces.

Parliamentary behaviour

The 'responsible party' model of representative government attracted many critics, not least for its imputation of voter rationality in choosing among parties on the basis of their policy offerings. None the less parties obviously cannot ignore the voters on whom their political survival depends. Klingemann and his colleagues found that in Western Europe there was indeed a reasonably close fit between the goals laid out in party election platforms and their subsequent conduct in office.[21] Even with coalitions blurring the lines between partners, governments took seriously the promises made to the electorate.

But this model cannot operate effectively without durable, cohesive political parties acting within parliament, whether to support or oppose the existing government. Established parties in Western Europe have both ideological and institutional bases for encouraging unified behaviour; they have the underlying cement of shared attitudes and loyalty, as well as carrots and sticks to foster party discipline. Political parties are not just sums of individual members; they are established, entrenched institutions with institutional interests that evolved slowly over a long period. New parties can (usually) be gradually socialised into the broader political culture. Within parliament, parties interact in a system of stable and relatively predictable patterns of interaction.

Although it was widely assumed that parties in new democracies would rather quickly become consolidated, cohesive entities, such development was slow and uneven. Parties that stood for election – and still more, parties that stood in alliance with other parties – did not provide the assured political support for coherent government or opposition. Only the successor parties could be relied upon to maintain their traditional levels of party discipline. Only ethnic parties maintained, by and large, a stable, loyal electorate. Otherwise the party fractions or clubs that formed in parliament did not match the contenders that had stood together at election time, nor did they remain stable. The nomadic behaviour of individual deputies eroded the relative strengths and political capacity of parliamentary parties. Deputies could not be relied upon to toe the party line. Ideological differences, conflicts of personality, and shifting perceptions of self-interest came into play. Parties defected from coalitions and even government ministers did not always vote with the government. Internal divisions weakened government effectiveness, in turn exacerbating divisions. When government popularity fell, electoral uncertainties increased, and space for new political entrepreneurs opened up. What looked stable could fall apart almost overnight.

Parliamentary party configurations retained considerable fluidity in Lithuania, Latvia, and Slovakia. Prospects for the institutionalisation of (ex)

Simeon II's National Movement in Bulgaria remained unclear after the 'earthquake election' of 2001. In Hungary, the Czech Republic, and Slovenia there was more evidence of growing party 'systemness'. In Hungary in particular a drastic reduction in the number of parliamentary parties facilitated greater party consolidation and more predictable patterns of competition. Czech parties also demonstrated solid party cohesion after 1998. Estonia saw some simplification of the political scene with the settling of its nation-building priorities; but personality politics remained writ large in tiny Estonia. Romania and Poland had strong left-wing parties, continuing fluidity on the right, and no discernible centre. In Poland Self-Defence and in Romania the Greater Romania Party were capable of providing further disruption and uncertainty.

Russia and the Ukraine were weakest of all in the development of their political parties. Strong communist parties had no clear vision of the future society they wished to shape. After 1999 Russia gained a presidential vehicle for the first time, as Unity and Fatherland combined forces. The Ukrainian parliament remained a shifting quicksand of pro- and anti-presidential factions. In neither case could responsiveness to the electorate be seen as a motor of politics. Indeed, the parties of power took the politics out of politics. They provided vague options of order and stability while themselves lacking both these attributes. Richard Rose wrote of (Russian) parties floating in and parties floating out. As he put it, '...elites have shown too much skill in forming, breaking, and avoiding parties... The ... free-floating party system destroys – or precludes – the central institutions necessary to create a representative and accountable democracy'.[22]

Conclusion

The multi-dimensional nature of the challenge of transition in post-communist Europe created unique conditions for democratisation. Reshaping the state and the political process were a necessary precondition of the economic, social, and cultural changes of the transformation agenda. It still seems extraordinary that so many countries made such momentous and rapid changes in such a short period of time. Free competitive elections provided the mechanism through which democracy was tested and survived throughout the former Soviet bloc, as well as in the newly independent states of the Baltic and Slovenia. Governments were formed from parliaments and accountable to them, subjecting themselves to the subsequent judgement of the electorate. The region weathered savage economic depression and individual suffering. Yet it did not descend into a cauldron of political instability, massive migration, ethnic wars, or populist authoritarianism.

The yawning gap between the successful democracies and post-Soviet Russia and the Ukraine remained a persisting feature of post-communist democratic development. Parliamentary democracy succeeded and presidentialism failed. With committed democrats in office it might have been otherwise. In practice unchecked executive power, personalism, and weak parliaments gave presidents the capacity to trade public resources for financial and political support without having to worry about the collapse of government. Unclear lines of responsibility and authority enabled presidents to divide and rule and increase the scope of their patronage.[23]

Russia and the Ukraine met few of the basic conditions for 'representative and responsible government'. The rule of law was not entrenched, and their size and resources made rent-seeking opportunities more highly developed than anywhere else. Their partial reform strategies created a set of incentives for the beneficiaries to delay further reform.[24] The fairness of elections was compromised by preferential media access for pro-presidential candidates, as well as lavish resources. Nor did elections lead to change; elections did not serve as a mechanism for 'getting the rascals out': indeed, Yitzhak Brudny argued that elections in Russia merely 'taught the ruling elite how it could use the electoral process to perpetuate its hold on power and destroy political opponents'.[25] Weak parliaments gave deputies little capacity to provide the people with public goods.

If there was a chasm between the non-democratic presidential and the democratic parliamentary systems, the latter were certainly imperfect reflections of the democratic model. The quality of post-communist democracy remained highly flawed in the years following the fall of the old regime. This is apparent in regard both to representation, the acting on behalf of, and its close twin accountability, being called to account for.

The populations of Central and Eastern Europe displayed many signs of their disappointment and disillusion with the practice of democracy. It does not follow that they rejected democratic principles, but it none the less presented serious potential problems for the continuing legitimacy of political systems. Even a minimalist concept of democracy as a mechanism for élite rule depends in some measure on the acceptance of the élites among whom voters are asked to choose. For participative concepts of democracy the chasm between ideals of a vibrant civil society, with multiple linkages of democratic bodies in society to democratic institutions of the state, and the existing socio-political landscape was far greater.

Voters began with very high expectations of what their politicians could deliver, and there was no realistic hope that even the most competent could have brought both freedom and prosperity in such a short space of time. Even when economic growth resumed it took some time just to get back to the original starting point of decline. At the same time inequalities were becoming more visible, as a stratum of *nouveau riche* and old *nomenklatura riche* engaged in highly conspicuous consumption. The world of politics was confusing, marked by politicians changing allegiance, parties splitting, merging or changing their names, government turbulence, scandals, and poor public services. Affective attachments had no time to form before a withdrawal process set in.

But the inexperience, incompetence, and in some cases the venality of the politicians also played a role. One legacy of the communist system was the importance of social networks, personal connections, and the exchange of favours. The initial conditions of democracy-building in a context of state ownership of the economy gave countless patronage opportunities to all élites, as well as scope for insider dealing. They could change or confirm the personnel of the state administration at national and regional level and staff new privatisation agencies, boards of directors, enterprise management, banks, stock exchanges, job centres, pension funds, broadcasting councils, and a host of others – in short a potential new *nomenklatura* for victorious parties. Every country without exception experienced perennial scandals arising from the abuse of power.

So the electorate was not always misguided in its perceptions of the emerging political class or its own sense of inadequate representation. 'Ordinary citizens have doubts as to the quality and trustworthiness of their political representatives and their mistrust and cynicism over the political process is widespread', Adolf Sprudzs noted of Latvia.[26] He could have been referring to virtually the whole of the region.

It is quite possible for political alienation to assume considerable proportions without obvious effects. People also get used to the way things are and see them as normal and natural. Democracy has its own path-dependent inertia. But flawed democracy can also be improved. Élites can gain experience, and there are ample instances of élite integrity and civic responsibility. Institutions do shape behaviour. New laws and procedural rules cannot remove informal or corrupt practices, but they subject such conduct to legal sanctions. Politicians can learn to communicate. Passive societies can mobilise and become active. Democracy-building is not a project that starts and ends. There is no representative democracy that cannot be improved.

Notes

Chapter 1

1. David Judge, *Representation. Theory and Practice in Britain*, London: Routledge, 1999, p. 11.
2. See Leon D. Epstein, *Political Parties in Western Democracies*, New Brunswick and London: Transaction Publishers, 1980 (rev. ed.), pp. 19–45.
3. Juan Linz and Alfred Stepan, *Problems of Democratic Transition and Consolidation. Southern Europe, South America, and Post-Communist Europe*, London: Johns Hopkins University Press, 1996, p. 56.
4. A. Schedler, 'What is Democratic Consolidation?' *Journal of Democracy*, vol. 9, no. 2, April 1998, pp. 91–107.
5. See Larry Diamond, 'Introduction: In Search of Consolidation' in Larry Diamond, Marc F. Plattner, Yun-han Chu, and Hung-mao Tien, eds, *Consolidating the Third Wave Democracies. Themes and Perspectives*, London: The Johns Hopkins University Press, 1997, p. xxv.
6. See for example, Scott Mainwaring and Timothy R. Scully, 'Introduction: Party Systems in Latin America' in Scott Mainwaring and Timothy Scully, eds, *Building Democratic Institutions. Party Systems in Latin America*, Stanford: Stanford University Press, 1995, pp. 1–34. Compare Gábor Tóka, 'Political Parties in East Central Europe' in Larry Diamond, Marc F. Plattner, Yun-han Chu, and Hung-mao Tien, eds, *Consolidating the Third Wave Democracies. Themes and Perspectives*, London: The Johns Hopkins University Press, 1997, pp. 93–134; Vicky Randall and Lars Svåsand, 'Party Institutionalisation and the New Democracies', Paper presented to the ECPR Joint Session of Workshops, Mannheim, March 1999.
7. Tóka, 'Political Parties in East Central Europe', p. 95. See also S.M. Lipset, 'The Indispensability of Parties', *Journal of Democracy*, vol. 11, 2000, pp. 48–55.
8. For an assessment of this thesis see José Ramón Montero and Richard Gunther, 'Introduction: Reviewing and Assessing Parties' in Richard Gunther, José Ramón Montero and Juan J. Linz, eds, *Political Parties. Old Concepts and New Challenges*, Oxford: Oxford University Press, 2002, pp. 3–8.
9. See Matthew Soburg Shugart and John M. Carey, *Presidents and Assemblies. Constitutional Design and Electoral Dynamics*, Cambridge: Cambridge University Press, 1992, pp. 55–75.
10. See M. Steven Fish, 'The Executive Deception: Superpresidentialism and the Degradation of Russian Politics' in Valerie Sperling, ed., *Building the Russian State. Institutional Crisis and the Quest for Democratic Governance*, Boulder: Westview Press, 2000, pp. 178–9.
11. Yeltsin did retreat in summer 1998, when his nomination of Chernomyrdin was clearly unacceptable to the Duma.
12. Vladimir Gelman, 'Electoral Democracy in Russia', *Russia on Russia*, Issue 3, October 2000, p. 68.

13. William V. Smirnov, 'Democratization in Russia: Achievements and Problems' in Archie Brown, ed., *Contemporary Russian Politics: A Reader*, Oxford: Oxford University Press, 2001, p. 527.
14. Thomas F. Remington, *The Russian Parliament. Institutional Evolution in a Transitional Regime, 1989–1999*, New Haven: Yale University Press, 2001.
15. Neil Robinson, *Russia. A State of Uncertainty*, London: Routledge, 2002; Ilya Prizel, 'Ukraine's Hollow Decade', *East European Politics and Societies*, vol. 16, no. 2, spring 2002, pp. 363–85.
16. Remington, *The Russian Parliament*, p. 189.
17. For a general discussion of different types of electoral system see David Farrell, *Electoral Systems: A Comparative Introduction*, Basingstoke: Palgrave, 2001.
18. Also see John Ishiyama and Ryan Kennedy, 'Superpresidentialism and Political Party Development in Russia, Ukraine, Armenia and Kyrgyzstan', *Europe-Asia Studies*, vol. 53, no. 8, 2001, pp. 1177–91.
19. For an analysis of this phenomenon see Sarah Birch, 'The Effects of Mixed Electoral Systems in Eastern Europe', Paper presented at the 30th Annual Conference of the University Association for Contemporary European Studies, Budapest 7–9 April, 2000.
20. Neil Robinson, 'Classifying Russia's Party System: The Problem of "Relevance" in a Time of Uncertainty', *The Journal of Communist Studies and Transition Politics*, vol. 14, nos 1, 2, 1998; p. 174.
21. Sarah Birch, Frances Millard, Marina Popescu, and Kieran Williams, *Embodying Democracy. Electoral System Design in Post-Communist Europe*, Basingstoke: Palgrave, 2002, p. 151.
22. cf. Fish, 'The Executive Deception . . .', p. 182.
23. Gary Cox and Matthew McCubbins, 'The Institutional Determinants of Economic Policy Outcomes' in Stephan Haggard and Matthew D. McCubbins, eds, *Presidents, Parliaments, and Policy*, Cambridge: Cambridge University Press, 2001, p. 37.
24. Radosław Markowski, 'Democratic Consolidation and Accountability: News from Eastern and Central European Democracies' in Radosław Markowski and Edmund Wnuk-Lipiński, eds, *Transformative Paths in Central and Eastern Europe*, Warsaw: Institute of Political Studies, Polish Academy of Science and Friedrich Ebert Foundation, 2001, pp. 70–1.
25. Jose Antonio Cheibub and Adam Przeworski, 'Democracy, Elections, and Accountability for Economic Outcomes' in Adam Przeworski, Susan C. Stokes, and Bernard Manin, eds, *Democracy, Accountability, and Representation*, Cambridge: Cambridge University Press, 1999, p. 225.
26. Maurice Duverger, *Political Parties. Their Organization and Activity in the Modern State* (1951), New York: John Wiley & Sons, 1963, p. xxxvi.
27. Nicholas Pano, 'The Process of Democratization in Albania' in Karen Dawisha and Bruce Parrott, eds, *Politics, Power, and the Struggle for Democracy in South-East Europe*, Cambridge: Cambridge University Press, 1997, pp. 304–48.
28. M. Steven Fish, 'The Dynamics of Democratic Erosion' in Richard D. Anderson Jr, M. Steven Fish, Stephen E. Hanson and Philip G. Roeder, *Post-Communism and the Theory of Democracy*, Princeton: Princeton University Press, 2001, Table 3.1, p. 46.
29. Zoltan Barany, 'Bulgaria's Royal Elections', *Journal of Democracy*, vol. 13, no. 2, 2002, pp. 141, 152.
30. Grigory Yavlinski, 'Going Backwards', *Journal of Democracy*, vol. 12, no. 4, October 2001, p. 79.

31. Archie Brown, 'Evaluating Russia's Democratization' in Archie Brown, ed., *Contemporary Russian Politics: A Reader*, Oxford: Oxford University Press, 2001, p. 568.
32. Neil Robinson, *Russia. A State of Uncertainty*, London: Routledge, 2002.
33. Michael McFaul, 'The Fourth Wave of Democracy *and* Dictatorship. Noncooperative Transitions in the Postcommunist World', *World Politics*, vol. 54, January 2002, p. 236.
34. Alexander Lukin, 'Electoral Democracy or Clanism?' in Archie Brown, ed., *Contemporary Russian Politics: A Reader*, Oxford: Oxford University Press, 2001, p. 544.
35. Lilia Shevtsova, 'Russia's Hybrid Regime', *Journal of Democracy*, vol. 12, no. 4, October 2001, p. 68.
36. Nadia Diuk and Myroslava Gongadze, 'Post-Election Blues in Ukraine', *Journal of Democracy*, vol. 13, no. 4, 2002, p. 158.
37. Shevtsova, 'Russia's Hybrid Regime', p. 66; McFaul, 'The Fourth Wave . . .', p. 236.
38. It is questioned however by Karen Dawisha and Stephen Deets, 'Intended and Unintended Consequences of Elections in Russia and Postcommunist States', unpublished paper, 31 March 2002.

Chapter 2

1. A.H. Birch, *Representation*, London and Basingstoke: Macmillan Press, 1972, p. 29.
2. J.S. Mill, *Considerations on Representative Government* (1861), New York: The Liberal Arts Press, 1958, p. 174; George Sanford, *Democratic Government in Poland. Constitutional Politics since 1989*, Basingstoke: Palgrave Macmillan, 2002, pp. 8–9.
3. For a history of French elections and electoral systems, see Alistair Cole and Peter Campbell, *French Electoral Systems and Elections since 1789*, Aldershot: Gower, 1989.
4. Cole and Campbell, *French Electoral Systems and Elections since 1789*, p. 10.
5. Hanna Pitkin, *The Concept of Representation*, Berkeley: University of California Press, 1967, p. 186.
6. Edmund Burke, 'Speech to the Electors of Bristol' in B.W. Hill, ed., *Edmund Burke, Government Politics and Society*, London: Fontana, 1975, pp. 156–8.
7. Edmund Burke, Letter to Sir Hector Langriche (1797), quoted in A.H. Birch, *Representative and Responsible Government*, London: George Allen & Unwin, 1964, p. 24.
8. David Judge, *Representation. Theory and Practice in Britain*, London: Routledge, 1999, p. 26.
9. Mill, p. 107.
10. Robert McKenzie and Allan Silver, *Angels in Marble. Working Class Conservatives in Urban England*, London: Heinemann, 1968.
11. F.J.C. Hearnshaw, *Conservativism in England* (London, 1933), pp. 293–4, cited in Samuel Beer, *Modern British Politics. A Study of Parties and Pressure Groups*, London: Faber and Faber, 1965, p. 102.
12. Gordon Smith, *Politics in Western Europe. A Comparative Analysis*, London: Heinemann Educational Books, 1976 (2nd edn), p. 42.
13. See Karl Marx, 'The Communist Manifesto' in Robert C. Tucker, ed., *The Marx-Engels Reader*, New York: W.W. Norton, 1972, pp. 331–62.
14. Stanley Henig and John Pinder, eds, *European Political Parties*, London: George Allen & Unwin Ltd, 1969, p. 43.
15. See, for example, Margareta Holmstedt and Tove-Lise Schou, 'Sweden and Denmark 1945–1982: Election Programmes in the Scandinavian Setting' in Ian Budge,

David Robertson, and Derek Hearl, *Ideology, Strategy and Party Change: Spatial Analyses of Post-War Election Programmes in 19 Democracies*, Cambridge: Cambridge University Press, 1987, p. 180. For the programmes of the German Social Democrats see Susanne Miller and Heinrich Potthoff, *A History of German Social Democracy from 1848 to the Present*, Leamington Spa: Berg, 1986, pp. 236–92.

16. See McKenzie and Silver, p. 63.
17. Maurice Duverger, *Political Parties. Their Organisation and Activity in the Modern State* (1951), New York: John Wiley & Sons, 1963, pp. 64–6.
18. Philip Williams, *Politics in Post-War France. Parties and the Constitution in the Fourth Republic*, London: Longmans, 1954, pp. 107–10.
19. S.M. Lipset and S. Rokkan, 'Cleavage Structures, Party Systems and Voter Alignments: An Introduction' in S.M. Lipset and S. Rokkan, eds, *Party Systems and Voter Alignments*, New York: Free Press, 1967, pp. 1–64.
20. Duverger, pp. 63–6.
21. Dieter Langewiesche, *Liberalism in Germany*, Basingstoke: Macmillan, 2000, p. 132.
22. George Bernstein, *Liberalism and Liberal Politics in Edwardian England*, London: Allen & Unwin, 1986, p. 4.
23. Duverger, pp. 45, 249.
24. Lipset and Rokkan, p. 50.
25. See Ian Budge, Hans-Dieter Klingemann, Andrea Volkens, Judith Bara, and Eric Tanenbaum with others, *Mapping Policy Preferences. Estimates for Parties, Electors and Governments 1945–1998*, Oxford: Oxford University Press, 2001.
26. Philip E. Converse and Roy Pierce, *Political Representation in France*, Cambridge, Massachusetts: The Belknap Press of Harvard University Press, 1986, pp. 499–501.
27. This is the theme of numerous chapters in Budge, Robertson, and Hearl, *Ideology, Strategy and Party Change*; also Richard Rose, *Do Parties Make a Difference?*, London: Macmillan, 1980, pp. 54–5.
28. Otto Kirchheimer, 'The Transformation of Western European Party Systems' in Joseph LaPalombara and Myron Wiener, eds, *Political Parties and Political Development*, Princeton: Princeton University Press, 1966, p. 184.
29. Kirchheimer, p. 190.
30. Ibid., p. 200.
31. Hans-Jürgen Puhle, 'Still the Age of Catch-allism? *Volksparteien* and *Parteienstaat* in Crisis and Re-equilibration' in Richard Gunther, José Ramón Montero and Juan J. Linz, *Political Parties. Old Concepts and New Challenges*, Oxford: Oxford University Press, 2002, pp. 68–9.
32. Alan Ware, *Political Parties and Party Systems*, Oxford: Oxford University Press, 1996, pp. 228–9; Puhle, p. 68.
33. Angelo Panebianco, *Political Parties: Organisation and Power*, Cambridge: Cambridge University Press, 1988, pp. 264–6.
34. Richard Katz and Peter Mair, 'Changing Models of Party Organisation and Party Democracy: The Emergence of the Cartel Party', *Party Politics*, vol. 1, no. 1, pp. 5–28.
35. Puhle, p. 71 [italics mine].
36. Ferdinand Müller-Rommel, ed., *New Politics in Western Europe. The Rise and the Success of Green Parties and Alternative Lists*, Boulder: Westview Press, 1989; Michael O'Neill, *Green Parties and Political Change in Contemporary Europe*, Aldershot: Ashgate, 1997.
37. See Mudde's inventory of characteristics: 19 of 26 definitions of right-wing extremism stressed anti-democracy as a defining feature; Cas Mudde, 'Right-wing extremism analyzed: A comparative analysis of the ideologies of three alleged

right-wing extremist parties (NPD, NDP, CP'86)', *European Journal of Political Research*, vol. 27, 1995, p. 207; also Piero Ignazi, 'The Silent Counter-revolution. Hypotheses on the Emergence of Extreme Right Parties in Europe', *European Journal of Political Research*, vol. 22, 1992, pp. 11–13.

38. Paul Hainsworth, 'Introduction. The Cutting Edge: The Extreme Right in Post-War Western Europe and the USA' in Paul Hainsworth, ed., *The Extreme Right in Europe and the USA*, London: Pinter Publishers, 1992, p. 10.

39. Cas Mudde, 'The Paradox of the Anti-Party Party. Insights from the Extreme Right', *Party Politics*, vol. 2, no. 2, April 1996, pp. 265–76.

40. Leonard Weinburg, 'Introduction' in Peter H. Merkel and Leonard Weinberg, *Encounters with the Contemporary Radical Right*, Boulder, San Francisco and Oxford: Westview Press, 1993, p. 8; also Hans-George Betz, 'The New Politics of Resentment: Radical Right-wing Populist Parties in Western Europe', *Comparative Politics*, vol. 25, no. 3, July 1993, pp. 416–18.

41. Oliver Marchant, 'Austria and the "Fourth Way"', *Capital and Class*, Issue 73, winter 2000, pp. 7–14.

42. Steven B. Wolinetz, 'Beyond the Catch-All Party: Approaches to the Study of Parties and Party Organisation in Contemporary Democracies' in Richard Gunther, José Ramón Montero and Juan J. Linz, *Political Parties. Old Concepts and New Challenges*, Oxford: Oxford University Press, 2002, pp. 149–64.

43. Pitkin, pp. 60–91.

44. Andrew Heywood, *Political Ideas and Concepts*, London: Macmillan, 1994, pp. 182–4.

45. A.H. Birch, *Representation*, pp. 55–60; Iain McLean, 'Forms of Representation and Systems of Voting' in David Held, ed., *Political Theory Today*, Cambridge: Polity Press, 1991, pp. 172–96.

46. Mill, pp. 175–85.

47. Pippa Norris and Joni Lovenduski, 'Women Candidates for Parliament – Transforming the Agenda?', *British Journal of Political Science*, vol. 19, no. 1, January, 1989, p. 107.

48. Anne Phillips, *Engendering Democracy*, Cambridge: Polity Press, 1991, p. 63.

49. Georgina Waylen, 'Women and Democratization: Conceptualizing Gender Relations in Transition Politics', *World Politics*, vol. 46, no. 3, 1994, pp. 327–54.

50. Pippa Norris, 'Women Politicians: Transforming Westminster', *Parliamentary Affairs*, vol. 49, no. 1, 1996, p. 91.

51. David Dollar, Raymond Fisman, and Roberta Gatti, 'Are women really the "fairer" sex? Corruption and women in government', *Journal of Economic Behavior and Organisation*, vol. 46, 2001, pp. 423–9.

52. See Anna G. Jónasdóttir, 'On the Concept of Interest, Women's Interests, and the Limitations of Interest Theory' in Kathleen B. Jones and Anna G. Jónasdóttir, eds, *The Political Interests of Gender. Developing Theory and Research with a Feminist Face*, London, Newbury Park and New Delhi: Sage, 1985, pp. 33–65.

53. Phillips, *Engendering Democracy*, pp. 72–3.

54. Norris, 'Women Politicians'; Martha Nussbaum, *Sex and Social Justice*, Oxford and New York: Oxford University Press, 1999.

55. Norris and Lovenduski, 'Women Candidates', pp. 114–5.

56. Mill, p. 174.

57. Williams, *Politics in Post-War France*, pp. 107–10.

58. Converse and Pierce, p. 500; Cole and Campbell, p. 10.

59. See Neil Harding, *Lenin's Political Thought*, London: Macmillan, 1977.

60. cf. G.V. Plekhanov, quoted in Tony Cliff, *Lenin*, London: Pluto Press, 1975, vol. 1, p. 106.
61. cf. Karl Marx, *The Civil War in France*, in Robert C. Tucker, ed., *The Marx-Engels Reader*, New York, W.W. Norton, 1972, pp. 554.
62. J. Arch Getty, 'State and Society under Stalin: Constitutions and Elections in the 1930s', *Slavic Review*, vol. 50, no. 1, 1991, pp. 26–35.
63. This was a mark of the inferior status of the 'People's Republics', which retained vestiges of earlier class politics.
64. For an overview of communist-era electoral systems, see Robert K. Furtak, ed., *Elections in Socialist States*, New York and London: Harvester Wheatsheaf, 1990.
65. L.G. Churchward, *Contemporary Soviet Government*, London: Routledge and Kegan Paul, 1968, p. 112.
66. R.J. Hill, 'Continuity and Change in USSR Supreme Soviet Elections', *British Journal of Political Science*, vol. 11, no. 1, 1972, pp. 47–67.
67. William F. Robinson, *The Pattern of Reform in Hungary: A Political, Economic and Cultural Analysis*, London: Praeger, 1973, p. 208.
68. Hans-Georg Heinrich, *Hungary, Politics and Economics*, London: Frances Pinter, 1986, p. 66.
69. Zoltan Barany, 'Elections in Hungary' in Robert Furtak, ed., *Elections in Socialist States*, New York: Harvester Wheatsheaf, 1990, p. 73.
70. Barnabas Racz, 'Political Participation and Developed Socialism: the Hungarian Elections of 1985', *Soviet Studies*, vol. XXXIX, no. 1, 1987, especially pp. 42–5; Barany, 'Elections in Hungary', especially pp. 78–80.
71. Rudolf Tőkés, *Hungary's Negotiated Revolution. Economic Reform, Social Change and Political Succession*, Cambridge: Cambridge University Press, 1996, p. 268.
72. Barnabas Racz, 'The Parliamentary Infrastructure and Political Reforms in Hungary', *Soviet Studies*, vol. XLI, no. 1, 1989, pp. 39–66.
73. Gabriella Ilonszki, 'Legislative Recruitment: Personnel and Institutional Development in Hungary, 1990–94 in Gábor Tóka, ed., *The 1990 Election to the Hungarian National Assembly. Analyses, Documents and Data*, Berlin: Sigma, 1995, pp. 90–1.
74. This section is based on April Carter, *Democratic Reform in Yugoslavia. The Changing Role of the Party*, London: Frances Pinter, 1982, pp. 132–56 and Wolfgang Höpken, 'Elections in Yugoslavia' in Robert Furtak, ed., *Elections in Socialist States*, New York: Harvester Wheatsheaf, 1990, pp. 118–42.
75. Höpken, pp. 124–7, 130–2.
76. See W. Hahn, 'Electoral "Choice" in the Soviet Bloc', *Problems of Communism*, vol. 36, no. 2, March–April 1987, pp. 29–39.
77. Alex Pravda, 'Elections in Communist Party States' in Stephen White and Daniel Nelson, eds, *Communist Politics. A Reader*, London: Macmillan, 1986, pp. 27–54; Victor Zaslavsky and Robert J. Brym, 'The Functions of Elections in the USSR', *Soviet Studies*, vol. 30, no. 3, 1978, pp. 362–71; Theodore H. Friedgut, *Political Participation in the USSR*, Princeton: Princeton University Press, 1979, pp. 137–44.
78. Danica Fink Hafner, 'Political Modernization in Slovenia in the 1980s and the Early 1990s', *The Journal of Communist Studies*, vol. 8, no. 4, December 1992, pp. 211–20; A. Bibic, 'The Emergence of Pluralism in Slovenia', *Communist and Post-Communist Studies*, vol. 26, no. 4, December 1993, pp. 367–86; Sabrina Ramet, 'Slovenia's Road to Democracy', *Europe-Asia Studies*, vol. 45, no. 5, 1993, pp. 869–86.
79. I have argued elsewhere that this strategy represented the last-gasp attempt of a helpless and exhausted regime; see Frances Millard, *The Anatomy of the New Poland. Post-Communist Politics in Its First Phase*, Aldershot: Edward Elgar, 1994,

p. 45. For an alternative, if speculative view see Sanford, *Democratic Government in Poland*, p. 53.

80. The fullest study of the Round Table is András Bozóki, *The Roundtable Talks of 1989. The Genesis of Hungarian Democracy*, Budapest: Central European University Press, 2002.

81. Jana Reschová, 'Nová politika s novými l'ud'mi: Federálne zhromaždenie v roku 1990', *Sociologicky Časopis*, vol. 28, no. 2, 1992, pp. 223–4.

82. See Martyn Rady, *Romania in Turmoil*, London: I.B. Tauris, 1992; Nestor Radesh, *Romania: The Entangled Revolution*, Westport, Connecticut: Praeger, 1991.

83. On the talks see Albert P. Melone, 'Bulgaria's National Roundtable Talks and the Politics of Accommodation', *International Political Science Review*, vol. 15, no. 3, 1994, pp. 257–73.

84. Bernard Grofman, Evald Mikkel, and Rein Taagepera, 'Electoral System Changes in Estonia, 1989–1993', *Journal of Baltic Studies*, vol. 30, no. 3, 1999, pp. 235–6.

85. This section relies heavily on the analysis of Sarah Birch, Frances Millard, Marina Popescu, and Kieran Williams, *Embodying Democracy. Electoral System Design in Post-Communist Europe*, Basingstoke: Palgrave, 2002.

86. Grofman, Mikkel and Taagepera, p. 238.

87. See Birch, Millard, Popescu, and Williams, pp. 48–66, for details of the Hungarian system.

88. The detail on Lithuania comes from Robertas Pogorelis, 'Votes and Parties in the Mixed Electoral System in Lithuania', draft PhD thesis, University of Essex, March 2003.

89. A complex mixed-parallel system was used briefly in Brazil in 1933 and 1934, but this early example was surely not known to post-communist institutional designers.

90. Anna Grzymala-Busse, *Redeeming the Communist Past*, Cambridge: Cambridge University Press, 2002, p. 6.

91. The best studies are Tőkés, *Hungary's Negotiated Revolution* and Patrick O'Neil, *Revolution from Within. The Hungarian Socialist Workers' Party and the Collapse of Communism*, Cheltenham: Edward Elgar, 1998.

92. Millard, *The Anatomy of the New Poland*, 1994, pp. 1–28.

93. Ole Nørgaard, Lars Johannsen, and Anette Pedersen, 'The Baltic Republics. Estonia, Latvia, and Lithuania: The Development of Multi-party Systems' in Bogdan Szajkowski, ed., *Political Parties of Eastern Europe, Russia and the Successor States*, Harlow: Longman Information and Reference, 1994, p. 51.

94. Emil Giatzidis, *An Introduction to Post-communist Bulgaria. Political, Economic and Social Transformations*, Manchester: Manchester University Press, 2002, p. 49.

95. Grzymala-Busse, pp. 83–4.

96. For a vivid analysis see Vladimir Tismaneanu, 'The Tragicomedy of Romanian Communism', *East European Politics and Societies*, vol. 3, no. 2, spring 1989, pp. 329–76.

97. For more details see Anatol Lieven, *The Baltic Revolution*, New Haven: Yale University Press, 1994; Andrejs Plakans, 'Democratization and Political Participation in Post-communist Societies: The Case of Latvia' in Karen Dawisha and Bruce Parrott, eds, *The Consolidation of Democracy in East-Central Europe*, Cambridge: Cambridge University Press, 1997, pp. 294–300.

98. Gábor Tóka, 'Seats and Votes: Consequences of the Hungarian Electoral Law' in Gábor Tóka, ed., *The 1990 Election to the Hungarian National Assembly. Analyses, Documents and Data*, Berlin: Sigma, 1995, pp. 63–5.

99. Stephen Ashley, 'Bulgaria', *Electoral Studies*, vol. 9, no. 4, 1990, pp. 312–18.
100. Tom Gallagher, 'Romania: The Disputed Election of 1990', *Parliamentary Affairs*, vol. 44, no. 1, 1991, pp. 79–93; Ashley, pp. 312–18; 'Constitution Watch. Bulgaria', *East European Constitutional Review*, vol. 2, no. 2, 1993, pp. 3–4.
101. See Dobrinka Kostova, 'Parliamentary Elections in Bulgaria, October 1991', *The Journal of Communist Studies*, vol. 8, no. 1, 1992, pp. 196–203.

Chapter 3

1. Maurice Duverger, *Political Parties. Their Organization and Activity in the Modern State* (1951), New York: John Wiley & Sons, 1963.
2. Angelo Panebianco, *Political Parties: Organisation and Power*, Cambridge: Cambridge University Press, 1988.
3. S.M. Lipset and S. Rokkan, 'Cleavage Structures, Party Systems and Voter Alignments' in S.M. Lipset and S. Rokkan, eds, *Party Systems and Voter Alignments: Cross-National Perspectives*, New York: Free Press, 1967, pp. 1–64; Lane and Ersson divide parties into those linked to social structure ('structural parties') and those not ('non-structural parties'), but their essential criterion is ideology; Jan-Erik Lane and Svante Ersson, *Politics and Society in Western Europe*, London: Sage, 1987, pp. 97–105.
4. Alan Ware, *Political Parties and Party Systems*, Oxford: Oxford University Press, 1996, pp. 18–62. See also Paul Lewis, *Political Parties in Post-Communist Eastern Europe*, London: Routledge, 2000, pp. 56–9.
5. cf. Ware, p. 23.
6. On inter-war agrarianism (populism) see George C. Jackson Jr, *Comintern and Peasant in East Europe 1919–1930*, New York: Columbia University Press, 1966, pp. 40–8.
7. In Western Europe populism became associated with the extreme right; see Hans-George Betz, *Radical Right-wing Populism in Western Europe*, Basingstoke: Macmillan, 1994; Paul Taggart, 'New Populist Parties in Western Europe', *West European Politics*, vol. 18, no. 1, January 1995, pp. 34–51.
8. The usually perspicacious Cas Mudde identifies a distinct 'political populism' which he attributes to the Leninist legacy. I cannot share this view; but see Cas Mudde, 'Populism in Eastern Europe – Part I', *East European Perspectives*, vol. 2, no. 5, 8 March 2000 and 'Populism in Eastern Europe – Part II', *East European Perspectives*, vol. 2, no. 6, 22 March 2000.
9. László Lengyel, 'The Character of Political Parties in Hungary (Autumn 1989)' in András Bozóki, András Körösenyi, and George Schöpflin, eds, *Post-Communist Transition. Emerging Pluralism in Hungary*, London: Pinter Publishers, 1992, p. 35.
10. Rudolf Tőkés, *Hungary's Negotiated Revolution. Economic Reform, Social Change and Political Succession*, Cambridge: Cambridge University Press, 1996, p. 363.
11. Rudolf Tőkés, 'Party Politics and Political Participation in Post-communist Hungary' in Karen Dawisha and Bruce Parrott, eds, *The Consolidation of Democracy in East-Central Europe*, Cambridge: Cambridge University Press, 1997, p. 118.
12. Zsolt Enyedi, 'Organising a Subcultural Party in Eastern Europe: the Case of the Hungarian Christian Democrats', *Party Politics*, vol. 2, no. 3, 1996, pp. 377–96.
13. See Frances Millard, 'The Polish Parliamentary Election of October 1991', *Soviet Studies*, vol. 44, no. 5, September 1992, pp. 837–55.
14. Algis Krupavičius, 'The Post-communist Transition and Institutionalization of Lithuania's Parties' in Richard Hofferbert, *Parties and Democracy*, Oxford: Blackwell Publishers, 1998, p. 57.

15. On the complexity of Czech neo-liberalism see Martin Dangerfield, 'Ideology and the Czech Transformation: Neoliberal Rhetoric or Neoliberal Reality', *East European Politics and Societies*, vol. 11, no. 3, fall 1997, pp. 437–68.

16. Michal Klíma, 'Consolidation and Stabilization of the Party System in the Czech Republic' in Richard Hofferbert, *Parties and Democracy*, Oxford: Blackwell Publishers, 1998, p. 72.

17. Karen Henderson, 'Czechoslovakia: the Failure of Consensus Politics and the Break-up of the Federation', *Regional and Federal Studies*, vol. 5, no. 2, 1995, pp. 111–33; Abby Innes, 'The Breakup of Czechoslovakia: The Impact of Party Development on the Separation of the State', *East European Politics and Societies*, vol. 11, no. 3, fall 1997, pp. 393–435; Gordon Wightman, 'The 1992 Parliamentary Elections in Czechoslovakia', *The Journal of Communist Studies*, vol. 8, no. 4, December 1992, pp. 293–301; David Olson, 'Dissolution of the State: Political Parties and the 1992 Election in Czechoslovakia', *Communist and Post-Communist Studies*, September 1993, pp. 301–14.

18. Georgi Karasimeonov, 'Sea-changes in the Bulgarian Party system', *The Journal of Communist Studies*, vol. 9, no. 3, 1993, p. 275.

19. *International Herald Tribune*, cited in Sabrina Ramet, 'Democratization in Slovenia – the Second Stage' in Karen Dawisha and Bruce Parrott, eds, *Politics, Power, and the Struggle for Democracy in South-East Europe*, Cambridge: Cambridge University Press, 1997, p. 201.

20. Vello Pettai and Marcus Kreuzer, 'Party Politics in the Baltic States: Social Bases and Institutional Context', *East European Politics and Societies*, vol. 13, no. 1, winter 1999, p. 154.

21. On Hungary see Attila Ágh, 'Defeat and Success as Promoters of Party Change', *Party Politics*, vol. 3, no. 3, 1997, pp. 427–44; and Attila Ágh '1998 Elections in Hungary: Defeat as Promoter of Change for the HSP', *East European Politics and Societies*, vol. 14, no. 2, 2000, pp. 288–315; on Poland Frances Millard, *Polish Politics and Society*, London: Routledge, 1999, pp. 77–101; on Lithuania Algis Krupavičius, 'Role of the Left-wing parties in Transition to and in Consolidation of Democracy: A Case of Lithuania', Paper presented to the First General ECPR Conference, University of Kent at Canterbury, 6–8 September 2001.

22. Daniel Ziblatt, 'The Adaptation of Ex-Communist Parties to Post-Communist East Central Europe: a Comparative Study of the East German and Hungarian Ex-Communist Parties', *Communist and Post-Communist Studies*, vol. 31, no. 2, pp. 133–4.

23. Orenstein probably over-stresses the trade union linkage; Mitchell Orenstein, 'A Genealogy of Communist Successor Parties in East-Central Europe and the Determinants of their Success', *East European Politics and Societies*, vol. 12, no. 3, pp. 486–93.

24. Algis Krupavičius, 'Role of the Left-wing Parties', p. 6, 17.

25. On the government crisis of spring 2000, see 'Constitution Watch: Slovenia', *East European Constitutional Review*, vol. 8, no. 3, summer 2000, pp. 39–40.

26. John Bell, 'Democratization and Political Participation in "Postcommunist" Bulgaria' in Karen Dawisha and Bruce Parrott, eds, *Politics, Power, and the Struggle for Democracy in South-East Europe*, Cambridge: Cambridge University Press, 1997, pp. 378–82.

27. Berhanu Kassayie, 'The Evolution of Social Democracy in Reforming Bulgaria', *The Journal of Communist Studies and Transition Politics*, vol. 14, no. 3, September 1998, pp. 121–4.

28. Tom Gallagher, *Romania after Ceauşescu. The Politics of Intolerance*, Edinburgh: Edinburgh University Press, 1995, p. 3; also Vladimir Tismaneanu, 'Romanian Exceptionalism? Democracy, Ethnocracy, and Uncertain Pluralism in Post-Ceauşescu Romania' in Karen Dawisha and Bruce Parrott, eds, *Politics, Power, and the Struggle for Democracy in South-East Europe*, Cambridge: Cambridge University Press, 1997, p. 426.

29. John Ishiyama and András Bozóki, 'Adaptation and Change: Characterizing the Survival Strategies of the Communist Successor Parties', *The Journal of Communist Studies and Transition Politics*, vol. 17, no. 3, 2001, p. 40.

30. Grigore Pop-Eleche, 'Romania's Politics of Dejection', *Journal of Democracy*, vol. 12, no. 3, July 2001, p. 162; Vladimir Tismaneanu and Gail Kligman, 'Romania's First Postcommunist Decade: From Iliescu to Iliescu', *East European Constitutional Review*, vol. 10, no. 1, winter 2001, p. 81.

31. Gordon Wightman, 'The 1994 Slovak Parliamentary Elections', *The Journal of Communist Studies and Transition Politics*, vol. 11, no. 4, 1995, p. 386.

32. Anna Grzymala-Busse, *Redeeming the Communist Past. The Regeneration of Communist Parties in East Central Europe*, Cambridge: Cambridge University Press, 2002, pp. 200–202.

33. Peter Juza, 'The Formation of the Coalition "Common Choice" and Its Election Results' in Soňa Szomolányi and Grigorij Meseþnikov, eds, *Slovakia: Parliamentary Elections 1994*, Bratislava: Slovak Political Science Association, 1995, pp. 226–7.

34. This is stressed by Tim Haughton, 'Explaining the Limited Success of the Communist-Successor Left in Slovakia: the Case of the Party of the Democratic Left (SDL')', *Party Politics*, forthcoming 2004.

35. RFE/RL Newsline, vol. 5, no. 219, Part II, 19 November 2001.

36. Grzymala-Busse saw the leadership as effectively in thrall to the party's conservative membership, pp. 147–8.

37. Seán Hanley, 'Towards Breakthrough or Breakdown? The Consolidation of KSČM as a Neo-Communist Successor Party in the Czech Republic', *The Journal of Communist Studies and Transition Politics*, vol. 17, no. 3, pp. 108–9.

38. Petr Matějů and Blanka Řeháková, 'Turning Left or Class Realignment? Analysis of the Changing Relationship between Class and Party in the Czech Republic 1992–1996', *East European Politics and Societies*, vol. 11, no. 3, fall 1997, pp. 501–42.

39. David J. Smith, 'Estonia: Independence and European Integration' in David J. Smith, Artis Pabriks, Aldis Purs, and Thomas Lane, *The Baltic States. Estonia, Latvia and Lithuania*, London: Routledge, 2002, p. 70.

40. Artis Pabriks and Aldis Purs, 'Latvia: The Challenges of Change' in David J. Smith, Artis Pabriks, Aldis Purs, and Thomas Lane, *The Baltic States. Estonia, Latvia and Lithuania*, London: Routledge, 2002, pp. 68–9.

41. Ilya Prizel, 'Ukraine's Hollow Decade', *East European Politics and Societies*, vol. 16, no. 2, spring 2002, p. 371.

42. Kay Lawson, 'Political Parties and Linkage' in Kay Lawson, *Political Parties and Linkage: A Comparative Perspective*, New Haven: Yale University Press, 1980, pp. 17–18.

43. Michael Urban and Vladimir Gel'man, 'The Development of Political Parties in Russia' in Karen Dawisha and Bruce Parrott, eds, *Democratic Changes and Authoritarian Reactions in Russia, Ukraine, Belarus and Moldova*, Cambridge: Cambridge University Press, 1997, p. 183.

44. See Peter Lentini, 'Electoral Associations in the 1993 Elections to the Russian State Duma', *The Journal of Communist Studies and Transition Politics*, vol. 10, no. 4, 1994, pp. 8–28 for discussion of their election programmes.
45. Ilya Prizel, 'Ukraine Between Proto-democracy and "Soft" Authoritarianism', in Karen Dawisha and Bruce Parrott, eds, *Democratic Changes and Authoritarian Reactions in Russia, Ukraine, Belarus, and Moldova*, Cambridge: Cambridge University Press, 1997, p. 346.
46. Maurice Duverger, *Political Parties. Their Organisation and Activity in the Modern State* (1951), New York: John Wiley & Sons, 1963, p. xxvii.
47. Sarah Birch, 'Nomenklatura Democratization, Electoral Clientelism and Party Formation in Post-Soviet Ukraine', *Democratization*, vol. 4, no. 4, 1997, pp. 40–62.
48. Grigorii V. Golosov, 'Who Survives? Party Origins, Organisational Development, and Electoral Performance in Post-communist Russia' in Richard Hofferbert, ed., *Parties and Democracy*, Oxford: Blackwell Publishers, 1998, p. 110.
49. Marko Bojcun, 'The Ukrainian Parliamentary Elections in March–April 1994,' *Europe–Asia Studies*, vol. 47, no. 2, March 1995, pp. 229–49; Radisława Gortat, *Ukraińskie Wybory. Elecja parlamentarna '98 a partie polityczne*, Warsaw: Fundacja Polska Praca, 1998, pp. 32–5.
50. Sarah Birch, 'Electoral Systems, Campaign Strategies, and Vote Choice in the Ukrainian Parliamentary and Presidential Elections of 1994', *Political Studies*, vol. 46, no. 1, 1998, p. 106.
51. Ilya Prizel, 'Ukraine's Hollow Decade', p. 374.
52. Neil Robinson, 'Classifying Russia's Party System: The Problem of "Relevance" in a Time of Uncertainty', *The Journal of Communist Studies and Transition Politics*, vol. 14, nos 1/2, 1998, p. 165.
53. Golosov, p. 109.
54. Ibid., p. 111.
55. Richard Sakwa, 'Left or Right? The CPRF and the Problem of Democratic Consolidation in Russia', *The Journal of Communist Studies and Transition Politics*, vol. 14, nos 1 and 2, 1998, pp. 140, 141.
56. Luke March, *The Communist Party in Post-Soviet Russia*, Manchester: Manchester University Press, 2002, especially pp. 259–64.
57. Sakwa, p. 144.
58. Jeffrey Mankoff, 'Russia's Weak Society and Weak State', *Problems of Post-Communism*, vol. 50, no. 1, January–February 2003, pp. 39–40.
59. Ieva Zake, 'The People's Party in Latvia: Neo-Liberalism and the New Politics of Independence', *The Journal of Communist Studies and Transition Politics*, vol. 18, no. 3, September 2002, pp. 109–31.
60. M. Steven Fish and Robin S. Brooks, 'Bulgarian Democracy's Organisational Weapon', *East European Constitutional Review*, vol. 9, no. 3, summer 2000, pp. 64–9.
61. Petr Kopecky and Cas Mudde, 'The 1998 Parliamentary and Senate Elections in the Czech Republic', *Electoral Studies*, vol. 18, no. 3, September 1999, p. 416.
62. An English summary of its programme is available at http://www.isamaaliit.ee.
63. Andras Bozoki, 'Hungary's Social-Democratic Turn', *East European Constitutional Review*, vol. 11, no. 3, summer 2002, p. 81.
64. Golosov, p. 113.
65. See Tom Gallagher, 'Nationalism and Post-Communist Politics: The Party of Romanian National Unity, 1990–1996' in Lavinia Stan, ed., *Romania in Transition*, Aldershot: Dartmouth, 1997, pp. 25–47.

66. Michael Shafir, 'The Greater Romania Party', *RFE/RL Report on Eastern Europe*, vol. 2, no. 46, 1991, pp. 25–30.
67. Petre Datculescu, 'Romania: Parties and Issues after 1989' in Kay Lawson, Andrea Römmele, and Georgi Karasimeonov, eds, *Cleavages, Parties, and Voters. Studies from Bulgaria, the Czech Republic, Hungary, Poland, and Romania*, London: Praeger, 1999, p. 176; also Michael Shafir, 'Radical Continuity in Romania: The Greater Romania Party' in Radical Politics in East-Central Europe, *East European Perspectives*, vol. 2, no. 16, 16 August 2000; Mark Temple, 'The Politicisation of History: Marshall Antonescu and Romania', *East European Politics and Societies*, vol. 10, no. 3, fall 1996, pp. 497–500.
68. Thomas Orr, 'The Far Right in the Czech Republic', *Uncaptive Minds*, vol. 6, no. 1, winter–spring 1993, p. 67.
69. For more details, see Aleks Szczerbiak, 'The Polish Peasant Party: A Mass Party in Postcommunist Eastern Europe', *East European Politics and Societies*, vol. 15, no. 3, fall 2001, pp. 554–88.
70. Klara Vlachová, 'Party identification in the Czech Republic: Inter-party Hostility and Party Preference', *Communist and Post-Communist Studies*, vol. 34, no. 4, December 2001, p. 487.
71. Robinson, p. 160.
72. Michael McFaul, 'Party Formation and Non-Formation in Russia', *Comparative Political Studies*, December 2001, p. 1183.
73. Timothy J. Colton and Michael McFaul, 'Reinventing Russia's Party of Power: "Unity" and the 1999 Duma Election', *Post-Soviet Affairs*, vol. 16, no. 3, 2000, p. 218.
74. Colton and McFaul, p. 206.
75. Mikhail Myagkov and Peter C. Ordeshook, 'The Trail of Votes in Russia's 1999 Duma and 2000 Presidential Elections', *Communist and Post-Communist Studies*, vol. 34, 2001, p. 368.
76. Kimitaka Matsuzato, 'Élites and the Party System of Zakarpattya *Oblast*': Relations among Levels of Party Systems in Ukraine', *Europe–Asia Studies*, vol. 54, no. 8, 2002, especially pp. 1280–9.
77. Sarah Whitmore, 'Fragmentation or Consolidation? Parties in Ukraine's Parliament', presented to the Annual Conference of the British Association of Slavonic and East European Studies, Cambridge, April 2002, pp. 4–5.
78. RFE/RL Newsline Part II, vol. 6, no. 8, 14 January 2002.
79. Andy Wilson, 'Ukraine's 2002 Elections: Less Fraud. More virtuality', *East European Constitutional Review*, vol. 11, no. 3, summer 2002, p. 93.
80. Taras Kuzio, 'Rukh-1 to Rukh-2: Yushchenko's Our Ukraine', RFE/RL Newsline, vol. 6, no. 54, Part II, 21 March 2002, Endnote, citing *Zerkalo nedeli/Dzerkalo tyzhnya*.
81. Kuzio, 'Rukh-1 to Rukh-2 . . .'.
82. Nadia Diuk and Myroslava Gongadze, 'Post-Election Blues in Ukraine', *Journal of Democracy*, vol. 13, no. 4, 2002, p. 158.
83. The DCR had reform competitors stressing the same themes; see Datculescu, p. 174.
84. See Rasmus Bing and Bogdan Szajkowski, 'Romania', in Bogdan Szajkowski, ed., *Political Parties of Eastern Europe, Russia and the Successor States*, Harlow, Essex: Longman, 1994, pp. 360–1 for a list of its 1993 constituents.
85. On internal disputes over how the SDK should function after the election see Peter Schutz, 'Playing the Numbers Game', *Transitions On-Line*, 9 February 2000 (http://www.tol.cz).

86. See Geoffrey Pridham, 'Coalition Behaviour in New Democracies in Central and Eastern Europe: The Case of Slovakia', *The Journal of Communist Studies and Transition Politics*, vol. 18, no. 2, June 2002, pp. 75–102.
87. On the election see Cas Mudde, 'Slovak Elections: Go West!', *RFE/RL East European Perspectives*, vol. 4, no. 21, 16 October 2002, pp. 1–8.
88. See RFE/RL Newsline, vol. 5, no. 185, Part II, 1 October 2001.
89. Smer's Programme (Programové tézy) is available in English at http://www. strana-smer.sk. See also Tim Haughton, 'Does Slovakia Need a Facelift?', *Central European Review*, vol. 3, no. 20, 4 June 2001.
90. M.A.G. Harper, 'The 2001 Parliamentary and Presidential Elections in Bulgaria', *Electoral Studies*, vol. 22, issue 2, June 2003, pp. 335–44.
91. David Arter, *Parties and Democracy in the Post-Soviet Republics: The Case of Estonia*, Aldershot: Dartmouth, 1996, p. 202.
92. See Soňa Szomolányi, 'Does Slovakia Deviate from the Central European Variant of Transition?' in Soňa Szomolányi and Grigorij Mesežnikov, eds, *The Slovak Path of Transition – to Democracy?*, Bratislava: Slovak Political Science Association & Interlingua, 1994, pp. 8–33.
93. Peter Toma and Dušan Kováč, *Slovakia. From Samo to Dzurinda*, Stanford: Hoover Institution Press, 2001, p. 266, 304; Vladimír Krivý, personal communication, November 2002.
94. Tim Haughton, 'HZDS: The Ideology, Organisation and Support Base of Slovakia's Most Successful Party', *Europe–Asia Studies*, vol. 53, no. 5, July 2001, pp. 745–70.
95. Kieran Williams, 'What Was Mečiarism?' in Kieran Williams, ed., *Slovakia After Communism and Mečiarism*, London: School of Slavonic and East European Studies, 2000, p. 7; John Gould and Soňa Szomolányi, 'Bridging the Chasm in Slovakia', *Transitions*, vol. 4, no. 6, November 1997, pp. 75–6. But Josette Bauer's thesis of the 'inevitability of Mečiarism' because of Slovak history and civic incompetence remains unconvincing; see Josette Baer, 'Boxing and Politics in Slovakia: "Meciarism" – Roots, Theory, Practice', *Democratization*, vol. 8, no. 2, summer 2001, pp. 97–116.
96. Abby Innes, 'Party Competition in Post-Communist Europe: The Great Electoral Lottery', *Comparative Politics*, vol. 35, no. 1, October 2002, pp. 85–104.
97. Innes, p. 102.
98. Jiri Pehe, 'Czech Elections: Victory for a New Generation', *RFE/RL East European Perspectives*, vol. 4, no. 17, 21 August 2002.

Chapter 4

1. Seymour Martin Lipset, *Political Man. The Social Bases of Politics*, New York: Anchor Books, 1963, pp. 226–9.
2. Mark Gray and Miki Caul, 'Declining Voter Turnout in Advanced Industrial Democracies, 1950 to 1997. The Effects of Declining Group Mobilization', *Comparative Political Studies*, vol. 33, no. 9, November 2000, pp. 1094–6; Mark Franklin, Patrick Lyons, and Michael Marsh, 'The Turnout Paradox: Why Changing Electoral Experiences Trump Changing Social Characteristics in Driving Voter Turnout in Advanced Democracies', Paper presented to the First General Conference of the European Consortium for Political Research, University of Kent, Canterbury, September 2001, Table 1.
3. Witness the views of Popular Front leader Edgar Savisaar in Estonia, as reported in Riina Kionka, 'How Democratic Will the Estonian Elections Be?', *Report on the USSR*, vol. 2, no. 9, 2 March 1990, pp. 21–3.

4. Turnout is measured as the percentage of voters casting valid and invalid ballots divided by the number of registered voters. This is consistent with the usage of Franklin *et al.*, but it differs from that of Gray and Caul, who use the eligible voting-age population: Gray and Caul, p. 1093. Since all countries in ECE have compulsory registration, our measure should be more or less reliable. Note that since official figures sometimes use the number of voters collecting a ballot paper (but not necessarily voting) as the numerator, our calculations may be slightly different than those of others.

5. Richard Sakwa, 'The Russian Elections of December 1993', *Europe-Asia Studies*, vol. 47, no. 2, 1995, p. 220; Hans Oversloot, Joop van Holsteyn, and Ger P. Van Den Berg, 'Against All: Exploring the Vote "Against All" in the Russian Federation's Electoral System', *The Journal of Communist Studies and Transition Politics*, vol. 18, no. 4, December 2002, no. 14, p. 47.

6. Iván Szelényi and Szonja Szelényi, 'The Vacuum in Hungarian Politics: Classes and Parties', *New Left Review* 187, May–June 1991, pp. 121–37; Róbert Angelusz and Róbert Tardos, 'Electoral Participation in Hungary, 1990–1994' in Gábor Tóka and Zsolt Enyedi, eds, *Elections to the Hungarian National Assembly 1994. Analyses, Documents and Data*, Berlin: Sigma, 1999, pp. 168–97; Radosław Markowski, 'Milcząca większość – O bierności politycznej społeczeństwa polskiego' in Stanisław Gebethner, ed., *Polska scena polityczna a wybory*, Warsaw: Fundacja Inicjatyw Społecznych 'Polska w Europie', 1993, pp. 57–86; CBOS 'Nieobecni w wyborach-przyczyny absencji wyborczej', Komunikat z badań BS/132/132/97, Warsaw, CBOS, October 1997; Darius Žeruolis, 'Rational Voters and Causes of Absenteeism' in Algis Krupavičus, ed., *Lithuania's Seimas Election 1996: The third Turnover. Analyses, Documents and Data*, Berlin: Sigma, 2001, pp. 196–212; Richard Rose and Neil Munro, *Elections without Order. Russia's Challenge to Vladimir Putin*, Cambridge: Cambridge University Press, 2002, p. 131.

7. Mark N. Franklin, 'Electoral Participation' in Lawrence LeDuc, Richard G. Niemi, and Pippa Norris, eds, *Comparing Democracies. Elections and Voting in Global Perspective*, London: Sage, 1996, p. 220.

8. The reasoning here is not dissimilar to that of Jackman, who stresses the role of strong bicameralism in discouraging voters; Robert Jackman, 'Political Institutions and Voter Turnout in Industrial Democracies', *American Political Science Review*, vol. 81, 1987, pp. 405–23.

9. Franklin, 'Electoral Participation', pp. 221–2. Jackman earlier found that proportionality, unicameralism, and 'nationally competitive districts' had some positive effect on turnout; Jackman, pp. 405–23.

10. Oversloot, van Holsteyn, and Van Den Berg, p. 33.

11. Kieran Williams, 'PR's First Decade in Eastern Europe', *Representation* (forthcoming 2004). The formula is $[(v_2\ s_2)/(v_1\ s_1)] * 100$, in which v represents the vote share of the first or second-largest party and s the percentage of seats awarded to those parties; see Aníbal Pérez-Liñán, 'Neoinstitutional Accounts of Voter Turnout: Moving Beyond Industrial Democracies', *Electoral Studies*, vol. 20, no. 2, June 2001, p. 291.

12. Marina Popescu, 'Turnout in Post-Communist Europe: the Salience of Elections and Information Flows', Paper presented to the ECPR Joint Workshop Sessions, Turin, 22–28 March 2002.

13. Franklin, Lyons and Marsh, p. 11.

14. This is the absolute difference between the percentage of seats won by the largest party and 50 taken as an indicator of the decisiveness of an election.

15. Among others see Sarah Birch, *Elections and Democratization in Ukraine*, Basingstoke: Macmillan Press, 2000, p. 32; D.W. Lovell, 'Trust and the Politics of Post-Communism', *Communist and Post-Communist Studies*, vol. 34, 2001, pp. 27–8.
16. Pérez-Liñán, pp. 281–97.
17. Gray and Caul, pp. 1112–15.
18. Alan Siaroff and John Merer, 'Parliamentary Election Turnout in Europe since 1990', *Political Studies*, vol. 50, no. 5, December 2002, p. 920.
19. But Angelusz and Tardos judged the mobilising capacity of the Hungarian socialists to be a factor increasing turnout in 1994; Angelusz and Tardos, p. 193.
20. I regard the political party and trade union membership figures used to test comparative hypotheses as well-nigh useless. Even accurate figures would need to take account of (*inter alia*) huge constituency variations in party membership, and great sectoral and ownership (public versus private) differences in trade union membership; but see Siaroff and Merer.
21. See also Algis Krupavičius, 'Party Systems in Central East Europe: Dimensions of Social Stability' in Dirk Berg-Schlosser and Raivo Vetik, eds, *Perspectives on Democratic Consolidation in Central and Eastern Europe*, Boulder: East European Monographs, 2001, p. 143.
22. David Mason, 'Attitudes toward the Market and Political Participation in the Post-communist States', *Slavic Review*, vol. 51, no. 2, summer, 1995, pp. 395–402; Lena Kolarska-Bobińska, *Aspirations, Values and Interests. Poland 1989–94*, Warsaw, IFiS, 1994, pp. 48–58; Daniel N. Nelson, 'Civil Society Endangered', *Social Research*, vol. 63, no. 2, summer 1996, pp. 345–68. Yet Bahry and Lipsmeyer found that in Russia neither objective economic dislocation nor dissatisfaction with economic conditions took people out of politics; indeed it was the relatively well-to-do who opted out; Donna Bahry and C. Lipsmeyer, 'Economic Adversity and Public Mobilization in Russia', *Electoral Studies*, vol. 20, no. 3, September 2001, pp. 371–98.
23. See, for example, William L. Miller, Stephen White, and Paul Heywood, *Values and Political Change in Postcommunist Europe*, Basingstoke: Macmillan Press, 1998, pp. 102–4; Peter A. Ulram and Fritz Plasser, 'Mainly Sunny with Scattered Clouds: Political Culture in East-Central Europe' in Geoffrey Pridham and Attila Ágh, eds, *Prospects for Democratic Consolidation in East-Central Europe*, Manchester: Manchester University Press, 2001, pp. 122–3. Choe addressed these factors in Yonhyok Choe, 'Institutional Trust and Electoral Turnout in New Democracies: A Comparative Study of Eastern and Central Europe' Paper presented at the First General Conference of the European Consortium for Political Research, University of Kent at Canterbury, September 2001.
24. Miller, White and Heywood, pp. 411, 170.
25. Miller, White and Heywood, pp. 169–70; Richard Rose, 'Mobilizing Demobilized Voters in Post-communist Societies', *Party Politics*, vol. 1, 1995, p. 551; *Rzeczpospolita*, 1–2 April 1995 (PBS data).
26. Richard Rose, 'A Bottom Up Evaluation of Enlargement Countries: New Europe Barometer 1', Glasgow: University of Strathclyde Centre for the Study of Public Policy, 2002.
27. Jacek Raciborski, 'How the Voters Respond: Poland' in Kay Lawson, Andrea Römmele and Georgi Karasimeonov, eds, *Cleavages, Parties, and Voters. Studies from Bulgaria, the Czech Republic, Hungary, Poland, and Romania*, London: Praeger, 1999, pp. 240–2.
28. Martin Bútora and Pavol Demeš, 'Civil Soviety Organizations in the 1998 Elections' in Martin Bútora, Grigorij Mesežnikov, Zora Bútorová, and Sharon Fisher, eds,

The 1998 Parliamentary Elections and Democratic Rebirth in Slovakia, Bratislava: Institute for Public Affairs, 1999, pp. 155–67; Karen Henderson, 'Problems of Democratic Consolidation in the Slovak Republic', *Society and Economy in Central and Eastern Europe*, no. 3, 1999, pp. 159–60.

29. Brigid Fowler, 'Hungary's 2002 Parliamentary Election', ESRC 'One Europe or Several? Programme, Briefing Note 2/02, May 2002.
30. Bernard Grofman, Evald Mikkel, and Rein Taagepera, 'Electoral System Changes in Estonia, 1989–1993', *Journal of Baltic Studies*, vol. 30, no. 3, 1999, p. 238; we do not have the invalid vote totals for that election.
31. Henry F. Carey, 'Irregularities or Rigging: The 1992 Romanian Parliamentary Elections', *East European Quarterly*, vol. XXIX, no. 1, March 1995, pp. 52–3.
32. Carey, pp. 49–55.
33. Dennis Deletant and Peter Siani-Davies, 'The Romanian Elections of 1996', *Representation*, vol. 35, nos 2, 3, 1998, pp. 159–67.
34. Office for Democratic Institutions and Human Rights, *Final Report. Romanian Parliamentary and Presidential Elections 3rd and 17th November 1996*, Warsaw: OSCE, n.d.
35. This is also why our election results differ from those of the Electoral Commission.
36. Grofman, Mikkel and Taagepera, p. 235.
37. See Gary Cox, *Making Votes Count: Strategic Coordination in the World's Electoral Systems*. Cambridge: Cambridge University Press, pp. 77–9.
38. Kenneth Benoit, 'Two Steps Forward, One Step Back: Electoral Coordination in the Hungarian Election of 1998', Paper presented to the 2000 Annual Meeting of the American Political Science Association, Mariott Wardman Park (31 August–3 September 2000).
39. Grofman, Mikkel and Taagepera, p. 238.
40. Robert Moser, 'The Impact of Parliamentary Electoral Systems in Russia' in Archie Brown, ed., *Contemporary Russian Politics. A Reader*, Oxford: Oxford University Press, 2001, p. 199.
41. Milan Zemko, 'Political Parties and the Election System in Slovakia' in Soňa Szomolányi and Grigorij Mesežnikov, eds, *Slovakia: Parliamentary Elections 1994* Bratislava: Slovak Political Science Association, 1995, pp. 40–55.
42. Steven Reed, 'Democracy and the Personal Vote: A Cautionary Tale from Japan', *Electoral Studies*, vol. 13, no. 1, 1994, pp. 17–28.
43. Grofman, Mikkel and Taagepera, p. 240.
44. Frances Millard, 'The Polish Parliamentary Elections of 1991', *Soviet Studies*, vol. 44, no. 5, 1992, p. 848. (837–55).
45. Birch, Millard, Popescu and Williams, pp. 41–2.
46. Frances Millard, 'Elections in Poland 2001: Electoral Manipulation and Party Upheaval', *Communist and Post-Communist Studies*, vol. 36, no. 1, March 2003, pp. 69–86.
47. Andrej Auersperger Matic, 'Electoral Reform as a Constitutional Dilemma', *East European Constitutional Review*, vol. 8, no. 3, summer 2000, pp. 77–81.
48. Petr Kopecký, *Parliaments in the Czech and Slovak Republics. Party Competition and Parliamentary Institutionalization*, Aldershot: Ashgate, 2001, p. 61.
49. According to the 1996 law, the ratings of a candidate were equal to the product of the election rating and the party rating. The election rating was obtained by adding the number of positive preferences to the number of voters for the list on which the candidate stood and subtracting the number of voters who crossed out the candidate's name. The party rating was obtained by adding one to the total

number of candidates on the list and subtracting the candidate's number on the list. The final order of candidates was established according to the candidates' ratings; see Robertas Pogorelis, 'Votes and Parties in the Mixed Electoral System in Lithuania', draft PhD thesis, University of Essex, March 2003, p. 19.

50. The election rating was made equal to the simple sum of the preference votes for a candidate when this sum exceeded 70; this considerably increased the voter's influence. At the same time the party rating was lowered: the party rating of the first candidate on the list had to be made 20 times higher than the party rating of the last candidate on the list, and the difference of party ratings of the candidates whose place on the list differed by one digit had to equal 19. This way the party rating of the candidate who is the last on the list was lower by one digit than the total number of candidates on the list, and the party rating of the first candidate on the list was 20 times higher than the party rating of the last candidate on the list; see Pogorelis, p. 20.

Chapter 5

1. Morgens Pedersen, 'The Dynamics of European Party Systems: Changing Patterns of Electoral Volatility', *European Journal of Political Research*, vol. 7, no. 1, 1979, pp. 14–15.
2. The most commonly used formula for assessing electoral volatility is that of Pedersen, pp. 4–5. It is half the sum of the absolute value of differences between the vote share of each party in two consecutive elections.
3. See the considerable range of volatility calculations in Paul Lewis, *Political Parties in Post-Communist Eastern Europe*, London: Routledge, 2000, Table 3.3, p. 85; also compare Algis Krupavičius, 'Party Systems in Central East Europe: Dimensions of Social Stability' in Dirk Berg-Schlosser and Raivo Vetik, eds, *Perspectives on Democratic Consolidation in Central and Eastern Europe*, Boulder: East European Monographs, 2001, p. 145; Jacek Bielasiak, 'The Institutionalization of Electoral and Party Systems in Postcommunist States', *Comparative Politics*, vol. 34, no. 2, January 2002, p. 199.
4. For example, the fact that the Christian National Union (ZChN) never stood under its own name in any Polish election created a source of confusion and error, not just for calculations of volatility; for example Iván Szelény, Éva Fodor, and Eric Hanley, 'Left Turn in PostCommunist Politics: Bringing Class Back In?', *East European Politics and Societies*, vol. 11, no. 1, winter 1997, p. 193, mistakenly list the Fatherland Coalition (*Ojczyzna*) as the ZChN's vehicle in 1991 (ZChN stood as Catholic Electoral Action in 1991 and as Ojczyzna in 1993).
5. Radosław Markowski, 'Party System Institutionalization in New Democracies: Poland – A Trend-Setter with no Followers' in Paul G. Lewis, ed., *Party Development and Democratic Change in Post-Communist Europe*, London: Frank Cass, 2001, pp. 57–61.
6. For a discussion of electoral volatility in a historical context in Western Europe, see Peter Mair and S. Bartolini, *Identity, Competition and Electoral Availability: The Stabilisation of European Electorates 1885–1985*, Cambridge: Cambridge University Press, 1990. For more recent assessment, see S. Ersson and Jan-Erik Lane, 'Electoral Instability and Party System Change in Western Europe' in Paul Pennings and Jan-Erik Lane, eds, *Comparing Party System Change*, London: Routledge, 1998, pp. 23–39.
7. Markowski, 'Party System Institutionalization ...', p. 60.
8. Michael Pinto-Duschinsky, 'Send the Rascals Packing', *Representation*, vol. 36, no. 1, 1998, pp. 117–26.

9. Kieran Williams, 'PR's First Decade in Eastern Europe', *Representation* (forthcoming).
10. Michael Shafir, 'Romania's Road to "Normalcy"', *Journal of Democracy*, vol. 8, no. 2, 1997, pp. 145–6.
11. Michael Shafir, 'The Ciorbea Government and Democratization: A Preliminary Assessment' in Duncan Light and David Phinnemore, eds, *Post-Communist Romania. Coming to Terms with Transition*, Basingstoke: Palgrave, 2001, p. 87.
12. Michael Shafir, 'The Greater Romania Party and the 2000 Elections – A Retrospective Analysis (Part 1)', *RFE/RL East European Perspectives*, vol. 3, no. 14, 22 August 2001.
13. See Algis Krupavičius, 'Political Results of the Seimas Election of 1996 and Formation of the Cabinet: The Third Turnover' in Algis Krupavičius, ed., *Lithuania's Seimas Election 1996: The Third Turnover. Analyses, Documents and Data*, Berlin: Sigma, 2001, p. 140.
14. Klaus von Beyme, *Political Parties in Western Democracies*, Aldershot: Gower, 1985, p. 29.
15. Slovene economic development is charted on the very accessible website of the Statistical Agency at http://www.stat.si/letopis_n.htm.
16. See Tim Haughton, 'HZDS: The Ideology, Organisation and Support Base of Slovakia's Most Successful Party', *Europe-Asia Studies*, vol. 53, no. 5, July 2001, pp. 745–70.
17. On the 1994 elections, see Gábor Tóka and Zsolt Enyedi, eds, *Elections to the Hungarian National Assembly 1994. Analyses, Documents and Data*, Berlin: Sigma, 1999.
18. Kenneth Benoit, 'Two Steps Forward, One Step Back: Electoral Coordination in the Hungarian Election of 1998', Paper presented to the 2000 Annual Meeting of the American Political Science Association, Mariott Wardman Park, 31 August–3 September 2000, pp. 13–16.
19. See Attila Ágh, '1998 Elections in Hungary: Defeat as Promoter of Change for the HSP', *East European Politics and Societies*, vol. 14, no. 2, pp. 299–315 for an analysis of their failings.
20. Frances Millard, 'The Polish Parliamentary Election of October 1991', *Soviet Studies*, vol. 44, no. 5, September 1992, pp. 837–55.
21. Aleks Szczerbiak, 'Electoral Politics in Poland: The Polish Election of 1997', *Journal of Communist Studies and Transition Politics*, vol. 14, no. 3, September 1998, p. 74.
22. Ieva Zake, 'The People's Party in Latvia: Neo-Liberalism and the New Politics of Independence', *The Journal of Communist Studies and Transition Politics*, vol. 18, no. 3, September 2002, pp. 120–7.
23. Nerijus Prekivicius and Terry D. Clark, 'Lithuanian Politics: Implications of the Parliamentary Elections', *ACE. Analysis of Current Events*, vol. 13, no. 1, February 2001, p. 1.
24. Vello Pettai and Marcus Kreuzer, 'Party Politics in the Baltic States: Social Bases and Institutional Context', *East European Politics and Societies*, vol. 13, no. 1, winter 1999, p. 156.
25. Uldis Ozoliņš, 'What's so New about New Era?', http://www.latviansonline.com/columns/cm020930ozolins.html.
26. Daunis Auers, 'Latvia's 2002 Eections – Dawn of a New Era?', *East European Constitutional Review*, vol. 11, no. 4 & vol. 12, no. 1, fall 2002–winter 2003, p. 106.
27. Claus Offe, 'Capitalism by Democratic Design? Democratic Theory Facing the Triple Transition in East Central Europe', *Social Research*, vol. 58, no. 4, winter 1991, pp. 865–92; see also Grzegorz Ekiert, 'Democratization Processes in East

Central Europe', *British Journal of Political Science*, vol. 21, no. 3, July 1991, pp. 285–314.

28. Martin Butora and Zora Butorova, 'Slovakia's Democratic Awakening', *Journal of Democracy*, vol. 10, no. 1, January 1999, pp. 80–95.

29. On AWS, see Michal Wenzel, 'Solidarity and Akcja Wyborcza Solidarność – An Attempt at Reviving the Legend', *The Journal of Communist Studies and Transition Politics*, vol. 31, no. 2, June 1998, pp. 139–56.

30. Michael Minkenberg, 'The Radical Right in Postsocialist Central and Eastern Europe: Comparative Observations and Interpretations', *East European Politics and Societies*, vol. 16, no. 2, spring 2002, p. 358; Jiri Pehe, 'Czech Elections. Victory for a New Generation', RFE/RL *East European Perspectives*, no. 17, 21 August 2002.

31. On 'red-brown coalitions', see John T. Ishiyama, 'Strange Bedfellows: Explaining Political Cooperation Between Communist Successor Parties and Nationalists in Eastern Europe', *Nations and Nationalism*, vol. 4, no. 1, 1998, pp. 61–85.

32. Michael Shafir, 'Radical Politics in East-Central Europe Part V: Bulgaria's Radical Transfigurations', RFE/RL *East European Perspectives*, vol. 2, no. 15, 2 August 2000.

33. Tim Haughton, 'Vladimir Mečiar and his Role in the 1994–1998 Slovak Coalition Government', *Europe-Asia Studies*, vol. 54, no. 8, December 2002, p. 1334.

34. In 1995 the ČSSD party congress had explicitly imposed a ban on agreement with the communists.

35. Christopher Williams and Stephen E. Hanson, 'The "Radical Right" in Russia' in Sabrina Ramet, ed., *The Radical Right in Central and Eastern Europe since 1989*, University Park: The Pennsylvania State University Press, 1999, pp. 265–9, class the KPRF as a party of the extreme right.

36. See Laura Bellin, 'Communist Party Consolidates Its Position on the Left', RFE/RL *Russian Election Report*, no. 8, 7 January 2000.

37. Cas Mudde, 'Extreme-right Parties in Eastern Europe', *Patterns of Prejudice*, vol. 34, no. 1, January 2000, pp. 5–27 offers a typology based on origins and tradition. Minkenberg identifies fascist-authoritarians, racist-ethnocentrists and religious fundamentalists but his party placements are highly contentious: Minkelberg, 'The Radical Right in Postsocialist Central and Eastern Europe' spring 2002, p. 347.

38. The Republicans favoured the retention of a single Czechoslovak state, while the Ukrainian National Assembly was Pan-Slav in its outlook; see Roman Solchanyk, 'The Radical Right in Ukraine' in Sabrina Ramet, ed., *The Radical Right in Central and Eastern Europe since 1989*, University Park: The Pennsylvania State University Press, 1999, pp. 292–3.

39. Katherine Verdery, *What Was Socialism and What Comes Next*, Princeton: Princeton University Press, 1996, pp. 196–7.

40. quoted in Solchanyk, p. 295.

41. Andor describes MIÉP unequivocally as 'neo-Nazi'; László Andor, 'New Striker in Old Team. Parliamentary Elections in Hungary, May 1998', *Labour Focus on Eastern Europe*, no. 60, 1998, p. 35.

42. Rudolf Rizman, 'Radical Right Politics in Slovenia' in Sabrina Ramet, ed., *The Radical Right in Central and Eastern Europe since 1989*. University Park, Pennsylvania: Pennsylvania State University Press, 1999, p. 152.

43. Marina Popescu, 'The Parliamentary and Presidential Elections in Romania, November 2000', *Electoral Studies*, vol. 22, issue 2, June 2003, pp. 325–35.

44. Michael Shafir, 'Anti-Semitism without Jews in Romania', *RFE/RL Report on Eastern Europe*, vol. 2, no. 26, 1991, p. 29.
45. Rizman, p. 155.
46. This case and that of HZDS well illustrate the problems of classifying parties by expert judgement when those judgements vary: see for example Karen Dawisha and Stephen Deets, 'Intended and Unintended Consequences of Elections in Russia and Postcommunist States' manuscript, 31 March 2002; Minkelberg; David Ost, 'The Radical Right in Poland: Rationality of the Irrational' in Sabrina Ramet, ed., *The Radical Right*, pp. 97–8.
47. But sympathy for Self-Defence (SO) in Poland was positively correlated with 'nostalgia for the pre-1989 regime and a distaste for democracy'; see Clare McManus-Czubińska, William Miller, Radosław Markowski, and Jacek Wasilewski, 'The New Polish "Right"?', Paper presented at the Workshop on the Central European Right and EU Enlargement, Foreign and Commonwealth Office, London, July 2002, p. 18.
48. Rizman, p. 152.
49. Michael Shafir, 'The Greater Romania Party and the 2000 Elections in Romania: A Retrospective Analysis' (Part I), *RFE/RL East European Perspectives*, vol. 3, no. 14, 22 August 2001 and 'The Greater Romania Party and the 2000 Elections in Romania: A Retrospective Analysis' (Part 2), *RFE/RL East European Perspectives*, vol. 3, no. 15, 5 September 2001. See also Tom Gallagher, 'Nationalism and Romanian Political Culture in the 1990s' in Duncan Light and David Phinnemore, eds, *Post-Communist Romania. Coming to Terms with Transition*, Basingstoke: Palgrave, 2001, p. 112.
50. However, one cannot agree with Baer that Slovak voters 'chose' the coalition; Josette Baer, 'Boxing and Politics in Slovakia: "Meciarism" – Roots, Theory, Practice', *Democratization*, vol. 8, no. 2, summer 2001, p. 99, p. 112.
51. Dawisha and Deets, 'Intended and Unintended Consequences of Elections in Russia and Postcommunist States', p. 9.

Chapter 6

1. Geoffrey Pridham, 'Comparative Reflections on Democratisation in East-Central Europe: A Model of Post-communist Transformation?' in Geoffrey Pridham and Attila Ágh eds, *Prospects for Democratic Consolidation in East-Central Europe*, Manchester: Manchester University Press, 2001, pp. 2–3.
2. Richard I. Hofferbert, 'Introduction: Party Structure and Performance in New and Old Democracies', in Richard Hofferbert, ed., *Parties and Democracy*, Oxford: Blackwells (the Political Studies Association), 1998, p. 1; G. Pasquino, 'Party Elites and Democratic Consolidation: Cross-national Comparison of Southern European Experience' in Geoffrey Pridham, ed., *Securing Democracy: Political Parties and Democratic Consolidation in Southern Europe*, London: Routledge, 1990, p. 53.
3. Scott Mainwaring and Timothy R. Scully, 'Introduction: Party Systems in Latin America' in Scott Mainwaring and Timothy Scully, eds, *Building Democratic Institutions. Party Systems in Latin America*, Stanford: Stanford University Press, 1995, p. 27.
4. Larry Diamond, 'Introduction: In Search of Consolidation' in Larry Diamond, Marc F. Plattner, Yun-han Chu, and Hung-mao Tien, eds, *Consolidating the Third Wave of Democracies. Themes and Perspectives*, Baltimore and London: The Johns Hopkins University Press, 1997, pp. xxii–xxiv.
5. Giovanni Sartori, *Parties and Party Systems. A framework for analysis*, Cambridge: Cambridge University Press, 1976, vol. 1, pp. 21–2.

6. See, for example, Maurizio Cotta, 'Structuring the New Party Systems after the Dictatorship. Coalitions, Alliances, Fusions and Splits during the transition and Post-transition Stages' in Geoffrey Pridham and Paul G. Lewis, eds, *Stabilising Fragile Democracies. Comparing New Party Systems in Southern and Eastern Europe*, London: Routledge, 1996, pp. 69–99; Iván Szelény, Éva Fodor, and Eric Hanley, 'Left Turn in PostCommunist Politics: Bringing Class Back In?', *East European Politics and Societies*, vol. 11, no. 1, winter 1997, pp. 190–224.

7. Sartori, p. 43.

8. See Alan Ware, *Political Parties and Party Systems*, Oxford: Oxford University Press, 1996, pp. 158–75.

9. Peter Mair, 'Party Systems and Structures of Competition' in Lawrence LeDuc, Richard Niemi and Pippa Norris, eds, *Comparing Democracies. Elections and Voting in Global Perspective*, London: Sage, 1996, pp. 89–105.

10. This is sometimes referred to as *apparentement*, but *apparentement* is more precisely a formal agreement between lists to pool their votes, rather than agreement on a common list. This was permitted in Poland in 1991, when it proved effective for the KPN.

11. Vello Pettai and Marcus Kreuzer, 'Party Politics in the Baltic States: Social Bases and Institutional Context', *East European Politics and Societies*, vol. 13, no. 1, winter 1999, p. 163; these authors use several indicators of fragmentation in addition to the 'effective number'.

12. Milan Zemko, 'Political Parties and the Election System in Slovakia' in Soňa Szomolányi and Grigorij Mesežnikov, eds, *The Slovak Path of Transition – to Democracy?*, Bratislava: Slovak Political Science Association & Interlingua, 1994, pp. 40–55.

13. Sartori, p. 123.

14. Ibid., pp. 122–3.

15. See Neil Robinson, 'Classifying Russia's Party System: The Problem of "Relevance" in a Time of Uncertainty', *The Journal of Communist Studies and Transition Politics*, vol. 14, nos 1/2, 1998, pp. 159–77.

16. R. Taagepera and M. Laakso, ' "Effective" Number of Parties: A Measure with Application to Western Europe', *Comparative Political Studies*, vol. 12, no. 1, April 1979, pp. 3–27. It is achieved by weighting the contribution of parties to the total number of parties by their respective votes (effective number of electoral parties) or seats (effective number of parliamentary parties): thus $N = 1/\Sigma p_i^2$, where p_i is each party's fractional share of seats or votes.

17. Taagepera and Laakso, p. 4 [italics mine].

18. For example, Algis Krupavičius, 'Party Systems in Central East Europe: Dimensions of Social Stability' in Dirk Berg-Schlosser and Raivo Vetik, eds, *Perspectives on Democratic Consolidation in Central and Eastern Europe*, Boulder: East European Monographs, 2001, p. 149; Karen Dawisha and Stephen Deets, 'Intended and Unintended Consequences of Elections in Russia and Postcommunist States', unpublished paper, 31 March 2002; Alan Siaroff's compendium, *Comparative European Party Systems*, New York: Garland Publishing, 2000, treats each election as generating a 'party system': 'a polity may . . . go through, or shift among, various party systems over time, or its party system may remain constant', p. 69; Olson recognises a number of problems, but he uses the formula anyway: David Olson, 'Party Formation and Party System Consolidation in the New Democracies of Central Europe' in Richard Hofferbert, ed., *Parties and Democracy*, Oxford: Blackwell Publishers, 1998, pp. 37–8.

19. Sarah Birch, 'Electoral Systems and Party Systems in Europe East and West' in Paul Lewis and Paul Webb, eds, *Pan-European Perspectives on Party Politics*, Leiden and Boston: Brill, 2003, p. 14–15.
20. Taagepera and Laakso, p. 23 [italics mine].
21. This still excludes the 'non-parties'; the number of seats won by the 'real parties' was 411, and the proportion of seats is based on that total.
22. See, for example, Darina Malová, 'Slovakia', *European Journal of Political Research*, vol. 26, no. 3–4, 1994, pp. 413–21; David Judge and Gabriella Ilonszki, 'Member-Constituency Linkages in the Hungarian Parliament', *Legislative Studies Quarterly*, vol. XX, no. 2, May 1995, pp. 161–76.
23. Pettai and Kreuzer, p. 161.
24. David Arter, *Parties and Democracy in the Post-Soviet Republics: The Case of Estonia*, Aldershot: Dartmouth, 1996, p. 178.
25. Judge and Ilonszki, 'Member-Constituency Linkages in the Hungarian Parliament', p. 166.
26. Attila Ágh, 'The Parliamentarization of the East Central European Parties: Party Discipline in the Hungarian Parliament, 1990–1996' in Shaun Bowler, David M. Farrell and Richard M. Katz, eds, *Party Discipline and Parliamentary Government*, Columbus: Ohio State University Press, 1999, p. 172.
27. Darina Malová and Kevin Deegan Krause, 'Parliamentary Party Groups in Slovakia' in Knut Heidar and Ruud Koole, eds, *Parliamentary Party Groups in European Democracies. Political Parties Behind Closed Doors*, London: Routledge, 2000, p. 199, 203.
28. David Olson, 'The New Parliaments of New Democracies: The Experience of the Federal Assembly of the Czech and Slovak Federal Republic' in Attila Ágh, ed., *The Emergence of East Central European Parliaments: The First Steps*, Budapest: Hungarian Centre of Democracy Studies, 1994, p. 39.
29. Pettai and Kreuzer, p. 161.
30. Data taken from the website of the Czech Parliament at http://www.psp.cz/cgi-bin/eng/sqw/snem.sqw?o = 1&p1 = 0&p2 = 0 (1992–6); http://www.psp.cz/cgi-bin/eng/sqw/snem.sqw?o = 2&p1 = 0&p2 = 0 (1996–98); http://www.psp.cz/cgi-bin/eng/sqw/snem.sqw?o = 3&p1 = 0&p2 = 0 (1998–2002); http://www.psp.cz/cgi-bin/eng/sqw/snem.sqw?o = 4&p1 = 0&p2 = 0 (2002–).
31. Sarah Whitmore, 'Fragmentation or Consolidation? Parties in Ukraine's Parliament', Paper presented to the Annual Conference of the British Association for Slavonic and East European Studies, Fitzwilliam College, Cambridge, April 2002, p. 1.
32. Malová and Krause, 'Parliamentary party groups in Slovakia', pp. 200–1 (Table 12.1).
33. Tivadar Pártay, quoted in Mark Pittaway and Nigel Swain, 'Hungary' in Bogdan Szajkowski, ed., *Political Parties of Eastern Europe, Russia and the successor States*, Harlow: Longman Information and Reference, 1994, p. 231.
34. Darina Malová, 'The National Council of the Slovak Republic: Between Democratic Transition and National State-Building', *Journal of Legislative Studies*, vol. 2, no. 1, 1996, p. 115.
35. Terry D. Clark, Stacy Holscher, and Lisa Hyland, 'The LDLP Faction in the Lithuanian Seimas, 1992–96', *Nationalities Papers*, vol. 27, no. 2, June 1999, p. 232.
36. Clark, Holscher and Hyland, pp. 237–9.
37. Robertas Pogorelis, 'Votes and Parties in the Mixed Electoral System in Lithuania', draft PhD thesis, University of Essex, March 2003, p. 29; also Jūrate Novagrockienė,

'Elections to the Seimas 2000: Party System Evolution or Its Transformation?' in Algimantas Jankauskas, ed., *Lithuanian Political Science Yearbook 2000*, Vilnius: Institute of International Relations and Political Science, 2001, pp. 146–8.
38. Arter, p. 160.
39. Ibid., p. 161.
40. Marko Bojcun, 'The Ukrainian Parliamentary Elections in March–April 1994,' *Europe-Asia Studies*, vol. 47, no. 2, March 1995, p. 231.
41. Thomas F. Remington, *The Russian Parliament. Institutional Evolution in a Transitional Regime, 1989–1999*, New Haven: Yale University Press, 2001, pp. 178–80, 192.
42. Remington, pp. 178–80, 192.
43. Ibid., p. 197.
44. Thomas F. Remington, 'Putin and the Duma', *Post-Soviet Affairs*, vol. 17, no. 4, p. 287.
45. Remington, 'Putin and the Duma', p. 293.
46. Whitmore, p. 15.
47. Nadia Diuk and Myroslava Gongadze, 'Post-Election Blues in Ukraine', *Journal of Democracy*, vol. 13, no. 4, 2002, p. 160; Andy Wilson, 'Ukraine's 2002 Elections: Less Fraud. More virtuality', *East European Constitutional Review*, vol. 11, no. 3, summer 2002, p. 94.
48. For a rather intemperate but broadly accurate view of the processes of 'inducement and blackmail', see Taras Kuzio, 'Loser Takes All: Ukrainian President Coopts Parliament', RFE/RL Newsline, vol. 6, no. 100, Part I, 30 May 2002 (Endnote).
49. Diuk and Gongadze, p. 164.
50. Alvidas Lukošaitis, The Context of Parliamentary Elections 2000: The Experience and Perspectives of Coalition Politics in Lithuania' in Algimantas Jankauskas, ed., *Lithuanian Political Science Yearbook 2000*, Vilnius: Institute of International Relations and Political Science, 2001, p. 159.
51. Peter Lebovič discusses the political manipulation of the amended electoral law in Peter Lebovič, 'Political Aspects of the Election Law Amendments' in Martin Bútora, Grigorij Mesežnikov, Zora Bútorová and Sharon Fisher, eds, *The 1998 Parliamentary Elections and Democratic Rebirth in Slovakia*, Bratislava: Institute for Public Affairs, 1999, pp. 155–67; also Karen Henderson, 'Problems of Democratic Consolidation in the Slovak Republic', *Society and Economy in Central and Eastern Europe*, no. 3, 1999, pp. 159–60.
52. Mel Huang, 'Estonia: Savisaar Key To Low Estonian Turnout', RFE/RL, 18 March 1999; Mart Linnart and Villu Kand, 'Estonia: Third Parliamentary Poll Since 1991 Determines Future Coalition', RFE/RL Newsline Part II, Endnote, 5 March 1999.
53. Whitmore, p. 8.
54. Alexander Kynev, ' The Role of Russia's Political Parties in Russia's 2002 Regional Elections', *Russia and Eurasia Review*, vol. 2, issue 8, 15 April 2003, available at www.jamestown.org/authors/rer_alexander_kynev.htm.
55. Remington, *The Russian Parliament*.
56. Whitmore, p. 15.
57. Anna Grzymala-Busse, *Redeeming the Communist Past. The Regeneration of Communist Parties in East Central Europe*, Cambridge: Cambridge University Press, 2002, pp. 241–44.
58. Gabriella Ilonszki, 'Parties and parliamentary party groups in the making, Hungary 1989–1997' in Knut Heidar and Ruud Koole, eds, *Parliamentary Party Groups in European Democracies. Political Parties Behind Closed Doors*, London: Routledge, 2000, p. 229.

59. Magdolna Balázs and Zsolt Enyedi, 'Hungarian Case Studies: The Alliance of Free Democrats and the Alliance of Young Democrats' in Paul G. Lewis, ed., *Party Structure and Organization in East-Central Europe*, Cheltenham: Edward Elgar, 1996, p. 63.
60. Bill Lomax, 'The 1998 Elections in Hungary: Third Time Lucky for the Young Democrats', *The Journal of Communist Studies and Transition Politics*, vol. 15, no. 2, June 1999, p. 114.
61. Csilla Kiss, 'From Liberalism to Conservatism: The Federation of Young Democrats in Post-Communist Hungary', *East European Politics and Societies*, vol. 16, no. 3, fall 2002, p. 758.
62. Ilonszki, 'Parties and Parliamentary Party Groups in the Making, Hungary 1989–1997', p. 228.
63. Andor, p. 35.
64. Gábor Tóka, 'Seats and Votes: Consequences of the Hungarian Electoral Law' in Gábor Tóka, ed., *The 1990 Election to the Hungarian National Assembly. Analyses, Documents and Data*, Berlin: Sigma, 1995, p. 56.
65. Kenneth Benoit, 'Two Steps Forward, One Step Back: Electoral Coordination in the Hungarian Election of 1998', Paper presented to the 2000 Annual Meeting of the American Political Science Association, Mariott Wardman Park, 31 August–3 September 2000, pp. 13–16; see also Lomax, pp. 121–2.
66. Kenneth Benoit, 'Like Déjà Vu All Over Again: The Hungarian Parliamentary Elections of 2002,' *The Journal of Communist Studies and Transition Politics*, vol. 18, no. 4, December 2002, p. 129.
67. Benoit, 'Two Steps Forward . . .', pp. 18–19.
68. Cas Mudde, 'Extreme-right parties in Eastern Europe', *Patterns of Prejudice*, vol. 34, no. 1, January 2000, p. 20.
69. Tomáš Kostelecký, *Political Parties after Communism. Developments in East-Central Europe*, Baltimore: The Johns Hopkins Press, 2002, p. 49.
70. Jiri Pehe, 'Czech Elections: Victory for a New Generation', *RFE/RL East European Perspectives*, vol. 4, no. 17, 21 August 2002.
71. Jeffrey M. Jordan, 'Patronage and Corruption in the Czech Republic (Part I)', *RFE/RL East European Perspectives*, vol. 4, no. 4, 20 February 2002; see also 'Patronage and Corruption in the Czech Republic (Part II)', *RFE/RL East European Perspectives*, vol. 4, no. 5, 6 March 2002.
72. Sabrina Ramet, 'Democratization in Slovenia – the Second Stage' in Karen Dawisha and Bruce Parrott, eds, *Politics, Power, and the Struggle for Democracy in South-East* Europe, Cambridge: Cambridge University Press, 1997, p. 212; see pp. 212–4 on the 'Janša affair' and the defence minister's conflicts with President Kučan.
73. Andrej Auersperger Matic, 'Electoral Reform as a Constitutional Dilemma', *East European Constitutional Review*, vol. 8, no. 3, summer 2000, p. 80.
74. Grigore Pop-Elecheș, 'Separated at Birth or Separated by Birth? The Communist Successor Parties in Romania and Hungary', *East European Politics and Societies*, vol. 13, no. 1, winter 1999, p. 125, pp. 139–40.
75. Petre Datculescu, 'Romania: Parties and Issues after 1989' in Kay Lawson, Andrea Römmele, and Georgi Karasimeonov, eds, *Cleavages, Parties, and Voters. Studies from Bulgaria, the Czech Republic, Hungary, Poland, and Romania*, London: Praeger, 1999, p. 170.
76. Jeremy Bransten, 'Estonia: Premier's Resignation Announcement Pitches Country Into Uncertainty' at http://www.rferl.org/nca/features/2001/12/20122001083 234.asp.

Chapter 7

1. Pippa Norris, 'Legislative Recruitment' in Lawrence LeDuc, Richard Niemi and Pippa Norris, eds, *Comparing Democracies*, London: Sage, 1996, p. 186.
2. Michael Gallagher and Michael Marsh, 'Conclusion' in Michael Gallagher and Michael Marsh, eds, *Candidate Selection in Comparative Perspective*, London: Sage 1988, p. 265.
3. Norris in LeDuc *et al.*, Table 7.1, pp. 188–9.
4. Eric A. Nordlinger, 'Representation, Governmental Stability, and Decisional Effectiveness' in J. Roland Pennock and John W. Chapman, eds, *Representation*, New York: Atherton, 1968, pp. 113–14.
5. Nordlinger, p. 114.
6. Iain McLean, 'Forms of Representation and Systems of Voting' in David Held, ed., *Political Theory Today*, Cambridge: Polity Press, 1991, p. 175.
7. Hanna Pitkin, *The Concept of Representation*, Berkeley: University of California Press, 1967, p. 63.
8. Steven Saxonberg, 'Women in East European Parliaments', *Journal of Democracy*, vol. 11, no. 2, April 2000, p. 146.
9. Peter Vanneman, *The Supreme Soviet: Politics and the Legislative Process in the Soviet Political System*, Durham, N.C.: Duke University Press, 1977; Daniel Nelson and Stephen White, *Communist Legislatures in Comparative Perspective*, London and Basingstoke: Macmillan, 1982; Robert Siegler, *The Standing Commissions of the Supreme Soviet*, New York: Praeger, 1982.
10. David Lane, *Politics and Society in the USSR*, London: Martin Robertson, 1978 (2nd edn), pp. 154–6.
11. Petr Kopecký, *Parliaments in the Czech and Slovak Republics. Party Competition and Parliamentary Institutionalization*, Aldershot: Ashgate, 2001, p. 61.
12. David Olson, 'The New Parliaments of New Democracies: The Experience of the Federal Assembly of the Czech and Slovak Republics' in Attila Ágh, ed., *The Emergence of Central European Parliaments: The First Steps*, Budapest: Hungarian Centre of Democracy Studies, 1994, pp. 42–3.
13. Gabriella Ilonszki, 'Legislative Recruitment: Personnel and Institutional Development in Hungary, 1990–94' in Gábor Tóka and Zsolt Enyedi, eds, *Elections to the Hungarian National Assembly 1994. Analyses, Documents and Data*, Berlin: Sigma, 1999, p. 85.
14. Richard Sakwa, 'The Russian Elections of December 1993', *Europe-Asia Studies*, vol. 47, no. 2, 1995, pp. 198–9.
15. E. János Farkas and Agnes Vajda, 'Candidates for Parliament' in Gábor Tóka, ed., *The 1990 Election to the Hungarian National Assembly. Analyses, Documents and Data*, Berlin: Sigma, 1995, p. 82 (Table 13).
16. G. Loewenburg, 'The New Political Leadership of Central Europe: The Example of the New Hungarian National Assembly' in Thomas F. Remington, ed., *Parliaments in Transition. The New Legislative Politics in the Former USSR and Eastern Europe*, Boulder: Westview Press, 1994, p. 45.
17. Jiri Pehe, 'Elections Result in Surprise Stalemate', *Transition*, vol. 2, no. 13, 28 June 1996, p. 36.
18. Ilonszki, 'Legislative Recruitment...', p. 91.
19. Lukáš Fila, 'Who is ANO: TV & Sports Figures, Field Experts but not Politicians', *Slovak Spectator*, 12–18 August 2002.

20. Timothy J. Colton and Michael McFaul, 'Reinventing Russia's Party of Power: "Unity" and the 1999 Duma Election', *Post-Soviet Affairs*, vol. 16, no. 3, 2000, pp. 201–24.
21. Richard Rose and Neil Munro, *Elections without Order. Russia's Challenge to Vladimir Putin*, Cambridge: Cambridge University Press, 2002, p. 138. Erik Herron depicts Yabloko's candidate recruitment as affected by strategic responses to the positive and negative incentives of the mixed system (as well as resource constraints); but he provides little supporting detail; Eric S. Herron, 'Mixed Electoral Rules and Party Strategies. Responses to Incentives by Ukraine's Rukh and Russia's Yabloko', *Party Politics*, vol. 8, no. 6, November 2002, pp. 719–33.
22. Kopecký, pp. 71–2.
23. Kopecký, p. 211.
24. Ilonszki, 'Legislative Recruitment: Personnel and Institutional Development in Hungary, 1990–94', pp. 92–101.
25. Bernard Tamas, 'Parties on Stage: Evaluating the Performance of Hungarian Parties' in Gábor Tóka and Zsolt Enyedi, eds, *Elections to the Hungarian National Assembly 1994. Analyses, Documents and Data*, Berlin: Sigma, 1999, p. 41.
26. Michael Gallagher and Michael Marsh, eds, *Candidate Selection in Comparative Perspective*, London: Sage, 1988.
27. Gabriella Ilonszki, 'Consolidation of Hungarian Democracy' in Dirk Berg-Schlosser and Raivo Vetik, eds, *Perspectives on Democratic Consolidation in Central and Eastern Europe*, Boulder: East European Monographs, 2001, p. 101.
28. See Aleks Szczerbiak, *Poles Together. Emergence and Development of Political Parties in Post-Communist Poland*, Budapest: CEU Press, 2001, pp. 51–5; Vello Pettai and Marcus Kreuzer, 'Party Politics in the Baltic States: Social Bases and Institutional Conflicts', *East European Politics and Societies*, vol. 13, no. 1, winter 1999, p. 162.
29. Rose and Munro, *Elections without Order*, p. 113.
30. See L. Wolosky, 'Putin's Plutocrat Problem', *Foreign Affairs*, vol. 79, no. 2, 2000, pp. 18–31.
31. Attila Ágh, 'The Hungarian Party System and Party Theory in the Transition of Central Europe', *Journal of Theoretical Politics*, vol. 6, no. 2, 1994, pp. 227, 230.
32. See, for example, Joel Hellman, Geraint Jones and Daniel Kaufman, 'Seize the State, Seize the Day: An Empirical Analysis of State Capture and Corruption in Transition Economies', World Bank Policy Research Working Paper 2444, World Bank: Washington, DC., 2000, pp. 1–41; Andrei Schleifer and Daniel Treisman, *Without a Map: Political Tactics and Economic Reform in Russia*, Cambridge: MIT Press, 2000.
33. Walter Connor, *Socialism, Politics and Equality*, New York: Columbia University Press, 1979.
34. Michael D. Kennedy, *Professionals, Power and Solidarity in Poland*, Cambridge: Cambridge University Press, 1991, Table 7.1, p. 245.
35. András Bozóki, 'Introduction' in András Bozóki, ed., *Intellectuals and Politics in Central Europe*, Budapest: Central European Press, 1999, p. 1; Marian Kempny, 'Between Tradition and Politics: Intellectuals after Communism' in Bozóki, ed., pp. 152–3.
36. J. Widacki, *Czego nie powiedział Generał Kiszczak*, Warsaw: BGW, 1992, pp. 45, 47.
37. George Schöpflin, 'Opposition and Para-Opposition: Critical Currents in Hungary, 1968–78' in Rudolf Tőkés, ed., *Opposition in Eastern Europe*, London: Macmillan, 1979, pp. 142–86.
38. Joni Lovenduski and Jean Woodall, *Politics and Society in Eastern Europe*, Basingstoke: Macmillan, 1987, pp. 237–45.

39. Kitschelt found that blue-collar workers are overrepresented in the new radical right parties of Western Europe; Herbert Kitschelt with Anthony McGann, *The Radical Right in Western Europe. A Comparative Analysis*, Ann Arbor: the University of Michigan Press, 1997, pp. 34–5.
40. Sarah Birch, 'Nomenklatura Democratization: Electoral Clientelism and Party Formation in Post-Soviet Ukraine', *Democratization*, vol. 4, no. 4, 1997, pp. 40–62.
41. N. Ryabov, cited by Peter Lentini, 'Elections and Political Order in Russia: The 1993 Elections to the State Duma', *The Journal of Communist Studies and Transition Politics*, vol. 10, no. 2, June 1994, p. 178; these totals apparently also included 494 standing for the Federation Council.
42. J. Reschová, 'Nová politika s novými l'ud'mi: Federálne zhromaždenie v roku 1990', *Sociologicky Časopis*, vol. 28, no. 2, 1992, p. 226.
43. Włodzimierz Wesołowski, *Partie: Nieustanne Kłopoty*, Warsaw: IFIS PAN, 2000, p. 116.
44. Farkas and Vajda, pp. 74–5.
45. Sakwa, 'The Russian Elections of December 1993', p. 211.
46. Jane L. Curry and Irena Panków, 'Social Movements and Pluralist Theory: The Conundrum of Solidarity in Poland's Democratization' in Dirk Berg-Schlosser and Raivo Vetik, eds, *Perspectives on Democratic Consolidation in Central and Eastern Europe*, Boulder: East European Monographs, 2001, p. 86.
47. Eighty per cent of candidates of the Revolutionary Workers' Party (Bécko) were workers and 30 per cent of candidates of the United Slovak Workers' Party; but together they fielded only 54 candidates.
48. Jiri Pehe, 'European Union Wins Czech Elections – Barely', *East European Constitutional Review*, vol. 11, no. 3, summer 2002, p. 88.
49. Sakwa, 'The Russian Elections of December 1993, p. 206.
50. However we should note that in Hungary about one-third of candidates voluntarily provided personal statements for the 2002 election; of these 37 per cent were engaged in economic activities, while 30 per cent were professionals and 23 per cent worked for the state.

Chapter 8

1. There are very few studies of women deputies, but there have not been many women to study and only rarely have there been cross-party women's parliamentary groups. But even in the unruly Russian Duma Iulia Shevchenko has argued that party is usually more important than gender; Iulia Shevchenko, 'Who Cares about Women's Problems?: Female Legislators in the 1995 and 1999 Russian State Dumas', *Europe-Asia Studies*, vol. 54, no. 8, December 2002, especially p. 1217. Dobrinka Kostova takes a similar view of the position in Bulgaria, seeing women deputies as altogether insensitive to gender issues; Dobrinka Kostova, 'Women in the Bulgarian Parliament – Continuity and Change', Paper presented at the Conference on Political Participation of Women in Post-socialist ECE-countries of the German Political Science Association, Berlin, 28–30 June 2002.
2. David Lane, *State and Politics in the USSR*, New York: New York University Press, 1985, p. 185.
3. Sarah Birch, 'Women and Political Representation in Contemporary Ukraine' in Richard E. Matland and Kathleen Montgomery, eds, *Women's Access to Political Power in Post-Communist Europe*, Oxford: Oxford University Press (forthcoming), Table 1.

4. Algis Krupavičius and Irmina Matonytė, 'Women's Political Recruitment and Representation in Lithuania', *Viešosios Politikos Studijos*, vol. 1, no. 1, 2001, p. 9.
5. Sharon Wolchik, *Czechoslovakia in Transition*, London and New York: Pinter Publishers, 1991, p. 71. The figure is for both chambers of the Federal Assembly and differs somewhat from those available elsewhere.
6. Zoltan Barany, 'Elections in Hungary' in Robert Furtak, ed., *Elections in Socialist States*, London: Harvester Wheatsheaf, 1990, p. 81.
7. Stephen White, John Gardner, George Schöpflin and Tony Saich, *Communist Political Systems. An Introduction*, Basingstoke: Macmillan, 1990 (3rd edn), p. 104.
8. Birch, 'Women and Political Representation...', Table 1.
9. Krupavičius and Matonytė, p. 9.
10. Barbara Labuda, quoted in Jacqueline Heinen, 'Polish Democracy is a Masculine Democracy', *Women's Studies International Forum*, vol. 15, no. 1, 1992, pp. 129–38.
11. Andrew Reynolds, 'Women in the Legislatures and Executives of the World: Knocking at the Highest Glass Ceiling', *World Politics*, vol. 51, July 1999, pp. 547–72.
12. Pippa Norris and Ronald Inglehart, 'Cultural Obstacles to Equal Representation', *Journal of Democracy*, vol. 12, no. 3, 2001, p. 132.
13. Norris and Inglehart, note 17.
14. Ibid., p. 134.
15. Ibid., pp. 135–7.
16. Ibid., p. 133.
17. Richard W. Wilson, 'The Many Voices of Political Culture. Assessing Different Approaches', *World Politics*, vol. 52, no. 2, January 2000, p. 264.
18. Georgina Waylen, 'Gender and Democratic Politics: A Comparative Analysis of Consolidation in Argentina and Chile', *Journal of Latin American Studies*, vol. 32, no. 3, 2000, pp. 765–93.
19. Miki Caul, 'Women's Representation in Parliament. The Role of Political Parties', *Party Politics*, vol. 3, no. 1, 1999, pp. 79–98.
20. Richard E. Matland, 'Institutional Variables Affecting Female Representation in National Legislatures: The Case of Norway', *Journal of Politics*, vol. 55, no. 3, 1993, pp. 737–55.
21. Herbert Kitschelt with Anthony McGann, *The Radical Right in Western Europe. A Comparative Analysis*, Ann Arbor: the University of Michigan Press, 1997, pp. 34–5.
22. Benedict Anderson, *Imagined Communities: Reflections on the Origin and Spread of Nationalism*, London: Verso, 1983, p. 7.
23. Michael Gallagher and Michael Marsh, eds, *Candidate Selection in Comparative Perspective*, London: Sage, 1988.
24. Joni Lovenduski and Pippa Norris, eds, *Gender and Party Politics*, London: Sage, 1993; Pippa Norris, 'Legislative Recruitment' in Lawrence LeDuc, Richard G. Niemi and Pippa Norris, eds, *Comparing Democracies*, London: Sage, 1996, pp. 184–215.
25. Norris, 'Legislative Recruitment', p. 209.
26. Michael Gallagher, 'Conclusion' in Gallagher and Marsh, pp. 248–52.
27. Norris and Inglehart, p. 129.
28. See the Global Database of Quotas for Women at http://www.idea.int/quota/country.cfm.
29. Norris in Lovenduski and Norris, p. 321. See also Richard E. Matland and Donley T. Studlar, 'The Contagion of Women Candidates in Single-Member district and Proportional Representation Electoral Systems: Canada and Norway', *Journal of Politics*, vol. 58, no. 3, August 1996, pp. 707–33.

30. Matland and Studlar, pp. 707–33; see also Richard E. Matland, 'Women's Legislative Representation in National Legislatures: A Comparison of Democracies in Developed and Developing Countries', *Legislative Studies Quarterly*, vol. 28, no. 1, 1998, pp. 109–25.
31. Norris, 'Legislative Recruitment', p. 199.
32. Gallagher and Marsh, p. 254.
33. Philip E. Converse and Roy Pierce, *Political Representation in France*, Cambridge, Mass. and London: The Belknap Press of Harvard University Press, 1986, p. 198.
34. Pippa Norris, *Politics and Sexual Equality*, Boulder: Lynne Riener, 1987, p. 130; Matland and Studlar, p. 709.
35. See, for example, Richard E. Matland, 'Legislative Recruitment: A General Model and Discussion of Issues of Special Relevance to Women' in Matland and Montgomery, eds, forthcoming (draft); Phillipe Schmitter, 'What is to be Done to make neodemocracies 'female friendly'? in Jane S. Jacquette and Sharon Wolchik, eds, *Women and Democracy. Latin America and Central and Eastern Europe*, Baltimore and London: The Johns Hopkins University Press, 1999, p. 226.
36. Norris, 'Legislative Recruitment', p. 199 and p. 201 (Table 7.7).
37. See, for example, Barbara Einhorn, 'Democratization and Women's Movements in Central and Eastern Europe: Concepts of Women's Rights' in Valentine Moghadam, ed., *Democratic Reform and the Position of Women in Transitional Economies*, Oxford: Clarendon Press, 1993, pp. 58–63; Henryk Domański, 'Równouprawnienie, Stereotyp tradycyjnego podziału ról' in Anna Titkow and Henryk Domański, *Co to Znaczy Być Kobietą w Polsce*, Warsaw: Polska Akademia Nauk, 1995, pp. 64–87; Alina Zvinkliene, 'Neo-Conservatism and Family Ideology in Lithuania. Between the West and the USSR' in Sue Bridger, ed., *Women and Political Change. Perspectives from East-Central Europe*, Basingstoke: Macmillan and New York: St. Martin's Press, 1999, pp. 135–50.
38. See the (overly) optimistic discussion in Wilma Rule and Nadezhda Shvedova, 'Women in Russia's First Multi-party Election' in Wilma Rule and Norma C. Noonan, eds, *Russian Women in Politics and Society*, Westport, Connecticut and London: Greenwood Press, 1996, pp. 40–59.
39. See Nanette Funk and Magda Mueller, *Gender Politics and Post-Communism*, London and New York: Routledge, 1993; Jacquette and Wolchik; Suzanne LaFont, 'One step forward, two steps back: women in the post-communist states', *Communist and Post-Communist Studies*, vol. 34, 2001, p. 216, argues that this may be changing.
40. The adverse effects of economic reform on women are well documented, though the link to women's participation is not always made. See, for example, chapters in Bridger, Rule and Noonan, and Moghadam; and Marilyn Rueschemeyer, ed., *Women in the Politics of Postcommunist Eastern Europe*, New York and London: M.E. Sharpe, 1998 (rev. ed.).
41. Norris's widely used model is in Pippa Norris, 'Conclusions: Comparing Legislative Recruitment' in Lovenduski and Norris, p. 311.
42. Sharon Wolchik, 'Transition Politics in the Czech Republic and Slovakia' in Jane S. Jacquette and Sharon Wolchik, eds, *Women and Democracy. Latin America and Central and Eastern Europe*, Baltimore and London: The Johns Hopkins University Press, 1999, p. 166; Julia Szalai, 'Women and Democratization: Some Notes on Recent Changes in Hungary' in Jacquette and Wolchik, p. 199.

43. Cited in Katarina Mallok, 'Frauen in den politischen Parteien der Slowakei', Paper presented to the Conference on Political Participation of Women in Post-socialist ECE-countries, German Political Science Association, Berlin, 28–30 June 2002.
44. Yudit Kiss, 'System Changes, Export-Oriented Growth and Women in Hungary', *Europe-Asia Studies*, vol. 55, no. 1, January 2003, p. 29.
45. The annual Polish *Rocznik Statystyczny* (Warsaw: GUS) provides unemployment data by gender and education.
46. Birch, 'Women and Political Representation ...'.
47. Kiss, p. 4, p. 10.
48. Attila Ágh, '1998 Elections in Hungary: Defeat as Promoter of change for the HSP', *East European Politics and Societies*, vol. 14, no. 2, 2000, p. 312.
49. Filadelfiova *et al.*, *Zeny w politike*, cited in Mallok, p. 4.
50. Michael Shafir, 'Radical Politics in East-Central Europe Part VIII: Radical Continuity in Romania: The Greater Romania Party (A), *East European Perspectives*, vol. 2, no. 16, 16 August 2000, citing the party's website, http://www.romare.ro (I could not find more recent data on this site).
51. Kristi Long, *We All Fought for Freedom: Women in Poland's Solidarity Movement*, Boulder, Colorado: Westview Press, 1996.
52. Gabriella Ilonszki, 'Introduction to Research Areas and Research Findings with Respect to Female Politicians in Hungary', Paper presented at the Conference on Political Participation of Women in Post-socialist ECE-countries, German Political Science Association, Berlin, 28–30 June 2002.
53. Grigorii Golosov, 'Political Parties, Electoral Systems and Women's Representation in the Regional Legislative Assemblies of Russia, 1995–1998', *Party Politics*, vol. 7, no. 1, 2001, pp. 45–68.
54. The broadly centre-right SDK was described as a rainbow of right, centre, and left elements by John Fitzmaurice, 'The Slovak Elections of 25th and 26th September 1998', *Electoral Studies*, vol. 18, no. 2, June 1999, p. 292.
55. Krupavičius and Matonytė, p. 21.
56. Ibid., p. 22.
57. Robert Moser, 'The Effects of Electoral Systems on Women's Representation in Post-communist States', *Electoral Studies*, vol. 20, 2001, pp. 353–69.

Chapter 9

1. Joseph Rothschild, *East Central Europe between the Two World Wars*, Seattle and London: University of Washington Press, 1974, p. 14.
2. Raymond Pearson, *National Minorities in Eastern Europe, 1848–1945*, London: Macmillan, 1983.
3. D. Smith, 'Retracing Estonia's Russians: Mikhail Kurchinskii and Inter-war Cultural Autonomy, *Nationalities Papers*, vol. 27, no. 3, 1999, pp. 455–74.
4. For example, Will Kymlicka and Magda Opalski, eds, *Can Liberal Pluralism be Exported? Western Political Theory and Ethnic Relations in Eastern Europe*, Oxford: Oxford University Press, 2001.
5. For example Paul Ellen Frankel *et al.*, eds, *The Communitarian Challenge to Liberalism*, Cambridge: Cambridge University Press, 1997.
6. See, for example, Donald Horowitz, *Ethnic Groups in Conflict*, Berkeley: University of California Press, 1985; Arend Lijphart, 'Democracies, Forms, Performance and Constitutional Engineering', *European Journal of Political Research*, vol. 25, 1994, pp. 1–17.

7. Tove Malloy, 'The "Politics of Accommodation" in the Council of Europe after 1989: National Minorities and Democratization', PhD thesis, Department of Government, University of Essex, 2002.

8. *Monitoring the EU Accession Process: Minority Protection*, Budapest: Central European Press, 2001, p. 16.

9. Katarzyna Warmińska, 'Polish Tatars: Ethnic Ideology and State Policy' in Cora Govers and Hans Vermeulen, eds, *The Politics of Ethnic Consciousness*, London and New York: Macmillan and St. Martin's Press, 1997, pp. 343–66.

10. Paul Brass, *Ethnicity and Nationalism. Theory and Comparison*, London: Sage, 1991, p. 20.

11. Graham Smith, Vivian Law, Andrew Wilson, Annette Bohr and Edward Allworth, *Nation-building in the Post-Soviet Borderlands*, Cambridge: Cambridge University Press, 1998, p. 120. See also Oxana Shevel, 'Nationality in Ukraine: Some Rules of Engagement', *East European Politics and Societies*, vol. 16, no. 2, spring 2002, p. 393.

12. Zoltan Barany, *The East European Gypsies. Regime Change, Marginality, and Ethnopolitics*, Cambridge: Cambridge University Press, 2002, p. 161.

13. John T. Ishiyama and Marijke Breuning, *Ethnopolitics in the New Europe*, London: Lynne Rienner, 1998, p. 22.

14. Dmitri Glinski, 'Russia and Its Muslims: The Politics of Identity at the International-Domestic Frontier', *East European Constitutional Review*, vol. 11, no. 1/2, winter–spring 2002, pp. 71–2.

15. Claus Offe, 'Capitalism by Democratic Design? Democratic Theory Facing the Triple Transition in East Central Europe', *Social Research*, vol. 58, no. 4, winter 1991, pp. 865–92.

16. On the international legal dimensions of 'internal self-determination' see Gábor Kardos, 'Human Rights: A Matter of Individual or Collective Concern?' in Istvan Pogony, *Human Rights in Eastern Europe*, Aldershot: Edward Elgar, 1995, pp. 179–81.

17. Michael Keating, 'So Many Nations, So Few States: Territory and Nationalism in the Global Era' in Alain-G. Gagnon and James Tully, eds, *Multinational Democracies*, Cambridge: Cambridge University Press, 2001, p. 44.

18. Keating, 'So Many Nations . . .', p. 56.

19. Peter Duncan, 'Russia. Accommodating Ethnic Minorities' in Don McIver, ed., *The Politics of Multinational States*, London: Macmillan, 1999, p. 64 (63–83).

20. Duncan, p. 77.

21. Richard Simeon and Daniel-Patrick Conway, 'Federalism and the Management of Conflict' in Alain-G. Gagnon and James Tully, eds, *Multinational Democracies*, Cambridge: Cambridge University Press, 2001, p. 263.

22. See, for example, M.M. Balzer and U.A. Vinokurova, 'Ethnicity or Nationalism? The Sakha Republic (Yakutia)' in Leokadia Drobizheva, Rose Gottemoeller, Catherine McArdle Kelleher, and Lee Walker, eds, *Ethnic Conflict in the Post-Soviet World*, London: M.E. Sharpe, 1996, pp. 157–78; Z.V. Anaiban and E.W. Walker, 'On the Problem of Inter-Ethnic Conflict: The Republic of Tuva', *Infra*, pp. 179–94; and Roza Musina, 'Contemporary Ethnosocial and Ethnopolitical Processes in Tatarstan', *Infra*, pp. 195–208.

23. Tomila Lankina, 'Local Government and Ethnic and Social Activism in Russia' in Archie Brown, ed., *Contemporary Russian Politics: A Reader*, Oxford: Oxford University Press, 2001, p. 405.

24. V. Gelman, 'Subnational Institutions in Contemporary Russia' in Neil Robinson, ed., *Institutions and Political Change in Russia*, Basingstoke: Palgrave-Macmillan, 2000, pp. 85–105.

25. Alexander Kynev, 'The Role of Political Parties in Russia's 2002 Regional Elections, *Russia and Eurasia Review*, vol. 2, issue 8, 15 April 2003, online at www.jamestown.org/authors/rer_alexander_kynev.htm.
26. Kynev.
27. Glinski, p. 76.
28. quoted in Darrell Slider, 'Russia's Governors and Party Formation' in Archie Brown, ed., *Contemporary Russian Politics: A Reader*, Oxford: Oxford University Press, 2001, p. 232.
29. Slider, p. 234.
30. Arend Lijphart is the foremost advocate of consociationalism; see *Democracies. Patterns of Majoritarian and Consensus Government in Twenty-one Countries*, New Haven: Yale University Press, 1984. Paul Brass criticised consociational institutions as élitist: segmental isolation promotes élites and discourages rather than encouraging wide political participation, and violates the rights of groups not recognised by the state and of individuals who do not wish to be identified with particular cultural groups; Brass, pp. 339–42; see also Dominique Arel, 'Political stability in Multinational Democracies', in Alain-G. Gagnon and James Tully, eds, *Multinational Democracies*, Cambridge: Cambridge University Press, 2001, pp. 66–7.
31. Abby Innes, *Czechoslovakia. The Short Good-Bye*, New Haven: Yale University Press, 2001; E. Stein, *Czecho/Slovakia, Ethnic Conflict, Constitutional Fissure, Negotiated Break-up*, University of Michigan Press, 1997; Michael Kraus and Allison Stanger, eds, *Irreconcilable Differences?*, Cambridge: Cambridge University Press, 2000.
32. Cited in Matthew Rhodes, 'National Identity and Minority Rights in the Constitutions of the Czech Republic and Slovakia', *East European Quarterly*, vol. XXIX, no. 3, September 1995, p. 361.
33. Renate Weber, 'Constitutionalism as a Vehicle for Democratic Consolidation in Romania' in Jan Zielonka, ed., *Democratic Consolidation in Eastern Europe*, Oxford: Oxford University Press, 2001 (vol. 1: *Institutional Engineering*), p. 234.
34. This has been noted by (among others) Mary Kaldor, 'Yugoslavia and the New Nationalism', *New Left Review*, no. 197, 1993, pp. 96–112; Katherine Verdery, 'Nationalism and National Sentiment in Post-Socialist Romania', *Slavic Review*, vol. 52, no. 2 (summer), 1993, pp. 184–5; Graham Smith, Vivian Law, Andrew Wilson, Annette Bohr and Edward Allworth, *Nation-building in the Post-Soviet Borderlands*, Cambridge: Cambridge University Press, 1998, pp. 101–2.
35. Jeff Chinn and Lise Truex, 'The Question of Citizenship in the Baltics', *Journal of Democracy*, vol. 7, no. 1, 1996, p. 135. On the debates surrounding the first citizenship laws see Vello Pettai, 'Estonia: Positive and Negative Institutional Engineering' in Jan Zielonka, ed., *Democratic Consolidation in Eastern Europe*, Oxford: Oxford University Press, 2001 (vol. 1: *Institutional Engineering*), pp. 118–20; Adolf Sprudzs, 'Rebuilding Democracy in Latvia: Overcoming a Dual Legacy' in Jan Zielonka, ed., *Democratic Consolidation in Eastern Europe*, Oxford: Oxford University Press, 2001 (vol. 1: *Institutional Engineering*), pp. 147–51.
36. Smith, Law, Wilson, Bohr and Allworth, *Nation-building in the Post-Soviet Borderlands*, p. 96.
37. Calculated from data in *Monitoring the EU Accession Process. Minority Protection*, p. 310.
38. *Monitoring the EU Accession Process. Minority Protection*, p. 181.
39. Ibid., p. 180.
40. See Sylvia Maier, 'Are the Baltic States Living up to their International Legal Obligations?', *East European Human Rights Review*, vol. 4, no. 1, 1998, pp. 1–52.

41. Organisation for Security and Co-operation in Europe, 'Annual Report 2001 on OSCE Activities (1 November 2000–31 October 2001)', from http://www.osce.org/docs/english/misc/anrep01e_activ.htm#00010.
42. *Monitoring the EU Accession Process. Minority Protection*, pp. 294–5.
43. Organisation for Security and Co-operation in Europe, 'Annual Report 2001 . . .'.
44. RFE/RL Newsline, vol. 6, no. 29, Part II, 13 February 2002.
45. *Monitoring the EU Accession Process*, p. 297.
46. See Jirina Siklova and Marta Miklusakova, 'Denying Citizenship to the Czech Roma', *East European Constitutional Review*, vol. 7, no. 2, spring 1998, pp. 58–64.
47. See Zoltan Barany, *The East European Gypsies*, pp. 157–201 on the deterioration of the Roma's socio-economic situation in the context of regime change. *Monitoring the EU Accession Process. Minority Protection* provides an assessment of diverse areas relevant to the protection of the Roma in EU candidate countries.
48. IDEA Handbook; Stephen Holmes, 'Designing Electoral Regimes'. *East European Constitutional Review*, vol. 3, no. 2, spring 1994, p. 41.
49. Stein Rokkan (with Angus Campbell, Per Torsvik and Henry Valen), *Citizens, Elections, Parties: Approaches to the Comparative Study of the Processes of Development*, Oslo: Universitetsforlaget, 1970, p. 157.
50. Sarah Birch, Frances Millard, Marina Popescu and Kieran Williams, *Embodying Democracy. Electoral System Design in Post-Communist Europe*, Basingstoke: Palgrave, 2002, p. 94.
51. Interview, Bucharest, September 1999.
52. See the Bulletins of committee hearings on the electoral law in *Biuletyn z posiedzenia Komisji Nadzwyczajnej do rozpatrzenia projektu ustawy Ordynacja wyborcza do Sejmu RP*, Nr.482/Ikad., 30 June 1992; *Biuletyn . . . 495/Ikad.*, 7 July 1992; *Biuletyn . . . 837/Ikad.*, 17 November 1992, *Biuletyn . . . 932/Ikad.*, 15 December 1992.
53. speech of Ion Popescu in the Ukrainian Rada, 10 July 2001, cited in Marina Popescu, and Gábor Tóka, 'Districting and Redistricting in Eastern and Central Europe: Regulations and Practices', Paper presented at Conference on Redistricting from a Comparative Perspective, University of California at Irvine, 6–8 December 2001.
54. Rasma Karklins, *Ethnopolitics and the Transition to Democracy: the Collapse of the USSR and Latvia*, Baltimore: the Johns Hopkins University Press, 1994; Ishiyama and Breuning, p. 4.
55. Ishiyama and Breuning, p. 15.
56. Brass, pp. 276–7.
57. Roper defines ethnic parties as cadre parties, with 'membership open only to those individuals who share the ethnic identity'; Stephen Roper, 'The Romanian Party System and the Catch-all Party Phenomenon', *East European Quarterly*, vol. XXVIII, no. 4, January 1995, p. 521. But this is rarely the case, and is not true of the Bulgarian Movement for Rights and Freedoms or the Hungarian Democratic Alliance of Romania, both of which he cites as having a closed membership.
58. Antonina Zhelyazkova, 'The Bulgarian Ethnic Model', *East European Constitutional Review*, fall 2001, pp. 62–3.
59. Ishiyama and Breuning, p. 26.
60. Ibid., p. 28.
61. Stephen Ashley, 'Ethnic Unrest during January', *RFE/RL Report on Eastern Europe*, vol. 1, no. 6, 1990, pp. 4–11.
62. Mary E. McIntosh, Martha Abele MacIver, Daniel Abele and David Noelle, 'Minority Rights and Majority Rule: Ethnic Tolerance in Romania and Bulgaria', *Social Forces*, vol. 73, no. 3, March 1995, p. 944.

63. Moreover, only 62 per cent endorsed the view that minorities should enjoy the right to preserve their culture through their own organisations and associations; McIntosh, MacIver, Abele and Noelle, p. 944.
64. Ishiyama and Breuning, p. 34.
65. Ibid.
66. Dobrin Kanev, 'Political Culture and the Prospects for Democracy' in Georgi Karasimeonov, ed., *The Bulgarian Grand National Assembly and the 1991 Election to the Bulgarian National Assembly. Analyses, Documents and Data*, p. 67.
67. One study estimated that some 3–5 per cent of Muslims and 8–10 per cent of Christians displayed mutual intolerance, Zhelyazkova, p. 65.
68. Kanev, pp. 66–7.
69. Tom Gallagher, '*Vatra Romaneasca* and Resurgent Nationalism in Romania', *Ethnic and Racial Studies*, vol. 15, no. 4, October 1992, pp. 573–4.
70. Verdery, p. 189.
71. Verdery, pp. 197–200; Gallagher, '*Vatra Romaneasca...*', pp. 589–90; Vladimir Tismaneanu, *Fantasies of Salvation. Democracy, Nationalism and Myth in Post-Communist Europe*, Princeton, New Jersey: Princeton University Press, 1998, pp. 65–87.
72. Tom Gallagher, 'Ethnic Tension in Cluj', *RFE/RL Research Report*, vol. 2, no. 9, 26 February 1993, pp. 27–33.
73. Tom Gallagher, 'Nationalism and Post-Communist Politics: The Party of Romanian National Unity, 1990–1996' in Lavinia Stan, ed., *Romania in Transition*, Aldershot: Dartmouth, 1997, pp. 39–40.
74. Michael Shafir, 'Ethnic Tension Runs High in Cluj', RFE/RL Research Report, vol. 3, no. 32, 19 August 1994, p. 25.
75. Michael Shafir, 'The Ciorbea Government and Democratization: A Preliminary Assessment' in Duncan Light and David Phinnemore, eds, *Post-Communist Romania. Coming to Terms with Transition*, Basingstoke: Palgrave, 2001, p. 95.
76. Tom Gallagher, 'Nationalism and Romanian Political Culture in the 1990s' in Duncan Light and David Phinnemore, eds, *Post-Communist Romania. Coming to Terms with Transition*, Basingstoke: Palgrave, 2001, p. 110.
77. Gallagher, 'Nationalism and Romanian Political Culture...', pp. 112–14; Shafir, 'The Ciorbea Government...', pp. 95–6.
78. RFE/RL Newsline, vol. 6, no. 45, Part II, 8 March 2002.
79. RFE/RL Newsline, vol. 6, no. 22, Part II, 4 February 2002.
80. Janusz Bugajski, *Ethnic Politics in Eastern Europe*, London: M.E. Sharpe, 1995, p. 346.
81. Zsusza Csergo, 'Beyond Ethnic Division: Majority–Minority Debate about the Postcommunist State in Romania and Slovakia', *East European Politics and Societies*, vol. 16, no. 1, 2002, p. 8.
82. Bugajski, p. 341.
83. Innes, *Czechoslovakia*, p. 98.
84. Eleonóra Sándor, 'The Political Parties of the Hungarian Minority in the 1998 Elections' in Martin Bútora, Grigorij Mesežnikov, Zora Bútorová and Sharon Fisher, eds, *the 1998 Parliamentary Elections and Democratic Rebirth in Slovakia*, Bratislava: Institute for Public Affairs, 1999, pp. 246–9.
85. Karen Henderson, *Slovakia. The Escape from Invisibility*, London: Routledge, 2002, p. 79.
86. Brigid Fowler has stressed that there were good reasons why the Status Law stirred up such a hornets' nest: 'At least implicitly the kin-state relationship challenges... the host-state's territorial sovereignty, its exclusive citizenship relationship with

its citizens and its assumption of a singular tie of loyalty and identity between the citizenry and the state'; Brigid Fowler, 'Fuzzing Citizenship, nationalising political space: A framework for interpreting the Hungarian 'status law' as a new form of kin-state policy in Central and Eastern Europe', ESRC One Europe or Several? Programme Working Paper 40/02, Sussex European Institute, 2002, p. 24.

87. By the mid-1990s Russians in Latvia appeared to be better integrated than their Estonian counterparts; Anton Steen, 'Ethnic Relations, Elites and Democracy in the Baltic States', *The Journal of Communist Studies and Transition Politics*, vol. 16, no. 4, December 2000, pp. 68–87.

88. Smith, Law, Wilson, Bohr and Allworth, *Nation-building in the Post-Soviet Borderlands*, p. 116.

89. Ishiyama and Breuning, p. 95.

90. Andrejs Plakans, 'Democratization and Political Participation in Postcommunist Societies: The Case of Latvia' in Karen Dawisha and Bruce Parrott, eds, *The Consolidation of Democracy in East-Central Europe*, Cambridge: Cambridge University Press, 1997, p. 280.

91. Mel Huang, 'Latvia's Marching Season', *Central European Review*, vol. 0, no. 25, 26 March 1999.

92. Vello Pettai and Marcus Kreuzer, 'Party Politics in the Baltic States: Social Bases and Institutional Context', *East European Politics and Societies*, vol. 13, no. 1, 1999, p. 169.

93. Artis Pabriks, 'The Real Face of the Pro-Russian forces', http://www.tautaspartija. lv/index.php?type = news&l = 3&id = 11.

94. Andrew Cave, 'Minority versus Minority', *Transitions-On-Line*, 26 March 2003 at www.tol.cz.

95. Klara Hallik, 'Ethnopolitical Conflict in Estonia' in Leokadia Drobizheva, Rose Gottemoeller, Catherine McArdle Kelleher, and Lee Walker, eds, *Ethnic Conflict in the Post-Soviet World*, London: M.E. Sharpe, 1996, pp. 91–2.

96. Hallik, p. 97.

97. Ibid., p. 102.

98. RFE/RL Newsline, vol. 5, no. 213, Part II, 8 November 2001.

99. RFE/RL Newsline, vol. 6, no. 42, Part II, 5 March 2002.

100. Zhelyazkova, p. 65.

101. See, for example, Rick Fawn, 'Czech Attitudes Towards the Roma: "Expecting More of Havel's Country"?', *Europe-Asia Studies*, vol. 53, no. 8, 2001, p. 1203.

102. Gabriel Andreescu, 'Multiculturalism in Central Europe: Cultural Integration and Group Privacy: Group Privacy and Integration in the Case of the Roma', *RFE/RL East European Perspectives*, vol. 4, no. 3, 6 February 2002 (Part III).

103. Martin Kovats, 'The Roma and Minority Self-government in Hungary', *Immigrants and Minorities*, vol. 15, no. 1, 1996, pp. 42–58.

104. Michal Vašečka, 'Roma and the 1998 Parliamentary Elections' in Martin Bútora, Grigorij Mesežnikov, Zora Bútorová and Sharon Fisher, eds, *The 1998 Parliamentary Elections and Democratic Rebirth in Slovakia*, Bratislava: Institute for Public Affairs, 1999, p. 255.

105. Barany, *The Gypsies*, p. 228.

106. *Monitoring the EU Accession Process*, p. 109.

107. Stephen Deets, 'Reconsidering East European Minority Policy: Liberal Theory and European Norms', *East European Politics and Societies*, vol. 16, no. 1, winter 2002, p. 46.

108. Deets, p. 48.
109. Ieva Zake, 'The People's Party in Latvia: Neo-Liberalism and the New Politics of Independence', *The Journal of Communist Studies and Transition Politics*, vol. 18, no. 3, September 2002, p. 111.

Chapter 10

1. Kieran Williams, 'What was Mečiarism?' in Kieran Williams, ed., *Slovakia After Communism and Mečiarism*, London: School of Slavonic and East European Studies, 2000, pp. 4–5.
2. The term is Jon Elster's: see Jon Elster, 'Constitution Making in Eastern Europe: Rebuilding the Boat in the Open Sea', *Public Administration*, vol. 71, spring–summer 1993, pp. 169–217.
3. Petr Kopecký, 'Developing Party Organisations in East-Central Europe: What Type of Party is Likely to Emerge?', *Party Politics*, vol. 1, no. 4, 1995, p. 518.
4. Maurizio Cotta, 'Structuring the New Party Systems after the Dictatorship. Coalitions, Alliances, Fusions and Splits during the Transition and Post-transition Stages' in Geoffrey Pridham and Paul G. Lewis, eds, *Stabilising Fragile Democracies. Comparing New Party Systems in Southern and Eastern Europe*, London: Routledge, 1996, pp. 69–99.
5. British Helsinki Human Rights Group, 'LATVIA 1993: The Elections – Democracy & Human Rights', http://www.bhhrg.org/CountryReport. aspè ReportID = 146& CountryID = 14.
6. Sarah Birch, Frances Millard, Marina Popescu and Kieran Williams, *Embodying Democracy. Electoral System Design in Post-Communist Europe*, Basingstoke: Palgrave, 2002, p. 151.
7. Ilya Prizel, 'Ukraine between Proto-democracy and "Soft" Authoritarianism' in Karen Dawisha and Bruce Parrott, eds, *Democratic Changes and Authoritarian Reactions in Russia, Ukraine, Belarus, and Moldova*, Cambridge: Cambridge University Press, 1997, p. 355.
8. *Orszaggyulesi Naplo*, 61. űlése (19 October 1989), p. 5035, quoted in Birch, Millard, Popescu and Williams, p. 59.
9. Clare McManus-Czubińska, William Miller, Radoslaw Markowski and Jacek Wasilewski, 'The New Polish "Right"?', Paper presented at the Workshop on the Central European Right and EU Enlargement, Foreign and Commonwealth Office, London, July 2002.
10. See Keith Darden on the Ukraine as a 'blackmail state': Keith Darden, 'Blackmail as a Tool of State Domination: Ukraine under Kuchma', *East European Constitutional Review*, vol. 10, nos 2, 3, spring–summer 2001, pp. 67–71.
11. Office for Democratic Institutions and Human Rights, 'Final Report. Romanian Parliamentary and Presidential Elections 3rd and 17th November 1996', Warsaw: OSCE, n.d.
12. ODIHR, 'Ukraine. Parliamentary Elections 31 March 2002', Warsaw: OSCE/ODIHR, 27 May 2002.
13. OSCE Office for Democratic Institutions and Human Rights, 'Russian Federation Elections to the State Duma 19 December 1999. Final Report', OSCE: Warsaw, 13 February 2000.
14. These figures exclude one constituency where the Movement won no seats.
15. OSCE, Russian Federation Elections . . . 1999'.
16. ODIHR, 'Ukraine. Parliamentary Elections . . . 2001'.

17. Andy Wilson, 'Ukraine's 2002 Elections: Less Fraud. More Virtuality', *East European Constitutional Review*, vol. 11, no. 3, summer 2002, pp. 91–8.

18. This was a 'frequently asked question'; see for example William Miller, Stephen White, and Paul Heywood, *Values and Political Change in Postcommunist Europe*, Basingstoke: Macmillan Press, 1998, p. 170.

19. CBOS, 'Czy w Polsce powinna powstać nowa partia polityczna?', Komunikat Badań, CBOS BS/14/2003.

20. Jacek Bielasiak, 'The Institutionalization of Electoral and Party Systems in Post-communist States', *Comparative Politics*, vol. 34, no. 2, January 2002, p. 199.

21. Hans-Dieter Klingemann, Richard Hofferbert and Ian Budge, *Parties, Policies and Democracy*, Boulder: Westview Press, 1994.

22. Richard Rose, 'How Floating Parties Frustrate Democratic Accountability: A Supply-Side View of Russia's Elections' in Archie Brown, ed., *Contemporary Russian Politics: A Reader*, Oxford: Oxford University Press, 2001, p. 216.

23. see Neil Robinson, *Russia. A State of Uncertainty*, London: Routledge, 2002, pp. 77–90.

24. Joel Hellman, 'Winners Take All: The Politics of Partial Reform in Postcommunist Transitions', *World Politics*, vol. 50, no. 2, 1998, pp. 203–234.

25. Yitzhak Brudny, 'Continuity or Change in Russian Electoral Patterns? The December 1999–March 2000 Election Cycle' in Archie Brown, ed., *Contemporary Russian Politics: A Reader*, Oxford: Oxford University Press, 2001, p. 178.

26. Adolf Sprudzs, 'Rebuilding Democracy in Latvia: Overcoming a Dual Legacy' in Jan Zielonka, ed., *Democratic Consolidation in Eastern Europe*, Oxford: Oxford University Press, 2001 (vol. 1: *Institutional Engineering*), p. 163.

Bibliography

Ágh, Attila, 'The Hungarian Party System and Party Theory in the Transition of Central Europe', *Journal of Theoretical Politics*, vol. 6, no. 2, 1994, pp. 217–38.

—— ed., *The Emergence of East Central European Parliaments: The First Steps*, Budapest: Hungarian Centre of Democracy Studies, 1994.

—— 'Defeat and Success as Promoters of Party Change', *Party Politics*, vol. 3, no. 3, 1997, pp. 427–44.

—— *The Politics of Central Europe*, London, Thousand Oaks and New Delhi: Sage, 1998.

—— 'The Parliamentarization of the East Central European Parties: Party Discipline in the Hungarian Parliament, 1990–1996' in Shaun Bowler, David M. Farrell and Richard M. Katz, eds, *Party Discipline and Parliamentary Government*, Columbus: Ohio State University Press, 1999, pp. 167–88.

—— '1998 Elections in Hungary: Defeat as Promoter of Change for the HSP', *East European Politics and Societies*, vol. 14, no. 2, 2000, pp. 288–315.

Anaiban, Z.V. and Walker, E.W., 'On the Problem of Inter-Ethnic Conflict. The Republic of Tuva' in Leokadia Drobizheva, Rose Gottemoeller, Catherine McArdle Kelleher, and Lee Walker, eds, *Ethnic Conflict in the Post-Soviet World*, London: M.E. Sharpe, 1996, pp. 179–94.

Anderson, Benedict, *Imagined Communities: Reflections on the Origin and Spread of Nationalism*, London: Verso, 1983.

Andor, László, 'New Striker in Old Team. Parliamentary Elections in Hungary, May 1998', *Labour Focus on Eastern Europe*, no. 60, 1998, pp. 28–42.

Andreescu, Gabriel, 'Multiculturalism in Central Europe: Cultural Integration and Group Privacy: Group Privacy and Integration in the Case of the Roma', *RFE/RL East European Perspectives*, vol. 4, no. 3, 6 February 2002 (Part III).

Angelusz, Róbert and Tardos, Róbert, 'Electoral Participation in Hungary, 1990–1994' in Gábor Tóka and Zsolt Enyedi, eds, *Elections to the Hungarian National Assembly 1994. Analyses, Documents and Data*, Berlin: Sigma, 1999, pp. 168–97.

Arel, Dominique, 'Political Stability in Multinational Democracies' in Alain-G. Gagnon and James Tully, eds, *Multinational Democracies*, Cambridge: Cambridge University Press, 2001, pp. 65–89.

Arter, David, *Parties and Democracy in the Post-Soviet Republics: The Case of Estonia*, Aldershot: Dartmouth, 1996.

Ashley, Stephen, 'Ethnic Unrest during January', *Report on Eastern Europe*, vol. 1, no. 6, 1990, pp. 4–11.

Ashley, Stephen, 'Bulgaria', *Electoral Studies*, vol. 9, no. 4, 1990, pp. 312–18.

Auers, Daunis, 'Latvia's 2002 Elections – Dawn of a New Era?', *East European Constitutional Review*, vol. 11, no. 4/vol. 12, no. 1, fall 2002–winter 2003, pp. 106–10.

Baer, Josette, 'Boxing and Politics in Slovakia: "Meciarism" – Roots, Theory, Practice', *Democratization*, vol. 8, no. 2, summer 2001, pp. 97–116.

Bahry, Donna and Lipsmeyer, C., 'Economic Adversity and Public Mobilization in Russia', *Electoral Studies*, vol. 20, no. 3, September 2001, pp. 371–98.

Balázs, Magdolna and Enyedi, Zsolt, 'Hungarian Case Studies: The Alliance of Free Democrats and the Alliance of Young Democrats' in Paul G. Lewis, ed., *Party Structure and Organization in East-Central Europe*, Cheltenham: Edward Elgar, 1996, pp. 43–65.

Balzer, M.M. and Vinokurova, U.A., 'Ethnicity or Nationalism? The Sakha Republic (Yakutia)' in Leokadia Drobizheva, Rose Gottemoeller, Catherine McArdle Kelleher, and Lee Walker, eds, *Ethnic Conflict in the Post-Soviet World*, London: M.E. Sharpe, 1996, pp. 157–78.

Barany, Zoltan, 'Elections in Hungary' in Robert Furtak, ed., *Elections in Socialist States*, London: Harvester Wheatsheaf, 1990, pp. 71–97.

—— 'Bulgaria's Royal Elections', *Journal of Democracy*, vol. 13, no. 2, 2002, pp. 141–55.

—— *The East European Gypsies. Regime Change, Marginality, and Ethnopolitics*, Cambridge: Cambridge University Press, 2002.

Beer, Samuel, *Modern British Politics. A Study of Parties and Pressure Groups*, London: Faber and Faber, 1965.

Bell, John D., 'Democratization and Political Participation in "Postcommunist" Bulgaria' in Karen Dawisha and Bruce Parrott, eds, *Politics, Power, and the Struggle for Democracy in South-East Europe*, Cambridge: Cambridge University Press, 1997, pp. 353–402.

Bellin, Laura, 'Communist Party Consolidates Its Position on the Left', *RFE/RL Russian Election Report*, no. 8, 7 January 2000.

Benoit, Kenneth, 'Votes and Seats: The Hungarian Electoral Law and the 1994 Parliamentary Elections' in Gábor Tóka and Zsolt Enyedi, eds, *Elections to the Hungarian National Assembly 1994. Analyses, Documents and Data*, Berlin: Sigma, 1999, pp. 108–38.

—— 'Two Steps Forward, One Step Back: Electoral Coordination in the Hungarian Election of 1998', Paper presented to the 2000 Annual Meeting of the American Political Science Association, Mariott Wardman Park, 31 August–3 September 2000.

—— 'Like Déjà Vu All Over Again: The Hungarian parliamentary elections of 2002,' *The Journal of Communist Studies and Transition Politics*, vol. 18, no. 4, December 2002, pp. 119–33.

Bernstein, George, *Liberalism and Liberal Politics in Edwardian England*, London: Allen & Unwin, 1986.

Betz, Hans-George, 'The New Politics of Resentment: Radical Right-wing Populist Parties in Western Europe', *Comparative Politics*, vol. 25, no. 3, July 1993, pp. 413–27.

—— *Radical Right-wing Populism in Western Europe*, Basingstoke: Macmillan, 1994.

Bibic, A., 'The Emergence of Pluralism in Slovenia', *Communist and Post-Communist Studies*, vol. 26, no. 4, December 1993, pp. 367–86.

Bielasiak, Jacek, 'The Institutionalization of Electoral and Party Systems in Postcommunist States', *Comparative Politics*, vol. 34, no. 2, January 2002, pp. 189–210.

Bing, Rasmus and Szajkowski, Bogdan, 'Romania' in Bogdan Szajkowski, ed., *Political Parties of Eastern Europe, Russia and the Successor States*, Harlow, Essex: Longman, 1994, pp. 343–405.

Birch, A.H., *Representative and Responsible Government*, London: George Allen & Unwin, 1964.

—— *Representation*, London and Basingstoke: Macmillan Press, 1972.

Brich, Sarah 'Nomenklatura Democratization: Electoral Clientelism and Party Formation in Post-Soviet Ukraine', *Democratization*, vol. 4, no. 4, 1997, pp. 40–62.

—— 'Electoral Systems, Campaign Strategies, and Vote Choice in the Ukrainian Parliamentary and Presidential Elections of 1994', *Political Studies*, vol. 46, no. 1, 1998, pp. 96–114.

—— *Elections and Democratization in Ukraine*, Basingstoke: Macmillan Press, 2000.

—— 'The Effects of Mixed Electoral Systems in Eastern Europe', Paper presented at the 30th Annual Conference of the University Association for Contemporary European Studies, Budapest 7–9 April 2000.

—— 'Electoral Systems and Party Systems in Europe East and West' in Paul Lewis and Paul Webb, eds, *Pan-European Perspectives on Party Politics*, Leiden and Boston: Brill, 2003, pp. 9–34.

—— 'Women and Political Representation in Contemporary Ukraine' in Richard E. Matland and Kathleen Montgomery, eds, *Women's Access to Political Power in Post-Communist Europe*, Oxford: Oxford University Press (forthcoming 2003).

Birch, Sarah, Millard, Frances, Popescu, Marina and Williams, Kieran, *Embodying Democracy. Electoral System Design in Post-Communist Europe*, Basingstoke: Palgrave, 2002.

Bojcun, Marko, 'The Ukrainian Parliamentary Elections in March–April 1994,' *Europe-Asia Studies*, vol. 47, no. 2, March 1995, pp. 229–49.

Bozóki, András, 'Introduction' in András Bozóki, ed., *Intellectuals and Politics in Central Europe*, Budapest: Central European Press, 1999, pp. 1–15.

—— 'Hungary's Social-Democratic Turn', *East European Constitutional Review*, vol. 11, no. 3, summer 2002, pp. 80–6.

—— *The Roundtable Talks of 1989. The Genesis of Hungarian Democracy*, Budapest: Central European University Press, 2002.

Brass, Paul, *Ethnicity and Nationalism. Theory and Comparison*, London: Sage, 1991.

British Helsinki Human Rights Group, 'LATVIA 1993: The Elections–Democracy & Human Rights', http://www.bhhrg.org/CountryReport.asp?ReportID = 146&Country ID = 14.

Brown, Archie, 'Evaluating Russia's Democratization' in Archie Brown, ed., *Contemporary Russian Politics: A Reader*, Oxford: Oxford University Press, 2001, pp. 546–68.

Brudny, Yitzhak, 'Continuity or Change in Russian Electoral Patterns? The December 1999–March 2000 Election Cycle' in Archie Brown, ed., *Contemporary Russian Politics: A Reader*, Oxford: Oxford University Press, 2001, pp. 154–78.

Budge, Ian, Klingemann, Hans-Dieter, Volkens, Andrea, Bara, Judith, and Tanenbaum, Eric with others, *Mapping Policy Preferences. Estimates for Parties, Electors and Governments 1945–1998*, Oxford: Oxford University Press, 2001.

Budge, Ian, Robertson, David and Hearl Derek, eds, *Ideology, Strategy and Party Change: Spatial Analyses of Post-War Election Programmes in 19 Democracies*, Cambridge: Cambridge University Press, 1987.

Bugajski, Janusz, *Ethnic Politics in Eastern Europe. A Guide to Nationality Politics, Organizations, and Parties*, London: M.E. Sharpe, 1995.

Burke, Edmund, 'Speech to the Electors of Bristol' in B.W. Hill, ed., *Edmund Burke, Government Politics and Society*, London: Fontana, 1975, pp. 156–8.

Bútora, Martin and Bútorová, Zora, 'Slovakia's Democratic Awakening', *Journal of Democracy*, vol. 10, no. 1, January 1999, pp. 80–95.

Bútora, Martin and Demeš, Pavol, 'Civil Society Organizations in the 1998 Elections' in Martin Bútora, Grigorij Mesežnikov, Zora Bútorová and Sharon Fisher, eds, *The 1998 Parliamentary Elections and Democratic Rebirth in Slovakia*, Bratislava: Institute for Public Affairs, 1999, pp. 155–67.

Bútorová, Zora and Bútora, Martin, 'Political Parties, Value Orientations and Slovakia's Road to Independence' in Gordon Wightman, ed., *Party Formation in East-Central Europe*, Aldershot: Edward Elgar, 1995, pp. 107–33.

Bútora, Martin, Mesežnikov, Grigorij, Bútorová, Zora and Fisher, Sharon, eds, *The 1998 Parliamentary Elections and Democratic Rebirth in Slovakia*, Bratislava: Institute for Public Affairs, 1999.

Carey, Henry F., 'Irregularities or Rigging: The 1992 Romanian Parliamentary Elections', *East European Quarterly*, vol. XXIX, no. 1, March 1995, pp. 43–66.

Carter, April, *Democratic Reform in Yugoslavia. The Changing Role of the Party*, London: Frances Pinter, 1982.

Caul, Miki, 'Women's Representation in Parliament', *Party Politics*, vol. 5, no. 1, 1999, pp. 79–98.

Cheibub, Jose Antonio and Przeworski, Adam, 'Democracy, Elections, and Accountability for Economic Outcomes' in Adam Przeworski, Susan C. Stokes, and Bernard Manin, eds, *Democracy, Accountability, and Representation*, Cambridge: Cambridge University Press, 1999, pp. 222–49.

Chinn, Jeff and Truex, Lise, 'The Question of Citizenship in the Baltics', *Journal of Democracy*, vol. 7, no. 1, 1996, pp. 133–45.

Choe, Yonhyok, 'Institutional Trust and Electoral Turnout in New Democracies: A Comparative Study of Eastern and Central Europe', Paper presented at the First General Conference of the European Consortium for Political Research, University of Kent at Canterbury, September 2001.

Churchward, L.G., *Contemporary Soviet Government*, London: Routledge and Kegan Paul, 1968.

Clark, Terry D., Holscher, Stacy and Hyland, Lisa, 'The LDLP Faction in the Lithuanian Seimas, 1992–96', *Nationalities Papers*, vol. 27, no. 2, June 1999, pp. 227–46.

Cliff, Tony, *Lenin*, London: Pluto Press, 1975, vol. 1.

Cohen, Shari J., *Politics without a Past. The Absence of History in Postcommunist Nationalism*, London: Duke University Press, 1999.

Cole, Alistair and Campbell, Peter, *French Electoral Systems and Elections since 1789*, Aldershot: Gower, 1989.

Colton, Timothy J. and McFaul, Michael, 'Reinventing Russia's Party of Power: "Unity" and the 1999 Duma Election', *Post-Soviet Affairs*, vol. 16, no. 3, 2000, pp. 201–24.

Connor, Walter, *Socialism, Politics and Equality*, New York: Columbia University Press, 1979.

Converse, Philip E. and Pierce, Roy, *Political Representation in France*, Cambridge, Mass. and London: The Belknap Press of Harvard University Press, 1986.

'Constitution Watch. Bulgaria', *East European Constitutional Review*, vol. 2, no. 2, 1993, pp. 3–4.

'Constitution Watch. Slovenia', *East European Constitutional Review*, vol. 8, no. 3, summer 2000, pp. 39–40.

Cotta, Maurizio, 'Structuring the New Party Systems after the Dictatorship. Coalitions, Alliances, Fusions and Splits During the Transition and Post-transition Stages' in Geoffrey Pridham and Paul G. Lewis, eds, *Stabilising Fragile Democracies. Comparing New Party Systems in Southern and Eastern Europe*, London: Routledge, 1996, pp. 69–99.

Cox, Gary, *Making Votes Count. Strategic Coordination in the World's Electoral Systems*, Cambridge: Cambridge University Press, 1997.

Cox, Gary and McCubbins, Matthew, 'The Institutional Determinants of Economic Policy Outcomes' in Stephan Haggard and Matthew D. McCubbins, eds, *Presidents, Parliaments, and Policy*, Cambridge: Cambridge University Press, 2001, pp. 21–63.

Crawford, Keith, *East Central European Politics Today: From Chaos to Stability?* Manchester: Manchester University Press, 1996.

Csergo, Zsusza, 'Beyond Ethnic Division: Majority–Minority Debate about the Postcommunist State in Romania and Slovakia', *East European Politics and Societies*, vol. 16, no. 1, 2002, pp. 1–29.

Curry, Jane L. and Panków, Irena, 'Social Movements and Pluralist Theory: The Conundrum of Solidarity in Poland's Democratization' in Dirk Berg-Schlosser and Raivo Vetik, eds, *Perspectives on Democratic Consolidation in Central and Eastern Europe*, Boulder: East European Monographs, 2001, pp. 82–92.

Dangerfield, Martin, 'Ideology and the Czech Transformation: Neoliberal Rhetoric or Neoliberal Reality', *East European Politics and Societies*, vol. 11, no. 3, fall 1997, pp. 437–68.

Darden, Keith, 'Blackmail as a Tool of State Domination: Ukraine under Kuchma', *East European Constitutional Review*, vol. 10, nos 2/3, spring–summer 2001, pp. 67–71.

Datculescu, Petre, 'Romania: Parties and Issues after 1989' in Kay Lawson, Andrea Römmele, and Georgi Karasimeonov, eds, *Cleavages, Parties, and Voters. Studies from Bulgaria, the Czech Republic, Hungary, Poland, and Romania*, London: Praeger, 1999, pp. 169–84.

Dawisha, Karen and Deets, Stephen, 'Intended and Unintended Consequences of Elections in Russia and Postcommunist States', unpublished paper, 31 March 2002.

Deets, Stephen, 'Reconsidering East European Minority Policy: Liberal Theory and European Norms', *East European Politics and Societies*, vol. 16, no. 1, winter 2002, pp. 30–53.

Deletant, Dennis and Siani-Davies, Peter, 'The Romanian Elections of 1996', *Representation*, vol. 35, nos 2/3, 1998, pp. 155–67.

Diamond, Larry, 'Introduction: In Search of Consolidation' in Larry Diamond, Marc F. Plattner, Yun-han Chu, and Hung-mao Tien, eds, *Consolidating the Third Wave Democracies. Themes and Perspectives*, London: The Johns Hopkins University Press, 1997, pp. xiii–xlvii.

Diuk, Nadia and Gongadze, Myroslava, 'Post-Election Blues in Ukraine', *Journal of Democracy*, vol. 13, no. 4, 2002, pp. 157–66.

Dollar, David, Fisman, Raymond and Gatti, Roberta, 'Are Women Really the "Fairer" Sex? Corruption and Women in Government', *Journal of Economic Behavior and Organization*, vol. 46, 2001, pp. 423–29.

Domański, Henryk, 'Równouprawnienie, Stereotyp tradycyjnego podziału ról' in Anna Titkow and Henryk Domański, *Co to Znaczy Być Kobietą w Polsce*, Warsaw: Polska Akademia Nauk, 1995.

Duncan, Peter, 'Russia. Accommodating Ethnic Minorities' in Don McIver, ed., *The Politics of Multinational States*, London: Macmillan, 1999, pp. 63–83.

Duverger, Maurice, *Political Parties. Their Organization and Activity in the Modern State* (1951), New York: John Wiley & Sons, 1963.

Einhorn, Barbara, 'Democratization and Women's Movements in Central and Eastern Europe: Concepts of Women's Rights' in Valentine Moghadam, ed., *Democratic Reform and the Position of Women in Transitional Economies*, Oxford: Clarendon Press, 1993, pp. 48–74.

Ekiert, Grzegorz, 'Democratization Processes in East Central Europe', *British Journal of Political Science*, vol. 21, no. 3, July 1991, pp. 285–314.

Elster, Jon, 'Constitution Making in Eastern Europe: Rebuilding the Boat in the Open Sea', *Public Administration*, vol. 71, spring–summer 1993, pp. 169–217.

Enyedi, Zsolt, 'Organising a Subcultural Party in Eastern Europe: the Case of the Hungarian Christian Democrats', *Party Politics*, vol. 2, no. 3, 1996, pp. 377–96.

Epstein, Leon D., *Political Parties in Western Democracies*, New Brunswick and London: Transaction Publishers, 1980 (rev. ed.).

Ersson, Svante and Lane, Jan-Erik, 'Electoral Instability and Party System Change in Western Europe' in Paul Pennings and Jan-Erik Lane, eds, *Comparing Party System Change*, London: Routledge, 1998, pp. 23–39.

Farkas, E. János and Vajda, Agnes, 'Candidates for Parliament' in Gábor Tóka, ed., *The 1990 Election to the Hungarian National Assembly. Analyses, Documents and Data*, Berlin: Sigma, 1995, pp. 67–83.

Farrell, David, *Electoral Systems: A Comparative Introduction*, Basingstoke: Palgrave, 2001.

Fawn, Rick, 'Czech Attitudes Towards the Roma: "Expecting More of Havel's Country"?', *Europe-Asia Studies*, vol. 53, no. 8, 2001, pp. 1193–1219.

Fish, M. Steven, 'The Executive Deception: Superpresidentialism and the Degradation of Russian Politics' in Valerie Sperling, ed., *Building the Russian State. Institutional Crisis and the Quest for Democratic Governance*, Boulder: Westview Press, 2000, pp. 177–92.

—— 'The Dynamics of Democratic Erosion' in Richard D. Anderson Jr, M. Steven Fish, Stephen E. Hanson and Philip G. Roeder, *Post-Communism and the Theory of Democracy*, Princeton: Princeton University Press, 2001, pp. 54–95.

Fish, M. Steven and Brooks, Robin S., 'Bulgarian Democracy's Organizational Weapon', *East European Constitutional Review*, vol. 9, no. 3, summer 2000, pp. 63–71.

Fitzmaurice, John, 'The Slovak Elections of 25th and 26th September 1998', *Electoral Studies*, vol. 18, no. 2, June 1999, pp. 291–5.

Flatan, Lubomir and Krivy, Vladimir, 'Slovakia: Changes in Public Administration' in Emil J. Kirchner, ed., *Decentralization and Transition in the Visegrad. Poland, Hungary, the Czech Republic and Slovakia*, Basingstoke and New York: Macmillan and St. Martin's Press, 1999, pp. 102–31.

Fowler, Brigid, 'Fuzzing Citizenship, Nationalising Political Space: A Framework for Interpreting the Hungarian 'Status Law' as a New Form of Kin-state Policy in Central and Eastern Europe', ESRC One Europe or Several? Programme Working Paper 40/02, Sussex European Institute, 2002.

—— 'Hungary's 2002 Parliamentary Election', ESRC 'One Europe or Several?' Programme, Briefing Note 2/02, May 2002.

Franklin, Mark N., 'Electoral Participation' in Lawrence LeDuc, Richard G. Niemi and Pippa Norris, eds, *Comparing Democracies. Elections and Voting in Global Perspective*, London: Sage, 1996, pp. 216–35.

Franklin, Mark, Lyons, Patrick and Marsh, Michael, 'The Turnout Paradox: Why Changing Electoral Experiences Trump Changing Social Characteristics in Driving Voter Turnout in Advanced Democracies', Paper presented to the First General Conference of the European Consortium for Political Research, University of Kent, Canterbury, September 2001.

Friedgut, Theodore H., *Political Participation in the USSR*, Princeton: Princeton University Press, 1979.

Funk, Nanette and Mueller, Magda, eds, *Gender Politics and Post-Communism*, London and New York: Routledge, 1993.

Furtak, Robert K., ed., *Elections in Socialist States*, New York and London: Harvester Wheatsheaf, 1990.

Gallagher Michael and Marsh, Michael, *Candidate Selection in Comparative Perspective*, London: Sage, 1988.

Gallagher, Tom, 'Romania: The Disputed Election of 1990', *Parliamentary Affairs*, vol. 44, no. 1, 1991, pp. 79–93.

—— '*Vatra Romaneasca* and Resurgent Nationalism in Romania', *Ethnic and Racial Studies*, vol. 15, no. 4, October 1992, pp. 570–98.

—— 'Ethnic Tension in Cluj', *RFE/RL Research Report*, vol. 2, no. 9, 26 February 1993, pp. 27–33.

—— *Romania after Ceauşescu. The Politics of Intolerance*, Edinburgh: Edinburgh University Press, 1995.

—— 'Nationalism and Post-Communist Politics: The Party of Romanian National Unity, 1990–1996' in Lavinia Stan, ed., *Romania in Transition*, Aldershot: Dartmouth, 1997, pp. 25–47.

—— 'Nationalism and Romanian Political Culture in the 1990s' in Duncan Light and David Phinnemore, eds, *Post-Communist Romania. Coming to Terms with Transition*, Basingstoke: Palgrave, 2001, pp. 104–24.

Ganev, Venelin, 'Bulgaria: The (Ir)relevance of Post-communist Constitutionalism' in Jan Zielonka, ed., *Democratic Consolidation in Eastern Europe*, Oxford: Oxford University Press, 2001 (vol. 1, *Institutional Engineering*), pp. 186–211.

Gelman, Vladimir, 'Electoral Democracy in Russia', *Russia on Russia*, Issue 3, October 2000, pp. 63–8.

—— 'Subnational Institutions in Contemporary Russia' in Neil Robinson, ed., *Institutions and Political Change in Russia*, Basingstoke: Palgrave-Macmillan, 2000, pp. 85–105.

Gel'man, Vladimir and Elizarov, Vitalii, 'Russia's Transition and Founding Elections' in Vladimir Gel'man and Grigorii Golosov, eds, *Elections in Russia, 1993–1996. Analyses, Documents and Data*, Berlin: Sigma, 1999, pp. 19–46.

Getty, J. Arch, 'State and Society under Stalin: Constitutions and Elections in the 1930s', *Slavic Review*, vol. 50, no. 1, 1991, pp. 26–35.

Giatzidis, Emil, *An Introduction to Post-communist Bulgaria. Political, Economic and Social Transformations*, Manchester: Manchester University Press, 2002.

Glinski, Dmitri, 'Russia and Its Muslims: The Politics of Identity at the International-Domestic Frontier', *East European Constitutional Review*, vol. 11, nos 1/2, winter-spring 2002, pp. 71–83.

Golosov, Grigorii V., 'Who Survives? Party Origins, Organizational Development, and Electoral Performance in Post-communist Russia' in Richard Hofferbert, ed., *Parties and Democracy*, Oxford: Blackwell Publishers, 1998, pp. 89–121.

Golosov, Grigorii, 'Political Parties, Electoral Systems and Women's Representation in the Regional Legislative Assemblies of Russia, 1995–1998', *Party Politics*, vol. 7, no. 1, 2001, pp. 45–68.

Gortat, Radislawa, *Ukraińskie Wybory. Elecja parlamentarna '98 a partie polityczne*, Warsaw: Fundacja Polska Praca, 1998.

Gould, John and Szomolányi, Soňa, 'Bridging the Chasm in Slovakia', *Transitions*, vol. 4, no. 6, November 1997, pp. 70–6.

Gray, Mark and Caul, Miki, 'Declining Voter Turnout in Advanced Industrial Democracies, 1950 to 1957. The Effects of Declining Group Mobilization', *Comparative Political Studies*, vol. 33, no. 9, November 2000, pp. 1091–1122.

Grofman, Bernard, Mikkel, Evald and Taagepera, Rein, 'Electoral System Changes in Estonia, 1989–1993', *Journal of Baltic Studies*, vol. 30, no. 3, 1999, p. 227–49.

Grumm, John, 'Theories of Electoral Systems', *Midwest Journal of Political Science*, vol. 2, no. 4, November 1958, pp. 357–76.

Grzymala-Busse, Anna, *Redeeming the Communist Past. The Regeneration of Communist Parties in East Central Europe*, Cambridge: Cambridge University Press, 2002.

Gunther, Richard, Montero, José Ramón and Linz, Juan J., *Political Parties. Old Concepts and New Challenges*, Oxford: Oxford University Press, 2002.

Hafner, Danica Fink, 'Political Modernization in Slovenia in the 1980s and the Early 1990s', *The Journal of Communist Studies*, vol. 8, no. 4, December 1992, pp. 210–26.

Hahn, W. 'Electoral "Choice" in the Soviet Bloc', *Problems of Communism*, vol. 36, no. 2, March–April, 1987, pp. 29–39.

Hainsworth, Paul, 'Introduction. The Cutting Edge: The Extreme Right in Post-War Western Europe and the USA' in Paul Hainsworth, ed., *The Extreme Right in Europe and the USA*, London: Pinter Publishers, 1992.

Hallik, Klara, 'Ethnopolitical Conflict in Estonia' in Leokadia Drobizheva, Rose Gottemoeller, Catherine McArdle Kelleher, and Lee Walker, eds, *Ethnic Conflict in the Post-Soviet World*, London: M.E. Sharpe, 1996, pp. 87–108.

Hanley, Seán, 'Towards Breakthrough or Breakdown? The Consolidation of KSČM as a Neo-Communist Successor Party in the Czech Republic', *The Journal of Communist Studies and Transition Politics*, vol. 17, no. 3, 2001, pp. 96–116.

Harding, Neil, *Lenin's Political Thought*, London: Macmillan, 1977.

Harper, M.A.G., 'The 2001 Parliamentary and Presidential Elections in Bulgaria', *Electoral Studies*, vol. 22, issue 2, June 2003, pp. 335–44.

Haughton, Tim, 'Does Slovakia Need a Facelift?', *Central European Review*, vol. 3, no. 20, 4 June 2001.

—— 'HZDS: The Ideology, Organisation and Support Base of Slovakia's Most Successful Party', *Europe-Asia Studies*, vol. 53, no. 5, July 2001, pp. 745–70.

—— 'Vladimir Mečiar and his Role in the 1994–1998 Slovak Coalition Government', *Europe-Asia Studies*, vol. 54, no. 8, December 2002, pp. 1319–38.

—— 'Explaining the Limited Success of the communist-sucessor Left in Slovaika: The Case of the Democratic Left (SDL')' *Party Politics*, 2004 (forthcoming).

Heinen, Jacqueline, 'Polish Democracy is a Masculine Democracy', *Women's Studies International Forum*, vol. 15, no. 1, 1992, pp. 129–38.

Heinrich, Hans-Georg, *Hungary, Politics and Economics*, London: Frances Pinter, 1986.

Hellman, Joel S., 'Winners Take All: The Politics of Partial Reform in Postcommunist Transitions', *World Politics*, vol. 50, no. 2, 1998, pp. 203–34.

Hellman, Joel, Jones, Geraint and Kaufman, Daniel, 'Seize the State, Seize the Day: An Empirical Analysis of State Capture and Corruption in Transition Economies', *World Bank Policy Research Working Paper 2444*, World Bank: Washington, DC., 2000, pp. 1–41.

Henderson, Karen, 'Czechoslovakia: the Failure of Consensus Politics and the Break-up of the Federation', *Regional and Federal Studies*, vol. 5, no. 2, 1995, pp. 111–33.

—— 'Problems of Democratic Consolidation in the Slovak Republic', *Society and Economy in Central and Eastern Europe*, no. 3, 1999, pp. 141–78.

—— 'The Path to Democratic Consolidation in the Czech Republic and Slovakia: Divergence or Convergence' in Geoffrey Pridham and Attila Ágh, eds, *Prospects for Democratic Consolidation in East-Central Europe*, Manchester: Manchester University Press, 2001, pp. 205–37.

—— *Slovakia. The Escape from Invisibility*, London: Routledge, 2002.

Henig, Stanley and Pinder, John, eds, *European Political Parties*, London: George Allen & Unwin Ltd, 1969.

Herron, Eric S., 'Mixed Electoral Rules and Party Strategies. Responses to Incentives by Ukraine's Rukh and Russia's Yabloko', *Party Politics*, vol. 8, no. 6, November 2002, pp. 719–33.

Heywood, Andrew, *Political Ideas and Concepts*, London: Macmillan, 1994.

Hill, R. J., 'Continuity and Change in USSR Supreme Soviet Elections', *British Journal of Political Science*, vol. 11, no. 1,1972, pp. 47–67.

Holmes, Stephen, 'Designing Electoral Regimes', *East European Constitutional Review*, vol. 3, no. 2, spring 1994, pp. 39–41.

Holmstedt, Margareta and Schou, Tove-Lise, 'Sweden and Denmark 1945–1982: Election Programmes in the Scandinavian Setting' in Ian Budge, David Robertson, and Derek

Hearl, *Ideology, Strategy and Party Change: Spatial Analyses of Post-War Election Programmes in 19 Democracies*, Cambridge: Cambridge University Press, 1987, pp. 177–206.

Höpken, Wolfgang, 'Elections in Yugoslavia' in Robert Furtak, ed., *Elections in Socialist States*, New York: Harvester Wheatsheaf, 1990, pp. 118–42.

Horowitz, Donald, *Ethnic Groups in Conflict*, Berkeley: University of California Press, 1985.

Huang, Mel, 'Estonia: Savisaar Key To Low Estonian Turnout', RFE/RL 18 March 1999.

—— 'Latvia's Marching Season', *Central European Review*, vol. 0, no. 25, 26 March 1999.

Ignazi, Piero, 'The Silent Counter-revolution. Hypotheses on the Emergence of Extreme Right Parties in Europe', *European Journal of Political Research*, vol. 22, 1992, pp. 3–34.

Illner, Michael, 'Territorial Government in the Czech Republic' in Emil J. Kirchner, ed., *Decentralization and Transition in the Visegrad. Poland, Hungary, the Czech Republic and Slovakia*, Basingstoke and New York: Macmillan and St. Martin's Press, 1999, pp. 80–101.

Ilonszki, Gabriella, 'Introduction to Research Areas and Research Findings with Respect to Female Politicians in Hungary', Paper presented at the Conference on Political Participation of Women in Post-socialist ECE-countries (German Political Science Association), Berlin, 28–30 June 2002.

—— 'Legislative Recruitment: Personnel and Institutional Development in Hungary, 1990–94' in Gábor Tóka and Zsolt Enyedi, eds, *The 1990 Election to the Hungarian National Assembly. Analyses, Documents and Data*, Berlin: Sigma, 1995, pp. 82–107.

—— 'Parties and Parliamentary Party Groups in the Making, Hungary 1989–1997' in Knut Heidar and Ruud Koole, eds, *Parliamentary Party Groups in European Democracies. Political Parties Behind Closed Doors*, London: Routledge, 2000, pp. 214–30.

—— 'Consolidation of Hungarian Democracy' in Dirk Berg-Schlosser and Raivo Vetik, eds, *Perspectives on Democratic Consolidation in Central and Eastern Europe*, Boulder: East European Monographs, 2001, pp. 93–106.

Innes, Abby, 'The Breakup of Czechoslovakia: The Impact of Party Development on the Separation of the State', *East European Politics and Societies*, vol. 11, no. 3, fall 1997, pp. 393–435.

—— *Czechoslovakia. The Short Good-Bye*, New Haven: Yale University Press, 2001.

—— 'Party Competition in Post-Communist Europe – The Great Electoral Lottery', *Comparative Politics*, vol. 35, no. 1, October 2002, pp. 85–104.

Ishiyama, John T., 'Strange Bedfellows: Explaining Political Cooperation Between Communist Successor Parties and Nationalists in Eastern Europe', *Nations and Nationalism*, vol. 4, no. 1, 1998, pp. 61–85.

—— 'Representational Mechanisms and Ethnopolitics: Evidence from Transitional Democracies in Eastern Europe', *East European Quarterly*, vol. XXXIII, no. 2, June 1999, pp. 251–79.

Ishiyama, John and Bozóki, András, 'Adaptation and Change: Characterizing the Survival Strategies of the Communist Successor Parties', *The Journal of Communist Studies and Transition Politics*, vol. 17, no. 3, 2001, pp. 32–51.

Ishiyama, John T. and Breuning, Marijke, *Ethnopolitics in the New Europe*, London: Lynne Rienner, 1998.

Ishiyama, John and Kennedy, Ryan, 'Superpresidentialism and Political Party Development in Russia, Ukraine, Armenia and Kyrgyzstan', *Europe-Asia Studies*, vol. 53, no. 8, 2001, pp. 1177–91.

Jackman, Robert, 'Political Institutions and Voter Turnout in Industrial Democracies', *American Political Science Review*, vol. 81, 1987, pp. 405–23.

Jackson, George, *Comintern and Peasant in East Europe 1919–1930*, New York: Columbia University Press, 1966, pp. 40–8.

Jaquette, Jane S. and Wolchik, Sharon, 'Women and Democratization in Latin America and Central and Eastern Europe' in Jane S. Jaquette and Sharon Wolchik, eds, *Women and Democracy. Latin America and Central and Eastern Europe*, Baltimore and London: The Johns Hopkins University Press, 1999, pp. 1–28.

Jeszensky, Géza, 'More Bosnias? National and Ethnic Tensions in the Post-Communist World', *East European Quarterly*, vol. XXXI, no. 3, September 1997, pp. 283–98.

Jónasdóttir, Anna G., 'On the Concept of Interest, Women's Interests, and the Limitations of Interest Theory' in Kathleen B. Jones and Anna G. Jónasdóttir, eds, *The Political Interests of Gender. Developing Theory and Research with a Feminist Face*, London, Newbury Park and New Delhi: Sage, 1985, pp. 33–65.

Jordan, Jeffrey M., 'Patronage and Corruption in the Czech Republic (Part I)', *RFE/RL East European Perspectives*, vol. 4, no. 4, 20 February 2002.

—— 'Patronage and Corruption in the Czech Republic (Part II)', *RFE/RL East European Perspectives*, vol. 4, no. 5, 6 March 2002.

Judge, David, *Representation. Theory and Practice in Britain*, London: Routledge, 1999.

Judge, David and Ilonszki, Gabriella, 'Member-Constituency Linkages in the Hungarian parliament', *Legislative Studies Quarterly*, vol. XX, no. 2, May 1995, pp. 161–76.

Juza, Peter, 'The Formation of the Coalition "Common Choice" and Its Election Results' in Soňa Szomolányi and Grigorij Mesežnikov, eds, *The Slovak Path of Transition – to Democracy?*, Bratislava: Slovak Political Science Association & Interlingua, 1994, pp. 220–40.

Kaldor, Mary, 'Yugoslavia and the New Nationalism', *New Left Review*, no. 197, 1993, pp. 96–112.

Kanev, Dobrin, 'Political Culture and the Prospects for Democracy' in Georgi Karasimeonov, ed., *The Bulgarian Grand National Assembly and the 1991 Election to the Bulgarian National Assembly. Analyses, Documents and Data*, Berlin: Sigma, 1997, pp. 59–78.

Karasimeonov, Georgi, 'Sea-changes in the Bulgarian Party system', *The Journal of Communist Studies*, vol. 9, no. 3, 1993, pp. 272–8.

—— 'The Transition to Democracy' in Georgi Karasimeonov, ed., *The 1990 Election to the Bulgarian Grand National Assembly and the 1991 Election to the Bulgarian National Assembly. Analyses, Documents and Data*, Berlin: Sigma, 1997, pp. 10–22.

Kardos, Gábor, 'Human Rights: A Matter of Individual or Collective Concern?' in Istvan Pogony, *Human Rights in Eastern Europe*, Aldershot: Edward Elgar, 1995, pp. 169–82.

Karklins, Rasma, *Ethnopolitics and the Transition to Democracy: the Collapse of the USSR and Latvia*, Baltimore: the Johns Hopkins University Press, 1994.

Kassayie, Berhanu, 'The Evolution of Social Democracy in Reforming Bulgaria', *The Journal of Communist Studies and Transition Politics*, vol. 14, no. 3, September 1998, pp. 109–25.

Katz, Richard and Mair, Peter, 'Changing Models of Party Organisation and Party Democracy: The Emergence of the Cartel Party', *Party Politics*, vol. 1, no. 1, January 1995, pp. 5–28.

Keating, Michael, 'So Many Nations, So Few States: Territory and Nationalism in the Global Era' in Alain-G. Gagnon and James Tully, eds, *Multinational Democracies*, Cambridge: Cambridge University Press, 2001, pp. 39–64.

Kempny, Marian, 'Between Tradition and Politics: Intellectuals after Communism' in András Bozóki, ed., *Intellectuals and Politics in Central Europe*, Budapest: Central European Press, 1999, pp. 151–65.

Kennedy, Michael D., *Professionals, Power and Solidarity in Poland*, Cambridge: Cambridge University Press, 1991.

Kionka, Riina, 'How Democratic Will the Estonian Elections Be?', *Report on the USSR*, vol. 2, no. 9, 2 March 1990, pp. 21–3.

Kirchheimer, Otto, 'The Transformation of Western European Party Systems' in Joseph LaPalombara and Myron Wiener, eds, *Political Parties and Political Development*, Princeton: Princeton University Press, 1966, pp. 177–200.

Kiss, Csilla, 'From Liberalism to Conservatism: The Federation of Young Democrats in Post-Communist Hungary', *East European Politics and Societies*, vol. 16, no. 3, fall 2002, pp. 739–63.

Kiss, Yudit, 'System Changes, Export-Oriented Growth and Women in Hungary', *Europe-Asia Studies*, vol. 55, no. 1, January 2003, pp. 1–37.

Kitschelt, Herbert with Anthony McGann, *The Radical Right in Western Europe. A Comparative Analysis*, Ann Arbor: the University of Michigan Press, 1997.

Kitschelt, Herbert, Mansfeldova, Zdenka, Markowski, Radosław and Tóka, Gábor, *Post-Communist Party Systems. Competition, Representation and Inter-Party Competition*, Cambridge: Cambridge University Press, 1999.

Klingemann, Hans-Dieter, 'Election Programmes in West Germany: 1949–1980, Explorations in the Nature of Political Controversy' in Ian Budge, David Robertson, and Derek Hearl, *Ideology, Strategy and Party Change: Spatial Analyses of Post-War Election Programmes in 19 Democracies*, Cambridge: Cambridge University Press, 1987, pp. 294–323.

Klingemann, Hans-Dieter, Hofferbert, Richard and Budge, Ian, *Parties, Policies and Democracy*, Boulder: Westview Press, 1994.

Klíma, Michal, 'Consolidation and Stabilization of the Party System in the Czech Republic' in Richard Hofferbert, ed., *Parties and Democracy*, Oxford: Blackwell Publishers, 1998, pp. 70–88.

Kolarska-Bobińska, Lena, *Aspirations, Values and Interests. Poland 1989–94*, Warsaw, IFiS, 1994.

Kopecký, Petr, 'Developing Party Organisations in East-Central Europe: What Type of Party is Likely to Emerge?', *Party Politics*, vol. 1, no. 4, 1995, pp. 515–34.

—— 'The Limits of Whips and Watchdogs. Parliamentary Parties in the Czech Republic' in Knut Heidar and Ruud Koole, eds, *Parliamentary Party Groups in European Democracies. Political Parties behind Closed Doors*, London: Routledge, 2000, pp. 177–94.

—— *Parliaments in the Czech and Slovak Republics. Party competition and Parliamentary Institutionalization*, Aldershot: Ashgate, 2001.

Kopecký, Petr and Mudde, Cas, 'The 1998 Parliamentary and Senate Elections in the Czech Republic', *Electoral Studies*, vol. 18, no. 3, September 1999, pp. 415–24.

Kornai, Janos, *The Road to a Free Economy*, New York: WW Norton & Company, 1990.

Kostelecký, Tomáš, *Political Parties after Communism. Developments in East-Central Europe*, Baltimore: The Johns Hopkins Press, 2002.

Kostova, Dobrinka, 'Parliamentary Elections in Bulgaria, October 1991', *The Journal of Communist Studies*, vol. 8, no. 1, 1992, pp. 196–203.

—— 'Women in Bulgaria. Changes in Employment and Political Involvement' in Jane S. Jaquette and Sharon Wolchik, eds, *Women and Democracy. Latin America and Central and Eastern Europe*, Baltimore and London: The Johns Hopkins University Press, 1999, pp. 203–21.

Kovács, Zoltán and Dinsdale, Alan, 'Whither East European Democracies? The Geography of the 1994 Hungarian Parliamentary Election', *Political Geography*, vol. 17, no. 4, 1998, pp. 437–58.

Kovats, Martin, 'The Roma and Minority self-government in Hungary', *Immigrants and Minorities*, vol. 15, no. 1, 1996, pp. 42–58.

Kraus, Michael and Stanger, Allison, *Irreconcilable Differences?*, Cambridge: Cambridge University Press 2000.

Krupavičius, Algis, 'The Post-communist Transition and Institutionalization of Lithuania's Parties' in Richard Hofferbert, ed., *Parties and Democracy*, Oxford: Blackwell Publishers, 1998, pp. 43–69.

—— 'Party Systems in Central East Europe: Dimensions of Social Stability' in Dirk Berg-Schlosser and Raivo Vetik, eds, *Perspectives on Democratic Consolidation in Central and Eastern Europe*, Boulder: East European Monographs, 2001a, pp. 141–64.

—— 'Political Results of the Seimas Election of 1996 and Formation of the Cabinet: The Third Turnover' in Algis Krupavičius, ed., *Lithuania's Seimas Election 1996: The Third Turnover. Analyses, Documents and Data*, Berlin: Sigma, 2001b, pp. 133–80.

—— 'Role of the Left-wing Parties in Transition to and in Consolidation of Democracy: A Case of Lithuania', Paper presented to the First General ECPR Conference, University of Kent at Canterbury, 6–8 September 2001c.

Krupavičius, Algis and Matonytė, Irmina, 'Women's Political Recruitment and Representation in Lithuania', *Viešosios Politikos Studijos*, vol. 1, no. 1, 2001, pp. 5–32.

Kuzio, Taras, 'Rukh-1 to Rukh-2: Yushchenko's Our Ukraine', RFE/RL Newsline, vol. 6, no. 54, Part II, 21 March 2002, Endnote.

—— 'Loser Takes All: Ukrainian President Coopts Parliament', RFE/RL Newsline, vol. 6, no. 100, Part I, 30 May 2002, Endnote.

Kymlicka, Will and Opalski, Magda eds, *Can Liberal Pluralism be Exported? Western Political Theory and Ethnic Relations in Eastern Europe*, Oxford: Oxford University Press, 2001.

Kynev, Alexander, 'The Role of Political Parties in Russia's 2002 Regional Elections, *Russia and Eurasia Review*, vol. 2, issue 8, 15 April 2003, www.jamestown.org/authors/rer_alexander_kynev.htm.

LaFont, Suzanne, 'One Step Forward, Two Steps Back: Women in the Post-communist States', *Communist and Post-Communist Studies*, vol. 34, 2001, pp. 203–20.

Lane, David, *Politics and Society in the USSR*, London: Martin Robertson, 1978 (2nd edn).

—— *State and Politics in the USSR*, New York: New York University Press, 1985.

Lane, Jan-Erik and Ersson, Svante, *Politics and Society in Western Europe*, London: Sage, 1987.

Langewiesche, Dieter, *Liberalism in Germany*, Basingstoke: Macmillan, 2000.

Lankina, Tomila, 'Local Government and Ethnic and Social Activism in Russia' in Archie Brown, ed., *Contemporary Russian Politics: A Reader*, Oxford: Oxford University Press, 2001, pp. 398–411.

Lawson, Kay, 'Political Parties and Linkage' in Kay Lawson, *Political Parties and Linkage: A Comparative Perspective*, New Haven: Yale University Press, 1980, pp. 3–24.

Lebovič, Peter, 'Political Aspects of the Election Law Amendments' in Martin Bútora, Grigorij Mesežnikov, Zora Bútorová and Sharon Fisher, eds, *The 1998 Parliamentary Elections and Democratic Rebirth in Slovakia*, Bratislava: Institute for Public Affairs, 1999, pp. 38–47.

Lengyel, László, 'The Character of Political Parties in Hungary (Autumn 1989)' in András Bozóki, András Körösenyi, and George Schöpflin, eds, *Post-Communist Transition. Emerging Pluralism in Hungary*, London: Pinter Publishers, 1992, pp. 30–44.

Lentini, Peter, 'Elections and Political Order in Russia: The 1993 Elections to the State Duma', *The Journal of Communist Studies and Transition Politics*, vol. 10, no. 2, June 1994, pp. 151–92.

—— 'Electoral Associations in the 1993 Elections to the Russian State Duma', *The Journal of Communist Studies and Transition Politics*, vol. 10, no. 4, December 1994, pp. 1–36.

Lewis, Paul G., *Political Parties in Post-Communist Eastern Europe*, London: Routledge, 2000.

Lieven, Anatol, *The Baltic Revolution: Estonia, Latvia, Lithuania and the Path to Independence*, New Haven: Yale University Press, 1994.

Lijphart, Arend, 'Democracies, Forms, Performance and Constitutional Engineering', *European Journal of Political Research*, vol. 25, 1994, pp. 1–17.

Linnart, Mart and Kand, Villu, 'Estonia: Third Parliamentary Poll Since 1991 Determines Future Coalition', RFE/RL Daily Newsline Part II, Endnote, 5 March 1999.

Linz, Juan and Stepan, Alfred, *Problems of Democratic Transition and Consolidation. Southern Europe, South America, and Post-Communist Europe*, London: Johns Hopkins University Press, 1996.

Lipset, S.M., *Political Man. The Social Bases of Politics*, New York: Anchor Books, 1963.

Lipset, S.M., 'The Indispensability of Parties', *Journal of Democracy*, vol. 11, 2000, pp. 48–55.

Lipset, S.M. and Rokkan, Stein, 'Cleavage Structures, Party Systems and Voter Alignments: An Introduction' in S.M. Lipset and S. Rokkan, eds, *Party Systems and Voter Alignments*, New York: Free Press, 1967, pp. 1–64.

Loewenburg, G., 'The New Political Leadership of Central Europe: The Example of the New Hungarian National Assembly' in Thomas F. Remington, ed., *Parliaments in Transition. The New Legislative Politics in the Former USSR and Eastern Europe*, Boulder: Westview Press, 1994, pp. 29–53.

Lomax, Bill, 'The 1998 Elections in Hungary: Third Time Lucky for the Young Democrats', *The Journal of Communist Studies and Transition Politics*, vol. 15, no. 2, June 1999, pp. 110–25.

Long, Kristi, *We all fought for freedom: Women in Poland's Solidarity Movement*, Boulder, Colorado: Westview Press, 1996.

Lovell, D.W., 'Trust and the Politics of Post-Communism', *Communist and Post-Communist Studies*, vol. 34, 2001, pp. 27–38.

Lovenduski, Joni and Norris, Pippa, eds, *Gender and Party Politics*, London: Sage 1993.

Lovenduski, Joni and Woodall, Jean, *Politics and Society in Eastern Europe*, Basingstoke: Macmillan, 1987.

Lukin, Alexander, 'Electoral Democracy or Clanism?' in Archie Brown, ed., *Contemporary Russian Politics: A Reader*, Oxford: Oxford University Press, 2001, pp. 530–45.

Lukošaitis, Alvidas, The Context of Parliamentary Elections 2000: The Experience and Perspectives of Coalition Politics in Lithuania' in *Lithuanian Political Science Yearbook 2000*, Vilnius: Institute of International Relations and Political Science, 2001, pp. 151–76.

Maier, Sylvia, 'Are the Baltic States Living up to their International Legal Obligations?', *East European Human Rights Review*, vol. 4, no. 1, 1998, pp. 1–52

Mainwaring, Scott and Scully, Timothy R., 'Introduction: Party Systems in Latin America' in Scott Mainwaring and Timothy Scully, eds, *Building Democratic Institutions. Party Systems in Latin America*, Stanford: Stanford University Press, 1995, pp. 1–34.

Mair, Peter, 'Party Systems and Structures of Competition' in Lawrence LeDuc, Richard Niemi and Pippa Norris, eds, *Comparing Democracies. Elections and Voting in Global Perspective*, London: Sage, 1996, pp. 89–105.

Mair, Peter and Bartolini, S., *Identity, Competition and Electoral Availability: The Stabilisation of European Electorates 1885–1985*, Cambridge: Cambridge University Press, 1990.

Mallok, Katarina, 'Frauen in den politischen Parteien der Slowakei', Paper presented to the conference on Political Participation of Women in Post-socialist ECE-countries, German Political Science Association, Berlin, 28–30 June 2002.

Malloy, Tove, 'The "Politics of Accommodation" in the Council of Europe After 1989: National Minorities and Democratization', PhD thesis, Department of Government, University of Essex, 2002.

Malová, Darina, 'Slovakia', *European Journal of Political Research*, vol. 26, nos 3–4, 1994, pp. 413–21.

—— 'The National Council of the Slovak Republic: Between Democratic Transition and National State-Building', *Journal of Legislative Studies*, vol. 2, no. 1, 1996, pp. 108–32.

Malová, Darina and Krause, Kevin Deegan, 'Parliamentary party groups in Slovakia' in Knut Heidar and Ruud Koole, eds, *Parliamentary Party Groups in European Democracies. Political Parties Behind Closed Doors*, London: Routledge, 2000, pp. 194–213.

March, Luke, *The Communist Party in Post-Soviet Russia*, Manchester: Manchester University Press, 2002.

Markowski, Radosław, 'Democratic Consolidation and Accountability: News from Eastern and Central European Democracies' in Radoslaw Markowski and Edmund Wnuk-Lipiński, eds, *Transformative Paths in Central and Eastern Europe*, Warsaw: Institute of Political Studies, Polish Academy of Science and Friedrich Ebert Foundation, 2001, pp. 47–72.

—— 'Party System Institutionalization in New Democracies: Poland – A Trend-Setter with no Followers' in Paul G. Lewis, ed., *Party Development and Democratic Change in Post-Communist Europe*, London: Frank Cass, 2001, pp. 55–77.

Markowski, Radosław, 'Milcząca Większość – O Bierności Politycznej Społeczeństwa Polskiego' in Stanisław Gebethner, ed., *Polska scena polityczna a wybory*, Warsaw: Fundacja Inicjatyw Społecznych 'Polska w Europie', 1993, pp. 57–86.

Marx, Karl, 'The Communist Manifesto', in Robert C. Tucker, ed., *The Marx-Engels Reader*, New York: W.W. Norton, 1972, pp. 331–62.

—— 'The Civil War in France' in Robert C. Tucker, ed., *The Marx-Engels Reader*, New York: W.W. Norton, 1972, pp. 526–77.

Mastropaolo, Alfo and Slater, Martin, 'Italy 1946–1979: Ideological Distances and Party Movements' in Ian Budge, David Robertson, and Derek Hearl, *Ideology, Strategy and Party Change: Spatial Analyses of Post-War Election Programmes in 19 Democracies*, Cambridge: Cambridge University Press, 1987, pp. 345–68.

Matland, Richard E., 'Women's Legislative Representation in National Legislatures: A Comparison of Democracies in Developed and Developing Countries', *Legislative Studies Quarterly*, vol. 28, no. 1, 1998, pp. 109–25.

—— 'Institutional Variables Affecting Female Representation in National Legislatures: The Case of Norway', *Journal of Politics*, vol. 55, no. 3, 1993, pp. 737–55.

—— 'Legislative Recruitment: A General Model and Discussion of Issues of Special Relevance to Women' in Richard E. Matland and Kathleen Montgomery, eds, *Women's Access to Political Power in Post-Communist* Europe, Oxford: Oxford University Press (forthcoming 2003).

Matland, Richard E and Studlar, Donley T., 'The Contagion of Women Candidates in Single-Member district and Proportional Representation Electoral Systems: Canada and Norway', *Journal of Politics*, vol. 58, no. 3, August 1996, pp. 707–33.

Marchant, Oliver, 'Austria and the "Fourth Way"', *Capital and Class*, Issue 73, winter 2000, pp. 7–14.

Mason, David, 'Attitudes toward the Market and Political Participation in the Post-communist States', *Slavic Review*, vol. 51, no. 2, summer 1995, pp. 395–402.

Matějů, Petr and Řeháková, Blanka, 'Turning Left or Class Realignment? Analysis of the Changing Relationship between Class and Party in the Czech Republic 1992–1996, *East European Politics and Societies*, vol. 11, no. 3, fall 1997, pp. 501–42.

Matic, Andrej Auersperger, 'Electoral Reform as a Constitutional Dilemma', *East European Constitutional Review*, vol. 8, no. 3, summer 2000, pp. 77–81.

Matsuzato, Kimitaka, 'Elites and the Party System of Zakarpattya *Oblast*': Relations among Levels of Party Systems in Ukraine', *Europe-Asia Studies*, vol. 54, no. 8, 2002, pp. 1267–99.

McFaul, Michael, 'Party Formation and Non-Formation in Russia', *Comparative Political Studies*, vol. 34, no. 10, December 2001, pp. 1159–87.

—— 'The Fourth Wave of Democracy *and* Dictatorship: Noncooperative Transitions in the Postcommunist World', *World Politics*, vol. 54, January 2002, pp. 212–44.

McIntosh, Mary E., MacIver, Martha Abele, Abele, Daniel and Noelle, David, 'Minority Rights and Majority Rule: Ethnic Tolerance in Romania and Bulgaria', *Social Forces*, vol. 73, no. 3, March 1995, pp. 939–68.

McKenzie, Robert and Silver, Allan, *Angels in Marble. Working Class Conservatives in Urban England*, London: Heinemann, 1968.

McLean, Iain, 'Forms of Representation and Systems of Voting' in David Held, ed., *Political Theory Today*, Cambridge: Polity Press, 1991, pp. 172–96.

McManus-Czubińska, Clare, Miller,William, Markowski, Radosław and Wasilewski, Jacek, 'The New Polish "Right"?', Paper presented at the Workshop on the Central European Right and EU Enlargement, Foreign and Commonwealth Office, London, July, 2002.

Melone, Albert P., 'Bulgaria's National Roundtable Talks and the Politics of Accommodation', *International Political Science Review*, vol. 15, no. 3, 1994, pp. 257–73.

Mill, J.S., *Considerations on Representative Government* (1861), New York: The Liberal Arts Press, 1958.

Millard, Frances, 'The Polish Parliamentary Election of October 1991', *Soviet Studies*, vol. 44, no. 5, September 1992, pp. 837–55.

—— *The Anatomy of the New Poland. Post-Communist Politics in Its First Phase*, Aldershot: Edward Elgar, 1994.

—— *Polish Politics and Society*, London: Routledge, 1999.

—— 'Elections in Poland 2001: Electoral Manipulation and Party Upheaval', *Communist and Post-communist Studies*, vol. 36, no. 1, March 2003, pp. 69–86.

Miller, Susanne and Potthoff, Heinrich, *A History of German Social Democracy from 1848 to the Present*, Leamington Spa: Berg, 1986.

Miller, William L., White, Stephen and Heywood, Paul, *Values and Political Change in Postcommunist Europe*, Basingstoke: Macmillan Press, 1998.

Minkenberg, Michael, 'The Radical Right in Postsocialist Central and Eastern Europe: Comparative Observations and Interpretations', *East European Politics and Societies*, vol. 16, no. 2, spring 2002, pp. 335–85.

Monitoring the EU Accession Process: Minority Protection, Budapest: Central European Press, 2001.

Montero, José Ramón and Gunther, Richard, 'Introduction: Reviewing and Assessing Parties' in Richard Gunther, José Ramón Montero and Juan J. Linz, *Political Parties. Old Concepts and New Challenges*, Oxford: Oxford University Press, 2002, pp. 3–8.

Moser, Robert, 'The Impact of Parliamentary Electoral Systems in Russia' in Archie Brown, ed., *Contemporary Russian Politics. A Reader*, Oxford: Oxford University Press, 2001, pp. 195–207.

—— 'The Effects of Electoral Systems on Women's Representation in Post-communist States', *Electoral Studies*, vol. 20, 2001, pp. 353–69.

Mudde, Cas, 'Right-wing Extremism Analyzed. A Comparative Analysis of the Ideologies of Three Alleged Right-wing Extremist Parties (NPD, NDP, CP'86)', *European Journal of Political Research*, vol. 27, 1995, pp. 203–24.

—— 'The Paradox of the Anti-Party Party. Insights from the Extreme Right', *Party Politics*, vol. 2, no. 2, April 1996, pp. 265–76.

—— 'Extreme-right Parties in Eastern Europe', *Patterns of Prejudice*, vol. 34, no. 1, January 2000, pp. 5–27.

—— 'Populism in Eastern Europe – Part I', *East European Perspectives*, vol. 2, no. 5, 8 March 2000.

—— 'Populism in Eastern Europe – Part II', *East European Perspectives*, vol. 2, no. 6, 22 March 2000.

—— 'Slovak Elections: Go West!', *RFE/RL East European Perspectives*, vol. 4, no. 21, 16 October 2002, pp. 1–8.

Müller-Rommel, Ferdinand, ed., *New Politics in Western Europe. The Rise and the Success of Green Parties and Alternative Lists*, Boulder: Westview Press, 1989.

Musina, Roza, 'Contemporary Ethnosocial and Ethnopolitical Processes in Tatarstan' in Leokadia Drobizheva, Rose Gottemoeller, Catherine McArdle Kelleher, and Lee Walker, eds, *Ethnic Conflict in the Post-Soviet World*, London: M.E. Sharpe, 1996, pp. 195–208.

Myagkov, Mikhail and Ordeshook, Peter C., 'The Trail of Votes in Russia's 1999 Duma and 2000 Presidential Elections', *Communist and Post-Communist Studies*, vol. 34, 2001, pp. 353–70.

Nelson, Daniel N., 'Civil Society Endangered', *Social Research*, vol. 63, no. 2, summer 1996, pp. 345–68.

Nelson, Daniel and White, Stephen, *Communist Legislatures in Comparative Perspective*, London and Basingstoke: Macmillan, 1982.

Nordlinger, Eric, 'Representation, Governmental Stability and Decisional Effectiveness' in J. Roland Pennock and John W. Chapman, eds, *Representation*, New York: Atherton, 1968, pp. 108–27.

—— *Conflict Resolution in Divided Societies*, Cambridge, Massachusetts: Harvard University, Center for International Affairs, 1972.

Norris, Pippa, 'Legislative Recruitment' in Lawrence LeDuc, Richard G. Niemi and Pippa Norris, eds, *Comparing Democracies. Elections and Voting in Global Perspective*, London: Sage, 1996, pp. 184–215.

—— 'Women Politicians: Transforming Westminster', *Parliamentary Affairs*, vol. 49, no. 1, 1996, pp. 89–102.

—— *Politics and Sexual Equality*, Boulder: Lynne Riener, 1987.

Norris, Pippa and Inglehart, Ronald, 'Cultural Obstacles to Equal Representation', *Journal of Democracy*, vol. 12, no. 3, 2001, pp. 126–40.

Norris, Pippa and Lovenduski, Joni, 'Women Candidates for Parliament: Transforming the Agenda' *British Journal of Political Science*, vol. 19, no. 1, 1989, pp. 106–15.

—— 'If Only More Candidates Came Forward: Supply Side Explanations of Candidate Selection in Britain', *British Journal of Political* Science, vol. 23, no. 4, 1993, pp. 373–408.

Novagrockienė, Jūratė, 'Elections to the Seimas 2000: Party System Evolution or Its Transformation?' in Algimantas Jankauskas, ed., *Lithuanian Political Science Yearbook 2000*, Vilnius: Institute of International Relations and Political Science, 2001, pp. 138–50.

Offe, Claus, 'Capitalism by Democratic Design? Democratic Theory Facing the Triple Transition in East Central Europe', *Social Research*, vol. 58, no. 4, winter 1991, pp. 865–92.

Office for Democratic Institutions and Human Rights, 'Final Report. Romanian Parliamentary and Presidential Elections 3rd and 17th November 1996', Warsaw: OSCE, n.d.

Olson, David, 'Dissolution of the State: Political Parties and the 1992 Election in Czechoslovakia', *Communist and Post-Communist Studies*, vol. 26, no. 3, September 1993, pp. 301–14.

—— 'The New Parliaments of New Democracies: The Experience of the Federal Assembly of the Czech and Slovak Federal Republic' in Attila Ágh, ed., *The Emergence of East Central European Parliaments: The First Steps*, Budapest: Hungarian Centre of Democracy Studies, 1994, pp. 35–47.

—— 'Party Formation and Party System Consolidation in the New Democracies of Central Europe' in Richard Hofferbert, ed., *Parties and Democracy*, Oxford: Blackwell Publishers, 1998, pp. 10–42.

O'Neil, Patrick, *Revolution from Within. The Hungarian Socialist Workers' Party and the Collapse of Communism*, Cheltenham: Edward Elgar, 1998.

O'Neill, Michael, *Green Parties and Political Change in Contemporary Europe*, Aldershot: Ashgate, 1997.

Orenstein, Mitchell, 'A Genealogy of Communist Successor Parties in East-Central Europe and the Determinants of their Success', *East European Politics and Societies*, vol. 12, no. 3, 1998, pp. 472–99.

Orr, Thomas, 'The Far Right in the Czech Republic', *Uncaptive Minds*, vol. 6, no. 1, winter–spring 1993, pp. 67–72.

Ost, David, 'The Radical Right in Poland: Rationality of the Irrational' in Sabrina Ramet, ed., *The Radical Right in Central and Eastern Europe since 1989*. University Park, Pennsylvania: Pennsylvania State University Press, 1999, pp. 85–107.

Oversloot, Hans, van Holsteyn, Joop and Van Den Berg, Ger P., 'Against All: Exploring the Vote "Against All" in the Russian Federation's Electoral System', *The Journal of Communist Studies and Transition Politics*, vol. 18, no. 4, December 2002, pp. 31–50.

Pachkova, Petya, 'Electoral Behavior During Political Transition' in Georgi Karasimeonov, ed., *The Bulgarian Grand National Assembly and the 1991 Election to the Bulgarian National Assembly. Analyses, Documents and Data*, Berlin: Sigma, 1997, pp. 44–58.

Panebianco, Angelo, *Political Parties: Organisation and Power*, Cambridge: Cambridge University Press, 1988.

Pano, Nicholas, 'The Process of Democratization in Albania' in Karen Dawisha and Bruce Parrott, eds, *Politics, Power, and the Struggle for Democracy in South-East Europe*, Cambridge: Cambridge University Press, 1997, pp. 285–352.

Pearson, Raymond, *National Minorities in Eastern Europe, 1848–1945*, London: Macmillan, 1983.

Pedersen, Morgens, 'The Dynamics of European Party Systems: Changing Patterns of Electoral Volatility', *European Journal of Political Research*, vol. 7, no. 1, 1979, pp. 1–26.

Pehe, Jiri, 'Elections Result in Surprise Stalemate', *Transition*, vol. 2, no. 13, 28 June 1996.

—— 'Czech Elections: Victory for a New Generation', *RFE/RL East European Perspectives*, vol. 4, no. 17, 21 August 2002.

—— 'European Union Wins Czech Elections – Barely', *East European Constitutional Review*, vol. 11, no. 3, summer 2002, pp. 87–90.

Pérez-Liñán, Aníbal, 'Neoinstitutional Accounts of Voter Turnout: Moving Beyond Industrial Democracies', *Electoral Studies*, vol. 20, no. 2, June 2001, pp. 281–97.

Pétry, François, 'France 1958–1981: The Strategy of Joint Government Platforms' in Ian Budge, David Robertson, and Derek Hearl, *Ideology, Strategy and Party Change: Spatial Analyses of Post-War Election Programmes in 19 Democracies*, Cambridge: Cambridge University Press, 1987, pp. 324–44.

Pettai, Vello, 'Estonia: Positive and Negative Institutional Engineering' in Jan Zielonka, ed., *Democratic Consolidation in Eastern Europe*, Oxford: Oxford University Press, 2001 (vol. 1, *Institutional Engineering*), pp. 111–38.

Pettai, Vello and Kreuzer, Marcus, 'Party Politics in the Baltic States: Social Bases and Institutional Context', *East European Politics and Societies*, vol. 13, no. 1, winter 1999, pp. 148–89.

Phillips, Anne, *Engendering Democracy*, Cambridge: Polity Press, 1991.

—— 'Democracy and Representation: Or, Why Should It Matter Who Our Representatives Are?' in Anne Phillips, ed., *Feminism and Politics*, Oxford and New York: Oxford University Press, 2000, pp. 224–40.

Pitkin, Hanna, *The Concept of Representation*, Berkeley: University of California Press, 1967.

Pittaway, Mark and Swain, Nigel, 'Hungary' in Bogdan Szajkowski, ed., *Political Parties of Eastern Europe, Russia and the Successor States*, Harlow: Longman Information and Reference, 1994, pp. 185–245.

Plakans, Andrejs, 'Democratization and Political Participation in Postcommunist Societies: the Case of Latvia' in Karen Dawisha and Bruce Parrott, eds, *The Consolidation of Democracy in East-Central Europe*, Cambridge: Cambridge University Press, 1997, pp. 245–89.

Pogorelis, Robertas, Votes and Parties in the Mixed Electoral System in Lithuania, draft PhD thesis, University of Essex, March 2003.

Pop-Eleches, Grigore, 'Separated at Birth or Separated by Birth? The Communist Successor Parties in Romania and Hungary', *East European Politics and Societies*, vol. 13, no. 1, winter 1999, pp. 117–47.

—— 'Romania's Politics of Dejection', *Journal of Democracy*, vol. 12, no. 3, July 2001, pp. 156–69.

Popescu, Marina, 'Turnout in Post-Communist Europe: the Salience of Elections and Information Flows', Paper presented to the ECPR Joint Workshop Sessions, Turin, 22–8 March 2002.

—— 'The parliamentary and presidential elections in Romania, November 2000', *Electoral Studies*, vol. 22, issue 2, June 2003, pp. 325–35.

Popescu, Marina and Tóka, Gábor, 'Districting and Redistricting in Eastern and Central Europe: Regulations and Practices', Paper prepared for the Conference, 'Redistricting from a Comparative Perspective', University of California at Irvine, 6–8 December 2001.

Pravda, Alex, 'Elections in Communist Party States' in Stephen White and Daniel Nelson, eds, *Communist Politics. A Reader*, London: Macmillan, 1986, pp. 27–54.

Prekivicius, Nerijus and Clark, Terry D., 'Lithuanian Politics: Implications of the Parliamentary Elections', *ACE. Analysis of Current Events*, vol. 13, no. 1, February 2001, pp. 1–5.

Pridham, Geoffrey, 'Coalition Behaviour in New Democracies in Central and Eastern Europe: The Case of Slovakia', *The Journal of Communist Studies and Transition Politics*, vol. 18, no. 2, June 2002, pp. 75–102.

Pridham, Geoffrey and Ágh, Attila, eds, *Prospects for Democratic Consolidation in East-Central Europe*, Manchester: Manchester University Press, 2001.

Prizel, Ilya, 'Ukraine between Proto-democracy and "Soft" Authoritarianism' in Karen Dawisha and Bruce Parrott, eds, *Democratic Changes and Authoritarian Reactions in Russia, Ukraine, Belarus, and Moldova*, Cambridge: Cambridge University Press, 1997, pp. 330–69.

—— 'Ukraine's Hollow Decade', *East European Politics and Societies*, vol. 16, no. 2, spring 2002, pp. 363–85.

Puhle, Jürgen, 'Still the Age of Catch-allism? *Volksparteien* and *Parteienstaat* in Crisis and Re-equilibration' in Richard Gunther, José Ramón Montero and Juan J. Linz, *Political Parties. Old Concepts and New Challenges*, Oxford: Oxford University Press, 2002a, pp. 58–83.

Raciborski, Jacek, 'How the Voters Respond: Poland' in Kay Lawson, Andrea Römmele, and Georgi Karasimeonov, eds, *Cleavages, Parties, and Voters. Studies from Bulgaria, the Czech Republic, Hungary, Poland, and Romania*, London: Praeger, 1999, pp. 239–59.

Racz, Barnabas, 'Political Participation and Developed Socialism: the Hungarian Elections of 1985', *Soviet Studies*, vol. XXXIX, no. 1, 1987, pp. 40–62.

—— 'The Parliamentary Infrastructure and Political Reforms in Hungary', *Soviet Studies*, vol. XLI, no. 1, 1989, pp. 39–66.

—— 'The Hungarian Socialists in Opposition: Stagnation or Renaissance', *Europe-Asia Studies*, vol. 52, no. 2, 2000, pp. 319–47.

Radesh, Nestor, *Romania: The Entangled Revolution*, Westport, Connecticut: Praeger, 1991.

Rady, Martyn, *Romania in Turmoil*, London: I.B. Tauris, 1992.

Rak, Vladimír, 'Candidates in Czechoslovakian Parliamentary Election in June 1990 – Their Structure, Views and Attitudes' in Ivan Gabal, ed., *The 1990 Election to the Czechoslovakian Federal Assembly. Analyses, Documents and Data*, Berlin: Sigma, 1996, pp. 70–92.

Ramet, Sabrina P., ed., *The Radical Right in Central and Eastern Europe since 1989*. University Park, Pennsylvania: Pennsylvania State University Press, 1999.

Ramet, Sabrina Petra, 'Democratization in Slovenia – the Second Stage' in Karen Dawisha and Bruce Parrott, eds, *Politics, Power, and the Struggle for Democracy in South-East Europe*, Cambridge: Cambridge University Press, 1997, pp. 189–225.

Ramet, Sabrina, 'Slovenia's Road to Democracy', *Europe-Asia Studies*, vol. 45, no. 5, 1993, pp. 869–86.

Randall, Vicky and Svåsand, Lars, 'Party Institutionalisation and the New Democracies', Paper presented to the ECPR Joint Session of Workshops, Mannheim, March 1999.

Reed, Steven, 'Democracy and the Personal Vote: A Cautionary Tale from Japan', *Electoral Studies*, vol. 13, no. 1, 1994, pp. 17–28.

Reeve, A. and Ware, A., *Electoral Systems: A Comparative and Theoretical Introduction*, London: Routledge, 1992.

Reich, Alfred, 'Meciar and Slovakia's Hungarian Minority', *RFE/RL Research Report*, 30 October 1992, pp. 13–20.

Remington, Thomas F., 'Putin and the Duma', *Post-Soviet Affairs*, vol. 17, no. 4, pp. 285–308.

—— *The Russian Parliament. Institutional Evolution in a Transitional Regime, 1989–1999*, New Haven: Yale University Press, 2001.

Reschová, Jana, 'Nová politika s novými l'ud'mi: Federálne zhromaždenie v roku 1990', *Sociologicky Časopis*; vol. 28, no. 2, 1992, pp. 222–36.

Reynolds, Andrew, 'Women in the Legislatures and Executives of the World: Knocking at the Highest Glass Ceiling', *World Politics*, vol. 51, July 1999, pp. 547–72.

Rhodes, Matthew, 'National Identity and Minority Rights in the Constitutions of the Czech Republic and Slovakia', *East European Quarterly*, vol. XXIX, no. 3, September 1995, pp. 347–69.

Rizman, Rudolf, 'Radical Right Politics in Slovenia' in Sabrina Ramet, ed., *The Radical Right in Central and Eastern Europe since 1989*, University Park, Pennsylvania: Pennsylvania State University Press, 1999, pp. 147–70.

Robinson, Neil, 'Classifying Russia's Party System: The Problem of "Relevance" in a Time of Uncertainty', *The Journal of Communist Studies and Transition Politics*, vol. 14, nos 1/2, 1998, pp. 159–77.

—— *Russia. A State of Uncertainty*, London: Routledge, 2002.

Robinson, William F., *The Pattern of Reform in Hungary: A Political, Economic and Cultural Analysis*, London: Praeger, 1973.

Rokkan, Stein (with Angus Campbell, Per Torsvik and Henry Valen), *Citizens, Elections, Parties: Approaches to the Comparative Study of the Processes of Development*, Oslo: Universitetsforlaget, 1970.

Roper, Steven, 'The Romanian Party System and the Catch-All Party Phenomenon', *East European Quarterly*, vol. XXVIII, no. 4, January 1995, pp. 519–32.

Rose, Richard, *Do Parties Make a Difference?*, London: Macmillan, 1980.

—— 'Mobilizing Demobilized Voters in Post-communist Societies', *Party Politics*, vol. 1, 1995, pp. 545–63.

—— 'How Floating Parties Frustrate Democratic Accountability: A Supply-Side View of Russia's Elections' in Archie Brown, ed., *Contemporary Russian Politics: A Reader*, Oxford: Oxford University Press, 2001, pp. 215–23.

—— 'A Bottom Up Evaluation of Enlargement Countries. New Europe Barometer 1', Glasgow: University of Strathclyde Centre for the Study of Public Policy, 2002.

Rose, Richard and Munro, Neil, *Elections without Order. Russia's Challenge to Vladimir Putin*, Cambridge: Cambridge University Press, 2002.

Rothschild, Joseph, *East Central Europe between the Two World Wars*, Seattle and London: University of Washington Press, 1974.

Rueschemeyer, Marilyn, ed., *Women in the Politics of Postcommunist Eastern Europe*, New York and London: M.E. Sharpe, 1998 (rev. ed.).

Rule, Wilma, 'Introduction: Equal Players or Back to the Kitchen?' in Wilma Rule and Norma C. Noonan, eds, *Russian Women in Politics and Society*, Westport, Connecticut and London: Greenwood Press, 1996, pp. 1–12.

Rule, Wilma and Shvedova, Nadezhda, 'Women in Russia's First Multi-party Election' in Wilma Rule and Norma C. Noonan, eds, *Russian Women in Politics and Society*, Westport, Connecticut and London: Greenwood Press, 1996, pp. 40–59.

Sakwa, Richard, 'The Russian Elections of December 1993', *Europe-Asia Studies*, vol. 47, no. 2, 1995, pp. 195–227.

—— 'Left or Right? The CPRF and the Problem of Democratic Consolidation in Russia', *The Journal of Communist Studies and Transition Politics*, vol. 14, nos 1/2, 1998, pp. 128–58.

Sándor, Eleonóra, 'The Political Parties of the Hungarian Minority in the 1998 Elections' in Martin Bútora, Grigorij Mesežnikov, Zora Bútorová and Sharon Fisher, eds, *The 1998 Parliamentary Elections and Democratic Rebirth in Slovakia*, Bratislava: Institute for Public Affairs, 1999, pp. 245–54.

Sanford, George, *Democratic Government in Poland. Constitutional Politics since 1989*, Basingstoke: Palgrave Macmillan, 2002.

Saxonberg, Steven, 'Women in East European Parliaments', *Journal of Democracy*, vol. 11, no. 2, April 2000, pp. 145–58.

Schedler, A., 'What is Democratic Consolidation?' *Journal of Democracy*, vol. 9, no. 2, April 1998, pp. 91–107.

Schleifer, Andrei and Treisman, Daniel, *Without a Map: Political Tactics and Economic Reform in Russia*, Cambridge: MIT Press, 2000.

Schmitter, Phillipe C., 'Contemporary Democratization: The Prospects for Women' in Jane Jaquette and Sharon Wolchik, eds, *Women and Democracy. Latin America and Central and Eastern Europe*, Baltimore and London: The Johns Hopkins University Press, 1999, pp. 222–37.

Schöpflin, George, 'Opposition and Para-Opposition: Critical Currents in Hungary, 1968–78' in Rudolf Tőkés, ed., *Opposition in Eastern Europe*, London: Macmillan, 1979, pp. 142–86.

Schutz, Peter, 'Playing the Numbers Game', *Transitions-on-Line*, 9 February 2000 (http://www.tol.cz).

Shafir, Michael, 'Anti-Semitism without Jews in Romania', *RFE/RL Report on Eastern Europe*, vol. 2, no. 26, 1991, pp. 20–32.

——— 'The Greater Romania Party', *RFE/RL Report on Eastern Europe*, vol. 2, no. 46, 1991, pp. 25–30.

——— 'Ethnic Tension Runs High in Cluj', RFE/RL Research Report, vol. 3, no. 32, 19 August 1994, pp. 24–32.

——— 'Romania's Road to "Normalcy" ', *Journal of Democracy*, vol. 8, no. 2, 1997, pp. 144–58.

——— 'Radical Politics in East-Central Europe Part V: Bulgaria's Radical Transfigurations', *RFE/RL East European Perspectives*, vol. 2, no. 15, 2 August 2000.

——— 'Radical Politics in East-Central Europe Part VIII: Radical Continuity in Romania: The Greater Romania Party (A)', *East European Perspectives*, vol. 2, no. 16, 16 August 2000.

——— 'The Ciorbea Government and Democratization: A Preliminary Assessment' in Duncan Light and David Phinnemore, eds, *Post-Communist Romania. Coming to Terms with Transition*, Basingstoke: Palgrave, 2001, pp. 79–103.

——— 'The Greater Romania Party and the 2000 Elections in Romania: A Retrospective Analysis' (Part I), *RFE/RL East European Perspectives*, vol. 3, no. 14, 22 August 2001.

——— 'The Greater Romania Party and the 2000 Elections in Romania: A Retrospective Analysis' (Part II), *RFE/RL East European Perspectives*, vol. 3, no. 15, 5 September 2001.

Shevchenko, Iulia, 'Who Cares about Women's Problems? Female Legislators in the 1995 and 1999 Russian State Dumas', *Europe-Asia Studies*, vol. 54, no. 8, December 2002, pp. 1201–22.

Shevel, Oxana, 'Nationality in Ukraine: Some Rules of Engagement', *East European Politics and Societies*, vol. 16, no. 2, spring 2002, pp. 386–413.

Shevtsova, Lilia, 'Russia's Hybrid Regime', *Journal of Democracy*, vol. 12, no. 4, October 2001, pp. 65–70.

Siaroff, Alan, *Comparative European Party Systems*, New York: Garland Publishing, 2000.

Siaroff, Alan and Merer, John, 'Parliamentary Election Turnout in Europe since 1990', *Political Studies*, vol. 50, no. 5, December 2002, pp. 916–27.

Siegler Robert, *The Standing Commissions of the Supreme Soviet*, New York: Praeger, 1982.

Siklova, Jirina and Miklusakova, Marta, 'Denying Citizenship to the Czech Roma', *East European Constitutional Review*, vol. 7, no. 2, spring 1998, pp. 58–64.

Simeon, Richard and Conway, Daniel-Patrick, 'Federalism and the Management of Conflict' in Alain-G. Gagnon and James Tully, eds, *Multinational Democracies*, Cambridge: Cambridge University Press, 2001, pp. 338–65.

Slider, Darrell, Russia's Governors and Party Formation' in Archie Brown, ed., *Contemporary Russian Politics: A Reader*, Oxford: Oxford University Press, 2001, pp. 224–34.

Smirnov, William V., 'Democratization in Russia: Achievements and Problems' in Archie Brown, ed., *Contemporary Russian Politics: A Reader*, Oxford: Oxford University Press, 2001, pp. 517–29.

Smith, David J., 'Retracing Estonia's Russians: Mikhail Kurchinskii and Inter-war Cultural Autonomy, *Nationalities Papers*, vol. 27, no. 3, 1999, pp. 455–74.

Smith, David J., Pabriks, Artis, Purs, Aldis and Lane, Thomas, *The Baltic States. Estonia, Latvia and Lithuania*, London: Routledge, 2002.

Smith, Gordon, *Politics in Western Europe. A Comparative Analysis*, London: Heinemann Educational Books, 1976 (2nd edn).

Smith, Graham, Law, Vivian, Wilson, Andrew, Bohr, Annette and Allworth, Edward, *Nation-building in the Post-Soviet Borderlands*, Cambridge: Cambridge University Press, 1998.

Solchanyk, Roman, 'The Radical Right in Ukraine' in Sabrina Ramet, ed., *The Radical Right in Central and Eastern Europe since 1989*, University Park: The Pennsylvania State University Press, 1999, pp. 279–96.

Sprudzs, Adolf, 'Rebuilding Democracy in Latvia: Overcoming a Dual Legacy' in Jan Zielonka ed., *Democratic Consolidation in Eastern Europe*, Oxford: Oxford University Press, 2001 (vol. 1: *Institutional Engineering*), pp. 139–64.

Steen, Anton, 'Ethnic Relations, Elites and Democracy in the Baltic States', *The Journal of Communist Studies and Transition Politics*, vol. 16, no. 4, December 2000, pp. 68–87.

Steiger, Stepan, 'The Far Right in the Czech Republic', *Labour Focus on Eastern Europe*, no. 49, 1994, pp. 81–87.

Stein, E., *Czecho/Slovakia, Ethnic Conflict, Constitutional Fissure, Negotiated Break-up*, University of Michigan Press, 1997.

Steiner, Jürg, *European Democracies*, New York and London: Longman, 1986.

Szajkowski, Bogdan, ed., *Political Parties of Eastern Europe, Russia and the Successor States*, Harlow, Essex: Longman, 1994.

Szalai, Julia, 'Women and Democratization. Some Notes on Recent Changes in Hungary', in Jane S. Jaquette and Sharon Wolchik, eds, *Women and Democracy. Latin America and Central and Eastern Europe*, Baltimore and London: The Johns Hopkins University Press, 1999, pp. 185–202.

Szczerbiak, Aleks, 'Electoral Politics in Poland: The Polish Election of 1997', *Journal of Communist Studies and Transition Politics*, vol. 14, no. 3, September 1998, pp. 58–83.

—— *Poles Together. Emergence and Development of Political Parties in Post-Communist Poland*, Budapest: CEU Press, 2001.

—— 'The Polish Peasant Party: A Mass Party in Postcommunist Eastern Europe?', *East European Politics and Societies*, vol. 15, no. 3, fall 2001, pp. 554–88.

Szelényi, Iván and Szelényi, Szonja, 'The Vacuum in Hungarian Politics: Classes and Parties', *New Left Review* 187, May–June, 1991, pp. 121–38.

Szelény, Iván, Fodor, Éva, and Hanley, Eric, 'Left Turn in PostCommunist Politics: Bringing Class Back In?', *East European Politics and Societies*, vol. 11, no. 1, winter 1997, pp. 190–224.

Szomolányi, Soňa and Mesežnikov, Grigorij, eds, *The Slovak Path of Transition – to Democracy?*, Bratislava: Slovak Political Science Association & Interlingua, 1994.

Taagepera, Rein and Laakso, M., '"Effective" Number of Parties: A Measure with Application to Western Europe', *Comparative Political Studies*, vol. 12, no. 1, April 1979, pp. 3–27.

Taggart, Paul, 'New Populist Parties in Western Europe', *West European Politics*, vol. 18, no. 1, January 1995, pp. 34–51.

Tamas, Bernard, 'Parties on Stage: Evaluating the Performance of Hungarian Parties' in Gábor Tóka and Zsolt Enyedi, eds, *Elections to the Hungarian National Assembly 1994. Analyses, Documents and Data*, Berlin: Sigma, 1999, pp. 13–51.

Temple, Mark, 'The Politicisation of History: Marshall Antonescu and Romania', *East European Politics and Societies*, vol. 10, no. 3, fall 1996, pp. 457–503.

Tismaneanu, Vladimir, 'The Tragicomedy of Romanian Communism', *East European Politics and Societies*, vol. 3, no. 2, spring 1989, pp. 329–76.

—— 'Romanian exceptionalism? Democracy, ethnocracy, and uncertain pluralism in post-Ceauşescu Romania' in Karen Dawisha and Bruce Parrott, eds, *Politics, Power, and the Struggle for Democracy in South-East Europe*, Cambridge: Cambridge University Press, 1997, pp. 403–51.

Tismaneanu, Vladimir, *Fantasies of Salvation. Democracy, Nationalism and Myth in Post-Communist Europe*, Princeton, New Jersey: Princeton University Press, 1998.

Tismaneanu, Vladimir and Kligman, Gail, 'Romania's First Postcommunist Decade: From Iliescu to Iliescu', *East European Constitutional Review*, vol. 10, no. 1, winter 2001, pp. 78–85.

Tóká, Gabor, 'Seats and Votes: Consequences of the Hungarian Electoral Law' in Gábor Tóka, ed., *The 1990 Election to the Hungarian National Assembly. Analyses, Documents and Data*, Berlin: Sigma, 1995, pp. 41–66.

—— 'Political Parties in East Central Europe' in Larry Diamond, Marc F. Plattner, Yun-han Chu, and Hung-mao Tien, eds, *Consolidating the Third Wave Democracies. Themes and Perspectives*, London: The Johns Hopkins University Press, 1997, pp. 93–134.

Tőkés, Rudolf, *Hungary's Negotiated Revolution. Economic Reform, Social Change and Political Succession*, Cambridge: Cambridge University Press, 1996.

—— 'Party politics and political participation in post-communist Hungary' in Karen Dawisha and Bruce Parrott, eds, *The Consolidation of Democracy in East-Central Europe*, Cambridge: Cambridge University Press, 1997, pp. 109–49.

Toma, Peter and Kováč, Dušan, *Slovakia. From Samo to Dzurinda*, Stanford: Hoover Institution Press, 2001.

Ulram, Peter A. and Plasser, Fritz, 'Mainly sunny with scattered clouds: political culture in East-Central Europe' in Geoffrey Pridham and Attila Ágh, eds, *Prospects for Democratic Consolidation in East-Central Europe*, Manchester: Manchester University Press, 2001, pp. 115–37.

Urban, Michael and Gel'man, Vladimir, 'The development of political parties in Russia' in Karen Dawisha and Bruce Parrott, eds, *Democratic Changes and Authoritarian Reactions in Russia, Ukraine, Belarus and Moldova*, Cambridge: Cambridge University Press, 1997, pp. 175–219.

Vanneman, Peter, *The Supreme Soviet: Politics and the Legislative Process in the Soviet political system*, Durham, N.C.: Duke University Press, 1977.

Vašečka, Michal, 'Roma and the 1998 Parliamentary Elections' in Martin Bútora, Grigorij Mesežnikov, Zora Bútorová and Sharon Fisher, eds, *The 1998 Parliamentary Elections and Democratic Rebirth in Slovakia*, Bratislava: Institute for Public Affairs, 1999, pp. 255–63.

Verdery, Katherine, 'Nationalism and National Sentiment in Post-Socialist Romania', *Slavic Review*, vol. 52, no. 2, (Summer) 1993, pp. 179–203.

—— *What Was Socialism and What Comes Next*, Princeton: Princeton University Press, 1996.

Vetik, Raivo, 'Multiculturalism as a Model for Democratic Consolidation' in Dirk Berg-Schlosser and Raivo Vetik, eds, *Perspectives on Democratic Consolidation in Central and Eastern Europe*, Boulder: East European Monographs, 2001, pp. 22–30.

Vlachová, Klara, 'Party identification in the Czech Republic: Inter-party Hostility and Party Preference', *Communist and Post-Communist Studies*, vol. 34, no. 4, December 2001, pp. 479–99.

von Beyme, Klaus, *Political Parties in Western Democracies*, Aldershot: Gower, 1985.

Ware, Alan, *Political Parties and Party Systems*, Oxford: Oxford University Press, 1996.

Warmińska, Katarzyna, 'Polish Tatars: Ethnic Ideology and State Policy' in Cora Govers and Hans Vermeulen, eds, *The Politics of Ethnic Consciousness*, London and New York: Macmillan and St. Martin's Press, 1997, pp. 343–66.

Waylen, Georgina, 'Gender and Democratic Politics: A Comparative Analysis of consolidation in Argentina and Chile', *Journal of Latin American Studies*, vol. 32, no. 3, 2000, pp. 765–93.

—— 'Women and Democratization: Conceptualising Gender Relations in Transition Politics', *World Politics*, vol. 46, no. 3, 1994, pp. 327–54.

Weber, Renate, 'Constitutionalism as a Vehicle for Democratic Consolidation in Romania' in Jan Zielonka, ed., *Democratic Consolidation in Eastern Europe*, Oxford: Oxford University Press, 2001 (vol. 1: *Institutional Engineering*), pp. 212–42.

Weinburg, Leonard, 'Introduction' in Peter H. Merkel and Leonard Weinberg, *Encounters with the Contemporary Radical Right*, Boulder, San Francisco and Oxford: Westview Press, 1993, pp. 1–15.

Wenzel, Michal, 'Solidarity and Akcja Wyborcza Solidarność – An Attempt at Reviving the Legend', *The Journal of Communist Studies and Transition Politics*, vol. 31, no. 2, June 1998, pp. 139–56.

Wesolowski, Wlodzimierz, *Partie: Nieustanne Kłopoty*, Warsaw: IFIS PAN, 2000.

White, Stephen, Gardner, John, Schöpflin, George and Saich, Tony, *Communist Political Systems. An Introduction*, Basingstoke: Macmillan, 1990 (3rd edn).

White, Stephen and Nelson, Daniel, eds, *Communist Politics. A Reader*, London: Macmillan, 1986.

Whitmore, Sarah, 'Fragmentation or Consolidation? Parties in Ukraine's Parliament', Paper presented to the Annual Conference of the British Association for Slavonic and East European Studies, Fitzwilliam College, Cambridge, April 2002.

Widacki, J., *Czego nie powiedział Generał Kiszczak*, Warsaw: BGW, 1992.

Wightman, Gordon, 'The 1992 Parliamentary Elections in Czechoslovakia', *Journal of Communist Studies*, vol. 8, no. 4, December 1992, pp. 293–301.

—— 'The 1994 Slovak Parliamentary Elections', *The Journal of Communist Studies and Transition Politics*, vol. 11, no. 4, 1995, pp. 384–92.

Williams, Christopher and Hanson, Stephen E., 'The "Radical Right" in Russia' in Sabrina Ramet, ed., *The Radical Right in Central and Eastern Europe since 1989*, University Park: The Pennsylvania State University Press, 1999, pp. 257–77.

Williams, Kieran, 'What Was Mečiarism?' in Kieran Williams, ed., *Slovakia After Communism and Mečiarism*, London: School of Slavonic and East European Studies, 2000, pp. 1–16.

—— 'PR's First Decade in Eastern Europe', *Representation* (forthcoming 2004).

Williams, Kieran, ed., *Slovakia After Communism and Mečiarism*, London: School of Slavonic and East European Studies, 2000.

Williams, Philip, *Politics in Post-War France. Parties and the Constitution in the Fourth Republic*, London: Longmans, 1954.

Wilson, Andy, 'Ukraine's 2002 Elections: Less Fraud: More virtuality', *East European Constitutional Review*, vol. 11, no. 3, summer 2002, pp. 91–8.

Wilson, Richard W., 'The Many Voices of Political Culture: Assessing Different Approaches', *World Politics*, vol. 52, no. 2, January 2000, pp. 246–73.

Wolchik, Sharon, *Czechoslovakia in Transition*, London and New York: Pinter Publishers, 1991.
—— 'Transition Politics in the Czech Republic and Slovakia' in Jane S. Jaquette and Sharon Wolchik, eds, *Women and Democracy. Latin America and Central and Eastern Europe*, Baltimore and London: The Johns Hopkins University Press, 1999, pp. 153–84.
Wolinetz, Steven B., 'Beyond the Catch-All Party: Approaches to the Study of Parties and Party Organization in Contemporary Democracies' in Richard Gunther, José Ramón Montero and Juan J. Linz, *Political Parties. Old Concepts and New Challenges*, Oxford: Oxford University Press, 2002, pp. 136–65.
Wolosky, L., 'Putin's Plutocrat Problem', *Foreign Affairs*, vol. 79, no. 2, 2000, pp. 18–31.
Yavlinski, Grigory, 'Going Backwards', *Journal of Democracy*, vol. 12, no. 4, October 2001, pp. 79–86.
Za kulisami bezpieki i partii. Józef Światlo ujawnia tajniki partii, reżymu i aparatu bezpieczeństwa, Warsaw: BIS, 1990.
Zaslavsky, Victor and Brym, Robert J., 'The Functions of Elections in the USSR', *Soviet Studies*, vol. 30, no. 3, 1978, pp. 362–71.
Zake, Ieva, 'The People's Party in Latvia: Neo-Liberalism and the New Politics of Independence', *The Journal of Communist Studies and Transition Politics*, vol. 18, no. 3, September 2002, pp. 109–31.
Zemko, Milan, 'Political Parties and the Election System in Slovakia' in Soňa Szomolányi and Grigorij Meseþnikov, eds, *Slovakia: Parliamentary Elections 1994*, Bratislava: Slovak Political Science Association, 1995, pp. 40–55.
úèruolis, Darius, 'Rational Voters and Causes of Absenteeism' in Algis Krupavičius, ed., *Lithuania's Seimas Election 1996: The third Turnover. Analyses, Documents and Data*, Berlin: Sigma, 2001, pp. 196–212.
Zhelyazkova, Antonina, 'The Bulgarian Ethnic Model', *East European Constitutional Review*, vol. 10, no. 4, fall 2001, pp. 62–66.
Ziblatt, Daniel, 'The Adaptation of Ex-Communist Parties to Post-Communist East Central Europe: a Comparative Study of the East German and Hungarian Ex-Communist Parties', *Communist and Post-Communist Studies*, vol. 31, no. 2, 1998, pp. 119–37.
Zielonka, Jan, ed., *Democratic Consolidation in Eastern Europe*, Oxford: Oxford University Press, 2001 (vol. 1: *Institutional Engineering*).
Zvinkliene, Alina, 'Neo-Conservatism and Family Ideology in Lithuania. Between the West and the USSR' in Sue Bridger, ed., *Women and Political Change. Perspectives from East-Central Europe*, Basingstoke: Macmillan and New York: St. Martin's Press, 1999, pp. 135–50.

Index